Praise for *Facing the Mountain*

"*Facing the Mountain* arrives at the perfect time, to remind us of the true meaning of patriotism. In Daniel James Brown's gifted hands, these overlooked American heroes are getting the glory they deserve. Read this book and know their stories."

—Mitchell Zuckoff, author of *Lost in Shangri-La*

"Daniel James Brown brings to life the gripping true story of Japanese Americans whose steely heroism fought Nazism abroad and racism at home. Bound by Japanese values of filial piety, *giri* (social obligation) and *gaman* (endurance), and forged in the crucible of brutal combat, these soldiers served the very country that locked their families in American concentration camps for no crime other than looking like the enemy, while camp resisters fought for justice denied."

—Lori L. Matsukawa, news anchor, KING-TV, Seattle

"The loyal and often heroic service of Japanese American soldiers is one of history's most inspiring responses to bigotry and oppression. Daniel James Brown brilliantly pairs these events in an epic of courage and resistance."

—David Laskin, author of *The Long Way Home*

"A must read. You will not be able to put it down."

—Scott Oki, former senior vice president, Microsoft; cofounder, Densho

"Riveting. *Facing the Mountain* is a book that is as much about the present as it is about the past. In it are vital lessons about courage, truth, justice, and an abiding love of country. Drawing on impeccable historic research, the narrative movingly shines the light of history on prejudice and discrimination and the unfinished struggle for a more just future."

—Ann Burroughs, president and CEO, Japanese American National Museum

FACING THE MOUNTAIN

ALSO BY DANIEL JAMES BROWN

*The Boys in the Boat: Nine Americans and Their Epic
Quest for Gold at the 1936 Berlin Olympics*

*The Indifferent Stars Above: The Harrowing
Saga of a Donner Party Bride*

*Under a Flaming Sky: The Great Hinckley
Firestorm of 1894*

FACING
THE
MOUNTAIN

A TRUE STORY OF
JAPANESE AMERICAN
HEROES IN WORLD WAR II

DANIEL JAMES BROWN

VIKING

VIKING
An imprint of Penguin Random House LLC
penguinrandomhouse.com

Grateful acknowledgment is made for permission to reprint the following:
Letters between Chaplain Hiro Higuchi and his wife, Hisako Higuchi,
are reprinted with permission of Royce Fukunaga.
Letters from the Saito family are reprinted courtesy of
the Japanese American National Museum.

Owing to limitations of space, image credits may be found on pages 523–24.

Maps by Jeffrey L. Ward

LIBRARY OF CONGRESS CATALOGING-IN-PUBLICATION DATA

Names: Brown, Daniel James, 1951– author.
Title: Facing the mountain: a true story of Japanese American heroes in
World War II / Daniel James Brown.
Other titles: True story of Japanese American heroes in World War II
Description: [New York, NY] : Viking, [2021] |
Includes bibliographical references and index.
Identifiers: LCCN 2020053098 (print) | LCCN 2020053099 (ebook) |
ISBN 9780525557401 (hardcover) | ISBN 9780525557418 (ebook) |
ISBN 9780593299814 (international edition)
Subjects: LCSH: United States. Army. Regimental Combat Team, 442nd. |
World War, 1939–1945—Campaigns—Europe. | Japanese American soldiers—
History—20th century. | World War, 1939–1945—Participation, Japanese American. |
World War, 1939–1945—Regimental histories—United States.
Classification: LCC D769.31 442nd .B76 2021 (print) |
LCC D769.31 442nd (ebook) | DDC 940.54/12730923956—dc23
LC record available at https://lccn.loc.gov/2020053098
LC ebook record available at https://lccn.loc.gov/2020053099

Printed in the United States of America
1st Printing

DESIGNED BY MEIGHAN CAVANAUGH

To Kats and Rudy and Fred and Gordon

And all those who held aloft the light of liberty

And led us over the mountain

when the darkness came

You know, to me, I felt all the guys who didn't make it, I hope they're watching from heaven so that they, too, can enjoy and say, "Look what we have done."

RUDY TOKIWA
MARCH 24, 2002

CONTENTS

FOREWORD

Twenty-five years ago, in 1995, before Google or smartphones, I spearheaded a group of inspired volunteers in an effort to interview, digitally preserve, and share the personal stories of our Japanese American ancestors incarcerated during World War II. We named the project Densho, a Japanese term meaning "to leave a legacy for future generations." At the time, my father said, with a pained expression, that this was a bad idea. Community members just wanted to forget the war years and the suffering.

This began a long discussion with a man who rarely told me what to do. At the end of the conversation, I told him I hoped he understood, but I *had* to do this project. This part of American history was barely taught in schools, and too many people had never even heard about the incarceration of 120,000 Japanese Americans. Those who lived through the experience were dying. We needed to hear and record their stories. When my father saw that I was really going to start interviewing people, he said there was something I needed to know: "There are deep divisions in the community that people won't want to talk about. Be sensitive and don't judge based on what you think you know. Life can change quickly."

In the years following that conversation, my father became my best adviser. He even agreed to be interviewed and often became an important liaison between Densho and Japanese American elders who were hesitant to share their stories.

Twenty years later, I stood on a sunny, outdoor stage at the Seattle Center to accept a Mayor's Arts Award for Densho's work preserving and sharing this history. As I scanned the audience for my eighty-eight-year-old father, who had come with me, I stood in front of the iconic Horiuchi mural, a seventeen-foot-high-by-sixty-foot-wide brightly colored glass mosaic created by the well-known Japanese American artist Paul Horiuchi. Through an interview I had done six years earlier with Paul's widow, Bernadette, I knew that Paul had had a hard time getting work as a Japanese American while they lived in Wyoming. The family was so poor, in fact, that when they visited relatives incarcerated at the Minidoka concentration camp in Idaho, Bernadette was envious of the children there who at least had warm food, shelter, and milk to drink. I remember feeling uneasy hearing Bernadette talk about wishing to live in this American concentration camp. Then I realized even more deeply how difficult those years must have been for her family. My father was right to tell me to listen and not judge.

When I turned away from the mural and faced the audience, my eyes caught the graceful lines of the Yamasaki Arches; five hundred-foot-high Gothic arches were created by the former Seattle architect Minoru Yamasaki for the 1962 Seattle World's Fair. They were supposed to be a temporary installation. However, they were so beautiful they became a permanent and historic landmark. Ironically, two of Yamasaki's other creations, these meant to be permanent, the Twin Towers in New York City, were destroyed by terrorists on September 11, 2001. In the days and months that followed, I remembered how horrified Japanese Americans felt as we watched Muslim and Arab Americans being feared, shunned, and seen as the enemy, echoing the Japanese American experience during World War II. Then I remembered my father's words: "Life can change quickly."

At the ceremony, Seattle's mayor introduced the work of Densho and then me. I began by dedicating the award to my father, but the whole time I was talking, I was searching the crowd for his face. I finally saw him waving from the third row back, off to the side. I'm guessing he sat in an out-of-the-way place so he wouldn't take a seat from a VIP, not knowing he was the most important person there that day.

When I returned to my seat on the stage, I sat next to another honoree, Daniel James Brown, a gentle, soft-spoken man being recognized for his book about the University of Washington crew, *The Boys in the Boat*. His book was a favorite of mine, and I admired his rich storytelling and historical research. We connected easily as we learned we both had worked at Microsoft at the same time and both had left to pursue our passions. Dan then told me he had long been interested in the experiences of Japanese Americans during World War II and was thinking about them as he considered ideas for his next book. Just before the program ended, we exchanged business cards and promised to stay in touch.

Five years later, I am now writing the foreword to the book that came, at least in part, from that conversation. Dan and I have now spent hours together, along with the Densho historian Brian Niiya, sharing story ideas and suggestions to make the book as historically accurate and authentic as possible, using Densho's oral history collection and other rich repositories in Hawai'i and California. I've watched as Dan and his wife, Sharon, spent years researching and traveling to build a full picture of the Japanese American experience during the war. At some point, my time with Dan and Sharon became opportunities for me to sit back and learn. I loved hearing the stories about the lives and letters of the chaplains of the 442nd. I cherished learning more about Fred Shiosaki, Rudy Tokiwa, and Gordon Hirabayashi, men who had generously spent hours with me when I conducted their oral histories and whose stories are now part of Dan's book.

When Densho began, I dreamed the stories we collected would humanize and educate others to stand against injustices. *Facing the Mountain* comes to us during a time of deep unrest, a time when our empathy for others is so needed to guide the choices we will make. This book will open hearts. Thank you, Dan.

Tom Ikeda

Tom Ikeda is executive director of Densho, a Seattle-based nonprofit dedicated to collecting, preserving, and sharing Japanese American history and promoting social justice and equity.

AUTHOR'S NOTE

n April 1946, in the aftermath of World War II, George Orwell wrote, "Political language—and with variations this is true of all political parties, from Conservatives to Anarchists—is designed to make lies sound truthful and murder respectable."

The events at the heart of this book richly illustrate the point. When the American government removed tens of thousands of Japanese Americans from their homes and incarcerated them in remote, desolate camps, it wrapped those actions in language calculated to filter, soften, obscure, and distort a number of hard and uncomfortable facts. Military and political leaders called the forced removal of citizens an "evacuation." They called the parents of those citizens, most of whom had lived in the United States for decades, "enemy aliens." They called the fairgrounds and racetracks where both citizens and their parents were first confined behind barbed wire "assembly centers." They called the more permanent facilities where more than a hundred thousand people lived out the war crammed into spartan barracks in desert wastelands "relocation centers." Almost without exception, the news outlets of the day adopted this language, and the authors of history books over the subsequent decades echoed it.

To tell a truthful story, one must use truthful language, so I have endeavored in this book to replace these euphemisms with more honest language. For example, I sometimes refer to the facilities I mention above as "concentration camps." Nobody should for a moment take this to mean that I equate them in any way with the horrific death camps and slave-labor camps of Nazi Germany, places like Auschwitz and Dachau. Nothing in modern history equates with the terrible reality of those places. But the fact remains that the "assembly centers" and "relocation centers" were indeed American concentration camps by any reasonable definition of that term.

I have also worked to be accurate and honest when re-creating conversations. Any dialogue I present here is taken directly from transcripts of interviews or other primary sources, and so it is faithful not only to the words spoken but also to the speaker's manner of speaking. I bring this up here, in part, because a number of the people you will meet in these pages spoke the Hawaiian creole known throughout the islands simply as pidgin. To the uninitiated, this language may sound coarse or even ignorant. It is neither. It is simply the warm, familiar language that has grown up in the cultural melting pot that Hawai'i is, combining words and expressions from English, Portuguese, Hawaiian, Cantonese, Japanese, Korean, Tagalog, and a bit of Spanish as a practical means of communicating across ethnic and linguistic boundaries. It ties together the larger Hawaiian *'ohana*, or family. And, as you will see, it plays a role in the story that follows.

DJB

PROLOGUE

We made the sacrifices. It was a sense of "Hey, I earned this. It's not that you owe me. It's this—that we have earned this."

FRED SHIOSAKI

One of the many pleasures of writing a book like this is meeting the extraordinary people who have lived the story you are telling. Usually, you meet them only virtually, through the letters or diaries or video recordings they have left behind. Occasionally, if you are lucky, you get to meet them in person.

Such was the case on a typically splendid Hawaiian afternoon in 2018 when my friend Mariko Miho ushered me into the Maple Garden Restaurant in Honolulu's McCully-Moʻiliʻili neighborhood. The place was loud with the clattering of dishes and lush with warm aromas arising from a buffet arrayed along one wall. Most of the people lined up at the buffet were there for the midweek, midday senior discount. We were there for the company.

Mariko led me to the back of the restaurant where half a dozen white-haired gentlemen, all in their nineties, were sitting at two large round tables, surrounded by their wives and sons and daughters. Mariko introduced me. Everyone smiled and waved a bit shyly and then resumed their conversations. Mariko seated me next to two of the gentlemen and introduced them to me as Roy Fujii and Flint Yonashiro. They were veterans of the 442nd Regimental Combat Team (RCT). During World War II, the regiment had fought the fascist powers in Europe so valiantly that they had emerged from the war as one of the most decorated units in American history. Roy and Flint had known and cared for each other for at least seventy-five years. They had fought together, lost friends together, bled together, been through hell together.

Soon, they were both regaling me with stories, and I was flinging questions at them. Roy patiently explained how to adjust the elevation settings on a 105-millimeter howitzer. They both talked about the terrifying sound of incoming artillery shells, about handing out candy bars to starving children in Italy, about swimming in the Mediterranean, and about picking their way through deadly minefields in Germany. I pulled out some maps, and soon both men were hunched over them, eagerly comparing notes, pointing out features of some terrain in France—mountains they had climbed, river crossings where friends had died. We talked for an hour or more, and through it all they were both so bright-eyed and clearheaded and vibrantly alive that you might have thought them twentysomething rather than ninetysomething. It was easy to see the eager, audacious, good-hearted young men they had once been.

When lunch was over and the veterans began to push their chairs away from the tables, family members scrambled for walkers and canes. Daughters who were themselves in their sixties or seventies rushed to help their fathers stand up. Sons cleared aisles for wheelchairs. When Roy Fujii rose to stand, he wobbled just a bit. A chair stood between him and the door, and it wasn't clear that he saw it. Faster than I could have, ninety-four-year-old Flint Yonashiro sprang to his feet, sprinted around the table, pushed the chair out of the way, steadied Roy, and handed him his cane.

It was a small thing, but I'll never forget it. It summed up in a gesture everything I have learned about not only those half a dozen men but thousands more just like them. For three-quarters of a century, all across the country, they have been coming together—at luncheons and dinners and *lūʻau*, in homes and restaurants and veterans' halls—needing to be in one another's presence again, needing to show again how much they love one another, needing to take care of each other, as brothers do. As they left the restaurant that afternoon, strangers made way for them, and a hushed reverence washed over the room. All of us knew that they would not be with us much longer, and all of us wished that were not so. And that is why I have set out here—with a great deal of help from some of them, and from their sons and daughters and friends and compatriots— to tell you their remarkable story as best I can.

SOME CAME FROM SMALL TOWNS, some from big cities. Some hailed from family farms in the American West, some from vast pineapple and sugarcane plantations in Hawaiʻi. By and large, they had grown up like other American boys, playing baseball and football and going to Saturday afternoon matinees. They performed in marching bands on the Fourth of July, went to county fairs, ate burgers and fries, messed around under the hoods of cars, and listened to swing tunes on the radio. They made plans to go to college or work in the family business or run the farm someday. They eyed pretty girls walking down school corridors clutching books to their chests, making their way to class. They studied American history and English literature, took PE and shop classes, looked forward to their weekends. And as the holiday season approached in 1941, it seemed as if the whole world lay before them.

But within hours of the Japanese attack on Pearl Harbor, all that changed. Within days, the FBI was banging on their doors, searching their homes, hauling their fathers away to undisclosed locations. Within weeks, many of them would watch as their immigrant parents were forced to sell their homes for pennies on the dollar and shutter businesses that they had spent decades building. Within months, tens of thousands of them or their family members would be living in barracks behind barbed wire or have family members who were.

For all their essential Americanness, the traumatic events of that December brought back into focus something they had always known: their place in American society remained tenuous. Millions of their countrymen regarded them with an unfettered animosity born of decades of virulent anti-Asian rhetoric spewing forth from the press and from the mouths of politicians. Local ordinances regulated where they could and could not live. Labor unions routinely barred them from employment in many industries. Proprietors of businesses could, at will, ban them from entering their premises. Public facilities were sometimes closed to them. State laws prohibited their parents from owning real estate. In many states they were not free to marry across racial lines. Their national government prohibited their parents from becoming citizens.

And they knew this, too: their lives, their very identities, were inevitably bound to their roots. The values that their parents had bestowed on them—the manner in which they approached others, the standards by which they measured success, the obligations they felt, the respect they owed to their elders, the traditions they celebrated, and a multitude of other facets of their individual and collective identities—were not things they could or would willingly cast aside. They were, in fact, things they cherished.

Because many of them had relatives living in Japan, they had seen the storm clouds growing over the Pacific long before most other Americans had. And they knew immediately on that first Sunday in December 1941 that straddling two worlds now suddenly at war would challenge them in ways that would shake the foundations of their lives.

For those young men there was no obvious path forward, no simple right way or wrong way to proceed with their lives. Some of them would launch campaigns of conscientious resistance to the deprivation of their constitutional rights. Others—thousands of them—would serve, and some would die, on the battlefields of Europe, striving to prove their loyalty to their country. Scores of their mothers would dissolve into tears as they saw grim-faced officers coming in past barbed-wire fencing bearing shattering news. But by the end of their lives almost all of them—whether they fought in courtrooms or in foxholes—would be counted American heroes.

At its heart, this is the story of those young men—some of the bravest Americans who have ever lived, the Nisei warriors of World War II, and how they, through their actions, laid bare for all the world to see what exactly it means to be an American. But it's also the story of their immigrant parents, the Issei, who like other immigrants before them—whether they came from Ireland or Italy, from North Africa or Latin America—faced suspicion and prejudice from the moment they arrived in America. It's the story of how they set out to win their place in American society, working at menial jobs from dawn to dusk, quietly enduring discrimination and racial epithets, struggling to learn the language, building businesses, growing crops, knitting together families, nurturing their children, creating homes. It's the story of wives and mothers and sisters who kept families together under extreme conditions. It's the story of the first Americans since the Cherokee in 1838 to face wholesale forced removal from their homes, deprivation of their livelihoods, and mass incarceration.

But in the end it's not a story of victims. Rather, it's a story of victors, of people striving, resisting, rising up, standing on principle, laying down their lives, enduring, and prevailing. It celebrates some young Americans who decided they had no choice but to do what their sense of honor and loyalty told them was right, to cultivate their best selves, to embrace the demands of conscience, to leave their homes and families and sally forth into the fray, to confront and to conquer the mountain of troubles that lay suddenly in their paths.

PART ONE

SHOCK

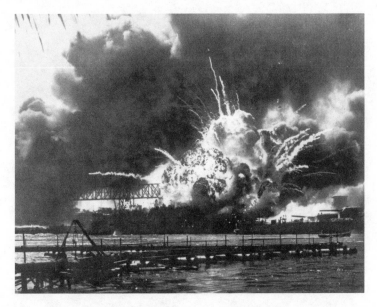

The USS *Shaw* explodes during the attack on Pearl Harbor

ONE

======

*If I ever meet a Japanese soldier, I'm going to knock him down
and kick him in the balls.*

TED TSUKIYAMA
UNIVERSITY OF HAWAIʻI STUDENT
DECEMBER 7, 1941

Katsugo "Kats" Miho was one of those kids you just couldn't help
but like. It didn't hurt that he was handsome. Even before he
put on a uniform, the girls at the University of Hawaiʻi thought
he looked pretty dreamy, almost like a movie star—"a Japanese Cary
Grant," they said. Especially when he slicked back his hair and tossed
you that easy, carefree smile of his. But it wasn't just his looks that drew
people to Kats Miho. It was the hand he always extended to you, the
look he gave you, the way it invited you in, the way it said, "Eh, let's get
to know each other, let's talk story, let's get somethin' going."

There was a casual grace, a natural optimism, a happy-go-lucky as-
suredness to him that you just couldn't turn away from.

Early on the morning of December 7, 1941, he was in Honolulu,
asleep at the Charles Atherton House, a stately shell-pink building that
the YMCA operated as a dormitory for students at the university, though
the place looked more like an English country manor house than a
dorm. As the sun rose over Oʻahu that morning, Kats stirred in his bed,

thinking about the day ahead. Ordinarily, he would have slept in late on a Sunday morning, but word among his friends was that there was an interesting new minister at the Church of the Crossroads just down the street. Better yet, he'd heard that a pair of particularly attractive sisters from the Big Island were going to be playing piano at the morning service. He and some buddies had decided to give the church a try. After church, he figured he would study for his last few exams and then start preparing to go home to Maui for Christmas break.

He couldn't wait to get home. His first semester at the university had been a great success. He'd joined the Reserve Officers' Training Corps (ROTC), made friends on campus and at Atherton House, was getting good grades, and was having the time of his life. But he missed his mother's cooking and the company of his siblings. And he was looking forward to hanging out on the beach with some of his old friends from Maui High, the ones who had gone from high school straight to work on the sugarcane and pineapple plantations. Maybe they'd play some barefoot football or have a cookout on the beach at Kīhei, the way they had when they were kids.

AT 6:26 THAT MORNING, just as Kats was beginning to wake up, the USS *Antares*, a navy cargo vessel, arrived in restricted water off Pearl Harbor, towing a five-hundred-ton steel barge. In the dim gray light of dawn, the skipper, Lawrence Grannis, noticed an odd cigar-shaped object in the water fifteen hundred yards off his starboard bow. Uncertain what he was looking at in the thin gray morning light, but suspecting that it might be some sort of strange submarine, Grannis radioed the nearby destroyer *Ward* and suggested that the ship's captain, William Outerbridge, and his crew investigate. At the same time, flying overhead in a navy PBY patrol plane, Ensign William Tanner also spotted the object. Thinking it was an American submarine in trouble, he dropped two smoke pots into the water near it to mark its position. The *Ward* turned toward the smoke and accelerated to twenty-five knots, bearing down rapidly on what soon everyone could see in the dawn light was indeed a submarine, but a very odd, very small one, definitely not American. At 6:45 the *Ward* opened fire and launched depth charges. The first shot missed, the shell sailing over the sub, but the second hit the vessel squarely at the intersection of the conning tower and the hull. Immediately the sub began to heel over and sink. Almost simultaneously one of the depth charges appeared to detonate directly under it and oil bubbled to the surface, confirming the kill. At 6:54, the *Ward* transmitted a message to Lieutenant Commander Harold Kaminski, the Fourteenth Naval District duty officer at Pearl: "We have attacked, fired upon, and dropped depth charges on a submarine operating in defensive sea areas."

Kaminski, startled, hesitated, uncertain whether to believe it. There had been a number of false sightings of hostile submarines in recent months. On the other hand, the news from East Asia had been growing more troubling for weeks. He picked up a telephone and began what would turn out to be a protracted game of phone tag involving multiple officers as over the next hour news of the incident slowly worked its way up the chain of command toward Admiral Husband E. Kimmel, commander in chief of the U.S. Fleet and Pacific Fleet.

Meanwhile, just eight minutes after the *Ward* first dispatched its alarming news, at the army's Opana mobile radar site on the northern tip of Oʻahu, Private George Elliott peered down into the screen of his oscilloscope and couldn't quite believe what he was seeing—a large blip, larger than anything he had ever seen on the newfangled machine. It looked to him like something on the order of fifty or more incoming aircraft flying directly toward the island from the north, about 132 miles out. Alarmed, he asked the only other man on duty, Private Joseph Lockard, to take a look. Lockard peered into the scope, then checked the equipment to see if it seemed to be working correctly. He, too, had never seen anything like it, but he figured it was most likely American planes and not worth reporting. Elliott, however, picked up the phone and called the U.S. Army Air Corps' information center at

Fort Shafter. He was told to wait for someone to call him back. More minutes ticked by. At about 7:15, Lieutenant Kermit Tyler called back, reaching Lockard. Tyler, figuring that what Elliott and Lockard had seen was most likely a flight of B-17s he expected to arrive from the mainland that morning, told Lockard, "Don't worry about it. It's okay." At about the same time, word of the *Ward*'s encounter with the small submarine finally reached Admiral Kimmel. Like Kaminski, he was dubious about the report's veracity. He decided to do nothing for the moment, choosing to wait for confirmation.

There was, in fact, a flight of B-17s from California approaching O'ahu that morning. But they didn't produce the blip on the radar that Elliott and Lockard saw. The blip was the radar reflection of 183 Japanese warplanes. The navigators of those planes, adjusting the tuners on their radios, had just begun to hear Hawaiian music—the soft sound of steel-string guitars and ukuleles—over the growling of their engines. It was Honolulu's radio station KGMB. At the request of the army, the station manager had agreed the evening before to stay on the air and keep the music playing all night. That way, the navigators of the incoming B-17s would be able to use the station's signal to home in on the most direct route to the Honolulu area. Now the Japanese navigators began to do exactly that, following the music toward Pearl Harbor.

But they were still half an hour from reaching O'ahu. At the Chuo Gakuin Japanese-language school on Honolulu's Nu'uanu Avenue, a Sunday school class was just getting under way, the teacher playing a piano, her students singing their school song. On the beach at Waikīkī, early morning swimmers laid towels on the soft coral sand and then waded out into the turquoise surf. For thirty minutes, coffee percolated in sunny kitchens, dogs wandered across deserted Sunday morning streets, the yellow blossoms of *hau* trees slowly opened, church bells rang, and mynah birds fussed and chattered among the fronds of palm trees as Pearl Harbor, its neighboring military bases, and the city of Honolulu went about the business of greeting another beautiful Hawaiian morning. Up at Atherton House, Kats Miho tossed aside his bed-sheets, got up, and headed for the shower room.

FOR MANY SURVIVORS, what happened next on Oʻahu was frozen in time for the rest of their lives.

At first, they looked insignificant, like swarms of black insects drifting across the pale, early morning sky. But then they looped around over the sea and the mountains and started to descend, spiraling down in groups of five or six, dropping dark objects from their bellies, the objects making white plumes in the water. The brain, trying to make sense of it, couldn't quite. Sailors and officers, soldiers and civilians alike stopped what they were doing and peered into the sky and wondered the same thing—what on earth was this? Not insects, but planes, but why? Some stunt? Flyboys goofing off again? Some kind of kooky Sunday morning military exercise? But as the planes grew nearer, one by one they suddenly assumed the form of something horrific, something compounded of gray steel, sleek glass, and huge black roaring engines. They came in low, some not more than fifty or sixty feet off the water, coming right at ships, at buildings, at trucks and houses and men standing on runways with their mouths agape, maybe even at you if you were unlucky—growling, spitting fire, flashing by overhead, big red disks under their wings and on their flanks. Then the brain finally, reluctantly, got it.

Japanese Zeros struck first at Kāneʻohe Bay Naval Air Station, sixteen miles northeast of Pearl Harbor at 7:48, raking aircraft parked on the ground with machine-gun fire, setting them ablaze, then circling back through billowing clouds of black smoke, strafing anything else that presented itself, cars racing toward the scene, men scrambling across the field trying to find cover, even private residences. About seven minutes later, many more planes—high-altitude bombers, dive-bombers, torpedo planes—struck, almost simultaneously, the naval air station on Ford Island in the middle of Pearl Harbor, the marine air base at ʻEwa, Wheeler and Bellows Army Air Fields, Schofield Barracks, and Hickam Field just south of Pearl. At many of these locations, American aircraft were grouped together—lined up wingtip to wingtip—the better to guard them against potential sabotage. Arrayed thus, they made easy targets for the attackers, and within minutes the American ability to mount an effective air defense simply vanished in a maelstrom of flames, shattered glass, twisted metal, and scattered bodies. At Ford Island, as bombs exploded right outside his window, Logan Ramsey, in charge of the command center, sprinted to the radio room, yelling at the radioman to broadcast an uncoded message, one that would quickly reach all the way to Washington, D.C.: "Air raid. Pearl Harbor. This is no drill."

Then the attackers wheeled their planes around and turned to the American fleet and their principal targets, seven enormous battleships lined up alongside Ford Island and an eighth, sitting helpless in dry dock. On the deck of one of those battleships, the USS *Nevada*, a military band was just striking up "The Star-Spangled Banner" for the 8:00 a.m. ritual of raising the American flag. Suddenly a Japanese torpedo plane roared in sixty feet off the water and sprayed machine-gun fire across the *Nevada's* deck, somehow missing all the band members but shredding the American flag halfway up the pole. The band kept playing until the anthem was finished. Then, flinging their instruments aside, men scrambled for cover. It was about the last lucky break the Americans would get that morning.

On the USS *Oklahoma*, a sailor screamed over the PA system, "Man your battle stations! This is no shit!" But almost immediately two torpedoes punched into the port side of the ship in rapid succession, and the ship began to list. Then a third hit, and minutes later it rolled over entirely, trapping hundreds belowdecks, its great gray hull turned to the sky like the belly of a dead whale. At about the same time, seven torpedoes and two aerial bombs hit the USS *West Virginia,* and it began to sink rapidly, trapping and drowning another sixty-six men belowdecks. Within minutes all eight battleships and a number of other, lesser ships had been hit.

Then the worst of it. Sometime between 8:04 and 8:10, an armor-piercing bomb penetrated the foredeck of the already damaged USS *Arizona* and detonated perhaps a million pounds of high explosives in its forward ammunition magazine. A fireball engulfed the ship. A shock wave pulsed out across Pearl Harbor. Men were blown off the decks of nearby ships. The *Arizona*—nearly thirty thousand tons of steel—jumped ten or fifteen feet in the air, ruptured, and sank rapidly, leaving only its devastated superstructure above water. Within moments 1,177 of its crew were dead, nearly half the ultimate death toll for the day.

Everywhere, without waiting for orders, men scrambled to get their hands on whatever sorts of guns they could—.50-caliber machine guns, antiaircraft batteries, rifles, pistols, anything that might hurl some lead or steel into the sky. On the *New Orleans*, which had lost electrical power, Chaplain Howell Forgy urged on men trying to manually load the ship's five-inch guns, bellowing, "Praise the Lord and pass the ammunition!" As the flight of thirteen unarmed American B-17s from California approached Oʻahu, their astonished pilots found themselves frantically dodging and weaving, trying to avoid fire from Japanese Zeros and the wild barrages of friendly fire coming up from the ground.

A deadly hailstorm of Japanese bombs and misdirected American antiaircraft shells began to fall on civilian areas of Honolulu, setting fire to houses, crumpling cars, taking, all told, forty-nine civilian lives. At the Japanese-language school on Nuʻuanu Avenue, a shell hit the auditorium. The blast sent desks, school satchels, books, and children flying. Beneath the rubble, seven-year-old Nancy Arakaki began to bleed to death. Eight-year-old Jacky Hirosaki ran from the school to his grandmother's nearby restaurant, the Cherry Blossom, where another shell exploded in the street outside, sending shrapnel flying, killing Jacky, his father, his brother, and his two-year-old sister, Shirley.

By now, a second wave of 167 attack planes had lifted off from the Japanese carriers north of Oʻahu and were bearing down on the island. Over the next two hours the carnage continued to unfurl in the harbor and in Honolulu—a swirling kaleidoscope of horrors. On the smoldering hulk of the *Arizona*, a big, husky cook sitting, staring mutely at the stump of his leg. Sailors wandering like zombies on bloodied decks, naked and ghostly white, their clothes and skin burned from them. Men in the water, covered in black oil. Oil on the surface of the water burning, surrounding the men, closing in on them. Suffocating black smoke. Deafening concussions. From inside the *Oklahoma*, the sound of someone pounding on its hull, desperately trying to find a way out, finding none. At a hospital in Honolulu, ambulance drivers in blood-soaked uniforms carrying in moaning victims, their bodies blackened. In the hospital morgue, a little girl, barefoot, wearing a red sweater, clutching the burned-off end of a jump rope.

A civilian home damaged during the Pearl Harbor attack

MANY OF THE JAPANESE PILOTS brought their planes in so low that morning that people on the ground could see the pilots looking back at them, making eye contact, sometimes stone-faced, sometimes grinning, sometimes even waving at them as they passed overhead. And those pilots, looking down, could not help but see that the faces looking back up at them in astonishment looked, in many cases, very much like faces they might see back home in Japan.

In 1941, nearly a third of Hawai'i's residents were of entirely Japanese ancestry.* As the horrors of that day unfolded, they, overwhelmingly, reacted with the same stunned fury and outrage as other Americans. One U.S. soldier, Akiji Yoshimura, later summed up what many of them felt that morning, saying he felt "deep anguish and despair because the land that I had been taught to honor by my parents had committed an act of war against the country that I loved."

Ronald Oba—a senior at the 'Iolani School in downtown Honolulu— was enjoying a regular Sunday morning treat, pancakes, with his family, when he heard what he thought were fireworks. As the sounds grew louder, he revised his thinking. It must be military exercises. But when a much larger explosion shook the house and rattled the windows, Ronald jumped out of his chair, sprinted down Kauhale Street, jogged across the railroad tracks, and came to a stop on the eastern shore of Pearl Harbor, staring dumbfounded at the pillars of dense black smoke rising from Ford Island and, beyond that, the wreckage of the *Arizona*. As he stood there, trying to make sense of it, another series of explosions rocked Battleship Row. When one of the planes banked and headed directly toward Ronald, he saw the Rising Sun insignia of imperial Japan and thought, "The nerve of these guys! They're our ancestors and come and attack us like that!"

Seventeen-year-old Daniel Inouye was getting dressed, listening idly to the Hawaiian music that KGMB had been playing all night to guide in the B-17s, when announcer Webley Edwards broke in with a bulletin, screaming into the mic—"This is no test! This is the real McCoy! Pearl Harbor is being bombed by the Japanese! Get off the streets!" Defying the advice, Inouye rushed from his house in Honolulu's Mo'ili'ili

---

*In the 1940 U.S. census, there were 128,947 people of Japanese descent living on the islands out of a population of 423,330.

neighborhood. He, too, saw the Rising Sun insignia on the wings of a Zero passing overhead and was immediately overwhelmed by a wave of anger and dread. "I thought my life was over," he later said. But he got on his bike and raced to a first aid station at the Lunalilo School, where he would spend most of the next three days and nights helping treat the wounded and carrying the dead to the morgue.

In the old plantation town of Waipahu on the north shore of Pearl Harbor, Flint Yonashiro, a high school student, heard planes roaring low overhead. He stepped from the small restaurant where his mother sold ice cream and saimin noodles just in time to see twin lines of bullets slamming into the ground in front of him, just missing him, chattering across pavement, kicking up dust, as a Japanese pilot fired on a nearby molasses storage tank, apparently mistaking it for a fuel tank. Flint watched the plane peel off, then stood mesmerized, horrified, and angry as enormous orange blossoms of flame erupted from across the water on Ford Island.

Jesse Hirato had been in the U.S. Army only five weeks when he heard the first radio bulletins that morning. He climbed into a friend's car and headed for his base at Schofield Barracks, but the traffic was snarled up all over Honolulu. Frustrated, Private Hirato, not yet in uniform, stepped out of the car to get a better look at the chaos of Pearl Harbor. While he stood watching, a shore officer stuck a pistol in his ribs and yelled to his superior, "This is a Jap. What do I do with him?" Jesse swallowed the cusswords rising in his throat and explained that he was an American soldier. They sent him on his way. When he arrived at Schofield, he found another scene of chaos—young men in uniform running in every direction, asking what they should do, unloading ammunition from trucks, furiously digging slit trenches in the parade grounds. Jesse headed for his tent, which he found riddled with bullets. Two spent Japanese bullets lay in his bed. He and some others set up a water-cooled machine gun in an open field, pointed it at the sky, and then simply stared at it. None of them had any idea how to use it.

. . .

AT ATHERTON HOUSE eighteen-year-old Takejiro Higa was serving breakfast in the cafeteria when a white woman suddenly burst into the room, shouting, nearly incoherent, "War, war, coffee, coffee!" Someone handed her a cup of coffee, but her hands were shaking so badly most of the coffee splashed out onto her saucer. "I just dropped my husband off at Pearl Harbor," the woman stammered. Takejiro, not yet comprehending what was going on, looked at the other boys working in the cafeteria, shook his head, and said softly, "Eh, this wahine, I think little bit cuckoo, yeah?"

Upstairs, Kats Miho was shaving when a commotion erupted downstairs—a bunch of fellows yelling, heavy footsteps running down the stairs, radios blaring. Curious, he leaned over a balustrade and shouted down Atherton House's open stairwell, "Eh, what's going on down there?" Someone shouted back, "Put on the radio! Listen to the radio!" Someone else yelled, "We're being attacked!"

By the time he got to a radio, Kats realized he could just make out a low rumbling off in the distance. He turned on the radio. An announcer was screaming something about Pearl Harbor. With shaving cream still on his face, Kats scrambled out onto the roof of Atherton House and looked northwest toward Pearl, where black pillars of smoke billowed high into the sky. Takejiro Higa and other boys from downstairs joined him on the roof, some clutching binoculars. They still weren't quite sure what they were seeing until a shell fell much nearer, in the vicinity of Nuʻuanu Avenue, just a mile away. Corrugated iron roofs cartwheeled through the sky. Then a thud. A flash. Smoke. A crater. And a fire, as another shell landed right in front of Atherton House.

Kats raced back to the radio in time to hear another urgent bulletin. All ROTC cadets were to report to the University of Hawaiʻi gym immediately. He threw on his khaki uniform and sprinted across University Avenue and onto the campus, joining a stream of young men, many of them Japanese American, rushing toward the gym.

Inside, five or six hundred boys were milling around noisily in adrenaline-fueled mass confusion. At first nobody seemed to be in charge, but Kats elbowed his way through the crowd and tracked down his ROTC squad leader, a thirty-year-old University of Hawai'i football coach, Francis Aiwohi. Someone dragged in some crates of old 1903 Springfield bolt-action rifles packed in Cosmoline, a thick, sticky petroleum-based rust preventative. Aiwohi set his squad to wiping the smelly concoction from the guns. Then they began trying to figure out how to fit the firing pins into the rifles. More confusion. Their training had not yet progressed to the point that they had yet been allowed to handle weapons. From time to time, they heard Japanese aircraft roaring low overhead. Nobody knew what to expect next or what, exactly, was happening outside. Aiwohi handed each of them a total of five cartridges for his rifle.

Then word began to spread, rippling through the circles of boys sitting anxiously on the hardwood floor of the gym clutching their guns. Reports had come in that Japanese paratroopers wearing blue uniforms were landing on St. Louis Heights, the hills right above campus. They rushed out into a field, peered up the hill, and sure enough, they could just make out figures moving through the keawe trees up on the heights. Someone ordered the stunned young men to form a skirmish line, advance to the base of the hills, and prepare to repel an enemy assault. Kats Miho stood staring up the hill, clutching his rifle, aghast.

TWO

*I remember that many times I prayed for white skin secretly in
my childhood. . . . It was an unwritten understanding that "if
you have yellow skin you cannot be promoted beyond a certain
level—you must be kept in your place."*

FUMIYE MIHO

Home, for as long as Kats could remember, had been the small
hotel his family ran in the port town of Kahului on the island of
Maui. Small as it was—and a bit rickety with termites relentlessly at work on its underpinnings—the Miho Hotel was nevertheless a
happy home, a vibrant place, pulsing year-round with interesting visitors and lively conversations. It was a place where guests and family
alike could enjoy home-cooked, Hiroshima-style Japanese dinners, bathe
in a large wood-fire-heated *ofuro*, fall asleep to the sound of palm fronds
rustling in the trade winds, and awaken in the morning to the shrill
whistles of small, stout steam locomotives pulling the sugar trains through
town.

Two stories tall, with fourteen small guest rooms, the hotel stood
wedged narrowly between Toda's Drug Store and Ah Fook's Grocery on
Kahului's wide Main Street. The family lived at the back of the hotel, in
small rooms centered on a larger tatami room. In the center of the hotel
was a small but lush, open-air courtyard, where Kats's mother, Ayano,

grew spectacular orchids and other tropical flowers—sweet explosions of pink, lavender, and red set among dark green foliage.

Kats's father, Katsuichi—a thin, dapper man with an impeccably trimmed mustache—presided over the hotel. A school principal by training in Japan, he'd become a businessman only by necessity after immigrating to Hawai'i. He studied Buddhism and Shintoism and the teachings of Confucius earnestly. He thought deeply about life. He spoke his opinions boldly and seldom shrank from controversy. Maui's large Japanese community held him in high esteem, and he spent most of his time bustling around town—one or another of his adult children driving him because his own driving was so erratic as to be life threatening—tending to community affairs, distributing a Japanese-language newspaper, cultivating Japanese culture, keeping the old ways alive. That was important to Katsuichi—staying in touch with family back home, celebrating Obon to honor his ancestors, conducting himself as he had been brought up to conduct himself.

He paid little heed to money. Extraordinarily generous, he wrote checks with abandon and with scant awareness of his account balance. He presided over the hotel, but it was Kats's mother who, by and large, ran the place. She watched the budget, paid the bills, supervised the small staff, and cooked the meals that made the Miho Hotel so popular with visiting businessmen from Honolulu and, occasionally, Tokyo.

Kahului was, for all practical purposes, a feudal town. Indeed, virtually all of Maui—with its vast sugarcane plantations—was a feudal fiefdom, ultimately owned and operated by the Baldwin family, descendants of Christian missionaries who had come to the island in the 1830s. The Baldwins had married into another missionary family, the Alexanders, and between the two of them the families had established a business and political dynasty that would effectively rule Maui well into the mid-twentieth century. They lived mostly apart from the rough-and-tumble life of Kahului, ensconced in several placid estates, mostly in Maui's tranquil up-country. They filled their leisure time playing polo, coddling their Pomeranian dogs, and feting one another and prominent visitors from the mainland with lavish *lū'au* and rounds of golf at the Maui Country Club.

The Baldwins exerted their control over the island indirectly, through the corporate auspices of Alexander & Baldwin and its elaborate web of subsidiaries—principal among them the Hawaiian Commercial & Sugar Company and the Kahului Railroad Company. It was the latter of these, the KRR, that mattered most in Kahului. The town was located on Maui's principal deepwater port, and its business was stevedoring—mostly unloading vast quantities of sugar and pineapples from the KRR trains and then loading them onto mainland-bound freighters.

Like the plantations in the surrounding countryside, Kahului was physically divided into "camps," clusters of inexpensive houses owned by different subsidiaries of Alexander & Baldwin. As on the plantations, the camps were segregated along ethnic lines, and pretty much the only people who didn't live in them were white North Americans—haoles in the local vernacular. They lived in comfortable homes hidden behind tall hibiscus hedges along a stretch of white sand known to locals as Haole Beach.

The largest camps, in the center of town, belonged to the KRR and housed Japanese stevedores and their families. Other camps, on the outskirts, bore names hinting at the ethnicity or occupation of their residents. Raw Fish Camp, near the harbor, housed Portuguese fishermen. Alabama Camp was home to Black laborers from the Deep South. At Kolo Camp, Hawaiians lived, as much as they could, as their ancestors had, plying Kahului Bay in outrigger canoes, gathering in family groups to steam taro corms, and pounding poi on long, wooden slabs using ancient basalt pestles.

Along Main Street, the KRR allowed merchants—mostly Japanese and Chinese immigrants—to lease land and build private businesses like Ah Fook's Grocery, Toda's Drug Store, and the Miho Hotel. Owning such businesses made families like the Mihos "town people" rather than "camp people," and thus conferred on them a somewhat elevated social status. It was a precarious advantage, though. The leases on the land were short term, only month to month. The company could snatch them away at any time, for any reason, or for no reason at all.

The biggest of the big homes stretched out along Haole Beach belonged to William Walsh, manager of the KRR, manager in fact of everything and everyone in Kahului. The Mihos, like everyone in town, knew that if they wanted to stay in business for more than thirty days, they'd best not run afoul of Boss Walsh. Or, for that matter, his wife, Mabel.

Accommodations had to be made. Whenever the proprietor of the Kahului Theater, for example, knew that the Walshes might be coming to watch a movie, he sent ushers out into the street to watch for their arrival, working himself into a nervous sweat as he awaited them, refusing to start the film until they had arrived and were comfortably seated. Every New Year's Day, townspeople, the Mihos among them, brought offerings to the Walshes' big house down on the beach—a gallon of sake one year, the next year a dainty red lacquered dressing table that Mabel Walsh had admired in the lobby of the Miho Hotel. Paying a bit of tribute helped to safeguard the future.

THE STRATIFIED SOCIAL STRUCTURE of Kahului—and all of Maui— was replicated across the Hawaiian Islands. From the time the first white missionaries had arrived, the history of the islands had been all about the exploitation of the land and its people. Coming mostly from New England, missionaries like the Baldwin and Alexander families were imbued with the Puritan notion that wealth was an indicator of divine favor. By the late nineteenth century their children and grandchildren— while holding fast to that notion—were also embracing the tenets of social Darwinism, particularly the idea that the Anglo-Saxon race was naturally superior to other races and so best suited for controlling society.

As they and their descendants gained control of the land and began to plant sugarcane and pineapples, they quickly found that they were going to require a great deal of labor to work their fields. Given their view of the world, that meant finding people with darker complexions than their own to do the actual work. It was a view that defined race relations in the islands. The Honolulu businessman Walter Dillingham stated it bluntly in 1921, "When you are asked to go in the sun and into the canebrake away from the tropical breeze you are subjecting the white man to do something that the good Lord did not create him to do. If He had, the people of the world, I think, would have had a white pigment of the skin and not variegated colors."

Initially, the planters turned to the native Hawaiians to work the fields. But there were far too few of them to meet the needs of the sprawling plantations. In 1853 a census of the Kingdom of Hawaiʻi had shown that Hawaiians made up 96 percent of the islands' population. But by 1884, they made up only 50 percent. And by 1896, they constituted barely 25 percent. It wasn't just that their numbers shrank but also that they were swamped by waves of immigrants whom the planters began to import, mostly from Asia—Chinese, Filipino, Korean, and Japanese contract laborers. By far the largest of those waves consisted of Japanese immigrants.

As the plantation system matured, the planters found it useful to play these ethnic groups off against one another. By segregating their housing into camps along racial lines, they adopted a kind of divide-and-conquer strategy, keeping their workforce from organizing in any meaningful way and fostering perceived resentments among the different groups as they competed for scant wages. It was an efficient, often ruthless system that enabled a small oligarchy of powerful families to wield enormous power over the lives of those who made them wealthy.

DESPITE THE DEEP RACIAL and economic inequities of life in Kahului, Kats Miho—like many of the camp kids he grew up with—had an exuberant childhood. Born in 1922, he was the baby of the family, the last of eight children, and much doted on by his older siblings, particularly his sister Fumiye and his brother Katsuaki.* The Miho Hotel was perpetually full of rambunctious young Mihos, all of them bursting with energy, optimism, and a determination to leave their mark on the world. They took much of their worldview from their father and from a central element of his philosophy—maintaining the right posture in the eternal dance between *giri* and *ninjo*. *Giri,* one's obligation to follow the strict rules and norms of society, often clashed with *ninjo*, one's natural feeling of warmth and compassion for fellow humans. Much in life, Katsuichi taught his children, depended on exhibiting both qualities, each in the correct measure, each at the correct time. But perhaps equally, the Miho kids modeled their behavior on their father's disregard for another widely held Japanese tenet, *otonashi*, the necessity of keeping one's place, remaining quiet, avoiding the appearance of knowing too much or voicing too many opinions. The Miho kids were all about getting involved, voicing their opinions, taking charge. And keeping their place was the last thing they intended to do.

In this happy milieu, Kats grew up mostly shoeless and carefree. One of his principal pleasures, in fact, was playing football barefoot, Hawaiian style. The games were wild affairs, boys scrabbling with one another in swirling clouds of red Maui dust, without benefit of helmets or pads or shoes. During the summers he sometimes had to arise at 2:00 in the morning to work in the cane fields, hoeing weeds or cutting cane until 2:00 in the afternoon and counting himself lucky if he earned a dollar for the twelve hours of work. But on weekends he spent long happy days and evenings on Maui's coral-sand beaches with his Boy Scout troop. There the boys threw themselves into the warm surf with abandon, wrestled in the water, lingered in the waves until well after dark, then cooked corned beef and cabbage over campfires. They strummed ukuleles and guitars, sang, gazed up at the vast night sky of Hawai'i, and

---

*All told, Kats had four older brothers—Katsuto (born and raised in Japan), Katsuro, Katsuso (who went by Paul), and Katsuaki. Their father had given them all names beginning, like his own, with "katsu," as a means of expressing the familial loyalty they owed to him and to one another.

talked quietly and confidentially as the surf pounded the sand just beyond the flickering light of their fires, speaking now not in their proper
school English but in the language they had always spoken among themselves, their easy, natural Hawaiian pidgin. When they couldn't get to
the beach, they fished for *manini*, yellow surgeonfish, under the pier in
Kahului Harbor, using bent pins for hooks, or they gathered little sand
crabs that their mothers would coat with batter and drop into hot ses-
ame oil to make sweet, crunchy tempura.

On weekdays Kats attended Kahului's public, English-language
school. In the afternoons he attended Japanese-language school, where
he struggled without much success to learn his parents' language but
took a deep interest in *shushin*, Japanese ethics. On Sundays, the Miho
family put on shoes, dressed up in fancy clothes, and went to the Kahului Union Church, where they sang songs with lyrics like "Jesus loves
me, this I know." After the services they walked down the street to the
Buddhist temple, where a priest in robes beckoned them in. They removed their shoes and sat on tatami mats while the priest, to everyone's
amusement, sometimes led them in singing, "Buddha loves me, this I
know."

Once a month or so, trucks drove through town preceded by rattling
drummers and young men distributing leaflets announcing Japanese
silent films to be played out in the cane fields that evening. On those
warm Maui nights, Kats and his brother Katsuaki crawled through the
cane on their bellies to avoid detection, quietly swatting away cane spiders the size of their hands, then slithered under canvas barriers to
watch the movies. The films—usually samurai movies like *The Forty-
Seven Ronin* and *The Treasury of the Loyal Retainers*—flickered on white
sheets while professional "movie talkers," or *benshi,* narrated them in
Japanese with dramatic flourishes. Most of the Japanese was lost on the
Miho brothers, but watching the films, they absorbed elements of a warrior tradition that would eventually serve them in ways they could not
yet imagine.

It was the Maui County Fair, though, that Kats dreamed about and

The Miho kids on Maui: (*left to right*) Paul, Kats, Fumiye, Katsuaki

anticipated all year long. Like fairs on the mainland, it was a feast for the senses, with the lowing of cows and squealing of piglets, the smoky scent of barbecue and grilled onions, the wheezing melodies and shrill whistles of a steam-powered carousel. There were amateur boxing matches, trapeze artists, horse races, livestock exhibitions, and dog shows. Kids gobbled popcorn and hot dogs, guzzled cold Coke and root beer, and sank their faces into pink swirls of cotton candy.

But this wasn't Iowa. Along with the cotton candy, Kats and his friends clutched paper cones of shave ice, served Japanese style, with a scoop of sweet bean paste at the bottom of the cup. Instead of funnel cakes, they lined up for Portuguese malasadas fresh out of hot oil and dusted with cinnamon and local sugar. They scooped the sweet orange flesh out of ripe papayas. In the agricultural exhibits they eyed mounds of mangoes and pineapples and 'uala, Okinawan purple sweet potatoes. At the sugarcane exhibit, wicked-sharp cane knives flashed in the sun as young men raced to see who could cut the most seed cane in a set period of time.

The fair also offered Kats a unique pleasure, one that would affect him later in life. Nearly all the sideshow people—the Bearded Lady, the World's Tallest Human, the Contortionist, Freckles the Clown, the Man with Two Stomachs—stayed at the Miho Hotel, drawn by Ayano's cooking and a desire to stay concealed from the townspeople lest they give them a free show.

They were kind to Kats. For hours at a time, they sat around card tables among the orchids in the hotel's garden courtyard, smoking cigarettes, playing dominoes, sipping sake, and regaling Kats with tall tales of carnival life. The Man with Two Stomachs demonstrated how he could swallow objects and regurgitate particular items on demand. The Bearded Lady confided that she was not, actually, a lady at all. The World's Tallest Human, an affable kid from Memphis, Willie Camper, proudly showed Kats his size 33 shoes and how he could hold a dozen eggs, unstacked, in the palm of his twelve-inch-long hand. At first, Kats thought the sideshow guests were funny, something to snicker about later with his friends down on the beach, but as he matured, and they kept coming back to the hotel each year, Kats soon came to empathize with them. Seeing the world through the eyes of "freaks," understanding their humanity, feeling the warmth of their goodwill toward him, added to what Kats had learned from his father about treating others with compassion.

It was when he entered Maui High, though, that Kats really came into his own. Located in the foothills of Mount Haleakala, Maui's massive shield volcano, where the trade winds kept things cool most days, the school was an improbable-looking place, its graceful, vine-covered California mission-revival architecture rising monumentally out of a vast sea of sugarcane like the temple of a lost civilization. And it was a kind of temple. Every school morning, hundreds of students arrived at a flagpole in front of the school, many of them walking in barefoot from the plantations on dusty footpaths among the cane fields. A corps of buglers summoned them to gather in a circle. They put their hands over their hearts and recited the Pledge of Allegiance as the American flag was slowly raised. Then they ascended a grand staircase to the main campus and trooped off to their first classes of the morning.

And the classes were exceptional. Aside from its architecture, what made Maui High special was its faculty. Inspired young teachers from the mainland taught Homer, English literature, Latin, astronomy, philosophy, cellular biology, and world history to the sons and daughters of plantation workers and railroad officials alike. The curriculum was so rich that even some of the Baldwin children enrolled, forsaking the usual practice among the planters of sending their children to private boarding schools on the mainland.

Right from the start, Kats threw himself enthusiastically into the life of the school. He played football—now with a uniform, a helmet, and proper shoes with cleats. He joined clubs, performed in plays, and got involved in student government, where he quickly discovered that he had a knack for public speaking and leadership. For the next four years, he spoke his opinion loudly and boldly in class discussions. He reached out and formed connections. And by his senior year he found himself wielding a gavel as the president of a student body of just over a thousand students. His friends, amused and impressed by his success, took to calling him Prezi.

Kats Miho at Maui High

After graduating, Kats spent a year working as a maintenance man at the Maui Pineapple cannery in Kahului to save up some money. In the fall of 1941—following in the footsteps of his older siblings Katsuaki and Fumiye—he moved to Honolulu, enrolled at the university, and moved into Atherton House.

And that's how he came to be there on the morning of the day that would change everything he had ever known, that would shut down the Miho Hotel, separate his parents, cost him a brother, isolate his sister, challenge his identity, and send him halfway around the world deep into the landscape of a nightmare.

THREE

The news had gotten around that my father was going to be taken soon after. And so my father was all prepared and he was dressed in his coat and tie. They had these gun bayonets. They said, "Hey! You are arrested! Come with us!" And they just grabbed him. Oh, we were all so scared, and we didn't know what to do.

LAURA IIDA MIHO

In 1941, there were forty-five million radios in the United States, and on any given Sunday most of them were likely to be turned on. Radio programming was enormously popular throughout the country, particularly on Sunday afternoons, after church, when life offered working Americans an opportunity to finally sit down, pick up some knitting needles or a newspaper or a panful of peas in need of shelling, and enjoy a broadcast. But when the first bulletins about Pearl Harbor came crackling across the airwaves that day, whatever they had been doing, whatever they had been listening to, faded instantly into insignificance for millions of Americans and their allies around the world. In Los Angeles and in Omaha, in London and in Toronto, people leaned closer to their radios, beckoned others to gather around, and listened intently. In those first few minutes, most of them understood that whatever else the news signified, it meant that a generation, their generation, was about to be defined forever.

ONE OF THE RADIOS TURNED on that day was in a small apartment over a small commercial laundry in a beaten-down neighborhood called Hillyard, on the shabby side of Spokane, Washington.

Hillyard was a rough-hewn place, a mile or so of old brick storefronts and small, wood-frame houses squatting on weedy lots alongside the sprawling five-hundred-acre rail yard of James J. Hill's Great Northern Railway. With a roundhouse capable of holding twenty locomotives at a time, massive sheds for the manufacture and repair of more locomotives, enormous tanks for storing oil, a lumber mill for making railroad ties, gravel pits, machine shops, and rows of boxcars with their wheels removed and converted into cheap housing for workers, the Great Northern yard was a bedlam of clanging steel, shrieking whistles, and engines belching steam, day and night. It was a world of grime and grease and grit, of soot and sweat, of perpetually soiled overalls and grubby work shirts—the kind of place that needed a laundry nearby.

Just half a block from the yard, the Hillyard Laundry occupied the downstairs portion of a narrow two-story building on East Olympic Avenue. The laundry's busy proprietors, Kisaburo and Tori Shiosaki, were at their ease that morning after another long week of work. Six days a week, the Shiosakis arose well before dawn to begin their sixteen-hour workdays, firing up the laundry's huge boilers, operating the whirring extractor that spun most of the water out of hundreds of pounds of wet clothes and bedsheets, wrestling the still wet laundry into two large electric dryers, pulling it all out, and then ironing, shaking, and folding it, until it was finally time to open the shop at 7:00 a.m. and greet the day's first customers.

Most of the Shiosakis' customers, indeed most of Hillyard's residents, were recent immigrants—mainly German, Irish, Scandinavian, or Italian laborers, the majority of whom worked for the Great Northern in one capacity or another. A few were Japanese, from a colony of railroad workers who lived in the boxcars on the other side of the tracks in a place called Dogtown, the only place in the Spokane area that could be called a step down from Hillyard. Whichever side of the tracks they came from, their customers were almost universally fond of the Shiosakis, whom they called Kay and Mrs. Kay, monikers that the pair liked and happily embraced for themselves. Pretty much everyone in town enjoyed stopping in for a few minutes to exchange pleasantries and a bit of morning gossip with Kay and Mrs. Kay before they dropped off their laundry and got on with their day's work.

Tori and Kisaburo Shiosaki at work in the Hillyard Laundry

But that December Sunday was a day for resting up, for Kisaburo to sit back, read the *Spokane Spokesman-Review*, and enjoy a few of the big White Owl cigars that he favored. It was a cold, mostly clear day in Hillyard, not quite freezing, but just on the edge of it. The snow from a storm the week before had mostly melted, but the streets were still icy, the ground rock hard, the vegetation in James J. Hill Park over on Nebraska Avenue brown and withered. Driven by a chilling north wind, a few high clouds scudded rapidly across a nearly white sky. Small as it was—just two bedrooms, a sitting room, and a kitchen—the apartment over the laundry was pleasant, cozy, and warm, the wet heat rising from the big boilers downstairs, steaming up the windows. And it was full of the usual comfortable Sunday morning smells—eggs frying, toast browning, tea brewing on the stove. If she had time, Tori Shiosaki thought she might go downtown to the Methodist Mission Church in Spokane to visit with some of the Japanese ladies there. After a week of struggling to communicate with her customers in English, she always enjoyed being able to speak Japanese.

THE SHIOSAKIS' SEVENTEEN-YEAR-OLD SON, Fred, had turned the radio on. He wasn't really looking forward to the next morning. The school week usually dragged for Fred. He was a competent but not particularly enthusiastic student at John R. Rogers High. He was vice president of the school's photography club and popular on the track team, but he really lived for his weekends, particularly his Saturdays. His Saturday mornings, like his weekday mornings, began at dawn with chores, mostly cutting and splitting the seemingly endless supply of firewood required for the boilers, but by afternoon he was free to play baseball with his friends in one of the town's many vacant lots, take photographs around town, ride his bike down to the Rialto Theater on Diamond Avenue to catch a matinee western, or wander among the sagebrush and ponderosa pines up in Spokane's dry, dusty hills, plinking at tin cans with his .22 rifle.

At five feet six, Fred was a slight, bespectacled young man, light-skinned with a tendency to pink up in the cheeks when the weather turned cold or he got excited. He had a twinkle in his eye, a ready smile, a surprisingly hearty laugh, and a ready willingness to poke fun at himself. He was polite and courteous as a first instinct. In a tough town like Hillyard—and it was a very tough town, particularly if you were a kid trying to hold your own out on its potholed streets—he looked at first glance like someone you could steamroll, pick a fight with, and walk away a winner. More than a few Hillyard boys had made that calculation over the years, and nearly all of them had quickly come to regret it.

For all his genuine good nature, Fred had a core of steel. If someone tried to take advantage of him, the politeness melted away in an instant. He wound up in so many scuffles that his father threatened to stop buying him new eyeglasses if he kept coming home with smashed pairs. At fifteen dollars a pair, it was straining the family budget. More often than not, the fights arose because in the ethnic stew of Hillyard race and ethnicity were often a bully's first and most potent line of attack. Fred would not abide being bullied, and above all he would not abide being called a Jap. It didn't matter a whit how big the boy hurling the epithet at him was. Defiance would rise in Fred like a cobra. With narrowed eyes and a clenched jaw, he would hiss out the first cussword he could think of, clench his fists, and go at the offender in a flash. He didn't always win, but he never backed down.

At 11:30 a.m., Fred was listening to the opening of *The World Today*, a regular CBS news show, when an agitated voice abruptly broke into the broadcast: "Go ahead, New York!" Then a different voice, the show's anchor, John Charles Daly, was suddenly on the air. This voice was urgent, crackling through the speaker: "The Japanese have attacked Pearl Harbor, Hawaii, by air, President Roosevelt has just announced." Fred looked up, startled, trying to comprehend it. Daly went on, "The attack also was made on all naval and military activities on the principal island of Oʻahu."* Fred called to his father in the next room, "Hey, Pop. The Japanese have attacked Hawaii." Fred's parents, his brother Floyd, and his sister, Blanche, all gathered around Fred and the radio. His parents suddenly looked drawn, pale, tense. After listening for a while, Kisaburo murmured, "It's not going to last long." But he didn't look con-

---

*Though Daly actually mispronounced the island's name as "Ohau."

vinced, and Fred couldn't decipher what exactly his father meant. Why wouldn't it last long? Troubling thoughts began to worm their way through his mind: What would happen to the laundry? What would his friends and neighbors do? What would happen at school the next day?

As the noon hour passed, Fred put his homework aside unfinished and sat in front of the radio stunned as the word began to pour out, over and over again, sounding more and more venomous each time. "The Japs." "The dirty Japs." "The dirty yellow Japs." This time, though, the word wasn't coming from adolescent bullies on the streets of Hillyard; it was coming from adults, from stern-voiced news announcers, from military officials issuing emergency proclamations, from figures of respect and authority. It was serious, sober, cold, official, and it seemed to be coming from the heart of America itself.

For Fred's parents the word, and the tone, came as no surprise. They had traveled a long, hard road from their previous lives in Japan. Since arriving in America they had been mistreated often enough, heard the word hurled at them often enough to know that as friendly as their customors in Hillyard might be, much of the country had long since hardened its heart against people who looked like them. Now, instinctively, Tori Shiosaki pulled down the blinds on the apartment's two little upstairs windows looking out onto the mean streets of Hillyard.

IN JAPAN, it was already December 8 when word of the attack reached civilians going about their morning business. Kats Miho's sister Fumiye was in suburban Tokyo, standing in the classroom where she taught English at a women's college when another teacher, a young Russian named Miss Zabriaski, rushed into her classroom.

"Miss Miho, Miss Miho! War between Japan, America!"

Fumiye smiled and laughed her off. "No, no, that's just propaganda," she said, and went on teaching. Miss Zabriaski, with little English, looked exasperated, stuttered something in Russian, and ran from the room.

Fumiye—fed up with the racial discrimination she had faced growing up on Maui—had come to Japan in the spring of 1940, shortly after graduating from the University of Hawai'i. The impetus for the move had come when a famous Oxford-educated Buddhist scholar, Dr. Junjiro Takakusu, visited the university, saw Fumiye's extraordinary academic potential, and suggested that she enroll for graduate studies at Japan's most prestigious university, Tokyo Imperial. Fumiye had enthusiastically embraced the chance and set sail for Japan almost without a second thought. Only when she arrived in Yokohama did she discover that her new mentor had overlooked one crucial detail: women were not allowed to enroll at Tokyo Imperial. Nevertheless, she moved in with her older sister Tsukie and her husband, a dentist.

Fumiye threw herself into her new life. She found jobs teaching English part-time. She took advanced lessons in ikebana and dutifully wore kimonos for tea ceremony every Friday. She developed a deep interest in Kabuki. She stopped speaking English at home with Tsukie.* And she thrilled to the rhythms and opportunities of her new life. For the first time, she felt a fully fledged part of the society in which she lived, as if she truly belonged and would not be judged by her appearance or held back by her race.

She knew that tensions between the country where she had been born and the country where she chose to live were on the rise, but she paid little attention to the saber rattling that seemed to emanate every day from the Japanese press. It seemed like the hyperbolic rhetoric of old men, political men, and it seemed incomprehensible that her two worlds would collide in any real way. She knew too many good, kind people on both sides in both countries. So when Miss Zabriaski rushed into her classroom shouting about war that morning, Fumiye had immediately put it out of her mind and turned her attention to her students.

---

*Tsukie had been born in Japan but had grown up on Maui and attended Maui High, where she went by Rosaline. But because Japanese-born immigrants could not become American citizens, she had returned to Japan in 1934.

But walking home that afternoon, she began to realize that something unusual was, in fact, going on. People were gathered in small knots on the streets, agitated, their conversations animated. As she passed open windows, she heard martial music blaring from radios. Lines had formed in front of shops selling more radios. People were smiling for a change. There was something electric in the air. Then she passed a radio airing an official bulletin from NHK, Japan's national broadcaster. Japan had "entered into a situation of war with the United States and Britain in the western Pacific before dawn." On a street corner she saw a shocking headline; apparently the entire U.S. Navy had been destroyed in Hawai'i.

Fumiye ran the rest of the way home, burst into the house, and fell into her sister's arms, the two young women sobbing, trying to comfort each other, quaking, wondering aloud and fearing silently what was happening to their parents and siblings back in Hawai'i.

DESPITE THE FLASHES on the radio, the news reached many people in the United States that day more slowly than one might have expected. Because it was a Sunday, many Americans were still at church or in movie theaters for early afternoon matinees. A few theaters flashed cards on the screen or made announcements over the PA systems, but many didn't. Thousands of moviegoers walked out into the light of day later that afternoon and were stunned to find newsboys shouting and holding up extra editions of the papers with banner headlines like the *Oakland Tribune*'s—JAPS DECLARE WAR; HAWAII BOMBED, HEAVY LIFE LOSS—or the *San Francisco Chronicle*'s simpler, four-inch-tall proclamation: WAR. For others, the news arrived by telephone as family members reached out to one another. Young women in telephone exchanges around the country worked frantically to make connections, but there were not nearly enough operators working on a Sunday afternoon to keep up with the load. In quiet neighborhoods, on farms and in towns, word traveled by mouth, directly from one neighbor to another, a doorbell ringing after Sunday afternoon dinner or a quick, startling conversation over a hedge or a picket fence.

In the first few hours, Americans' reactions ran the gamut from rage to fear to relief. The last of those, relief, sometimes came as a surprise even to those who felt it most acutely. The country had spent the years since World War I assiduously trying to ignore what was happening in the rest of the world, convincing itself that the growing global mayhem was someone else's problem even as it became more and more obvious that it wasn't. Now that line of reasoning was suddenly extinct. The endless uncertainty was over. Benjamin Fox, a young police officer standing on Market Street in San Francisco that day, said the feeling was like a rubber band that had been stretched too far for too long and had finally been allowed to snap. "Now it's come and it's a good thing and I think everyone thinks so." A waitress in Boston proclaimed to her customers, "There's been too much talk and not enough action. Let's get going." Many young men, particularly those already in uniform, suddenly saw their futures as more interesting, vibrant with the possibility of glory awaiting them just over the western horizon. A soldier on leave at the Rialto Theater in Atlanta crowed, "Oh boy. This is it!" A sailor added, "That's what we've been waiting for." Another soldier, in Portland, Oregon, turned to a friend, smiled, and said, "We'd better polish up our shootin' irons."

But most people were, unsurprisingly, just plain angry—deeply angry and raring to do something about it. At Pilgrim Congregational Church in St. Louis, Sunday worshippers agreed that "they ought to blow the Japanese navy out of the water." In Kansas City, a newsboy hawking an extra edition yelled, "Gotta whip those Japs," as his customers nodded, handed him coins, and took their papers. In Buffalo, ninety-five-year-old John Caudell—a man old enough to have fought in the Civil War—growled at a reporter, "I hope we knock hell out of them, but don't say hell. It won't look good."

And right from those first moments of realization, anti-Asian racial animus that had long festered—particularly in the American West—bubbled to the surface and fueled the fury of millions. A motorist in San

Francisco pulled in to a filling station and exclaimed, "Down the street I almost ran over a Jap on a motorcycle. Maybe I should have hit him. That would be my contribution." In Topeka a man at a field trial for hunting dogs snarled, "I guess our hunting will be confined to those God-damned slant-eyed bastards from now on."

AT THE EPICENTER of it all, in Honolulu, Kats Miho found himself in a city gripped by terror that night. The widespread—and not unreasonable—assumption was that the air raids had merely been preparation for a full-scale invasion of Hawai'i. At 4:25 p.m., the territorial governor, Joseph Poindexter, had imposed martial law, and now a total blackout plunged the city into utter darkness. Virtually the only light illuminating the Pearl Harbor area was from the fires still burning on shattered battleships and in the ruins of aircraft hangars. Sirens wailed in the darkness. From time to time, thundering volleys of antiaircraft fire lit up the sky as anxious gunners at Pearl shot at imagined aircraft. Drivers desperate to get home or to find loved ones drove, without aid of headlights or traffic lights, through blackened streets, despite a military curfew. Except for occasional bulletins, commercial radio stations went off the air to prevent any additional Japanese aircraft from following their signals toward O'ahu.

In the official silence, wild rumors raced unchecked through the darkened city. Word was that Japanese nationals living in Hawai'i had poisoned the water supply; that SS *Lurline*—a Matson Company luxury liner that carried thousands between Honolulu and California each year—had been sunk en route to Los Angeles with 840 passengers aboard;* that Japanese plantation workers had cut large arrows in the cane fields to

---

*In fact, the *Lurline* arrived safely at Pier 32 in San Francisco a little after 2:00 a.m. on December 10, but only after its crew had daubed black paint on all its portals and ordered passengers not even to strike a match after twilight, its skipper put it on a zigzag course and brought it up to its maximum speed, and terrorized passengers had tried vainly to fall asleep fully dressed and wearing life jackets.

direct enemy planes toward Pearl; that Japanese troops had come ashore on certain beaches on the north shore of Oʻahu; that Kauaʻi was already occupied; that San Francisco was being bombed; that Japanese Americans armed with machine guns had opened fire on Hickam Field from milk trucks.

Kats stood in the dark on a street corner down in Iwilei—a raw industrial landscape of fuel-storage tanks, railroad tracks, cranes, and rusting machinery near Honolulu Harbor—carrying an old rifle he still didn't really know how to use, peering into the night. The waterfront was black all the way down through Waikīkī to Diamond Head, the lights of the grand hotels along the beach extinguished. Even the red and green navigation lights in the harbor had been turned off, so it was hard to make out anything but shadows and silhouettes in the moonlight. From time to time, an unexpected sound startled Kats—the sudden bark of a dog, someone dropping something into a trash can, a door slamming—and he flinched, crouched, and put his finger back on the trigger.

Earlier in the day he and his fellow ROTC cadets from the University of Hawaiʻi—virtually all Americans of Japanese ancestry—had been transferred into an entirely new entity, the Hawaiʻi Territorial Guard. Their mission was to guard Oʻahu's critical infrastructure—power plants, pumping stations, fuel depots, and the like—against the expected Japanese invasion. The earlier reports of paratroopers landing on St. Louis Heights had turned out to be false, just some hikers apparently trying to get a better view of what was happening at Pearl Harbor. But now in the dark, everything that moved, every ambiguous shape, every unexpected sound, seemed a potentially lethal threat. More young men like Kats were stationed at other spots along the waterfront, every fifty yards or so. Everyone was jittery, trigger-happy. Occasionally someone actually pulled the trigger, and the crack of a shot split the night, boys unwittingly shooting at dogs and cats and rats, at anything that walked, crept, or crawled through shadows in the moonlight.

Still, Kats was proud. After a long day of feeling angry and helpless, he was in uniform, armed, and finally doing something—serving his country, protecting it from those who would do it harm. But what Kats didn't know was that while he stood guard with his gun in Honolulu, other men with guns were leading his father away into the Kahului night at the point of a bayonet as Ayano Miho stood in the doorway of their hotel, weeping. As he was taken out the door, Katsuichi, believing he was about to be executed, turned to his wife and hastily offered his final advice: "Don't do anything that will bring shame to the family and the Japanese race. Do your best no matter what. Keep your self-dignity."

KATSUICHI MIHO WAS just one of hundreds of mostly older men taken from their homes that evening and one of thousands taken over the next several weeks as federal agents arrested and jailed Japanese nationals both in Hawai'i and on the U.S. mainland. Almost all were Issei men—first-generation immigrants, the heads of households. Most of them had lived lawfully in the United States for decades, though by law they were not allowed to naturalize as citizens. Their second-generation, American-born children—the Nisei—were American citizens and theoretically protected by the Constitution from unwarranted arrest, though that protection would soon turn out to be illusory.

Well before the attack on Pearl Harbor, the U.S. government had laid detailed plans for what it might do about alien residents from hostile nations in the event of war. Relying on the authority of the Alien Enemies Act of 1798, the Office of Naval Intelligence, the War Department's Military Intelligence Division, and the FBI had begun during the 1930s to compile lists of Japanese, Italian, and German nationals living in the United States. By 1936, as tensions with Japan heightened, Japanese immigrants in Hawai'i came under particular scrutiny as authorities examined with whom they associated. One major point of focus was Japanese commercial ships stopping in Honolulu. Often, they carried

Japanese naval personnel who mingled with local Issei and Nisei, carrying news and letters from family in Japan. On August 10 of that year, President Roosevelt proposed to the chief of naval operations that "every Japanese citizen or non-citizen on the Island of Oahu who meets these Japanese ships [arriving in Hawai'i] or has any connection with their officers or men should be secretly but definitely identified and his or her name placed on a special list of those who would be the first to be placed in a concentration camp in the event of trouble." By 1941, the military intelligence services and the FBI, at the direction of J. Edgar Hoover, had developed an extensive, hierarchical system for identifying and categorizing those whom they suspected might pose a danger. Termed the Custodial Detention List, the list was organized with the names of suspect individuals divided into three categories—A, B, and C. In the A category were the people considered most dangerous: members of ultranationalistic German, Italian, or Japanese organizations, as well as international fascist or communist organizations. One step down, in the B category, were members of cultural or religious organizations that might promote "foreign" values, such as Japanese community associations, Buddhist temples, and Shinto shrines. The C category included a much wider variety of people, such as those doing business in Japan or simply individuals whom someone had identified as "suspicious."

Now, in the wake of Pearl Harbor—both in Hawai'i and on the mainland—the FBI cast a wide net, working through the lists as quickly as they could, sweeping up everyone on them in all three categories, whether of Japanese, German, or Italian ancestry.* In Hawai'i and on the West Coast, most of the names on the list were far and away Japanese. FBI agents fanned out, seizing Buddhist and Shinto priests,

---

*More than 1.2 million people in the United States had been born in Germany, and 5 million had two German-born parents. The nation's ethnic Italian community was even larger. During the war, the Department of Justice incarcerated roughly 11,500 individuals of German ancestry and 3,000 of Italian ancestry. However, neither Italian Americans nor German Americans were ever subject to the sweeping, all-inclusive incarcerations that would follow for Japanese Americans and their parents.

Japanese-language schoolteachers, business leaders, anyone who had corresponded with the Japanese consulate, the owners of fishing boats, Japanese-language newspaper editors, members of Japanese literary societies, Japanese flower arranging clubs, and many others. Most of the people taken were men, and most were taken from their homes or businesses with only the clothes on their backs, without charges, and without a word to them or to their families about where they were being taken. The suddenness and seeming randomness of the arrests sent a shock wave of dread and uncertainty through Japanese families both on the mainland and in Hawai'i. Nobody could be sure who would be taken and who wouldn't.

Agents arresting Issei men

At Sumi Okamoto's wedding in Spokane, agents raided the reception and led several Issei guests away. In San Pedro, California, as they climbed off their boats, unaware of what had happened in Hawai'i, several hundred fishermen were herded into chicken-wire enclosures on the waterfront. In San Diego, Margaret Ishino, a student at San Diego High, watched as federal agents searched her family home. Her mother lay in bed, having just delivered her little brother, Thomas. Suspecting the bed held contraband, one of the agents ripped away the blankets and sheets, exposing her mother. Then they took away her father. In Hood River, Oregon, agents pounded on doors at 3:30 on Monday morning, ransacking houses and taking away a dozen community leaders. Among them was Tomeshichi Akiyama, whose son George was then serving in the U.S. Army.* In Stockton, California, as Yasaburo Saiki was being led away from the boardinghouse he ran, he said, "Wait, wait, you might need these," reached into his pocket, and handed his son Barry—a student at the University of California at Berkeley—a bundle of U.S. defense bonds he had purchased before the attack. In Honolulu's Wai'alae neighborhood, Matsujiro Otani was sick in bed, dressed only in pajamas, when the FBI arrived. They stuck a pistol in his ribs, ordered him out of bed, and marched him outside barefoot. His wife pleaded with them, "If you are going to take him, take me along too!" The agents snapped, "You keep out of this," and shoved Otani toward their waiting car. Mrs. Otani dashed back into the house, grabbed a raincoat and a pair of shoes, and threw them into the car just before the doors closed and the car pulled away. In downtown Honolulu, the Yokohama Specie Bank on Merchant Street had been seized and turned into a station for booking the Issei men as they were brought in. One of them, a temple priest so bent and stooped by age that he could hardly walk, was escorted by a young Japanese American soldier. Mortified by what he was being required to do, the soldier stared glumly at the ground and refused to talk to anyone about it. Some of the older men being questioned spoke little English and simply did not understand what was happening to them. One asked his son and daughter-in-law, "What means Jap?"

---

*George Akiyama would subsequently earn a Silver Star for his extraordinary courage in battle.

FOUR

I step outside the tent and look up at the stars twinkling in the sky, as if laughing at man's wretched state. Earth continues to spin, carrying its two billion inhabitants who behave like crazed people. Tomorrow will follow today. Our tent squeaks under the slanting Nu'uanu winds, and I feel like saying a prayer.

OTOKICHI OZAKI
SAND ISLAND DETENTION CENTER

I n Spokane, Fred Shiosaki awoke on Monday morning as he had fallen asleep Sunday evening, deeply anxious, unsettled, his stomach in a knot. He stayed home from school and remained indoors all day. He knew he could scrap with the best of them, one-on-one, but he was one of only a few Japanese American students at Rogers High, and he wasn't at all sure the whole school wouldn't jump him the moment he walked into the building. Suddenly, for the first time in his life, he felt that he would be utterly alone once he ventured out onto the streets of Hillyard.

The day had not started off well at the laundry. His parents opened at the usual hour—7:00 a.m.—but by mid-morning no customers had come in. Kisaburo drove over to the home of Will Simpson—a print-shop proprietor, the editor of the *Hillyard News,* and a longtime friend—to pick up Simpson's laundry as he did every Monday morning. For more than twenty years, Simpson had been Kisaburo's principal mentor and an important ally in town. A prominent Democrat, appointed Spokane's postmaster by FDR, he was widely respected, not just in Hillyard but throughout Washington State and beyond. Now, when Kisaburo appeared at his back door, Simpson stepped outside and held up the front page of the *Spokane Spokesman-Review*. The headline, a four-inch black banner, read WAR LIST BIG. Under that were the first horrifying casualty figures from Pearl Harbor. "Kay, look at this! What do you think of that?" Simpson demanded. Kisaburo glanced down. He didn't know what to say. Finally, he murmured, "It was dumb of them. I'm sure it will be over soon." Simpson stared at him, hard, as if he were seeing him for the first time, and said, "Well, Kay, I'm afraid I can't do business with you anymore. I have a political position I have to be careful of." And with that he stepped back into the house and shut the door in Kisaburo's face.

When he returned to the laundry, Kisaburo Shiosaki found his family waiting, hoping he would come with work, with something to do. But Fred could see at a glance that his father was empty-handed and utterly crestfallen. Kisaburo muttered, "Mr. Simpson said, well, he's not going to do business with us anymore." Then he sat quietly behind the counter for the rest of the morning, contemplating the apparent ruination of all that he had worked for over three decades in the United States. Fred had never seen him so crushed.

FRED'S FATHER HAD COME to America with a wicker suitcase, a head full of dreams, and a heart yearning to realize them. As the third son of a tenant farmer in a village near the city of Kakegawa in rural Shizuoka-ken, he had been born with no prospects at all in Japan, nothing beyond a life of stoop labor and extreme poverty.

A deep financial depression had settled over Japan in the late 1870s and the 1880s. Then in 1883 a major drought seared the landscape and wiped out millions of yen worth of rice and other crops, only to be followed in 1884 by a major storm that caused widespread flooding and destroyed still more crops. By the middle of the decade, the poorest of Japan's farmers were reduced to eating rice husks and the dregs of bean paste mixed with weeds and grass as they huddled in small, dark homes heated only by charcoal fire pits or hibachis. Emigration fever swept over large parts of Japan as thousands of young men, desperately seeking a way out, climbed onto steamers bound first, in the 1880s, for the sugarcane and pineapple plantations of Hawai'i and later, in the first decade of the twentieth century, for the West Coast.

So when recruiters for the Oriental Trading Company came to his village seeking workers for the Canadian Pacific Railroad, Kisaburo Shiosaki lunged at the opportunity and boarded a steamer. The company paid for his passage to Canada, though not without first taking out an insurance policy on his life so that it could recoup its investment should he die en route.

He arrived alive and healthy in Vancouver in 1904—a twenty-one-year-old with a steely ambition in his eyes—and went to work laying and repairing track for the railroad. It was desperately hard work and paid low wages, just a dollar or two a day. Kisaburo and his fellow Japanese immigrants lived in boxcars or tent encampments, enduring the long, dark, bitter winters of British Columbia and Alberta. They worked stooped over, with frozen hands, wielding picks and shovels in relentless sleet and snow, and then huddled at night around campfires, cooking rice and bits of fish or whatever else they could afford on their meager wages. In the summers, they toiled under a broiling sun, shoveling gravel, toting heavy railroad ties, swinging sledgehammers, driving spikes. Because vegetables were expensive and hard to come by in the Canadian interior, many of them suffered from scurvy. Others were torn apart by high explosives or crushed under tons of falling rock. It was a miserable existence. Mere survival was the best a man could hope for.

When a section of line that he was working on brought him close to the U.S. border, Kisaburo decided he'd had enough. He slipped across

the border and began to work his way westward along the Great Northern line toward Washington State, doing odd jobs, searching for any
open opportunity, still seeking a way to make his dreams come true. He
finally found it, not in the snowy woods, or on a bleak stretch of railroad
track, but in the nearest thing the Pacific Northwest had to a genuine
palace.

The Davenport Hotel in Spokane was by far the most opulent lodg-
ing and dining establishment between Minneapolis and Seattle. Many
thought it the finest west of the Mississippi, a marvel of refinement, good
taste, and elegance. To walk off Spokane's gritty streets into its cavern-
ous, Spanish Revival lobby was to step into another world, a world of
hushed, refined elegance. By day, natural light filtered down through
opalescent glass skylights, flooding the vast interior, reflecting off polished marble floors, burnished brass railings, and massive framed mirrors. By night, lamps in the form of white scallop shells set atop gilded
ten-foot-tall columns bathed the room with warm yellow light. Carved
walnut and mahogany furniture upholstered with fine embroidered fab-
rics invited guests to sit and simply soak in the splendor. Movie stars,
financiers, captains of industry, and political giants all regularly disembarked from the Great Northern Railway and swept through the front
doors, interrupting their transcontinental journeys simply for a chance
to enjoy the Davenport's luxurious appointments and fine dining.

For such distinguished visitors, a night or two at the hotel was an
indulgence. For a young man who had grown up stooped over in sodden
fields, living in the squalor and cramped poverty of rural Japan, simply
walking into the lobby was a revelation. This was a world Kisaburo
Shiosaki could not have dreamed of before he saw it with his own eyes.
When he secured a job at the Davenport, it was his salvation, and he
knew it.

The work was anything but elegant. Men his own age called him
"boy." He cleared tables, picked up scraps of food fallen to the floor, toted
stacks of greasy plates into the kitchen, swept up cigarette butts, emptied
spittoons and ashtrays, mopped restrooms, scrubbed dishes, did what-

ever was asked of him for nine or ten hours a day, six days a week. But for Kisaburo, after years toiling on the railroad, it seemed a golden opportunity. He poured his heart into every task, however menial.

Within a year he had so impressed his employers at the Davenport that they wrote him a glowing letter of recommendation, and with that in hand he sailed for home to find a wife. Wearing a crisp new Sears, Roebuck suit and toting a silk umbrella as evidence of his prosperity, he wasn't long in securing one. He found her in the village of Hatsuma, within walking distance of his own. Tori Iwai was eighteen and beautiful, and the two were promptly married with the blessings of both sets of parents. Kisaburo returned to Spokane and bought the laundry in Hillyard in 1917, and Tori soon followed. He and she joined hands and leaped into their suddenly bright future together, laboring long hours, making friends in the community, becoming Kay and Mrs. Kay, and building a family.

By early 1941, the Shiosakis were secure. They were not the kind of people who could stay at the Davenport, or even take a meal there. And in Spokane, as in many cities throughout the American West, signs on certain ice rinks and restaurants and swimming pools sometimes informed them that they and their children were not allowed to enter. There were neighborhoods in Spokane where local ordinances would prevent them from buying a home, even if they had had the money to do so. Random strangers on the street might still sneer at them and call them "Japs," as they had since the first day they had set foot on American soil. But at least they had a thriving business, a home, an automobile, a few modern conveniences, and children who were obtaining educations that would almost certainly allow them to rise eventually into the American middle class. Now they could afford to take the family to the movies at the Rialto Theater or spend an afternoon at Ferris Field watching the Spokane Indians play baseball, a particular passion of Tori's, who had by then become the most knowledgeable Issei lady in Spokane on the subject of baseball. Life in America, though still constrained by racial barriers, was finally at least beginning to live up to what Kisaburo had dreamed of decades before. But that had all been before that first Sunday in December 1941.

ON MONDAY MORNING, dread hung heavy in the air in Honolulu. Billows of dense black smoke still rose from the oil-slicked waters of Pearl Harbor. The big luxury hotels on Waikīkī Beach were ghostly quiet, the nearby streets nearly deserted now except for a few bewildered guests venturing out for the first time since the attack, shock, horror, and disbelief etched onto their faces. The beach itself was devoid of sunbathers. Instead, soldiers were already erecting concrete barricades on the sand and stringing barbed wire between them. Fears of an imminent invasion had only intensified shortly after dawn that morning when the commander of a Japanese mini-submarine—the twenty-four-year-old ensign Kazuo Sakamaki—struggled out of the water and collapsed on Waimānalo Beach on the eastern shore of Oʻahu. When Sakamaki looked up from the sand, he found himself the first Japanese POW of World War II, staring down the barrel of a pistol wielded by a startled young member of the Hawaiʻi National Guard, David Akui.

Up at Atherton House, Kats Miho was finally resting up after a long, anxious night on the Honolulu waterfront. The only casualty of the newly formed Hawaiʻi Territorial Guard's first night on watch had been a cow that wandered too near a water-pumping station, failed to respond to the boys' repeated commands to halt, and provoked a volley of rifle fire lethal to the cow but nobody else. As Kats contemplated what had happened in the past twenty-four hours and how it might change his life, he did not yet know that his father was sitting that morning in the Maui County Jail.

KATS'S FATHER WAS NOT BORN a Miho. He was born Katsuichi Imamura in the village of Kure, just a few miles south of Hiroshima, in 1884. As a young man on his way to school, he began lingering each day in front of the house of an attractive young woman named Ayano Miho, the daughter of a prosperous nori merchant. The two began talking over a fence. When a maid in the Miho household came across a love letter Katsuichi had written to Ayano, the family erupted in an uproar. Romance was not the usual way of finding a wife in Japan. This was a dangerous, subversive development. But Mr. Miho decided to investigate the young man, and the more he investigated, the more he liked what he found. The two families conferred and grew fond of each other, and the couple was finally allowed to marry on one condition. Ayano's father had no son to carry on the Miho family name and the nori business. If Katsuichi wanted the Mihos' eldest daughter, he would have to agree to be adopted by Mr. Miho and take his name.

Katsuichi accepted, and the young couple married. Both finished their schooling and became teachers in Hiroshima prefecture. In time, Ayano bore a son and two daughters, and Katsuichi became the principal of the Fujisaki Elementary School in Hiroshima-ken. All seemed settled. But then—when he was twenty-eight and Ayano was twenty-six—Katsuichi caught the emigration bug.

Word was that the sugar and pineapple plantations in Hawai'i were seeking educators for the thousands of Nisei children being born to the immigrant workers who had arrived there in the previous decades. With the plantations reputedly offering much higher teaching wages than in rural Japan, it seemed a ripe opportunity to Katsuichi and Ayano. The problem was, Katsuichi would need his adopted father's permission, and that would be hard to get. If he left Japan, there would be no one to carry on the family name and business, the very reason that Mr. Miho had adopted Katsuichi in the first place.

After much arguing and negotiating, father and adopted son came to an agreement, but the terms were brutally hard. Katsuichi and Ayano would have to leave their firstborn son, Katsuto, and their firstborn daughter, Hisae, behind in Japan to serve as heirs. Reluctantly, the couple agreed, taking only their infant daughter, Tsukie, with them and saying they would be back in a few years to resume parenting their first two children once they had saved up some money.

In October 1911, they sailed from Kobe on a steamer, arrived a couple of weeks later in Honolulu, and were processed through the same immigration facility that thousands of Japanese immigrants had already passed through on their way to Hawai'i's cane fields. Once they were released from the immigration system, though, the couple found to their disappointment that no jobs requiring their advanced educations were readily to be found on O'ahu. Needing some way to support his family, Katsuichi went to work picking macadamia nuts instead.

Over the next few years he worked at various jobs, traveling on to California for a time to try his hand first at railroad work, then at strawberry farming, and finally at beekeeping. Eventually he returned to Honolulu, where, to his great relief, he at last landed a job worthy of his education—as the principal of a Japanese-language school. He seemed finally on his way to a secure, if not prosperous, future. But his tenure there ended abruptly—and characteristically for Katsuichi—over a matter of ethics.

Although subject to crushing racial prejudice themselves—particularly on the sugarcane and pineapple plantations, where the owners and the foremen called *luna* had free hands to exploit them brutally—some Japanese immigrants harbored prejudices of their own. Those who hailed from one prefecture in Japan often looked down on those from another. At the very bottom of the heap were those who had come from Okinawa. With their distinctive appearance, dialect, culture, and cuisine, Okinawans struck many Japanese—particularly those from the more urban prefectures—as foreign and inferior. To Katsuichi Miho that sort of intolerance and injustice was abhorrent, and he would not abide it. When he selected Steven Chinen—an Okinawan boy—for the honor of delivering a speech to some visiting Japanese sailors, the school's PTA rose up in anger. "No, no, no. You can't have him. He's from Okinawa," parents insisted. Soon the whole school was in an uproar. But Katsuichi, above all, was a man of strong principles. He held firm against the parents. "So what?" he said. "This is not ken against ken, province against province. We're simply selecting a student to represent the school." Still the parents raged. Finally, Katsuichi threw up his hands, "You either accept him as our representative or I'll resign from your school." They resisted. He resigned.

By now the Mihos' brood was rapidly expanding, with five more American children eventually being added to the three born in Japan. More than ever, they needed money. They moved to Kahului, on Maui, where Katsuichi went to work first as an itinerant teacher, traveling from plantation to plantation on Maui's red-soil cane roads in a horse-drawn wagon, then as a bookkeeper, and finally as a manager at the Onishi Store, a general store just across the street from what would soon become the Miho Hotel. But it wasn't until Ayano talked Katsuichi into buying the hotel in 1929 that the Mihos' fortunes finally turned and they began to make serious advances on the American dream. To be sure, the hotel still stood on land they leased from the KRR and the Baldwin family, and so it could be snatched away at any time. But, nevertheless, there, in the hotel, the family finally settled in and began to prosper. It was there the Miho children grew up exuberant, barefoot, and ambitious, and there that Katsuichi became, by the early 1940s, one of the community's most trusted and respected elders, widely admired for his principled stands and frequently consulted for his wisdom. Until they took him away.

WHEN THE FBI HAD COME for him on December 7, Katsuichi had been frightened but not really surprised. In the prior two years, federal agents had shown up at the Miho Hotel more than once to interrogate him about family connections in Japan and the work Katsuichi had done helping other families in Hawai'i register their children's births with the Japanese consulate. From that point on—though he knew nothing about the FBI's A-B-C list—he had assumed he was under some kind of suspicion. He understood that his activities aimed at keeping Japanese culture alive among his fellow immigrants would likely look nefarious to American authorities on the lookout for spies and saboteurs. It was the price of being in America but not an American. Prohibited, in fact, from becoming an American. In Japanese terms, it required the application of *gaman*, recognition that it was one of those things that couldn't be helped. But as agents led him away and he realized they didn't intend to execute him, he knew also that it was going to be excruciatingly hard to be separated from his wife and children, not knowing when or if he would see them again.

He was taken from the Maui County Jail and transported to Sand Island—a bleak expanse of sand and dead coral just across the mudflats from the immigration center in Honolulu where he had first entered the country thirty years earlier. There, soldiers armed with bayonets herded him and roughly 450 other Issei—all of them men—from all over Hawai'i into a five-acre enclosure surrounded by a fifteen-foot-tall fence topped with barbed wire. Eight guard towers, each manned by soldiers with machine guns, stood at regular intervals around the perimeter. Whatever meager possessions the Issei men had brought were taken from them. They were assigned to canvas tents—each with eight cots laid directly on the mud and coral.

It rained for days on end that December, and the tents quickly flooded. Several times a day, the men were forced to stand in the driving rain for roll call. With almost no changes of clothes available, they shivered in wet clothes through long damp nights on the cots. The guards referred to them as POWs. Some were made to clean toilets with their bare hands. When a spoon went missing, they were strip-searched. They had no access to phones, radios, newspapers, pens, paper, wristwatches, or even bars of soap. They had little idea of what was happening in the outside world and no idea at all about what was going to happen to them. For weeks, they were allowed no family visits. With Pearl Harbor and Hickam Field just four miles to the west, military aircraft roared low overhead and the ground shuddered day and night as the navy fired practice rounds at barges towed back and forth out in Māmala Bay.

Amid the rain, the roar of the planes, and the thunder of the big guns, Katsuichi walked daily along the perimeter fence around the Sand Island Detention Center, looking out across a narrow waterway at Honolulu, where, unbeknownst to him, Kats—just a long stone's throw away—was patrolling the waterfront each night, armed with his old carbine, ready to repel the enemy.

IN SPOKANE, Fred Shiosaki returned reluctantly to school. His mother insisted. Getting there was the worst of it. It was a long, cold, lonely walk through Hillyard's bleak winter streets—four blocks down Market Street alongside the clattering railroad yard, then a right turn and fourteen more blocks past rows of modest houses fronting East Wellesley Avenue. Passing them, Fred thought he saw people peeking out from behind curtains, watching him go by. As each step brought him closer to school, the prospect of entering the building seemed more dreadful. By the time he finally arrived in front of John R. Rogers High, with its red-and-yellow-brick art deco facade, his heart was racing, his stomach churning. He took a deep breath, pushed his way through one of the four massive front doors, and made his way into the school's clamoring hallways. Students were huddled in clusters, talking excitedly about the war. People seemed too absorbed by the headlines, the latest casualty figures, the prospect that the boys among them would all soon be in uniform, to take any particular note of Fred. If anything, people seemed to avert their eyes from him. He made his way to his first class. By midmorning, to his enormous relief, he found that his friends were still his friends. His buddies on the track team still wanted to talk about the upcoming season. His friends in the photography club were already making assignments for next June's yearbook.

But those were his friends. And those were just the first few hours. As that day wore on, and others followed it, Fred soon realized that while nobody was going to assault him at school, he now stood apart from most of the student body at John Rogers. Conversations dissolved into silence when he attempted to join them. Friendly glances were returned with blank stares. Backs were suddenly turned as he approached. When teachers talked about the war, Fred wished he could turn invisible. When he walked the halls of the school, he felt as if a black cloud were following him everywhere. He trudged home every afternoon to find the laundry still nearly lifeless, the machinery quiet, the racks devoid of laundry, the cash register empty, his parents still idle and despondent.

THE WAR NEWS just kept getting worse. The Japanese imperial forces appeared to be unstoppable. Hours before the attack on Hawai'i had begun, they had stormed the beaches of Malaya. As Japanese bombs were falling on O'ahu, they were also falling on Wake Island. And that same day, with wreckage in Pearl Harbor aflame, the Japanese had seized Hong Kong, invaded Thailand, and bombed Guam and airfields in the Philippines. On December 10, off the coast of Malaya, they sank two enormous British warships—HMS *Prince of Wales* and HMS *Repulse*—with the loss of more than eight hundred men. On December 12 they began to land troops on Luzon in the Philippines. On December 14 they invaded Burma. They even returned to Hawai'i. At dusk on December 15 a Japanese submarine surfaced off Maui and lobbed ten shells into Kahului, damaging the pineapple cannery where Kats had worked the previous year. Only two chickens died in the attack, but it had its desired effect, terrorizing guests at the Miho Hotel as well as the town's other inhabitants and reinforcing the belief that a Japanese invasion of Hawai'i was imminent.

By Christmas Eve, General Douglas MacArthur was abandoning Manila and fleeing across Manila Bay to Corregidor as General Jonathan Wainwright led thousands of Allied troops retreating toward the Bataan Peninsula. By Christmas morning huge pillars of flame and smoke rose into an otherwise clear blue sky on the outskirts of Manila as Filipino troops set fire to oil storage facilities to keep the fuel from falling into the hands of the advancing Japanese troops.

As the bad news continued to roll in, the nation's angriest voices soon became the loudest, unleashing a torrent of racist rhetoric that all but drowned out the voices of those who were still able to take a step back and distinguish between friend and foe. Cartoons appeared in newspapers depicting Japanese people as rats, insects, skunks, monkeys, lice, or rabid dogs. One cartoon strip, titled *How to Spot a Jap*, featured instructions for distinguishing between Japanese and Chinese Americans: "A Jap is shorter and looks as if his legs are joined directly to his chest. . . . The Jap has buck teeth. . . . The Chinese strides. The Jap shuffles." Restaurant owners put signs in their front windows: THIS RESTAURANT POISONS BOTH RATS AND JAPS. When "Jap" didn't seem a degrading enough epithet, sign makers and cartoonists alike went with "Nip" or "yellow vermin." Some of the country's most influential editorial writers began to feed the hatred. Talking about the American-born Nisei, the *Los Angeles Times* editorialized, "A viper is nonetheless a viper wherever the egg is hatched." Smaller newspapers chimed in as well. Fred Shiosaki's hometown newspaper, the *Spokane Spokesman-Review*, ran an editorial calling for people like his parents to be imprisoned: "All Japanese nationals on our islands and our mainland should be rounded up and placed in concentration camps for the duration of the war."

Politicians who had long known how racial hatred could fuel campaigns and advance legislative or personal agendas seized a ripe opportunity, and their rhetoric quickly became brazenly toxic. Representative John Rankin of Mississippi declared, "This is a race war. . . . I say it is of vital importance that we get rid of every Japanese. . . . Damn them! Let's get rid of them now!" Another member of Congress, Oklahoma's Jed Johnson, demanded the forced sterilization of all Japanese living in the United States. Chase Clark, governor of Idaho, said, "The Japs live like rats, breed like rats, act like rats."

None of these degrading tropes, images, and sentiments were new to most Americans. From the earliest days of Asian immigration in the nineteenth century, first print media and later Hollywood had promoted the notion of a "Yellow Peril"—an unrelenting wave of Asian immigration that threatened to overwhelm and destroy not just the United States but the entire western world. Particularly from the 1880s onward, editorial cartoons in major newspapers routinely depicted Asian figures as rodents, cockroaches, snakes, and other vermin swarming ashore on American beaches. Magazine covers offered up lurid images of sinister Asian men with long fingernails ravaging white women or seducing them in dingy opium dens. Beginning in 1929, Hollywood brought Americans the specter of the evil Fu Manchu, bent on destroying the western world. Soon a host of other unsavory Asian characters, either servile and cringing or inscrutable and threatening—and almost always played by white actors— were regular fare in American movie houses.

Now, as the rhetoric continued to escalate, the old sterotypes and the hatred were already thoroughly ingrained in the minds of millions of Americans, and the consequences for Japanese Americans and their Issei parents quickly grew ever more wrenching. In Hawai'i, martial law remained in effect throughout the islands. The writ of habeas corpus was suspended. Military courts replaced civilian courts and hundreds of Issei and Nisei were summarily arrested on suspicions of disloyalty. The sudden arrests of hundreds of Issei men, in particular, decapitated the leadership of Japanese communities, causing enormous, systematic disruptions in every one of them throughout the territory. Buddhist temples were ordered closed. So were Japanese-language schools and community centers. Japanese-language newspapers were shut down. Bank accounts were frozen. Issei fishermen were prohibited from taking their boats out to sea.

On the mainland, children were taunted on their way to school, barred from public amusement parks, turned away at the doors to theaters. The proprietors of small businesses of all sorts—among them restaurants, barbershops, hair salons, auto repair shops, pharmacies, veterinary clinics, and dental offices—refused to serve Japanese American customers. Many people boycotted businesses owned by Japanese Americans and their parents. The president of the University of Arizona forbade the library to lend books to Japanese American students, declaring that "these people are our enemies."

The Nisei, most of whom were no more than high school or college age, worried how their immigrant parents, unprotected by citizenship, would fare. The Issei worried how they could continue to support their young American families as harsh new economic realities ravaged their lives. Railroad companies, restaurants, nurserymen, landscapers, mining companies, and all manner of industrial plants abruptly laid off men who had worked faithfully for them for decades. Within weeks, cities rescinded the business licenses of Japanese proprietors, shuttering grocery stores, laundries, beer halls, florists, and other small businesses. The Treasury Department closed Japanese banks, freezing assets and throwing tellers, clerks, and account managers out of work. Families were limited to one hundred dollars per month in withdrawals from their bank accounts. Travel restrictions prohibited anyone of Japanese descent, American or not, from traveling more than a few miles from home or from venturing anywhere near certain critical facilities such as power plants and dams.* On Bainbridge Island, just west of Seattle, the Black Ball Ferry Line barred anyone of Japanese descent—again American or not—from boarding its boats.

The Shiosaki family hunkered down in Hillyard. As 1942 approached, their world shrank to the nearly lifeless laundry and its immediate vicinity. Unable to draw freely from their bank account, with revenue from the laundry reduced to a trickle, and unable to travel even as far as the lakes outside Spokane where Kisaburo liked to fish on Sundays, they told Fred and his siblings to tread lightly, to avoid making themselves conspicuous: "Don't go where there are crowds, where there are people you don't know who might do something overt. Stay away from people you don't know."

---

*The Issei very seldom married people of other nationalities and races in the early twentieth century, so for all practical purposes a Japanese surname was considered evidence of Japanese ancestry.

. . .

As THE NEW YEAR BEGAN, a tidal wave of young American men rushed to join the military services, sleeping on the pavement and waiting in long lines in front of recruiting offices that stayed open sixteen to eighteen hours a day, emerging later with broad smiles on their faces, clutching enlistment papers. The streets and restaurants, the bars and dance halls, of every American city were suddenly full of men proudly wearing navy white or army green uniforms. Everywhere they went, the new sailors and soldiers drew compliments and friendly nods when they entered a room, pats on the back from men too old to fight, admiring glances from young women they passed on the street.

Perhaps none of those young men were prouder to be in uniform than the members of the Hawai'i Territorial Guard. More than three-quarters of them were Japanese Americans, and they wore their uniforms with particular pride for that reason. From the moment they had first heard the news of Pearl Harbor—or witnessed the attack with their own eyes—they knew that they would bear a unique burden in this war. They knew that their faces and last names suggested an affinity with the enemy, and they were determined to prove that they were as American as the next Joe and just as eager to fight. So, for nearly six weeks, Kats Miho and his fellow guardsmen—the majority of them eighteen- or nineteen-year-old kids—patrolled O'ahu, mostly by night, guarding reservoirs, telephone exchanges, fuel storage facilities, electrical plants, hospitals, and piers, carrying their old bolt-action rifles.

But then, on January 19, 1942, in the predawn hours of a moonless night, came a blow that they never expected. Kats and his squad were camped in a pyramid tent behind an electric substation on School Street. It was a routine night. The boys took turns, two at a time, standing at attention in front of the substation with fixed bayonets. From time to time, night-shift defense workers would pass by along School Street on their way to work, always singing or talking loudly or knocking on fences to make sure the Territorial Guard boys knew they were coming and didn't get trigger-happy. A few even dragged cans tied on strings behind them, just to make sure.

At about 2:00 a.m. the squad got a radio call to pack up and prepare to move out. This was not at all routine. Alarmed but excited, not sure where they were about to be deployed, or why, the boys got ready. Then they waited. It wasn't until 5:30 a.m. that a flatbed truck finally lumbered up School Street, picked them up, and took them to Lanakila School. There they found the entire Territorial Guard milling around in the dark on an athletic field, trying to figure out what was happening.

Finally, one of their commanding officers began to explain. Captain Nolle Smith was a large man, a halfback from the University of Hawai'i football team. He began stuttering as he spoke, tears welling in his eyes. As a Black man, he knew something about discrimination. He said that he had tried to stop what was about to happen, that all the local officers had tried, but that they'd been overruled by someone in Washington. Then another officer, Rusty Frazier, took over and got bluntly to the heart of the matter. Apparently, some of the brass visiting from the mainland had been upset to see young men with Japanese faces carrying guns. Orders had come down. "The reason why you are here this morning is because you—all you Americans of Japanese ancestry—because of your ethnic background, you are being discharged herein. As of now, you have been discharged from the Hawaiian Territorial Guard."

Kats Miho stood stock-still, his mouth open, stunned. They were all stunned. Angry. Frustrated. Humiliated. One young man, Ted Tsukiyama, would say many years later that that moment was the low point of his life, the most traumatic moment of the entire war, a war in which he would see many traumatic moments. "If a bomb had exploded in our midst, it couldn't have been more devastating," he recalled. All they had wanted since December 7 was to serve, to do what young men were doing all across the country, to stand tall and proud like all the others. Now that opportunity was gone in a single instant, replaced by a sudden re-alization that they were not trusted. And worse. Not even seen as truly American.

For a few moments there was only silence. Then Kats began to hear young men weeping softly in the darkness all around him.

PART TWO

EXILE

Seattle spectators watch as Japanese Americans are
made to board a train waiting below

FIVE

One man took my little sewing kit—you know, those little travel kits. He took that. I said, "I can't make a bomb with that, but I need it." He looked at me just like, "You don't have a right to say anything."

LILY YURIKO HATANAKA
DECEMBER 14, 2009

I n 1942, spring came early, as it often does, in California's Salinas valley, where vast fields of lettuce, Swiss chard, spinach, and artichokes stretched from the Gabilan Mountains in the east all the way out to the great blue crescent of Monterey Bay in the west. By early February, daytime temperatures were reliably in the sixties, sometimes the low seventies. The Gabilans had shifted from autumnal brown to vernal green. Bright yellow mustard flowers already bloomed alongside the valley's irrigation ditches. Men driving tractors plowed up sweet-smelling black soil as swirling clouds of screeching seagulls followed them, diving to earth, feasting on fat earthworms. Meadowlarks perched on fence posts, trying out their spring songs, their clear bell-like notes spiraling upward toward pale blue skies.

This was Steinbeck country, the end of a long, brutally tough road for the thousands of dust bowl refugees who had flooded into the valley in the preceding few years, their epic journey memorialized by the haunting photographs of Dorothea Lange and the publication, just three years before, of *The Grapes of Wrath*. The Okies, as many derisively called them, had arrived—gaunt, hollow-eyed, and exhausted—in jalopies and battered trucks piled high with rocking chairs and wash pans and old sewing machines, expecting to find an American Eden. And in many ways, they had. But they also found that they were not alone. They were just the latest addition to a rich mix of refugees and immigrants who had come to the valley before them. Less than a century after Yankee Americans had swept into California in search of gold, displacing the Mexican families who had owned the valley's original sprawling ranchos, white Americans now owned most of the land. But it was mostly Chinese, Filipino, and Japanese immigrants who worked that land. It was they who grew, harvested, and shipped east the bulk of the nation's fresh green produce, they whose labor had, by the 1930s, turned the valley into "America's Salad Bowl." The work they did was tough, unrelenting, and poorly paid, and so were many of the kids who grew up in the valley, whatever their ethnicity. Few of them, though, were tougher than sixteen-year-old Rudy Tokiwa. And Rudy was hopping mad.

On the day of the Pearl Harbor attack he had stood in a field of lettuce leaning on a hoe, watching his sister Fumi running across the field toward him, stumbling over furrows, waving her arms, yelling, bringing the news. Rudy had been alarmed but not surprised. His first thought was "Well, it had to happen." Then, almost immediately, a second thought—a question—came to mind. If this was war, war with Japan, what would he do if called upon to fight? For Rudy that was a complex question.

It's not that he was averse to fighting. Far from it. He'd been a fighter all his short life. Small, born prematurely and not expected to survive, beset by childhood asthma, prone to passing out when he got excited, he'd had to struggle for every breath and for his own survival from the very beginning. From the time he was five, he had worked in the fields, tending to the crops his family raised on rented expanses of deep, rich, alluvial soil. Working stooped over, pulling weeds, he'd always known that nothing much was likely to come easy to a Japanese American farm

kid in California. And as he got older, he'd found that, like Fred Shiosaki's Hillyard, Salinas was a place where a boy had to know how to use
his fists if he wanted to hold his head high.

Beginning when he was twelve, Rudy—like many young Japanese
Americans of his generation—had spent some time in Japan, living with
family members, learning the language, and acquainting himself with
his parents' culture. He had agreed to go only because his older siblings
had outright refused to go, and his father had finally convinced him
that somebody in the next generation should at least know the language
in order to stay in touch with relatives. Then, too, as the smallest, youngest member of the family, he tended to get bossed around by his siblings.
Maybe in Japan, he figured, he'd be free from that.

But as a schoolboy in his family's ancestral prefecture, Kagoshima in
southern Japan, he had found Japanese life to be far harder and harsher
than he had expected. In school, his teachers would brook no dissension
or discussion. His instruction consisted almost entirely of endless rote
memorization of new Japanese words and characters. When he walked
to school, if he failed to bow and pay respects to any upperclassmen he
happened to pass along the way, they were apt to slap him to the ground
for his insolence. If an upperclassman ordered him to kneel and shine
his shoes, Rudy soon learned to do so, lest he be unceremoniously slapped
or kicked again. He did it, but he hated it. And he wasn't one to back
down indefinitely. He began taking judo lessons.

When he came to the age at which all boys were required to participate in Japanese military training, he and his classmates were subjected
to being suddenly summoned from their beds at any hour of the night
by the blaring of a bugle and sent out on maneuvers in the Kagoshima
countryside. Sometimes the maneuvers went on for more than forty-
eight hours straight, thirteen-year-old boys stumbling across fields in
the dark of night, in rain or fog, staggering under the weight of heavy
rucksacks. If Rudy hadn't thought to have food ready to bring with him,
he went hungry. If he complained, he was berated. After maneuvers, he
went not home but straight back to school, fed or unfed.

In his scant leisure time, Rudy witnessed firsthand the privations of everyday life in Japan. A U.S. oil embargo—designed to punish Japanese aggression in China—meant that buses, cars, and taxis ran on coal and steam rather than gasoline or diesel. When the underpowered buses couldn't make it up a hill, everyone had to get out and push them. The air was dirty and foul with coal soot. Seventy percent of Japan's economy was devoted to military expenditures, and consumer goods were scarce. Necessities, even rice, were rationed. Western-style dress—suits and fedoras, silk ties and stylish boots—all but disappeared from the stores as it became unfashionable, even unpatriotic, to display any kind of prosperity in these times of national austerity. Life in Japan had become gray and gloomy, and people dressed to match the mood. And as the national mood darkened under the strain of the oil embargo, the inevitability of war against America was on everyone's lips. In the fall of 1939, Rudy's uncle decided it was time to take him to Yokohama and put him on a boat, the *Tatsuta Maru*, bound for San Francisco.

Despite the harsh life he was leading, Rudy would have preferred to stay in Japan longer. He had finally begun to make friends and earn respect at school. He could talk with some facility about English nouns and verbs and pronouns, and other students had begun to come to him, begging for English lessons. The principal of the school had started inviting Rudy to sit with him and help him evaluate students giving speeches in English. And nobody at school called him a Jap.

That October, Rudy sailed under the Golden Gate Bridge and arrived back home in California. Lean, lithe, and hardened by his experiences in Japan, he enrolled in John Steinbeck's old alma mater, Salinas High. He took up gymnastics, track, and wrestling. He joined the Salinas Cowboys football team along with his older brother, Duke, the team's star quarterback. Without much difficulty, he stepped back into the all-American life he had known before his time abroad. He and his mostly white friends from school hung out at soda fountains downtown, went to the movies, and took an interest in cars and how to fix them, and in girls.

Rudy Tokiwa

But Rudy's outlook on life was not the same as it had been before he left, and not the same as that of most of his friends. He felt that he had become a better young man in Japan—tougher, better able to cope with adversity, more aware of the virtues of hard work and discipline. He had come home deeply proud of his Japanese heritage and aware of the Japanese view of what was happening on the world stage, how isolated and besieged the Japanese felt. From the time he'd arrived back in the valley, he had known far better than his classmates at Salinas High, or most Americans for that matter, just how close war was, how inevitable it seemed from the Japanese point of view. So Rudy had not been surprised when his sister delivered the news of Pearl Harbor as he stood in a field of lettuce on December 7.

That evening, the Tokiwa family had done what thousands of Japanese families across America did. Up and down the West Coast in particular, they fired up oil stoves and woodstoves or kindled fires in fireplaces. They threw family photographs, their daughters' precious Hinamatsuri dolls, and volumes of Japanese literature into the flames. They smashed Japanese phonograph records. They disassembled Buddhist and Shinto shrines and hid them. They gave away lovely old kimonos, antique vases, and heirloom samurai swords to astonished neighbors. They discarded anything made in Japan—cameras, binoculars, dinnerware. Going through an old steamer trunk, Rudy's father, Jisuke—a veteran of World War I—carefully laid his U.S. Army uniform on top of the pile of clothes inside, to make sure that anyone searching the trunk would see it first.

The next morning, as Rudy and Duke walked toward school, half a dozen of the dust bowl boys suddenly stepped in front of them, jabbed fingers in their chests, and snarled, "Them dirty Japs. Let's beat the shit out of them." Rudy and Duke exchanged glances. Then Duke growled, "Aw, just a bunch of Okies. We can handle them." They squared off and cocked their fists, but before they could engage, a voice behind them shouted, "All right, you Tokiwa brothers, step aside. We'll handle it." It was a good portion of the Salinas Cowboys football team. The Tokiwas stepped to one side, the football boys stepped forward, and the Oklahomans took off running. When Rudy and Duke entered the school, though, and walked down the halls, more kids began jeering at them: "There go them Japs." Rudy was fed up. He stormed into the principal's office and said he and his brother were going home. "We don't have to take this harassment," Rudy exploded. "I have anybody come up to my face and call me a 'Jap,' it's the last one he'll ever call!" The principal told Duke he had to stay at school. But he didn't like Rudy's attitude. He sent him home, making it clear he thought Rudy was a troublemaker and was going to suffer consequences for his outburst.

When Rudy got home, there was more trouble. The FBI arrived at the Tokiwas' farmhouse on River Road southwest of Salinas in a big black sedan while the family was out working in the field. By the time they got to the house, agents had broken down the front door and were ransacking the place, pulling out drawers, dumping their contents on the floor, rummaging through closets, climbing up into the attic with flashlights, searching for contraband items—shortwave radios, binoculars, cameras, anything that might be useful to saboteurs or suggest loyalty to the Empire of Japan. The Tokiwas sat watching solemnly. When agents opened the family's steamer trunk and found Jisuke's World War I uniform, one of them held it up and said, "What's this?"

"That's my uniform," Jisuke replied quietly.

"This is an American uniform."

"Well, I was in the American army. I went to France."

"Aw, the American army never took no Japs."

They threw the uniform on the floor and trampled it underfoot as they continued to search the house. That was too much for Rudy. He leaped to his feet and screamed, "Go to hell! Go to hell!" His parents restrained him, but as Rudy stood there seething, watching the agents finally leave, he thought to himself, "This country does not like Japanese. Does not like Orientals. You gotta be white."

Now, eight weeks after Pearl Harbor, Rudy was even angrier. One thing after another was being denied him and his family. First his parents had been told they couldn't travel more than twelve miles from home without permission, which meant they couldn't get into downtown Salinas to buy supplies. Then, when his sister Fumi had gone to the feed store to buy seed, she'd been quietly told to come back later when there weren't any white customers in the store to see the transaction. Finally his family had to turn in flashlights and radios and a set of bows and arrows. Flashlights.

And rumors were circulating. Word was that thousands of Japanese American families—perhaps his among them—might soon be forced out of their homes and locked up in concentration camps, like criminals. Of course, that wasn't really likely, Rudy thought. At least not whole families. After all, the Nisei like himself were American citizens. At Salinas High, he'd learned a little about the Constitution in his history class, and American citizens had rights. They couldn't just lock him up for nothing. He knew that much. But what, he wondered, was going to become of his parents?

. . .

IN HAWAI'I, Kats Miho was devastated by his expulsion from the Territorial Guard and decided to go home to Maui. He had no stomach for staying at the university while many of his male classmates prepared to go off to war, not if he couldn't join them.

Maui was quickly being converted into a training and staging area for the looming battles in the Pacific. More than fifty military facilities were under construction all across the island—jungle training camps, machine-gun ranges, a mortar and artillery impact area, a bazooka training area, coastal defense batteries, cave-fighting encampments, barracks, canteens, and, especially, airfields. On an island that previously offered almost no job opportunities off the plantations, good jobs now went begging, and in a place where white men seldom did manual labor, most of those jobs fell to young men of Japanese, Chinese, Filipino, and native Hawaiian ancestry. If he couldn't serve in the military, Kats figured he might as well make himself useful to the country doing defense work. He found a hammer, a saw, and a square at the Miho Hotel. Proclaiming himself an apprentice carpenter, he went to work helping to build barracks at the sprawling Pu'unēnē Naval Air Station in the great green swath of Maui's central valley. He worked ten- or twelve-hour days, seven days a week, hauling roof shingles on his shoulders, crawling across rafters, pounding nails, laboring shirtless under the Hawaiian sun. The pay was decent—seventy-five cents an hour—and he was glad to be busy.

But he had a front-row seat from which to watch the burgeoning American war effort, and the view only demoralized him even more. When he visited the beaches where he and his friends had camped as kids, he found eager young men wading out of the surf clutching rifles over their heads, practicing amphibious landings. When he drove up into the hills around Maui High, he met scores of green army jeeps bouncing down cane roads. As he sat in the shade eating sandwiches on his lunch break at the naval air station, he watched silently day after day as more troops poured off transport planes, eager to get into it. The disappointment and shame he had felt that early morning in January when he and all the other Nisei troops were expelled from the Hawai'i Territorial Guard kept creeping back. It ate at his gut.

IN HILLYARD, Fred Shiosaki's parents gnawed on an unrelenting worry, fearful that at any moment men in trench coats might yet arrive and lead Kisaburo away. For weeks, one by one other Issei men in Spokane had simply disappeared. Many of their families had not heard from them since. Then, finally, FBI agents did show up.

They rummaged through the apartment above the laundry. They confiscated a shortwave radio, a pair of binoculars, Fred's .22 rifle, and, most crushing for Fred, his beloved camera. They didn't take his father away, but they ordered him and Tori to report to their office downtown immediately. Fred and his sister, Blanche, drove their parents into Spokane in the family's old Maxwell touring car. As they sat in the car waiting outside the building, hours ticked by and the Shiosaki kids worried that their father would vanish, as other fathers had vanished. When their parents did finally emerge from the building, they were together. They climbed into the car and announced quietly that they were now something called enemy aliens.

A few days later, Fred was called down to the principal's office at school, where an older man in a suit and fedora was waiting for him. The man pulled out a badge and announced sternly, "I'm from the FBI. You were seen taking pictures of the building. What were you doing?" Fred froze, terrified. He found himself stammering, desperate to get words out but babbling, making little sense. He tried to explain that he was the photo editor for the school annual, that he'd borrowed a camera to get the pictures he needed, that he hadn't meant any harm. Finally, he made himself understood, and the agent eased up. Apparently, a woman driving by the school had seen Fred out front, taking the pictures, and decided that he was a spy. "Just cut it out," the agent concluded as he left. But Fred went home shaken.

· · ·

THE WOMAN WHO LOOKED at Fred and saw a spy was just one of millions of Americans who believed that Japanese treachery was all around them that winter, lurking behind the counter at the laundry, concealed in the heart of the gardener mowing the lawn, hidden by the smiling face of the old man selling produce at the public market. Surely, many thought, only some sort of domestic espionage could account for such a sudden and devastating catastrophe as Pearl Harbor. Surely more treachery was at hand. In Rudy Tokiwa's Salinas, the citizenry forced priests at a Buddhist temple to remove their large bronze gong because they believed Japanese Americans might use it to summon an invading Japanese army.

What had started as wild rumors of sabotage and betrayal swirling through the streets of Honolulu and raging up and down the West Coast on December 7 soon began to gain the imprimatur of official legitimacy. Just a week after Pearl Harbor, Frank Knox, secretary of the navy, released a statement to the press: "I think the most effective fifth column of the war was done in Hawaii."* That same day, Congressman John Rankin of Mississippi strode onto the floor of the House of Representatives and declared, "I'm for catching every Japanese in America, Alaska, and Hawaii now and putting them in concentration camps." Some in the Roosevelt administration pushed back, citing the lack of evidence and concerns over what the law allowed. A debate began to rage behind the scenes, both about the facts (whether there had been any disloyalty) and about policy (how to safeguard against it in the future). On the one hand, the War Department, under Henry Stimson, and military commanders, particularly Lieutenant General John DeWitt, pushed for mass incarcerations. On the other hand, within the Justice Department, key aides to Attorney General Francis Biddle argued vehe-

---

*"Fifth column," a term for domestic espionage, had recently come into widespread use during the Spanish Civil War.

mently that such an action would constitute a massive civil rights violation. Throughout late January and early February, the two sides debated the issue in a series of contentious meetings. All the while, pressure mounted on Roosevelt, applied by military officials, West Coast journalists, and both Democratic and Republican politicians. They wanted those people removed, now. Increasingly, Roosevelt seemed inclined to agree with them.

Eleanor Roosevelt did not. Immediately after Pearl Harbor, Mrs. Roosevelt had flown to the West Coast, where, when she learned that the bank accounts of Issei farmers had been frozen, she successfully lobbied the Treasury Department to allow them to make monthly withdrawals of one hundred dollars. During her visit, she made a point of posing with a group of Nisei and making a radio address on January 11 in which she pointed out that the Issei were long-term residents of the country and yet they had always been denied the right to apply for citizenship. Back at the White House, she tried to gain the president's ear.

Then two titanic voices weighed in. On February 12, America's most respected columnist, the generally liberal Walter Lippmann, wrote, employing extraordinarily tortured logic, that the very absence of any sabotage thus far proved that it was about to occur: "Since the outbreak of the Japanese war there has been no important sabotage on the Pacific Coast. From what we know about Hawaii and about the Fifth Column in Europe this is not, as some have liked to think, a sign that there is nothing to be feared. It is a sign that the blow is well-organized and that it is held back until it can be struck with maximum effect." Four days later, on February 16, perhaps the most vitriolic columnist in the country, the conservative James Westbrook Pegler, weighed in, quoting Lippmann's piece but taking it further: "The Japanese in California should be under armed guard to the last man and woman and to hell with habeas corpus until the danger is over."

On February 19, 1942, three days after the Pegler column, Franklin Roosevelt signed Executive Order 9066, authorizing the secretary of war or his military commanders to designate areas of the country from

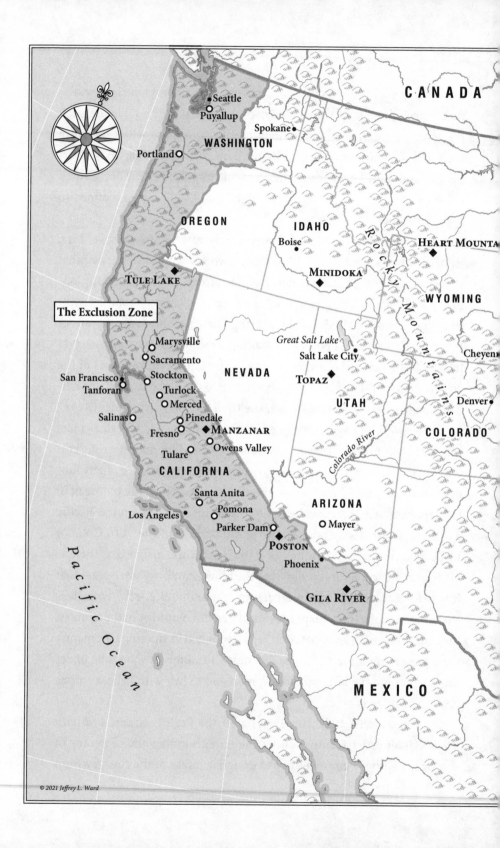

CANADA

Seattle
Puyallup
Spokane
WASHINGTON
Portland

OREGON

IDAHO
Boise

HEART MOUNTAIN

MINIDOKA

WYOMING

TULE LAKE

The Exclusion Zone

Marysville
Sacramento
Stockton
San Francisco
Tanforan
Turlock
Salinas
Merced
Pinedale
Fresno
MANZANAR
Tulare
Owens Valley

Great Salt Lake
Salt Lake City

NEVADA
TOPAZ

UTAH

Cheyenne

Denver

COLORADO

CALIFORNIA

Santa Anita
Pomona
Los Angeles
Parker Dam

ARIZONA
Mayer

POSTON
Phoenix

GILA RIVER

Pacific Ocean

MEXICO

© 2021 Jeffrey L. Ward

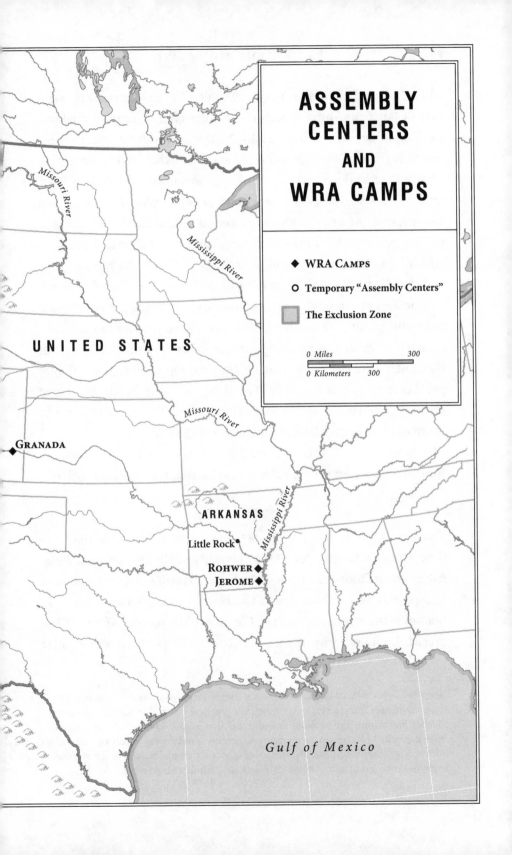

ASSEMBLY CENTERS AND WRA CAMPS

◆ WRA Camps

○ Temporary "Assembly Centers"

The Exclusion Zone

0 Miles   300

0 Kilometers   300

Missouri River

Mississippi River

UNITED STATES

Missouri River

◆ GRANADA

ARKANSAS

Mississippi River

Little Rock●

ROHWER ◆
JEROME ◆

Gulf of Mexico

which "any and all persons may be excluded." The order made no mention of Japanese Americans, nor any other ethnic group. It made no distinction between citizens and noncitizens. It did not specify what was to become of whoever was excluded, where they were to be sent, or what was to be done with them. All that was to be left to the military authorities. But even as Germany continued to expand its iron grip on Europe, most American eyes were directed toward the Pacific now, and everyone knew whom the order was aimed at—anyone and everyone with a Japanese surname living near the West Coast. The rationale that had prevailed within the Roosevelt administration was that with no way to quickly and thoroughly vet the loyalties of Japanese Americans and their immigrant parents, they posed an existential threat to the coast's military bases and burgeoning defense industry. And the politics of the matter were straightforward. A National Opinion Research Center poll taken in March indicated that 93 percent of respondents favored removing the Issei from the West Coast. Only 25 percent objected to incarcerating the Nisei, their American children, as well.

When Eleanor Roosevelt learned of Executive Order 9066, she confronted the president about it. He refused to discuss the matter with her.

THE MACHINERY OF GOVERNMENT whirred to life, with cold, wartime efficiency. General John DeWitt issued a public proclamation designating an exclusion zone from which both Japanese Americans and their Issei parents were to be removed, forcibly if necessary—the western sections of Washington, Oregon, and California, and parts of Arizona.* The overwhelming majority of America's Issei and Nisei lived within these

---

*For a brief period that March, Japanese Americans were encouraged to "voluntarily" remove themselves from the exclusion zone. As a practical matter this was virtually impossible for most families to accomplish within the time allowed. With their bank accounts frozen, they had nowhere to go, no means to get there, and no way to support themselves once they got there. Additionally, threats of mob violence and hostile public statements from the governors of many inland states left most families afraid to take the chance.

boundaries. The only other large concentration—and it was very large— was in Hawai'i. There, the Roosevelt administration realized, it would be impossible to remove so many people without plunging the economy of the entire territory into a catastrophic state of ruin. That could not be allowed to happen, both because the big sugar and pineapple interests would be devastated and because in the months to come, Hawai'i would be crucial as the platform from which the war in the Pacific was to be prosecuted. So in Hawai'i, only those who had found their way onto the FBI's lists would be incarcerated, and they would be kept in separate federal detention sites, mostly on the mainland, far away from their families.*

On March 1, DeWitt issued another proclamation, establishing an 8:00 p.m. to 6:00 a.m. curfew for all people of Japanese ancestry, citizens or not. On March 18, Franklin Roosevelt signed a second executive order, 9102, establishing a new agency, the War Relocation Authority (WRA). The mission of the WRA was to carry out the work of systematically incarcerating people removed from the exclusion zone on the mainland. Then, on March 27, DeWitt issued yet another proclamation, this one prohibiting Japanese Americans from "voluntarily" relocating farther east of their own volition, leaving them with no option except forced removal and incarceration.

Shock waves and confusion ran through Japanese American communities up and down the coast. The sweeping orders seemed clean, clear-cut, and efficient from the military's and the administration's points of view, but from the point of view of the people whose lives they touched, they were anything but clear-cut.

Anyone whose ancestry was so much as one-sixteenth Japanese— anyone with even a single Japanese great-great-grandparent—was now required to register for removal from the exclusion zone. The ratio in

---

*A relatively small number of both Issei and Nisei detainees were incarcerated in Hawai'i, held first at Sand Island and then, beginning in 1943, at Honouliuli, a particularly spartan camp in a hot, mosquito-infested gulch in the hills northwest of Honolulu.

itself was absurd and irrelevant. The Issei had been born in Japan and were virtually all entirely Japanese in their ancestry. Almost all Nisei had two Japanese parents. And most Nisei were too young to have children of their own. In effect, anyone with any Japanese ancestry at all was subject to removal. But there were other complications. Some older Nisei did have spouses of other races. Those couples would have to figure out whether to separate or to be incarcerated together. There were Japanese orphans, some living in orphanages and others who had been adopted by people of other races. There were foster children as well. They would all have to be taken from their orphanages or their foster homes. And then what was to be done with the bedridden elderly? Pregnant women about to give birth? The chronically ill? The mentally disabled? People recovering from surgeries in hospitals? All would—somehow—have to move.

Scores of other questions came to the minds of mothers and fathers, sons and daughters. What would become of students who were halfway through their academic years? What about high school and college students who were just months from graduating with degrees they had all but earned? In an age when polio and tuberculosis and influenza were still major public health threats, how could epidemics be avoided in crowded camps?

As the news reverberated through Japanese American households and the questions multiplied, work got under way on seventeen temporary "assembly centers" in which to house those who were about to be forcibly removed from their homes. The exact number of people who would ultimately be incarcerated in those temporary centers and the more permanent "relocation centers" to follow is difficult to ascertain precisely, but it amounted to at least 108,000 and might have included as many as 120,000. On March 24, the army issued the first of what would become a series of area-specific civilian "evacuation" orders. This first one applied to 271 people of Japanese ancestry living on Bainbridge Island in Washington State. It gave them six days to prepare to leave, taking with them only what they could carry. That week, men in trucks drove around Bainbridge, hanging out the windows, looking to take advantage. "Hey, you Japs! You're going to get kicked out of here tomorrow. I'll give you ten bucks for that refrigerator. . . . I'll give you two bucks and fifty cents for that washing machine."

In Salinas, Rudy Tokiwa was apoplectic.

SIX

All I think about is you. Whatever I'm doing, whether it's
eating or even laughing, I just can't seem to get away from
the situation and am constantly on the verge of tears. In the
evenings I look at the moon and pray for your homecoming.
When the wind blows, I pray to the wind. Seeing the small
birds flying free brings tears to my eyes, and I appeal to the
airborne birds for your return.

HANAYE MATSUSHITA, INCARCERATED AT MINIDOKA,
WRITING TO HER HUSBAND, IWAO, INCARCERATED
AT FORT MISSOULA, MONTANA
SEPTEMBER 27, 1942

Rudy Tokiwa's father, Jisuke, didn't know what to do. He was
sixty-two years old, a U.S. Army veteran, the head of the family,
the one who made the decisions, the one to whom everyone
turned for guidance. In the forty-two years since he had left Japan as a
young man without prospects, he had been a houseboy, a student, a la-
borer, an American soldier, a farmer, a husband, and a father. Now he
and Fusa owned a tractor and a family car. Their rented house contained most of the amenities of modern American life—indoor plumb-
ing, a radio, electric lights, beds with mattresses and box springs. The
land he worked was so fertile and the sweat he poured into it so profuse
that most years he produced such an abundance of produce that some of

it was shipped by rail all the way to the East Coast. As he had begun to look toward his old age, he had finally come to believe that he and Fusa would be reasonably comfortable, that they could begin to enjoy life a little and let their sons carry more of the weight of running the farm in the years to come.

But now he just plain didn't know what to do.

His sons were assaulted on their way to school. His daughter was turned away at the feed store. The spring crops were already in the fields, but blazing headlines in newspapers, posters plastered on telephone poles, and stern-sounding bulletins on the radio were all telling him that by April 30 he would be required to "evacuate"—to walk away from the land, leaving his crops to wither and die. It seemed more than a man his age should have to bear.

THE TOKIWA FAMILY did not own the land they farmed. Japanese immigrants were prohibited from owning any sort of land by virtue of a set of anti-Asian laws that had roots reaching back to the arrival of Chinese laborers in California during the gold rush of 1849. Right from the start, many white Californians had resented the Chinese immigrants, who often worked harder and for lower wages than they were willing to accept. Sporadic violence against the Chinese soon broke out in the goldfields and then spread up and down the coast and worked its way inland. By the 1880s the violence had become more or less endemic. Eighteen eighty-five was particularly grim. In that one year, hundreds of Chinese families had their homes burned and were driven out of towns throughout the West. In April, at least five Chinese miners died when explosives were deliberately set off under their cabin in Anaconda, Montana. On September 2, roughly 150 white miners carrying rifles surrounded the Chinese district of Rock Springs, Wyoming. As they moved into Chinatown, they began beating Chinese men to the ground with the butts of their rifles, then robbing them as they lay in the streets. With a crowd of white women cheering them on from a plank bridge nearby, the mob set fire to Chinese homes. As people ran out of the flames, the men began shooting them down. The carnage continued into the night. Some victims were burned alive in their homes. Some were hanged. At least one was scalped. The survivors fled, many of them wounded, into the nearby hills and watched from that vantage point as white families searched through the ruins of their homes for gold and other valuables. Approximately fifty Chinese immigrants were killed. In 1882, President Chester A. Arthur signed the Chinese Exclusion Act, entirely barring the immigration of Chinese laborers.

Then the anti-Asian forces turned their attention to the Japanese. In February 1905, the *San Francisco Chronicle* launched what would become a drumbeat of fiercely anti-Japanese editorials: THE JAPANESE INVASION: THE PROBLEM OF THE HOUR; JAPANESE A MENACE TO AMERICAN WOMEN; CRIME AND POVERTY GO HAND IN HAND WITH ASIATIC LABOR. In 1913, California passed the Alien Land Act, prohibiting "all aliens ineligible for citizenship" from owning land. Other western states soon did the same. In June 1919, Senator James Phelan of California testified before Congress, seething about what he considered the unfair advantage Japanese immigrants gained by working too hard or being too ingenious: "They are tireless workers and persevering and clever agriculturalists. They know how to get the last penny out of the soil. . . . I regard them in their economic destructiveness, their competitive ability, as enemies to be rejected, to keep away from as a plague of locusts, not to be compromised with but to be eliminated."

In 1922, the U.S. Supreme Court ruled against Takao Ozawa—a twenty-eight-year resident of the United States, a graduate of Berkeley High School, a former student at UC Berkeley, the father of two American children, and a practicing Christian—in his quest to become a U.S. citizen. Because he was neither a "free white man" nor a person of African descent, the Court ruled, his race precluded him from any right to citizenship under the Naturalization Act of 1906. Finally, in May 1924, President Calvin Coolidge signed the Johnson-Reed Act, effectively shutting the doors to further Japanese immigrants, starting July 1 of that year.

In the United States, the Issei shuddered. There could be no illusion now. Prohibited from becoming citizens, with their relatives in Japan now ineligible to immigrate, and with the two nations drifting into increasingly bellicose stances, their lifelines to Japan were cut off. Their future lay entirely in the hopes and dreams they nourished for their American children. They, at least, seemed to have a future in America.

But in the spring of 1942, that future suddenly darkened. Now they and those children together faced wholesale forced removal from their homes, deprivation of their livelihoods, curtailment of their rights, and mass incarceration.

A family being forcibly removed from Bainbridge Island

NOT ALL THEIR COUNTRYMEN had hardened their hearts against their Japanese neighbors, though. As the deadline for the Tokiwa family's eviction from their home approached in Salinas, a measure of relief came suddenly and unexpectedly from some young friends reaching out, trying to help them at a time when helping anyone with a Japanese name was decidedly unpopular.

Some years before, a pair of brothers living just down River Road from the Tokiwas—Ed and Henry Pozzi—had suddenly been orphaned. The Pozzis were immigrants themselves, an Italian Swiss family, and in the manner of the old country they had always run their property as a dairy operation. Growing up, Rudy and his siblings enjoyed hanging out with the family, sitting in their barn on bales of hay, eating fresh-made Swiss cheese and salami sandwiches. The Pozzi boys had grown equally close to the Tokiwas, stopping by the house often, joking around, calling Fusa and Jisuke "Mom and Dad." But when, just out of high school, they had been orphaned, the boys found themselves, just as the Great Depression was at its peak, abruptly in charge of a dairy operation they didn't know how to run. Before long, the bank was threatening to foreclose on them.

Desperate, they went to the Tokiwas for advice. Jisuke pointed out to them that they were raising cows on some of the most fertile land in the country.

"Turn it into a farm," he said.

"But we don't know nothing about farming."

"We will teach you how to farm," Jisuke reassured them.

And he set about doing just that, instructing them on everything from tractor maintenance to seed selection. Within months, the boys were farming.*

Now the Tokiwa family, like nearly all Japanese American families, faced a flurry of practical dilemmas. The most immediate was how to deal with their possessions. Because they did not own the land they farmed, there was no way to know when, or even whether, they would ever return to the Salinas valley. Much of the little wealth they had ac-

---

*In time Pozzi Brothers would become a multimillion-dollar lettuce-growing operation, thriving well into the twenty-first century.

cumulated was tied up in the things they did own—their furniture, their car, their clothing, their farm equipment. There seemed little alternative but to sell it all off to any buyer they could find, at any price.

That's when the Pozzi brothers came to them, eager to help.

"You store everything in our place," they said.

"Are you sure you want to do that? You might get in trouble."

"No, no, you people are like family to us. You store your car and everything. We will jack it up so the tires don't rot, and we'll come start it every so often."

They even agreed to take care of Fumi's dog.

In all this, the Tokiwas were blessed by their neighbors. And to be sure, there were many other families who stepped forward to help their departing friends, neighbors, and business associates. But there were many more who couldn't wait to see them go, and to swoop in and exploit the opportunities created by their absence—gobbling up leases on homes and farmland, buying out businesses for fractions of their worth, looting possessions put in storage, vandalizing orchards and greenhouses, breaking into warehouses full of merchandise.

ON APRIL 30, Rudy watched angrily as his father turned the latch on the front door of their now empty house for the last time. The Pozzi brothers drove the family downtown to the National Guard Armory on Howard Street. Outside the armory, they joined hundreds of other people milling around on the sidewalk. Rudy stared at the scene. He hadn't seen so many Japanese faces in one place since leaving Japan. Many people had come dressed in their Sunday best—men in three-piece suits and ties and fedoras; women wearing white gloves, pumps, and church hats; little girls decked out in plaid skirts and shiny black patent-leather shoes. As Rudy watched, more people arrived. They came pushing Grandfather in a wheelchair, holding Grandmother by the arm. They came carrying bags and suitcases, dragging steamer trunks, cradling babies and jewelry boxes. One woman, with several teenage daughters in tow, had stuffed one of her two duffel bags with nothing but Kotex sanitary pads. Another woman toted a large tin laundry tub full of clothes, with a small tricycle tied on top. The Tokiwas piled their possessions on the growing mountain of suitcases and duffel bags and household goods and stood back and looked at them wistfully, wondering if they'd made the right choices.

Families with personal possessions stacked
in front of the Salinas Armory

Men in military uniforms attached paper tags—like luggage tags— each bearing a number, to the bundles of possessions. Then they attached matching tags to Rudy, to his parents, to his siblings, and to everyone else. More men in uniforms directed them into a clamoring auditorium full of people where they sat on folding chairs waiting to register for incarceration. Eventually their names were called. They went to the front of the room, filled out some forms, then trooped back outside and climbed reluctantly onto a Greyhound bus. Olive-green army trucks arrived to transport their luggage.

Rudy stared out green-tinted windows at a crowd of curious onlookers gathered across the street. Occasionally someone on the bus forced a

smile or waved a handkerchief out a window at a friendly face they recognized in the crowd. But when the bus pulled away, the smiles faded
rapidly, and a grim silence settled over the passengers as the reality of
what was happening sank in.

It was a short ride, just across town to the Salinas Rodeo Grounds.
When he got off the bus, Rudy was shocked. He had tried to imagine it
in advance, to prepare himself for it, but the sight of barbed-wire fencing surrounding acres of tar-paper-and-pine-plank barracks drove home
the reality of his future and deepened his outrage at the injustice it represented. Army trucks arrived, bringing the possessions they had left
piled on the sidewalk in front of the armory. An enormous mountain of
baggage grew near the gates to the camp. The Tokiwas found their be-
longings and began to drag them through the dust, past a row of tall
eucalyptus trees and a barbed-wire gate, and into what was now officially called the Salinas Assembly Center.

They found their assigned barracks and peeked into the single room
they were all to occupy. It was almost entirely empty, roughly twenty by
twenty feet, devoid of furniture except for some metal cots lined up
against a wall, a couple of lightbulbs hanging from the ceiling, and a
kerosene stove in the middle of the room. The Tokiwas stepped into the
room and stood looking around for a few minutes, stunned, bewildered,
not sure what to do next, not sure how they could make a home out of
so little. The plywood partition between their room and the room next
door did not even reach the ceiling, and they could hear every word the
family next door spoke as they, too, moved in. Rudy and Duke began to
haul in the luggage and started scouting around the camp for scraps of
lumber they could cobble together to make some kind of basic furniture, or at least some shelves on which to place things, and perhaps some
nails they could hang their clothes from.

Over the next few days, Rudy explored the camp, though there was
not much to discover except dust and weeds among the long rows of
identical tar-paper-clad barracks. When he went to the men's latrine, he
found he needed to stand in a long line and that the toilets were nothing

more than planks with holes placed over earthen pits. There were no partitions between the "toilets," and so no privacy. And the place stank. The urinals were simply zinc troughs that emptied directly onto the ground outside the building, where the urine pooled on hard, com-pacted soil. In the men's bathhouses, shower faucets had been placed seven feet high on the walls, too high for many boys and some adults to reach.

When he went to one of the mess halls for his first meal, Rudy dis-covered that it, too, required standing in a long line—sometimes for forty or forty-five minutes—and that when he finally got his food, it was sparse at best. With a food budget of only thirty-three cents per day al-located by the War Relocation Authority for each internee, there was usually rice or potatoes but seldom any kind of meat, perhaps a bit of tongue or liver at most. One meal consisted of what an official report termed "a codfish concoction," derived from twelve pounds of fish di-vided among six hundred people.

But the worst of it for Rudy, as for most people there, was the simple, stark presence of the barbed wire around the perimeter of the camp, the gatehouse at the entrance, and, above all, the guard towers manned by uniformed men carrying guns, watching them.

CONDITIONS WERE MUCH the same at the sixteen other hastily built "assembly centers"—what newspapers around the country had taken to calling "Jap Camps"—in Washington, Oregon, California, and Arizona. At the Santa Anita racetrack in Arcadia, California, as at several other centers, dozens of families were housed in horse stalls still reeking of manure and urine. The only shower facilities at Santa Anita were those designed to wash horses, not humans. Old women found themselves having to stand, naked and humiliated, among other women, under torrents of water pouring from oversized showerheads in the middle of a wide-open room. The women's latrines housed porcelain flush toilets set in a row along a wall, but there were no partitions between them.

Mothers and daughters took turns holding up sheets around each other to provide a modicum of privacy.

At the Puyallup Fairgrounds, south of Seattle—where the "assembly center" was euphemistically named Camp Harmony—relentless spring rains had turned the open lanes between barracks into soupy, muddy mires, into which people sank up to their ankles every time they stepped outside. In the barracks, grass and dandelions grew up through floorboards laid directly on wet sod. Here, as in all the camps, the walls between the rooms were so thin that one could hear every word, every sound, that one's neighbors made—the shrill arguments, the muttered confidences, the gossip, the mundane chitchat, the lovemaking.

The mess halls at Camp Harmony had no fresh fruits or vegetables that first week. Day after day, the internees were fed canned Vienna sausages and stewed tomatoes, and soon nearly everyone had diarrhea. People rushed to the latrines in the middle of the night but found they had to stand in long lines in the rain and the mud with machine guns trained on them and searchlights playing over the scene as they inched forward, each of them desperately hoping they could hold out long enough to make it into the building. It was deeply humiliating, and starkly dehumanizing.

BY THE MIDDLE of that spring, Kats Miho's father found himself living in Oklahoma in a canvas tent on a windswept bit of prairie. On the morning of March 17, he and 165 men—all of them Issei, all of them considered too close to Japanese family members or Japanese culture and institutions to be allowed to remain free in Hawai'i—had been marched off Sand Island in Honolulu and down into the hold of the USS *Grant*, a decrepit old screw steamer built in Germany in 1907. The next morning, the ship weighed anchor and headed for San Francisco, bound not for the "assembly centers" set up for Japanese Americans but for separate prison camps run by the military and the Department of Justice. Conditions in the hold were hot, dank, and miserable. The lights

Barracks at Camp Harmony at the Puyallup Fairgrounds

were kept on twenty-four hours a day. The men were not allowed on deck, could not take showers, and could relieve themselves only by lining up at the latrine every three hours. Many of the older men couldn't last three hours, and so they passed a can around the soon-stinking hold.

The voyage was long and tedious as the boat followed a zigzag route to avoid Japanese submarines. Told that they might be attacked at any time, Katsuichi Miho sat for hours on end, leaning against the hull, wearing a life jacket, listening to the churning engines, gazing into space, trying not to think about the Japanese subs that might be lurking out there in the cold, dark sea just beyond the steel plates of the hull. When the *Grant* finally arrived at San Francisco's Pier 7 on March 30, the men emerged into the California sunshine stunned and disoriented. For the next nine days they were held on Angel Island, where thousands of Chinese immigrants had entered the country in the previous century. Then armed soldiers loaded them onto a train in Oakland, destination unknown. Although it was a passenger train, the windows were covered with wire mesh. The cars, Katsuichi realized, were cages on wheels. For several days the men sat bolt upright in their seats or occasionally leaned against each other, trying to catch a few minutes of sleep, as the train rolled on, carrying them deeper into the American heartland and to a fate that still remained utterly mysterious to them.

Finally, they climbed off the train at Fort Sill, Oklahoma, just north of the Texas border. The place was nearly treeless, a windy, flat landscape unlike anything most of the men from Hawai'i had ever seen. Soldiers herded them into a stockade surrounded by an inner and an outer fence, the outer one topped with rolls of barbed wire. Overlooking the stockade stood a guard tower with searchlights and a .30-caliber machine gun. The men crawled wearily into the four-man pup tents to which they had been assigned and fell asleep.

A day or two later, they were told to assemble in the stockade under a hot Oklahoma sun. Temperatures rose into the high nineties. For a long while, nothing happened, except that some of them began to grow faint. Eventually each of them was in turn called into a makeshift clinic and told to strip. Expecting to be inoculated, Katsuichi stood naked, waiting patiently for a doctor to arrive with a syringe. Instead, someone came into the room and slowly and deliberately wrote a number across his bare chest with a red pen. The number, from that moment forward, was to be his identity as far as the government was concerned.

As the spring of 1942 dragged on, most of the men living in tents at Fort Sill had little to think about other than the problems that their wives and children might be confronting back home in the islands. Who was paying the bills, tending to crops, managing the family business, getting the car tuned, running the store? Who might be sick? Who was making sure that Grandmother was taking her medicine? Word was they might never return home, that after the war they might just all be shipped back to Japan.

None of them was more pressed by such worries than Kanesaburo Oshima, a fifty-eight-year-old father of eleven from the Kona coast of

the Big Island. Oshima had come to Hawai'i to work on a sugar plantation in 1907, but after three years of brutal labor in the cane fields he'd
struck off on his own, eventually opening a combined general store, barbershop, and taxi business in the little roadside town of Kealakekua. Now,
more than thirty years later, his businesses were thriving, and he had
children ranging from age twenty-six down to four. With so many lines
of business, it took the whole family to keep things running.

But since arriving at Fort Sill in March, Oshima had been deeply
depressed. Lately, he'd begun acting erratically, muttering to himself
about home and his family. At about 7:30 on the morning of May 12, he
began asking around for a hatchet so he could cut some wood. It was
odd. There was no wood to be found on the barren patch of dust and
prairie grass within the stockade, and no one imprisoned there would
have had a hatchet at any rate. Then, suddenly, he began to walk toward
the double fencing surrounding the compound, shouting, "I want to go
home, I want to go home!" He began to scale the first ten-foot fence.
Some of his fellow internees tried to pull him down, but he climbed
quickly, scrambled over the top, and dropped into the narrow strip of
weedy ground between the fences. A guard pulled a pistol and shouted
at him to stop, then began firing. The first three shots missed. Oshima
began running along the space between the fences, then turned and
started climbing the second fence, shouting again, "I want to go home!"
As he reached the barbed wire at the top, he paused, apparently perplexed. The other inmates shouted, "Don't shoot him. He is insane!"
The guard hesitated, but a second guard pulled a pistol and fired. A bullet struck the back of Oshima's head, and he dropped immediately to
the ground, flat on his back, dead.

Issei men, alarmed by the commotion, came running from their tents
and gathered at the scene, staring at the body sprawled out in the weeds,
but then quickly moved back as soldiers in the guard tower swung the
barrel of the machine gun in their direction and shouted, "Disperse! Do
not congregate! Go back to your tents or you will be shot."

That night, the wind blew hard. Katsuichi Miho lay on his cot in the dark, staring at the canvas above his head as the searchlight played over the tents, probing every dark corner of the stockade. Lying there, listening to the wind whistle and his tentmates snore, he tried to conjure up the Miho Hotel—the pink and white orchids Ayano grew in the courtyard, the smell of ginger and shoyu drifting from the kitchen, the soothing warm water of his wood-heated *ofuro*, the laughter of his children. But try as he might, he couldn't hold on to it. Couldn't hold on to home. It was just too hard to imagine. It seemed an abstraction now, something out of reach, rapidly receding, dissipating and disappearing into an irrevocable past.

The next day, more than seven hundred Issei prisoners stood solemnly in ranks as a hearse carried Oshima's body out through the gate, beyond the barbed wire. In the following weeks, the mood among the men at Fort Sill grew darker. A question hung in the air: Who would be the next among them to crack, to go crazy? One of the men—Otokichi Ozaki—had been watching his fellow inmates deteriorate. Writing on a scrap of canvas on May 14 he noted, "If we continue to live like this for two or three years we will become living corpses. Everyone's eyes are beginning to look like those of dead fish."

SEVEN

*There is nothing wrong with the Constitution. . . . If the
promised protections did not materialize, it is because those
entrusted to uphold it have failed to uphold it. Ultimately, the
buck stops here, with me, with us, the citizens. . . . It is up to us.*

GORDON HIRABAYASHI

ordon Hirabayashi was halfway across the campus when it
hit him.

He was in a hurry, on his way home. Home, for now, was a
small room in the dingy basement of the YMCA across the street from
the University of Washington in Seattle, where Gordon tended to the
furnace and worked in the building's small restaurant in exchange for
room and board.* The room wasn't much of a home, really, nothing to
sit on but a bed and no furniture to speak of except for a desk. But Gordon didn't care much about material things. He was much more interested in all things spiritual and philosophical, in matters of the mind,
the heart, and the soul.

A few minutes before, he'd been at Suzzallo Library, working with
some of his classmates, when they'd reminded him that he might not

---

*This was the same basement where a few years earlier an Olympic rower named Joe
Rantz had lived.

make the 8:00 p.m. curfew for Japanese Americans if he didn't get a hurry on. He made his apologies and dashed out of the library. Then, suddenly, walking briskly across Parrington Lawn, he'd stopped dead in his tracks.

For the first time, really, the illogic and the unfairness of what he was being required to do settled on him. Why, precisely, did he have to be home by 8:00 p.m. when none of his classmates did? On what basis, other than race, was there a distinction between him and them? And if it was only race, how could that be consistent with the Constitution he had studied in high school?

He turned around and headed back to the library. His classmates, startled to see him reappear, said, "Hey! What are you doing here?"

"I'll go back when you guys are ready to go."

And with that he sat down, opened his books, and resumed working.

Gordon was, in many ways, an odd young man, certainly a young man who was determined to find his own path through life, however much it might diverge from the usual course. Slight and a bit owlish in appearance, peering out at the world from behind large glasses, he was soft-spoken but exceptionally eloquent. He chose his words carefully and deliberately, deploying them in a slow, measured cadence that invited close attention to each and every one of them. His manner was resolute and unflappable.

He had grown up in the White River valley, south of Seattle, where his family grew vegetables. His parents were followers of the Mukyokai movement in Japan—a Christian sect that rejected the church's dogma, liturgy, and ritual but focused instead on developing a personal relationship with God, doing good works, and following the dictates of conscience. As a result, Gordon grew up believing that nothing was more important than following his moral compass, defending just principles, and aligning his actions with his beliefs. His motivating principle, in all things, was to live a courageous life, and the essence of courage, as he saw it, was holding fast to fundamental truths, regardless of inconvenient or painful consequences.

An outstanding student, he had skipped through grammar school at an accelerated pace, entered high school at age twelve and a half, and graduated when he was just barely seventeen. When he had entered the University of Washington, he'd enrolled in the ROTC program, but after participating in a debate over conscription at a student leadership conference, he had moved toward pacifism and become active in the American Friends Service Committee, the Quakers. By 1940, well before Pearl Harbor, he had left the ROTC and registered with the Selective Service as a conscientious objector.

Now, as he sat in the library and the clock ticked past 8:00 p.m., he set himself on a journey that would eventually lead him to a cell in a federal prison.

LIVING EAST OF THE COLUMBIA RIVER as they did—and therefore outside Washington State's portion of the exclusion zone—Fred Shiosaki and his family were not incarcerated in one of the camps. The war was much on their minds, though. They had heard nothing from Fred's oldest brother, George, who had been studying in Japan when the war broke out. Letters sent via the Swiss embassy had gone unanswered.

In the apartment over the laundry, the family sat around the kitchen table at night making contingency plans. Nobody could be sure that at some point Fred's father might not yet be taken away, as so many other Issei men had been. There really was no telling who might be taken and when. If it happened to Kisaburo, Tori and the kids would have to run the laundry themselves to keep the family afloat financially. Fred found the conversations unsettling. The plans didn't jibe with what he had in mind. Fred's older brother Roy, who ran a laundry in Montana, had been drafted in early January, during a brief interlude between Pearl Harbor and the period when the Selective Service stopped drafting Japanese Americans. Fred had resolved that as soon as he turned eighteen, he, too, would sign up. For now, he was keeping that to himself.

Things were looking up at the laundry, though. As the war effort geared up, thousands of troops and millions of tons of war matériel began to move from industrial centers in the East toward the West Coast and the Pacific theater of operations. Much of it passed through the Great Northern's rail yard in Hillyard. The yard, busier than ever, was generating an enormous volume of greasy, sooty, grimy work clothes—the kind of dirty laundry that the Shiosakis specialized in. Customers began to drift back into the laundry. Before long, they began to flood back. Soon Kay and Mrs. Kay had more business than they could handle.

Then one day Will Simpson, the printer, walked into the laundry carrying a bundle of white work shirts. The family hadn't seen him since the day after Pearl Harbor, when he'd shut his door in Kisaburo's face. But apparently printer's ink was as difficult to remove as industrial grease.

"Kay, I can't find anybody to do my shirts right," Simpson said. "Would you do them?" Kisaburo paused for a moment, savoring the glee rising in his chest. Then he put on a mournful face, shook his head sadly, and said, "Jeez. Sorry. I'm just too busy."

RUDY TOKIWA STOOD each morning peering through the perimeter fence of the Salinas Assembly Center, trying to catch a glimpse of his friends on school buses passing by on their way to Salinas High. The first day, nearly everyone on the bus saw Rudy, and most waved to him as they passed. A few friends came after school that day and visited with him through the fence. Some of his football teammates came. The Pozzi brothers came. Everybody agreed it just wasn't fair what was happening to Rudy's family. After all, a lot of them were Italian Americans. Italy was at war with the United States, and they weren't locked up. The whole situation didn't make much sense to the young men on either side of the fence.

But as the days passed, life on the outside went on. Rudy's buddies were getting ready to enlist when they graduated in June. Fewer and fewer kids waved as the bus passed each morning. Eventually, nobody waved. Rudy realized he was becoming invisible to them. Still, he watched the bus each day and imagined what his old friends were thinking now: "Ah, he's one of the Japs. We can't be friends with him."

He realized he was going to go stir-crazy if he didn't find something to do other than stare out through the fence. At the mess hall one day, he approached Mr. Abe, the head cook. Abe, an Issei immigrant, had learned to cook for large numbers of people while feeding Japanese work crews on the Union Pacific Railroad. He didn't speak much English, but Rudy's Japanese was pretty good, so they got into a conversation. Rudy said he was bored and he'd like to learn to cook. Abe, impressed that someone as young as Rudy was willing to put in long hours in the kitchen, didn't hesitate. "I will teach you to cook," he said.

Rudy threw himself into the job. He worked seven days a week, sometimes from 4:00 a.m. until after 8:00 p.m., helping to feed more than a thousand people at a time, three times a day. He brewed huge pots of coffee, poured fifty-pound sacks of rice into enormous vats of boiling water, scrambled scores of eggs at a time on a griddle. There were times when the work hours seemed like too much, as if it might be better just to hang out with some of the other boys who loafed around the camp all day. But Mr. Abe had a way of leveling a look at him over a vat of rice and saying in quick, emphatic Japanese, "If you have free time, your mind wanders and you get in trouble." It reminded Rudy of the stern way his teachers in Japan had talked, and while he hadn't liked it then, he found Abe's gruff manner reassuring now. There was a certainty to it, a firmness that seemed lacking elsewhere in his life. The work, the rigor of it, the discipline it required—it all seemed to help him cope with the situation. He decided to keep his head down and continue working.

THE FORCED REMOVAL of Japanese Americans and their parents from the exclusion zone took place over a period of weeks that spring. In each area, they were given deadlines by which they had to close down their affairs, appear at assembly points, and climb on buses to be taken away.

As the deadline approached in Seattle, Gordon Hirabayashi dropped out of the University of Washington and went to work for the local Quaker chapter, aiding the families of Issei men who had already been incarcerated by the Department of Justice. With their husbands and fathers gone, many Issei wives and younger Nisei needed help preparing for their own impending incarcerations—selling their possessions, closing businesses, packing up, figuring out how much they could carry to the buses. As Gordon soon found, old women and old men with canes couldn't carry much of anything. Mothers carrying infants couldn't also carry a cradle or diapers or extra clothing for the baby. Furniture, automobiles, cherished heirlooms, couldn't be carried at all, and so had to be given away, sold for pennies on the dollar, or stored for who knew how long at who knew what cost.

In some ways personal possessions were the least of it. Gordon soon realized that the situation was exacting a terrible psychological toll. Anxiety, angst, depression, and fear stalked whole communities. He helped as parents sat children down and explained that they would have to give up beloved pets. He counseled students who realized they would have to quit classes in mid-semester, say goodbye to their closest friends, forgo

An elderly man in Hayward,
California, waiting to be taken
to an "assembly center"

senior proms, perhaps even forgo diplomas they had all but earned. He sought out business experts and solicited practical advice he could pass on to the anxious proprietors of businesses that had been nurtured over decades but now would have to be shuttered. Inventory somehow had to be liquidated, accounts receivable forgotten about. Long-standing and hard-earned customers would inevitably go to the competition. Contracts would be voided. Greenhouses full of orchids and azaleas and chrysanthemums left to die. Thousands of acres of crops abandoned. Could any of it ever be recovered?

For weeks, Gordon helped people onto the buses and waved solemnly as they pulled away. But as the date approached on which he, too, would be required to get on a bus, he began to realize that when the time came, he wouldn't—he couldn't—do it. Not if he were to remain true to his principles. As an American, he could not simply surrender his constitutional rights as if they meant nothing, as if they were mere words scrawled on an old piece of parchment.

Once he had made up his mind, his principal concern was that he didn't want to get his Quaker associates or his friends at the YMCA in trouble for harboring a fugitive. He wanted to be as transparent as possible, to make it clear that he alone was responsible for what he was about to do. He had already begun keeping a diary that documented his ongoing defiance of the curfew. Now he began to tell a few select friends what he planned. Then he phoned his parents to tell them. It was a hard conversation. They had expected him to be home in the White River valley by now to join them on their own bus journey into incarceration. When Gordon told them he was not going to allow himself to be taken away, his mother began to cry. She agreed with him in principle, respected his position, admired him for his courage, but she was desperately afraid of what might befall him. "Please put your principles aside on this occasion, come home, and move with us. Heaven knows what will become of you if you confront the government. . . . The worst of all would be if we are separated now, we may never get together again!" she pleaded. She was afraid they would put him in front of a firing squad,

A young girl in Oakland,
California, tagged and ready to
be sent to an "assembly center"

she said. "I'd like to," Gordon said, "but I wouldn't be the same person if I went now." As he put down the phone receiver that day, Gordon was crying, too. But he would not budge. Not even for his mother.

On May 12, the same day that Kanesaburo Oshima was shot at Fort Sill, the last bus carrying Seattle's Japanese Americans to Camp Harmony pulled out of town. Gordon was not on it. He was now the last Japanese American living in Seattle. The next day, he sat down at a typewriter in the basement of the YMCA and pecked out a statement addressed to the FBI. Titled "Why I Refuse to Register for Evacuation," it began by discussing the natural rights of man, then focused on the situation immediately at hand:

> These fundamental moral rights and civil liberties are included in the Bill of Rights, U.S. Constitution, and other legal records. They guarantee that these fundamental rights shall not be denied without due process of law. . . . If I were to register and cooperate under these circumstances, I would be giving helpless consent to the denial of practically all of the things which give me incentive to live. I must maintain my Christian principles.

I consider it my duty to maintain the democratic standards for which this country lives. Therefore, I must refuse this order for evacuation.

He made duplicates of the statement and handed copies to officials at the YMCA, the director of the ROTC program, and several of his Quaker friends.

On Saturday, May 16, Gordon arose early. A friend drove him downtown to the offices of Arthur Barnett, a Quaker attorney. Barnett walked Gordon over to the Vance Building at Third and Union and into the offices of the FBI. Barnett handed Gordon's statement to Special Agent Francis Manion, who glanced at it and said, "Oh we already have that. We've been expecting you." Apparently, someone at the YMCA or the ROTC had already sent the statement on to the FBI. Barnett spoke up. "We feel it is appropriate for us to come here to present this to you. We are not trying to hide anything." Gordon also wanted to make it abundantly clear that he was surrendering voluntarily, not because someone had intercepted his statement or turned him in. "Here is the original," he said. "I'd like to leave you with it." "Okay," Manion said. "We'll take it."

But now that they had him, the FBI couldn't figure out what on earth to do with Gordon. Manion and some other agents drove him over to Maryknoll School, where Japanese Americans were supposed to register. Someone put a paper in front of him.

"That looks like the same registration form I saw a few days ago," Gordon said. "Has there been any change in it?"

"Well, no."

"Well, I can't sign it then."

"But you have to sign it. Everyone has to sign it," Manion said.

Gordon, always implacable, replied, "Have you signed it?"

Taken aback, Manion said, "If you don't sign it, you are breaking the law, and you're subject to some punishment."

"I can't do it. What you are going to do as a result of my inability to sign, that's for you to determine. I don't make my decisions on the basis of what I think you are going to do."

Manion opened the diary that Gordon had kept. In it, Gordon had frankly confessed his curfew violations.

"Were you out after 8:00 p.m. last night?" Manion asked.

"Yes, like you and other Americans," Gordon replied.

"Oh, then you violated the curfew. That would be a 'count two' violation."

Gordon smiled, looked him in the eye, and replied softly, "Are you turning yourself in for curfew violation, since you did exactly as I did and we are both Americans?"

"Ah, but you are of Japanese ancestry."

"Has the Constitution been suspended?"

Manion had no answer for that. He had not expected anything like this. Some of the people being incarcerated had grown angry. Some had complained. But none, as far as he knew, had simply refused to cooperate. Perplexed, he made phone calls to the Presidio in San Francisco, asking for instructions, then drove Gordon to another location, where someone else put the same form in front of him. Gordon refused to sign. Manion took him to Fort Lawton, a U.S. Army base in Seattle. Gordon refused to sign. As they drove from one location to another, Gordon chatted with Manion. There were no hard feelings on either side. This was new territory for everyone.

Finally, late in the day, Manion took Gordon to the King County Jail in downtown Seattle and left him in Tank 3C, the federal holding tank. Gordon had never seen the inside of a jail before, and for the first time he was a bit nervous. Some of the men he found himself among were serious criminals awaiting trial on federal charges—wire fraud, counterfeiting, bank robbery, racketeering, smuggling. Others were in for lesser crimes like narcotics violations or petty larceny, but they had made the mistake of committing them on federal property or an Indian reservation. The place was a bedlam of noise—inmates shouting, laughing, doing calisthenics, playing cards, flushing toilets, and cussing one another. The only furnishings were metal tables and benches screwed to the concrete floor. Men were pacing back and forth like caged animals.

Gordon soon settled in, though, and began to chat with his fellow inmates and started to feel more comfortable. On Monday morning, a military officer, Captain Michael Revisto of the Wartime Civil Control Administration, showed up. Revisto was cordial, even charming, but clearly upset. "I've been looking forward to meeting you," he told Gordon. "You'll be glad to know that in Southern California, the biggest numbers of people went through. Hundred percent success. Northern California, next big headquarters, everything went through. Hundred percent success. And then when we finish this discussion, we'll be hundred percent here, too."

Gordon stared at him. Slowly it dawned on him what the man was saying. His defiance meant that Revisto's sector was the only one on the West Coast that didn't have a perfect record—100 percent compliance with the "evacuation" orders. Gordon was stunned. He had assumed

Gordon sitting on steps with
a big smile

that perhaps a hundred other Nisei would have done what he had done by now. Apparently, he was the only one.* Revisto continued, "You know you violated a lotta things and if they add these on, tack on consecutively, you're gonna have a long jail sentence. But they're willing to forget all that and they're giving you a clean slate. And soon as you sign this statement here, we're all set. I've got a car here ready to take you to Puyallup."

Gordon was sympathetic to the man's problem. He wanted to be helpful, but he wasn't about to sign the form. "You know," he said, "I have one suggestion by which you could get your hundred percent. You've got your car here all ready to take me down there. I'm not physically objecting to your doing this. It's just that I can't consent, give you the consent myself under the circumstances. . . . But I don't see why you can't take me down there without my consent. And all you need to do is just get a couple of your guys to escort me down to the car, throw me in the back, and drive down forty miles, open up the barbed wire, drive me in front of the administration building, put me down, plunk me down there, drive out, close the gate, I'm there."

Revisto, startled, replied, "We can't do that!"

"Why not?"

"That'd be breaking the law."

"You mean you think breaking the law, putting me in without signing, is worse than a hundred and twenty thousand people that were forced to be moved out?"

"Well, I can't do that," Revisto muttered. And with that, shaking his head, he gave up and left as perplexed as Manion had been.

On June 1, Gordon was arraigned in federal court on two counts: violating Civilian Exclusion Order No. 57 and violating the 8:00 p.m. to 6:00 a.m. curfew. He entered a plea of "not guilty," on the basis that both

---

*In fact, Gordon wasn't the only Japanese American to deliberately disobey the curfew and forced removal. Both Minoru Yasui in Oregon and Fred Korematsu in California took similar actions.

the exclusion order and the curfew were racially motivated and denied him due process of law and were thus unconstitutional. He was offered bail, but because he could not be released into the exclusion zone and he still refused to register for removal to one of the camps, he was returned to the King County Jail to await trial on charges with the potential to keep him imprisoned for years to come.

EIGHT

The soldier said, "Let me help you, put your arm out." He proceeded to pile everything on my arm. And to my horror, he placed my two-month-old baby on top of the stack. He then pushed me with the butt of the gun and told me to get off the train; knowing when I stepped off the train my baby would fall to the ground, I refused. But he kept prodding and ordering me to move.

SHIZUKO TOKUSHIGE, ON HER ARRIVAL AT POSTON

B y the summer of 1942, most Americans had come together to pull alongside one another with a single-mindedness, determination, and cohesion that they had not known in generations, perhaps since the Revolution of 1776. Their firm resolve was fueled not just by their immediate anger over what had happened at Pearl Harbor but also by their deeper recognition that something profoundly evil was afoot in Europe and in Asia, an evil given face and form by soulless men who wielded racial hatred, demagoguery, blind nationalism, and brute violence as the means by which to seize and hold power. In the face of this overwhelming darkness, Americans, like their overseas allies, held firm to the belief that they stood on the moral high ground, that the values they lived by—liberty, democracy, and the simple notion that all men were created equal—were inviolable and sacred and now under an existential threat. To meet that threat, they resolved to manifest their best selves, to give, as Lincoln had taught their grandparents and great-grandparents, the last full measure of their devotion to the high ideals underlying their national identity.

So by the millions they awoke every morning that summer and happily took their coffee without sugar so that the troops could have candy bars on the battlefield. In the evening they harvested vegetables from the victory gardens in their backyards so that the boys would sometimes have more than K rations to eat. They poured their earnings into War Savings Bonds. They scoured their homes for bits of rubber—extra toilet plungers, rubber bands, old galoshes, automobile floor mats, even rubber girdles—that might help the military offset the loss of rubber from plantations in Japanese-held Southeast Asia. They launched campaigns to collect scrap metal. In Seattle alone they gathered almost twenty-five million pounds of material, heaping it in mountains so large that they covered entire city blocks and became tourist attractions. They dutifully poured the fat from frying sausages and bacon into tin cans and took the fat to collection centers for the making of glycerin for high explosives. Women by the tens of thousands donned greasy overalls, grabbed monkey wrenches, and went to work in industrial plants, helping to turn out vast quantities of war matériel, including an astonishing sixty thousand aircraft in that one year. College girls spent their weekends standing on street corners selling "victory corsages" for a dollar apiece. Hundreds of major-league baseball players—among them superstars like Joe DiMaggio and Ted Williams—enlisted in the military. So did movie stars like Henry Fonda, Clark Gable, and Jimmy Stewart.

In cities as large as Los Angeles and towns as small as Casa Grande, Arizona, Boy Scout troops were trained to provide emergency support in case of an air raid. Men ineligible to serve volunteered as ambulance drivers and air raid wardens and utility repair crews. Doctors walked away from lucrative private practices to serve in military hospitals and on hospital ships. Entertainers like Bob Hope and Carole Lombard climbed onto planes and departed for remote sand spits and atolls in the South Pacific to entertain the boys. Everyone was chipping in. Everyone could do something to help. Everyone was part of something larger and much more important than themselves.

But for Gordon Hirabayashi in the King County Jail, for Fred Shiosaki in Hillyard, for Rudy Tokiwa in the Salinas Assembly Center, for Kats Miho pounding nails on Maui—and for thousands of young Japanese American men and women like them—the summer and fall of 1942 were seasons of profound discontent and angst. Assumptions they had held all their lives seemed suddenly to have been turned on their heads. Even their sense of self, of who they were and how they fit into the larger world, seemed suddenly uncertain. They arose every morning, went to mirrors to wash their faces and comb their hair, and saw Americans looking back at them. But each and every day, they confronted fresh reminders, in the starkest terms imaginable, that many of their countrymen saw them not as Americans but as enemies, enemies of all that America stood for and all that they themselves believed in. And there didn't seem to be much they could do about it. Many of them and their parents—more than a hundred thousand people—now lived behind barbed wire in America.

ON THE EVENING of the Fourth of July, Rudy Tokiwa and his family found themselves under guard, sitting in a darkened railway car, traveling south through a country busily but quietly celebrating the birth of liberty. As the train rolled through California's Central Valley that night, fireworks bloomed here and there in the skies over small towns. But the fireworks were sparse compared with prior years, their production greatly curtailed by war needs. And Rudy and the other passengers couldn't see them at any rate. They had been ordered to keep the shades in their coaches pulled down so that nobody could catch a glimpse of them as they passed.

The next morning, in the tiny hamlet of Parker, Arizona, they stepped down off the train and into the blast furnace of an Arizona summer. The thermometer in Blythe, just a few miles away, across the California-Arizona border, registered 112 degrees Fahrenheit. None of them had ever known heat like this. In spite of that, insisting on their dignity, many of the women were again wearing their Sunday best; some of the men were wearing coats and ties. Sweating, bleary-eyed from a mostly sleepless night on the train, they climbed into the backs of green army trucks.

Half an hour later and twelve miles to the south, they arrived at what was to be their new home for the foreseeable future—the Colorado River Relocation Center. Located at Poston, Arizona, two and a half miles east of a slow, sluggish section of the Colorado River, the center had been built on the Colorado River Indian Reservation—home to the Mojave and Chemehuevi people. The reservation's governing Tribal Council had objected to the camp's construction on the grounds that they did not want to be a part of an injustice. When the Office of Indian Affairs overruled them, a contractor—the Del E. Webb Construction Company—scraped seventeen thousand acres of the northernmost Sonoran Desert clean of sagebrush and began building.* Now, on this vast expanse of raw, sunbaked sand, stretching three miles from one end to the other, stood row upon row of black tar-paper-clad barracks. The facility was divided into three sub-camps—Poston I, II, and III—though the people incarcerated there would soon come to call them "Camp Roastin', Camp Toastin', and Camp Dustin'."

As Rudy and his family climbed off the trucks at Poston III, guards with rifles stood by watching them. Young Mojave men wearing cowboy boots and hats began to unload baggage from the trucks. Humidity from the nearby river made it feel even hotter here than it had in Parker. Almost immediately people began to faint. People who had arrived earlier

---

*The Office of Indian Affairs later became the Bureau of Indian Affairs. Del Webb later became well known for constructing Sun City, Arizona, the first community in America designed specifically for senior citizens.

rushed to the newcomers, handing out salt tablets and water. Young Nisei women helped older and disabled people off the backs of the trucks and sat them down in the sand in narrow margins of shade alongside the barracks.

Rudy, squinting against the glare, looked around him in disbelief. Heat waves shimmered over the roofs of the barracks. The molten air tasted of rocks and minerals. A fine gray dust had settled over everything—the sagebrush surrounding the camp, the rocks, bits of scrap lumber lying on the ground where carpenters building the barracks had left them. From time to time a gust of hot, dry wind stirred the dust up, but the wind was searing and offered no relief. Horned lizards skittered this way and that. Off in the distance, in the direction of some purple mountains, dust devils danced across the desert floor. It was hard, Rudy thought, to imagine a more godforsaken place.

Although the camp had opened in May, the WRA administrators who ran the place were still struggling to cope with the flood of incoming families. Mostly, the newcomers had to fend for themselves or rely on earlier arrivals, some of whom had been assigned specific duties by the administrators but were themselves still trying to figure out how to make things work. The newly arrived had to sort through mountains of baggage to find their own, wander through a maze of identical buildings to locate their quarters, explore still-unfinished latrines to find a place to relieve themselves. When the Tokiwas finally found their assigned barracks in Block 213, someone handed them empty sacks and pointed them to bales of straw outside. "Fill it up with hay. That's your mattress." Fusa and Fumi started stuffing mattress covers. It was even hotter inside the barracks than outside. Drifts of dust had blown up between the pine planks of the floorboards into the one room that was to be their living space. Fusa borrowed a broom and began to sweep, but every time another hot gust of wind came up, more dust wafted into the room. As in Salinas, there was no furniture, so Rudy and his brother Duke again began to gather scrap lumber with which to improvise simple shelving, tables, and chairs.

Stuffing mattresses at Poston

As evening approached, someone discovered that the refrigerators in the mess hall contained some food, but no one had been assigned to cook for the new arrivals in this corner of the camp. A crowd gathered in front of the kitchen, trying to figure out what to do about it. Everyone was starting to get hungry. Because Rudy had worked as a cook in Salinas, some of the younger men approached him.

"Rudy, how about cookin' here? We gotta have someone cook the meals."

Rudy peered into the kitchen. The only stove was a coal burner. There was dust and sand on the floor and all over the equipment. He was irritated. Why didn't they clean the place up and cook for themselves? he thought. Why him? Why a sixteen-year-old kid?

"Naw, hell. I ain't going to cook in this heat," he growled. "No way! Any of you guys want to get stuck in there?"

The young men backed off. But they knew Rudy, and they knew how to get to him. A few minutes later a group of stern-faced older men appeared and, speaking Japanese now, reopened the case with Rudy.

"We have to have someone cooking, Rudy. And you know us old men. We're old and we can't take this. It's going to have to be you young guys. So please, will you take the kitchen over?"

This time Rudy said yes. As fractious and recalcitrant as Rudy could sometimes be, he wasn't one to ignore the pleas of his elders. And he was the right man for the job. He quickly organized a crew of young men and set them to sweeping the place out while he fired up the coal stove. As the temperature in the kitchen approached 110, he rummaged through the storage cabinets and refrigerators organizing their contents. When he realized that there weren't enough knives and forks in the kitchen, he sent volunteers out to gather desert ironwood and mesquite and begin whittling primitive chopsticks. But as he looked at the supplies, his anxiety and frustration ratcheted up. How was he going to feed hundreds of hungry people with these meager ingredients? It was mostly going to have to be fried Spam. He wasn't looking forward to hearing the complaints. But he began to cook.

It was nearly midnight by the time everyone had been fed. As he shut off the coal stove, Rudy was exhausted and still sweating despite the late hour. But as pathetic as the meal had been, he had pulled it off, and as people had come through for their meals, instead of complaining, they had thanked him, the old men and women nodding, saying, "*Domo arigato*"—"thank you very much."

Rudy wandered out into the night air. He was proud of what he had done and proud of his people. They were tough. Uncomplaining. As unfair as the whole situation was, it was nice to feel that he was part of a community and contributing to making things a little better for them. The moon had not yet risen, and the black sky was ablaze with stars. Temperatures were finally starting to drop, but it was still too hot in the barracks for sleep, so Rudy did as some of the other young men were doing, dragging their straw mattresses out of the building and stretching them out on the sand. But as the moon rose a little after 1:00 a.m., lighting up the desert floor, one of the other boys called out in alarm, "Hey, look at all these damned things crawling around under our beds!" Rudy sat up and looked, and sure enough they were everywhere, dozens of scorpions scurrying this way and that in the silvery light, attracted by the boys' body heat. He didn't know much about the creatures except that if one stung you, it would hurt like hell. Still, he figured he'd take his chances. He wasn't going to let some creepy bugs force him back into the suffocating barracks. He rolled over and went to sleep.

GORDON HIRABAYASHI SPENT THAT Independence Day in the King County Jail writing letters. In the weeks since he'd been arrested, he had fallen into an unexpectedly warm fellowship with the other inmates, "our exclusive company," as he liked to call them: a rogues' gallery of men—mostly older than Gordon—who had run afoul of the law for various reasons. There were tough longshoremen and grizzled old alcoholics; there were pimps and pickpockets; there were petty thieves and bootleggers. They came from all over the world and spoke with a dozen different accents. Disputes among them were frequent and often grew violent. Early in his stay, an exceptionally tall Black man got into a wild brawl with a Native American. Buckets, mop handles, fists, and shoes all became weapons as the two careened around the tank attacking each other amid the cheering and hooting of the other inmates. In the end the Native American inmate, bloody and subdued, got the worst of it and both men were dragged off and thrown into solitary cells. On other occasions, the inmates ganged up on one another, stripping perceived offenders naked and hurling them into cold showers for infractions like sitting in someone else's seat. One of the jailers—a thuggish character named Barney who often showed up for work drunk—seemed to relish provoking the fights and spent much of his time lounging outside the tank whispering snide remarks through the bars, demeaning and irritating the men, seeing if he could set something off, just for the fun of it. At first, Gordon, deeply averse to both cussing and violence, stayed out of everyone's way during the outbursts. He spent much of his time writing letters, reading Oscar Wilde's *De Profundis* and Irving Stone's *Clarence Darrow for the*

Defense, or maintaining the diary he was keeping in a spiral-ring stenographer's notebook.

As time went on, though, Gordon sometimes felt the need to intervene. One of the other inmates had not showered or shaved for weeks. His hair was matted, and he smelled foul. The others began threatening to beat him up. Gordon approached the fellow quietly one day and asked him if he was going to shave. The man glared at him defiantly.

"Why?"

"Looks like you need one. Might make you feel better."

The man paused, looked baffled for a moment, and then walked away. The next time he passed by, Gordon asked quietly again, "Would you like a razor blade?"

"Yeah."

When he'd shaved, he asked Gordon to give him a haircut. Gordon suggested he take a bath and shampoo so his hair would be ready for the clippers. He did. By the next morning he looked as if he were ready to go to church.

A few days later, his fellow inmates approached Gordon with a proposition. They had been watching him, seeing how he dealt with others, how careful he was with his words, how determined he was when he set his mind on something. This soft-spoken, peculiar young man was different from them, and they knew it. Now, they said, they wanted to elect him "mayor of the tank," to resolve disputes and to act as their spokesman when dealing with the guards and the jail's administrators. Gordon was wary. "Well . . . I don't think I'm the one to do that for you," he said. "You get somebody else." But they wouldn't back off. He was the only one who could do the job, they said. Finally, Gordon agreed tentatively. "I'll take the position for a week. And at the end of the week, we'll assess whether I should continue or not. And I'll do it my way, and a lot of you people won't like it because I believe in nonviolence and I believe in negotiating for things, even if I'm not getting too far." The men eagerly agreed. "Well, that's fine. You do your own thing, and we'll support it," they said.

The job stayed his. In the weeks that followed, Gordon threw himself into it with characteristic determination, resolving disputes and negotiating with the jail's administrators for better living conditions. Slowly things began to improve. Men came to him with complaints about each other rather than cussing or striking each other. When Gordon discovered that many of them were illiterate and could not understand the court documents they were given, he read them aloud and explained their significance. Then he began to write letters on their behalf to the court, adding to his already voluminous correspondence with his own lawyers, friends, and advocates. Soon it was a full-time job, and he appointed a committee of three other inmates to help him manage the work flow.

But on that Fourth of July in 1942, Gordon put aside his mayoral duties. He was in a reflective mood. He fully expected that when his case came to trial in the fall, he would lose. After all, he had admitted to violating the curfew, and he still had not registered for incarceration in one of the camps. But the law was clearly unconstitutional, and his conviction would almost certainly lead to the Supreme Court. And there—he had to believe—his rights as an American citizen would surely be vindicated. Meanwhile, though, his family was living in a desolate concentration camp, and it was they he was thinking of now. On this day, of all days, it seemed important to meditate on what was happening to them. He sat down, opened his spiral-ring notebook, and wrote,

July 4, 1942, King County Jail. One hundred and sixty-six years ago today a band of earnest and far-seeing individuals drafted and signed a document—the Declaration of Independence. Because of their vision and conviction, we, the people of these United States, have made tremendous advancements in the liberation of mankind from political, social, economic, and religious slavery. . . . But even though this is America, these things happening today are not American. They are the results of mis-interpretations, mis-emphasis of the right thing to do, hysteria, and short-sightedness. It is up to those of us who feel that a wrong has been committed, that we have fallen short, to bear witness to that fact. It is our obligation to show forth our light in times of darkness, nay, our privilege. The risk is great; the consequences unpleasant. But there is the vision of those seekers of independence. We must carry the torch.

Below that he scrawled, "Just a rambling thought in remembrance of the 4th. Incarceration of liberty."

Not long after writing this, Gordon received a letter from his mother, Mitsu. Although more firmly committed than ever to the course of action he'd taken, he'd felt guilty for weeks about the last tearful phone conversation he'd had with her, for disregarding her pleas to join his family in camp. To go against her wishes violated everything Gordon had been taught about filial piety. And he just plain hated to upset her. So he opened her letter with apprehension.

After having been held for more than two months at the Pinedale Assembly Center near Fresno, California, Gordon's family had just arrived at the Tule Lake Relocation Center. Constructed on a dry, ancient lakebed set amid the jumble of the rough volcanic outcrops and sagebrush-covered hills that make up much of Modoc County in Northern California, Tule Lake was among the bleakest of the eight WRA camps in operation by the summer of 1942. It was also, after the camps in Arizona, probably the hottest. When the Hirabayashis first arrived, the temperature was in the vicinity of 115. The only way Mrs. Hirabayashi could find any relief was to crawl under her bed and lie on the cement floor of her barracks. But she also had pleasant news for Gordon. As she had been unpacking her suitcase, there had been a knock on her door. When she answered it, she found two Issei ladies from Los Angeles covered in dust from head to foot but wearing broad, warm smiles. One of the ladies bowed and said, "We had to walk about a mile and a half, so we're kind of dusty here now. But we heard that the family . . . whose boy is in Seattle fighting the case for us was arriving, so we wanted to be here to say welcome, and to say thank-you for your son."

It was, Mrs. Hirabayashi wrote to Gordon, a moment that gave her a huge lift, that made her proud. What she didn't tell him was that every evening she stepped outdoors at Tule Lake, searched for the North Star, and, gazing at it, talked to the star as if it were her son up in Seattle, and then said a little prayer on his behalf.

IN HAWAI'I, Kats Miho spent his days that summer putting roofs on barracks at the naval air station at Pu'unēnē and contemplating the sudden dissolution of his family and the world in which he had grown up. Although Maui's population was burgeoning with the military buildup, the island had become a profoundly lonely place for Kats. Six months after Pearl Harbor, he and his mother were now the only Mihos still living on Maui. His father, apparently, was somewhere on the mainland in some kind of military prison. Katsuaki, just three years older than Kats—and closest to him among his brothers—was in Honolulu, living at Atherton House, working as a paramedic and hospital volunteer while applying to medical schools on the mainland.* Their much older brother Katsuro was also in Honolulu, working as an attorney. Yet another brother, Paul, was in Connecticut, attending divinity school at Yale. But the sibling he missed the most and thought about most was his sister Fumiye.

In the evenings, Kats sometimes went after work to stand alone on the beach at Kīhei, where he and his Boy Scout troop had camped and played in the surf just a few years earlier. There, standing barefoot on soft coral sand, watching the sun sink into the Pacific, he gazed toward Japan and pondered what his big sister Fumiye might be doing. Her departure in 1940 had left a hole in his life. Fumiye was much like

---

*Like Kats, Katsuaki was out of sorts, upset that he could not contribute to the war effort, writing in his journal on his twenty-third birthday, "Why stay here and rot? I'd rather rot in the fields of France."

Kats—introspective, kind, exceptionally smart, and funny, with a dry sarcastic wit. Kats missed their long talks in the courtyard of the Miho Hotel, grilling each other about everything from world affairs to religion and philosophy. Since the war had come, there had been a few letters, but they were heavily censored, and now it felt as if an enormous gulf separated them. He wondered what her life might be like now, whether she—a young American—was being treated well, whether she missed their old life in the hotel, whether she wished she was back home, whether he would ever see her again.

WHEN FRED SHIOSAKI GRADUATED from John R. Rogers High School in Spokane that June, the last of his friends—some of them already in uniform, some still in civvies—disappeared almost overnight, climbing onto trains at the Great Northern depot, waving farewell to parents and girlfriends and pals, shouting goodbyes to well-wishers, nervous but happy to be on their way to win the war.

For the first few days of summer, Fred wandered the dry, rocky hills above Hillyard, sat alone in movie theaters on weekends, worked long hours beside his parents and younger siblings in the laundry, and vowed silently to himself that the day he turned eighteen he would enlist. In the meantime, though, he wanted to get out of town. He signed on with the U.S. Forest Service as a firefighter and wound up in Idaho spending his days being trucked from one brush fire to another, digging trenches, clearing brush, grubbing out roots, building fire lines. The work was brutally hard, but Fred didn't much mind it. He was growing lean and lithe and strong, and he figured it would all be good preparation for basic training and the war.

When he turned eighteen in late August, Fred came home to Hillyard, took a bus into downtown Spokane, and strode into a Selective Service office eager to finally sign up. But living as he did in a small, mostly white community outside the exclusion zone, Fred had missed one essential piece of news about Japanese Americans and the service. Back in

January—a month after Pearl Harbor—the War Department had decreed that Japanese Americans were ineligible to serve in the U.S. military and that they were, in fact, to be classified 4-C, "enemy aliens," by their local draft boards. When Fred told the young officer behind the desk that he wanted to enlist, the man simply stared at him, blank-faced, for a moment, and then said, "You can't sign up. You're an enemy alien." Stunned, Fred replied, "No I'm not! I was born in America. *I'm a citizen.*" "Well, the War Department says you're an enemy alien, so you're an enemy alien."

Fred emerged onto the sidewalk outside the building shocked and devastated. It was a hot day, in the nineties, and Spokane's sunbaked streets were nearly deserted. As he rode the bus home, he brooded on what had just happened. It defied common sense that a native-born American could be considered either an alien or an enemy, that simply placing the characters "4-C" next to his name on a draft card meant that he couldn't serve his country. Looking around, he saw that the only people on the bus who were anywhere near his age were young women. He sank a little lower in his seat, wishing the driver would hurry up and get him home to Hillyard.

THE END OF that summer saw Rudy Tokiwa lying in bed in the Poston camp hospital as doctors wielding scalpels and tweezers slowly and painfully scraped and pulled bits of dead flesh from his badly burned body.

It had been a long, hard, hot summer for Rudy. His first night of cooking for the camp had quickly turned into a full-time job. Once the Poston camp was up and running, the WRA had begun—as at the seven other permanent camps then in operation—to employ the people incarcerated there to carry on much of the day-to-day business of feeding, policing, educating, caring for, and cleaning up after themselves. The pay scale—deliberately set below the scale for American GIs to counteract accusations that they were being coddled—ranged from fourteen dollars per month for ordinary workers like Rudy up to nineteen dollars per month for professionals, like dentists and doctors. It wasn't much money by any measure, but salaries from those jobs sometimes allowed people to fulfill obligations left over from their lives before "evacuation"— to pay off business loans or income taxes, or to pay for storage of their possessions. More immediately, those bits of income allowed people to order a few necessities from the Sears, Roebuck and Montgomery Ward catalogs—a new pair of jeans, a dress for a daughter's birthday, a tricycle, some hair curlers, a pair of work boots. Mostly, though, people spent their scant earnings in the camps' co-ops. Set up and organized originally by Quaker and Mennonite volunteers, the nonprofit co-ops were owned and run by those incarcerated in the camps. For a five-dollar investment, they were able to join the co-op, shop for a variety of basic products, and earn periodic dividends to boot. It was there that they went to buy most everyday items—cigarettes, chewing gum, razor blades, fresh fruits, or canned goods.

As in Salinas, Rudy found himself cooking for hundreds almost every day, often from the time the sun rose until well after dark. With temperatures climbing to well over a hundred most days, Rudy took to rising at 3:00 a.m., swimming by moonlight in the camp's recently constructed pool, then firing up the kitchen's coal stove before dawn. His first task each morning was to set a thirty-gallon pot of water on the stove to boil and dump a sack of coffee in, brewing it hobo style, getting ready for the morning rush. Then, as the sun rose, he took his place at the stove, where he would work on and off for the rest of the day. It wasn't easy to put decent meals on the long tables in the mess halls that summer. The food was provided by the government, but the WRA had allocated only fifty cents' worth of rations per day for each person in camp, only a slight improvement over the thirty-three-cent budget that had prevailed at the "assembly centers." With the U.S. Army Quartermaster Service supplying the actual provisions, Rudy often found himself working with stuff the army had a surplus of—cheap canned meat, soggy canned vegetables, old potatoes, a few fresh fruits, and only evaporated milk. The fare offered little in the way of nutritional value and even less in the way of flavor. But Rudy did what he could, and the people at the tables continued to thank him for his efforts.

When he wasn't working in the kitchen, Rudy headed for rocky playing fields scratched out of the desert. To combat the interminable boredom, frustration, and anger that otherwise threatened to consume them, the camp's young men and women had scraped sagebrush away to make baseball diamonds and football fields. They'd set up basketball hoops on the ends of barracks. They'd even smoothed out patches of sand and sunk tin cans in them to make "greens" for an improvised desert golf course. Then they'd formed an elaborate network of sports teams, complete with leagues and divisions based on block and camp assignments for all the major sports—baseball, football, basketball, volleyball. Rudy's brother Duke soon became a superstar playing for Block 213's basketball team, the Terrors. Rudy himself was athletic but also small, not nearly as big and muscular as Duke. Nevertheless, he threw himself into the games wherever he could, even if simply to serve as the yell leader for the Terrors. The games often ended abruptly when blinding, choking dust storms swept in off the Sonoran Desert, sending everyone scurrying for the shelter of the barracks clutching wet cloths to their faces as it grew nearly as dark as night outside.

As people began to settle into life at Poston—trying to maintain some sense of normalcy—they did much more than make playing fields. They undertook an ambitious program to build a complete infrastructure to meet their needs. They constructed schools, complete with auditoriums and stages for theatrical productions, building them out of adobe bricks they made themselves from mud and straw. They turned spare barracks into Christian and Buddhist churches. To improve the fare in the mess halls, they established poultry and hog farms to supply fresh eggs and meat. They irrigated the surrounding desert and cultivated crops to supply fresh produce. They organized an internal police force and a fire department. They ran health clinics, beauty shops, barbershops, and camp newspapers. They organized Boy Scout

Young men playing basketball at Poston

troops and PTAs. And they initiated a wide variety of clubs and social activities.

Rudy tried to take advantage of it all. He surprised himself by signing up for dancing lessons. He learned to waltz and jitterbug and, for the first time, how to hold a girl in his arms. He resumed his education at the camp's high school and was even asked to teach agricultural classes. He began to make friends among the young men with whom he worked and played.

As he got to know them, Rudy began to look up to a couple of the other young men in particular. There was big Lloyd Onoye, who came from the same part of Salinas as Rudy. Lloyd was a gentle giant, an imposing physical specimen so powerful that when he grabbed other boys in wrestling matches or tackled them in football games, he sometimes inadvertently squeezed them so hard they passed out. He was slow to anger, but during one basketball game, playing for the Terrors, he became enraged over a series of foul calls and wound up dragging six other boys around the court as they tried to keep him from throttling the referee. Finally, one of the boys yelled at the referee, "If you want to live, Mac, you'd better get out of here!"

And then there was Harry Madokoro, another member of the Block 213 Terrors. Harry's father and sister had both died before the war, leaving Harry as his mother Netsu's only child. To make ends meet, Harry had worked on a vegetable farm and helped his mother run a small candy shop in Watsonville, near Salinas. Now the two of them lived together in the same block as the Tokiwas.

Harry was thirteen years older than Rudy and served as chief of police on Camp II's police force. Thoughtful and sober-minded but always friendly, Harry projected a certain gravitas and commanded a kind of respect that Rudy and the younger men found inspiring and reassuring. Instead of dangling a cigarette from his lips as many of the boys had taken to doing, Harry smoked a pipe. The younger men gravitated toward him, tending to follow wherever he led. When they had squabbles among themselves, they generally sought Harry's counsel, and his counsel almost always proved wise.

By midsummer, Rudy figured he was as content as he was likely to be, living in a desert behind barbed wire against his will. Then the accident happened. Early on the morning of August 8, as he was carrying a thirty-gallon stainless steel pot of boiling coffee from the stove to a counter, Rudy slipped on a rubber hose on the wet floor. His feet went out from under him. The scalding coffee went up in the air, then landed square on his chest and right arm. Rudy screamed. Another boy, Tom Yamamoto, knelt by him and ripped Rudy's coffee-stained shirt open. Already the skin was lobster red and beginning to blister. Men rushed in and hauled Rudy, moaning and in shock, away to the camp hospital.

Nearly a month later, Rudy was still in the hospital, watching patiently but flinching from time to time as a doctor taught him how to use tweezers to peel back layers of burned skin, bit by bit, until he exposed the pink shiny, granulating flesh underneath—the skin that, despite it all, was struggling to heal and to live.

BY OCTOBER, Gordon Hirabayashi's trial date was approaching in Seattle. One night, a jailer appeared a little after midnight outside his sleeping cell in the King County Jail. Most of the men in the cellblock were asleep, and Gordon was drifting off himself. But one of his unofficial jobs as "mayor of the tank" was to greet new arrivals and help them integrate into life in the jail. "Where should I put this guy?" the jailer asked. Gordon roused himself and went to the bars. "Why don't you bring them in the daytime when it's easy to do these things?" he groused. Gordon glanced at the newcomer, a short, older Japanese man. Then he did a double take. "Hey, that's my dad!" He was surprised. He had been told that his mother might be summoned to testify in his trial, to positively identify him, but he had not expected to see his father.

Shungo Hirabayashi looked exhausted. Federal agents had awakened both him and Gordon's mother early that morning at the Tule Lake camp in California. They'd been sitting in the backseat of a car since then, traveling north. Shocked to see his father so tired and haggard, Gordon welcomed him into the cell, had a brief conversation with him, gave him a bunk, and put him to bed. Gordon couldn't fall asleep, though. He lay awake in his bunk until 4:00 a.m., unsettled at the sight of his father in a prison cell.

Meanwhile, his mother had, in fact, arrived in the women's tank upstairs. As the door closed behind Mitsu Hirabayashi, she looked nervously around. The only familiarity she had with the notion of jail or prison was what she had read in Alexandre Dumas's *The Count of Monte Cristo*. She had imagined something more like a dungeon, and she was relieved to see that at least there were no rats scurrying around in dark corners. Despite the late hour, the room was brightly lit. Women were sitting on metal benches reading or standing around in clusters, chatting casually as if at an after-church social. Most of the inmates here were being held on county charges—prostitution, shoplifting, petty thievery. Mitsu noticed a broken-down old upright piano in one corner of the room. She sat down and began to plunk out a tune. Some of the keys didn't work, but the women gathered around her. She played Stephen Foster's "Old Folks at Home." More women gathered. They began to sing. Mitsu, a bit embarrassed by the attention, said, "No, no. Somebody else play. All I know are some songs like this and church hymns, and you don't want to hear church hymns, so somebody else play." And in a chorus the women said, "No, no. Nobody plays here. You play." And she played, deep into the night as the women stood behind her and sang along.

The next morning, the jail's matron brought her a green prison uniform and told her to change into it. Mitsu eyed it and said, defiantly, "No. I'm not a criminal. I'm a witness. I shouldn't be here in the first place." When the matron persisted, Mitsu demanded to see Gordon's lawyers, right now. The matron quickly backed down as the women in the tank looked on with amazement and growing admiration. Bright, outspoken, and strong-willed, Mitsu Hirabayashi—like her son—was nobody's fool.

Until now Gordon had seldom mentioned his own legal jeopardy in the diary he'd been keeping. Mostly he'd reflected on what he'd been reading, mused about religious and philosophical issues, fretted about the legal woes of his cellmates in the federal tank, and commented on news he'd heard from his family and others incarcerated in the camps. But now, with his trial date just a few days off, he wrote on October 15,

> The case is clear. I have refused to be evacuated; I have vio-
> lated curfew orders. I [did] these things with an open eye and
> a clear mind. I did not do these things sneakily; neither did
> I act defiantly. . . . And what should be understood is that
> I am a good American citizen. Therefore, for the witnesses and

for myself, we should have nothing to fear. Merely state the truths.

ON TUESDAY, October 20, Gordon's trial, with Judge Lloyd Llewellyn Black presiding, commenced, a fact *The Seattle Times* noted under the headline CURFEW TRIAL OF JAP STARTED. It turned out to be a short and somewhat farcical affair. The federal courtroom was long and narrow. Fifteen-foot-tall windows along one wall illuminated rows of burnished black walnut benches. By the time Gordon arrived, the room was packed with his fellow university students, Quaker friends, and supporters from the ACLU. Gordon's mother and father quietly took a seat on a bench near the front of the room. Shortly after a jury of ten men and two women was sworn in, the government's prosecuting attorney, Allan Pomeroy, rose and called Gordon's father to the stand.

Shungo Hirabayashi was nervous. He had never been in a courtroom. His English was far from fluent, and his answers, nearly inaudible, were hesitant and unclear. The judge asked, "Is there anyone here in this place who can interpret for the witness?" Nobody stepped forward. Gordon looked around the room. The only other Japanese faces he saw were his parents'. Finally, he spoke up. "Well, I can interpret for him, if you'll accept the defendant." The judge hesitated but agreed. Gordon approached the stand and began translating the prosecutor's questions into Japanese and his father's answers into English.

"Where were you born?" Gordon asked his father.

"In Japan," Gordon replied, translating his father's answer.

"Do you have any children here in the United States?"

"Yes."

"Is one of them here?"

"Yes."

"Can you point to your son?" Gordon asked.

Shungo, looking confused, pointed in Gordon's direction. Gordon smiled, turned to the judge, and said, "Well, in regards to that question, apparently he's confirming that I am his son." The whole exchange was, as Gordon said later, a bit "like a side-show."

When the prosecution rested, Gordon's attorney, Frank Walters, rose and called Gordon to the stand. Gordon quietly gave an account of his experiences growing up in America. He'd been educated in public schools, he said. He'd spent much of his teenage years working on his parents' farm, driving tractors and delivery trucks. He had never been to Japan. He'd been an enthusiastic member of the Boy Scouts of America, an assistant scout master, in fact. He was a Christian, a Quaker most recently. He'd played baseball in high school, joined the High Y, was the vice president of the University of Washington YMCA. All in all, he'd had a pretty typical American upbringing. When the judge dismissed Gordon from the stand, witnesses from the community came forward and attested to his good character and his community involvement. Then Walters rose again. He did not dispute that Gordon had violated the curfew and the exclusion order. Instead, he argued that Executive Order 9066, the subsequent region-specific exclusion orders, and the military curfew order all individually and collectively deprived Gordon of his liberty without due process of law and thus violated his Fifth Amendment rights under the Constitution.

When the defense rested, the judge prepared to read the jury their instructions. Gordon and Walters knew what was coming. In a preliminary hearing Judge Black had already tossed aside their constitutional concerns, proclaiming that wartime expediencies trumped constitutional rights and then going on to lump together the nation's Japanese enemies and what he called "their kind." "They are shrewd masters of tricky concealment among any who resemble them. With the aid of any artifice or treachery they seek such human camouflage and with uncanny skill discover and take advantage of any disloyalty among their kind."

Now he turned to the jury and said, "You can forget all the talk about the Constitution by the defense. What is relevant here is the public proclamation issued by the Western Defense Command. You are to determine this: Is the defendant a person of Japanese ancestry? If so, has he complied with the military curfew and exclusion orders, which are valid and enforceable laws? It is your duty to accept the law as stated by the Court."

Ten minutes later the jury returned their verdicts, guilty on both counts.

PART THREE

KOTONKS AND BUDDHAHEADS

Nisei soldiers on a train to Camp Shelby

NINE

===

You'll probably be terribly disappointed having waited a lonely year with hopeful expectations, but please don't cry. . . . Let's think of the families of soldiers who are fighting in the heat of the tropics or in the cold snow, what they must be feeling.

IWAO MATSUSHITA, INCARCERATED AT FORT MISSOULA,
MONTANA, TO HIS WIFE, HANAYE
DECEMBER 7, 1942

It was a lonely Christmas. I spent it crying. Seeing happy families gathering together brought a lump to my throat. I imagine you spent a lonely Christmas too. This year's was more sad and lonely than last year's or any I've had.

HANAYE MATSUSHITA, INCARCERATED AT MINIDOKA,
IDAHO, TO HER HUSBAND, IWAO
DECEMBER 30, 1942

No Christmas season in modern history was more poignant, emotionally wrought, and traumatic—in the United States and around the world—than that of 1942. A year into the world's first truly global war, a war on which the sun would never set for another two and a half years, millions of Americans and their allies sat around cabinet radios that December, thinking about someone who wasn't there, writing them long letters full of small happenings at home, listening with tears in their eyes to Bing Crosby crooning "White Christmas."* In the United States, five million servicemen were away from home. Before the war was over, sixteen million would be in uniform. Service flags with blue stars hung on porches and in the front windows of millions of American homes. Each week, at an ever-increasing pace, flags with gold stars replaced them.†

On Christmas Eve, at the Poston concentration camp in Arizona, more than seven thousand Japanese American children gathered for "block parties," where they opened presents donated by churches and placed under scraggly Christmas trees decorated with construction-paper ornaments they had made themselves. In barracks and mess halls, they sang "Silent Night" and "Jingle Bells," performed Christmas skits, and were entertained by the arrival of two Santas—one from the North Pole and one from the South Pole. Older youth went from one barracks to another singing Christmas carols under a black desert sky spangled with stars.

In the South Pacific, as army troops moved in to replace them, thousands of stunned young marines wearily climbed aboard ships bound for Australia after months of bloody and harrowing fighting in the jungles of Guadalcanal. But thousands of their comrades now lay dead in hastily dug graves on the island they were leaving behind. In the Philippines, captured Americans and Filipinos labored and died by the thousands, bludgeoned, brutalized, and murdered in steaming, stinking, malaria-ridden Japanese POW camps. On the heaving back of the North Atlantic, thousands of merchant marines plotted zigzag courses through towering black seas, their skippers desperately trying to avoid being spotted by German U-boats lurking beneath the surface. In Great Brit-

---

*"White Christmas" would eventually become the largest-selling single in history as rated by *Guinness World Records*.
†The tradition of displaying service flags emblazoned with blue stars to indicate the number of family members serving in the military and gold stars to indicate the number of family members killed in service began during World War I.

ain, tens of thousands of American, Canadian, Indian, New Zealander, and Australian servicemen and servicewomen joined their British allies celebrating Christmas in pubs and canteens and private homes, downing pints of warm beer, dancing with the locals, tossing darts, and tentatively tasting plum puddings. And at the Auschwitz-Birkenau death camp in Poland, German SS men erected a Christmas tree for the inmates. Then they piled the bodies of murdered Jews and Poles around the base of the tree as "Christmas presents."

Much of the dying and the incalculable suffering of World War II still lay in the future. But in many ways the tide of events was already slowly turning that Christmas, largely unseen under the daily fog of battle reports, casualty figures, and troop movements. A great force, a massive, coordinated, unified human effort unlike anything the world had ever seen, was in motion, gathering momentum across the globe, bent on destroying the dark, cynical forces of authoritarianism.

And it was at this moment in history that something suddenly changed for thousands of young Japanese American men, the Nisei, something that defied both their own and the larger world's expectations. With the entire country mobilizing for the war, with mounting losses in the South Pacific, with tens of thousands of women having to fill in for men in heavy manufacturing jobs, with men as old as thirty-seven now subject to the draft, the U.S. military was straining to build a fighting force large enough and potent enough to wage war effectively in both the Pacific and Europe.

Ever since the Pearl Harbor attack, Japanese American leaders in Hawai'i and on the mainland had been lobbying the Roosevelt administration to allow Nisei men to enlist. And increasingly, they were winning the argument. It just didn't make sense to have tens of thousands of fit young men idling their time away in Hawai'i or sitting behind barbed-wire fences in the American West. Beginning in early January 1943, secret memos began circulating among the War Department, the Selective Service, Army Intelligence, and the FBI about the possibility of allowing Nisei men to volunteer for a segregated, all–Japanese American combat team in the U.S. Army.

ON FEBRUARY 1, Franklin Roosevelt made it official, signing a memo to Secretary of War Stimson that read, in part, "Americanism is not, and never was, a matter of race or ancestry. A good American is one who is loyal to this country and our creed of liberty and democracy. Every loyal American should be given the opportunity to serve this country."*

Among the first civilians in Hawai'i to get the news was Kats Miho's brother Katsuaki, who was still living at Atherton House in Honolulu, still working as a paramedic for the city. He'd been accepted for medical school at Tulane and was saving money for tuition. His dream was to become a doctor and bring much-needed medical services to the plantation towns of rural Maui. But the news electrified him, and in an instant his plans changed. On February 2 he wrote in his journal, "Once in every man's life, he is forced to make a decision that may decide his whole future. I made mine. For a minute—I must confess—I was too overcome to think clearly. . . . But my mind was made up and I was happy. And I have to go back to Maui and tell mother."

But when he arrived home at the Miho Hotel to tell his mother, Kats was there waiting for him, and Kats had other ideas. He, too, was ablaze with the news, and he told his brother he should go instead. That was the last thing Katsuaki wanted to hear. No, Katsuaki insisted, he would go. They argued, then discussed, then argued again. The dispute simmered for several days, finally culminating in an all-night marathon of point and counterpoint. Soaking in the hot water of the *ofuro*, leaning across the dining table, sitting under the stars in the lush courtyard of the Miho Hotel, surrounded by their mother's orchids, the two brothers tried to dissuade each other from volunteering, each wanting to take the

---

*Although often attributed to FDR himself, the memo was authored by Elmer Davis, who ran the Office of War Information.

entire risk upon himself. They argued vehemently through the night, their words infused not with rancor but with brotherly love.

The way Kats saw it, someone needed to represent the family in the war effort. Honor demanded it. The Japanese ethics their father had taught them required it, even though the enemy now was Japan itself. Their oldest brother Katsuro had glaucoma; the next oldest brother, Paul, was at divinity school. So it would have to be one of the two of them. And Kats was desperately sick of pounding nails and watching others go off to war. He appealed to his brother's respect for *giri*, social obligation. Katsuaki owed it to his community to bring much-needed medical services to Maui. "You're already accepted to medical school. Your future is to become a doctor and be a professional. I will volunteer. I will represent the family."

But Katsuaki wasn't buying it. It was about more than his dreams or the family honor or even Maui's needs. It was about conscience. "No, no, no, it's an individual matter," he insisted. "Look, if both you and I, we survived this war and then came this business of, 'What did the Nisei do during World War II?' What is either of us going to tell his kids, that 'I didn't volunteer because I went to medical school'?" By dawn, they had worn each other down. They would both go.

A few weeks later, as they climbed aboard an interisland steamer bound for Oʻahu, they joined what had already turned into a tsunami of eager young Japanese American men heading for the same place. Throughout the islands, they had flooded Selective Service offices. In some offices there weren't enough typewriters to type up all the paperwork, and more had to be borrowed from local business schools. The army had called for fifteen hundred Nisei volunteers from Hawaiʻi. Nearly ten thousand had turned out.

IN ARIZONA, the old men at Poston's Camp III arose before sunup each morning and built bonfires out in the desert to warm their bones. The predawn hours were chilly, and the men enjoyed standing around the fire, luxuriating in the sweet, pungent scent of burning mesquite. They watched the last stars fade away and the sun rise over the purple mountains far to the east. They listened to the mourning doves cooing in the first gray light of day. They rubbed their hands together and smoked cigarettes and talked quietly, mostly in Japanese, about the war. Some of them believed Japan would win the war. Some tried to disabuse them of that notion. They argued, but softly, without much passion. They looked at one another and saw old men, in a desert, imprisoned and far removed from any place of consequence. There wasn't much they could do about the war, or anything else for that matter. At 7:00 a.m. the breakfast gong sounded three times, and they threw sand on the fires and trooped into the mess hall for coffee, pancakes, and fried eggs.

Rudy Tokiwa was no longer making the coffee and frying the eggs. When he was released from the hospital following his accident, Rudy had been given a day pass to work outside the camp in nearby Parker, where supplies for the camp arrived by train. There, he'd made friends with some of the white employees of a local liquor store.

When the old men in the camp got wind of that, they approached Rudy with a proposition, just as they had approached him about working in the kitchen months earlier. They would very much enjoy a little beer, they said, but alcohol was prohibited at Poston. They wondered if Rudy might be able to smuggle a little into the camp. Rudy was still only seventeen and, by his own reckoning, too young to drink. But he was always eager to oblige his elders. And he was, at heart, a rascal. So he collected a little money from the old men and talked to his liquor store friend. Then he talked to another friend, the fellow who drove the big water truck around camp, trying to keep the never-ending dust down. Before long they had a small-scale bootlegging operation going. Once or twice a week, Rudy picked up a few cases of beer at the back door to the liquor store, then met the water-truck driver out in the desert, dropped the beer into the truck's water tank, and sent it through the camp gates undetected. When no one was watching, the old men retrieved the beer, pulling it out of the cold water and sitting in groups behind the barracks, savoring it.

. . .

On February 9, the day the White House released FDR's memo announcing the eligibility of Nisei to enlist in the military, the staff of the camp's newsletter, the *Poston Chronicle,* reprinted the entire thing on the paper's front page. At Poston, and in all ten of the mainland concentration camps, the news set off an explosion of exultation, anger, confusion, fear, and fierce debate. Nobody was quite sure what to make of the sudden change in policy or what to do about it, but one thing was immediately clear: the initial reaction in the camps was very different from what it had been in Hawai'i. Seen from behind barbed wire, the invitation to fight and die for America struck many as less than tempting. For some, it seemed downright insulting.

That same afternoon, Lieutenant John Bolton from the U.S. Army convened a question-and-answer session at the Poston Camp III, a first step in trying to recruit as many Nisei soldiers as possible out of the camp. Nearly two thousand young men and their families crowded into the camp's new school auditorium. Bolton addressed mostly practical concerns: When would inductions begin? Would the Nisei soldiers be fighting against the Germans in Europe or against the Japanese in the South Pacific? Could their parents receive their paychecks? What ranks and pay grades would be open to them?

But Bolton had no answers for the larger, more troubling questions that still hung over the young men as they trooped out of the auditorium that afternoon. Why should they lay their lives on the line for a country that had forced them and their parents into bleak concentration camps? Why, if they fought for America, would America not at least release their family members, grant their parents citizenship, and restore their civil rights? And Bolton had said that the all–Japanese American fighting unit would be just that, a segregated unit, like the Black Ninety-second Division. Why were they to be segregated? If they were willing to fight and die like white soldiers, how was it that they would not be allowed to eat in commissaries and sleep in barracks and fight and die in the same foxholes as their white countrymen? There was another big sticking point, too. Bolton had said that they and their families—every adult in the camps, in fact—were now required to sign a special loyalty oath, whether or not they planned to enlist. Why was that required only of them and not of other Americans? For many of the young men at Poston—and for their sisters, wives, mothers, and fathers as well—it just didn't add up.

Rudy, his brother Duke, and their friends from their Block 213 and adjacent blocks huddled after the meeting, discussing and arguing about it, unable to come to a consensus. Bolton had told them registration would take place in the mess hall by the end of the week, just four days away. They needed to figure it out. Finally, Rudy's friend big Lloyd Onoye called for a meeting the next day. Every young man sixteen or older, he said, should attend.

The next morning, they gathered out in the desert, down in a dry wash where a few mesquite trees offered a scant bit of shade. Off in the distance, cactus wrens made their strange, dry clicking call, like small car engines trying and failing to turn over. About forty young men had turned out. They formed a rough circle, some sitting on boulders, some leaning against the twisted black trunks of the mesquite trees. They kicked nervously at rocks, picked up sticks, and idly scratched designs in the sand, waiting for someone to take command of the situation. Harry Madokoro, the police chief, stepped into the middle of the circle and got things going. As far as he was concerned, he said, they should all sign up and do it right away, but he wanted to hear what the younger men thought. One of the boys piped up, "Why in the hell should we go out, fight for a damn country that locks us up?" Others nodded their heads in agreement. One stood up and said, "Either way you look at it, it just seems a little foolish. Here you're in the damned concentration camp, and you're going to go volunteer to fight for that country?" Again, boys nodded and murmured their assent.

Rudy sat quietly, staring at the ground. Harry Madokoro got up again and said he was going to volunteer anyway. It wasn't a choice, he said. It was a duty. And besides, it was also an opportunity. When the war was over, either they would return from the camps still stigmatized as "Japs" or they would return as Americans who had served, maybe even as war heroes. Lloyd Onoye stood up and said he was in, too. But most of the younger boys were still skeptical. They eyed one another nervously, looking for signs, poking at imaginary things on the ground with sticks. Finally, Rudy stood up. He was the youngest one there, and he was in many ways more "Japanese" than many of the others, being fluent in the language and having gone to school there. But in the end, he knew he wasn't Japanese. He was an American. An angry one. And that's what it came down to for him now. He deserved respect. His father and his mother deserved respect in their home. His sister deserved respect when she went to the feed store. If he had to fight to earn respect, he'd fight.

"All right," he said. "Say nobody volunteers out of the camps. What can Roosevelt say? Well, he can say that we're more loyal to Japan than the United States, that's what. Well, do you guys want to live in Japan?"

One of the boys replied, "Naw, I couldn't. I wouldn't be able to make it in Japan. I can't hardly speak Japanese."

Rudy went on. "As an American it doesn't make no difference if they throw you in a concentration camp . . . if you can't turn around and be able to stand up later and say, 'I did my share.'"

Another nodded and said, "Well, if we plan to settle in this country, we'd better be able to prove ourselves."

As the meeting went on, a consensus slowly formed, and by the time it broke up, nearly every boy there had committed to registering by the end of the week.

Not all the young men at Poston were convinced, though. That night, Rudy and his friends learned that many who hadn't attended the meeting were furious at those who had and were on their way to Block 213 to beat up Rudy and the others who had argued for volunteering. Rudy and his friends quickly gathered some pick handles and baseball bats and formed a defensive line. When the others arrived and saw them well armed, they beat a hasty retreat.

A few days later, Rudy and Duke walked together back to Block 213, returning from the impromptu registration center in the mess hall, uncertain how their parents would react to what they had just done. When they entered their quarters, their father looked up and immediately asked Duke what he had done.

"Oh, I volunteered."

Jisuke Tokiwa thought for moment. He had served in World War I but had never been granted citizenship. Now the government for which he had fought had destroyed his livelihood and locked his family up in a desert wasteland. Would the army keep whatever promises they had made his son? But he nodded gravely. *Shikata ga nai*, he thought. It can't be helped.

"Well, you have to do what you think you should do. You can't let other people tell you what to do."

Rudy said he'd also volunteered. His father nodded solemnly again.

"If you believe this is what you must do, I'm glad that you are man enough to do what you think is right."

But his mother, Fusa, was less sanguine.

"*Bakatere!*" You fool! she exclaimed. But then she began to cry. "Oh, he's nothing but a little kid yet! How can they take him?"

"Well, I don't have to go until I'm eighteen," Rudy said. "So let's not worry about it until then."

OVER THE NEXT FEW DAYS and weeks, both the issue of volunteering and, even more, the issues surrounding the loyalty questionnaire that Bolton had said all adults in the camps were now required to complete opened fault lines at Poston and the other nine WRA camps. At the heart of the controversy were two specific items on the questionnaire. Question 27 asked Nisei men if they were willing to serve in combat duty whenever and wherever ordered. Question 28 asked both the Nisei and their parents if they would swear unqualified allegiance to the United States and forswear any allegiance to the emperor of Japan. On principle, many Nisei, although they were willing to serve, deeply resented the fact that—simply because of their race—they were made to sign an oath that other American citizens were not required to sign. Equally they resented that they were being asked to renounce a loyalty they had never held in the first place. Their parents faced a different problem in regard to question 28. Renouncing loyalty to Japan would terminate their Japanese citizenship at a time when they were not allowed to become American citizens. That would leave them entirely stateless, with no citizenship at all. In the end, the vast majority of both Nisei and Issei—93.7 percent at Poston—nevertheless answered yes to both questions. Anyone who answered no to either question, or declined to answer them, or took the opportunity to write statements of protest on the form, was promptly reclassified as "disloyal" by the War Relocation Authority. Once thus labeled, they were to be segregated from the "loyal" inmates.

Before long, people at Poston and all the other camps were watching solemnly as some of their friends and family members—among them the young men who would eventually come to be called no-no boys—were loaded onto the backs of flatbed trucks and driven out through the camp gates, on their way to live out the war in some unknown destination.*

IN SEATTLE, Gordon Hirabayashi continued to wage his own quiet war on behalf of the principles he believed in. In many ways, his was simply a different front in the same battle. Like the no-no boys, who

---

*About twelve thousand of the seventy-eight thousand people over the age of seventeen to whom the questionnaire was distributed answered no, refused to answer, or did not answer one question or the other affirmatively.

refused to sign oaths that set them apart from other Americans, Gordon continued to defy both the incarcerations and the curfews for the same reason—that they set Japanese Americans apart from other Americans purely on the basis of race.

Early on the morning of February 12, 1943, Gordon said goodbye to his many friends in the King County Jail and walked out the door onto a bustling Third Avenue. His attorneys at the ACLU and the American Friends Service Committee had worked out a deal with the court. While out on bail, he could live in Spokane and await a Supreme Court ruling on his case. In Spokane, he was to establish a Quaker office to help Japanese American families living in the camps or resettling in western Washington and Idaho. Gordon was thrilled. It was precisely the kind of work he had wanted to do, anyway. But he wasn't yet a free man. Harry Ault, a federal marshal, immediately took him into custody and drove him to Tacoma, where Gordon needed to fill out some paperwork.

He was in good spirits, happy to be out, but a bit frail. During his stint in jail, meals had arrived twice a day in buckets, the contents of which were inevitably some combination of beans, boiled meat, and potatoes. It was difficult to tell what was what and hard to pick through the mess to find parts that were palatable. His weight had plummeted from 145 pounds to 135. But when the paperwork was finished in Tacoma, Gordon got to experience, literally, his first taste of freedom. Ault walked him across the street to a café for lunch—a hamburger, custard pie, and good coffee. The memory of that meal, the smell of it, the texture of it, the rich, creamy sweetness of the pie, in particular, would stick with Gordon for decades. Then he and Ault returned to Seattle, picked up a police officer and another prisoner being transferred to a facility in eastern Washington, and boarded an overnight train to Spokane.

When he arrived in Spokane the next morning, Gordon found lodgings with some fellow Quakers, then went to meet with his principal mentor, Floyd Schmoe. Shortly after Pearl Harbor, Schmoe—an accomplished mountaineer, a marine biologist, and a Quaker activist—had resigned from a faculty position at the University of Washington in order to work full-time championing the rights of incarcerated Issei and Nisei. From the beginning, he had been one of Gordon's fiercest defenders and advocates. So Gordon couldn't wait to see him. And perhaps even more, he couldn't wait to see Schmoe's eighteen-year-old daughter.

Esther Schmoe—a nursing student at the University of Washington and a Quaker activist like her father—was a slender, vibrant young woman, about the same height as Gordon, with blond curls, a sprinkle of freckles, and luminous blue eyes. She was also intellectually keen, highly social, and brimming over with youthful hope and idealism. For nine months, while Gordon was in jail, Esther had been visiting him weekly, first in the company of her father but then increasingly by herself, just she and Gordon sitting on cold metal benches, talking with bars between them, sharing their ideas about life and religion, getting to know each other, and starting to fall in love.

Now, in Spokane, Gordon joined Esther in helping her father to set up the new American Friends Service Committee office. Together the three of them—Floyd, Gordon, and Esther—rolled up their sleeves, went to work, and waited to hear from the Supreme Court, confident that the eight wise men there would soon vindicate their faith in the Constitution and set Gordon truly free.*

ACROSS TOWN, for months, Fred Shiosaki had been doing his best to flunk out of his hometown college Gonzaga University. The school, a Jesuit men's college, had lost nearly its entire student body to the war effort in the months following Pearl Harbor. In order to survive, it had reinvented itself as primarily a naval training academy. Except for a few white students classified 4-F, Fred was virtually the only young man on

---

*Eight because there was, at the time, a vacancy on the court.

campus who wasn't in uniform. Formations of naval cadets in blue uniforms and white caps drilled endlessly on the campus quad, now turned into a parade ground. Officers in dress whites walked the halls, now renamed "corridors" in navy parlance. Floors were now "decks," the dining room a "canteen," beds in the dormitories "bunks." Military brass bands played martial music on the parade ground at dawn every morning. Young men grunted and heaved and sweated their way through a 740-yard-long, twenty-seven-station obstacle course—the Victory Course—said to be the toughest in the country. And for months Fred skulked his way around the campus, trying to remain invisible but knowing that everywhere he went, he stood out like the sorest of sore thumbs, not just as a civilian, but as a civilian who looked a whole lot like the enemy. As each week went by, all he wanted was to be somewhere else. Anywhere else.

So when rumors started spreading about an all–Japanese American fighting unit, Fred wasted no time. He got up early one morning, quietly took a bus downtown, and walked into the Selective Service office where in August he'd been told he was an enemy alien. This time there was a woman sitting behind the desk. "What's going on?" Fred asked. The woman smiled and replied, "Well, all you have to do is sign up and you're in." She handed Fred a pen and a piece of paper. He glanced at it, signed, thanked the woman, and headed for home. The whole thing had taken only minutes.

As he arrived home at the laundry that afternoon, he paused for a moment before opening the front door. His parents were behind the counter, working as usual. Fred knew that they weren't going to take the news well. In the Shiosaki family, as in many Japanese American families, the father was not just the head of the household; he was the decider, the final arbiter of all controversies, the last word on anything and everything that required an opinion or choice. It was he who had decided Fred should attend Gonzaga. That was the plan. He would expect his son to follow through on it, or to have been consulted about any change to that plan, certainly something as momentous as his son going off to war. He was going to be angry. Fred took a deep breath, opened the door, stepped into the familiar warm, wet smell of the laundry, nodded at his parents, and said nothing.

LATE IN THE AFTERNOON on March 28, Kats and Katsuaki Miho, along with twenty-six hundred other newly enlisted Nisei soldiers, assembled on the grounds of 'Iolani Palace—the lovely old residence and former seat of power of the Hawaiian royal family in downtown Honolulu—for a formal aloha ceremony. As the young men stood at ease in ranks, wearing crisp new khaki uniforms, coeds from the University of Hawai'i placed white leis around their necks. Overhead, *manu-o-Kū*, fairy terns, circled in dazzling white loops above broad-branched banyan trees. An artillery band played on the bandstand. The Royal Hawaiian Glee Club sang the lovely, stately old Hawaiian anthem, "Hawai'i Pono'ī"— written in 1874 by King Kalākaua in honor of King Kamehameha.

> *Hawai'i pono'ī*
> Hawai'i's own true sons
> *Nana i na ali'i*
> Honor give to your chiefs
> *Na pua muli kou*
> Of kindred race are we.

Standing on a speakers' balcony on the third story of the palace, officials made long-winded speeches thanking the new soldiers for what they were about to do. The mayor of Honolulu, however, spoke only briefly, saying, "I know you young men well enough to know you don't want a fuss made over you." Roy Vitousek, Speaker of the Territorial House of Representatives, said that by enlisting in such large numbers, the boys had "vindicated the liberal policies of this territory regarding racial matters. You have shown that the people of these islands, although of many varied racial strains, are amalgamated as one." It was a nice ceremony, but what the Miho brothers and most of the young men there that day would remember later wasn't the speakers. It was the crowd. Nearly twenty thousand people—one of the largest gatherings Honolulu had ever seen—had crowded onto the palace grounds, climbing into the banyan trees, perching on nearby buildings, overflowing into nearby King Street, craning their necks to catch a glimpse of the boys, calling out to those they knew, *"Aloha," "Aloha nui loa," "Genki de!"* wishing them well.

Over the next few days, Kats, his brother, and the other new enlistees purchased life insurance, bought war bonds, arranged for allotments from their paychecks to be sent to their parents, and visited friends and family to say what they all knew, but few really believed, might be their final farewells. And over and over again, when sons came to shake their

Farewell ceremony for Nisei volunteers at 'Iolani Palace

fathers' hands, they heard the same thing: "Be a good soldier. Come home alive if you can. But whatever you do, don't bring shame on yourself or your country or the family."

On April 5, they moved out. Details of their departure were supposed to be a military secret, but somehow word had gotten out, and as they marched in a rough column down King Street toward Honolulu's Pier 7, they found that once again thousands of friends and family had turned out to see them off. Mothers and wives and sisters and aunties had brought bento boxes full of treats that they tried to hand to the boys as they marched by, staggering under overstuffed duffel bags they could hardly manage to hoist. Out of step, hot, and exhausted, they presented a bedraggled appearance. As one of their number later remembered it, "We were not soldiers at that point, no training. Our uniforms didn't fit and we carried ukuleles and guitars and all kinds of things like that, very unmilitary-like. . . . [W]e looked like prisoners." Adding to that impression were scores of military police lining the route, carrying rifles, separating the boys from their friends and relatives, shouting at them to "keep back!"

The Matson luxury liner SS *Lurline* was waiting for them at the harbor. Since 1933, the elegant ship, with its trademark gleaming white hull, had arrived every other week in Honolulu disgorging legions of well-heeled tourists who strolled down gangways under the city's iconic Aloha Tower to have leis placed around their necks before heading for the grand hotels and beaches of Waikīkī. But the ship the boys boarded now was transformed. The *Lurline* had been painted battleship gray to make it less visible to Japanese submarines, and its portals were blacked out. As the boys moved into their quarters belowdecks, they found that cabins intended for two people were to house as many as twelve of them, with bunks stacked two and three high against every available wall.

When the ship departed, at a little after 2:00 p.m., they stood on deck watching the Aloha Tower recede in the distance, not yet knowing how often and how keenly they would think of it in the months to come, how achingly they would long to see it and the *manu-o-Kū* circling above the city and beyond that the lovely green mountains wreathed in white clouds.

BY THE TIME the *Lurline* set sail that day, perhaps six million Americans were already under arms. Millions more, like the young men from Hawai'i, were on their way to training camps or about to leave them for distant battlefields, determined to lend their strength to the Allied effort. The war they were all about to enter now raged on a scale humankind had never seen before.

In the South Pacific, Japanese naval forces had been crippled by their staggering defeat at the Battle of Midway, and Allied troops had finally driven them from Guadalcanal after a long and horrifically bloody series of battles. But Japan still held Burma, parts of China, and a long string of island fortresses that would have to be taken one by one before the Allies could even begin to contemplate conquering the Japanese archipelago itself.

In Europe, Allied bombing raids had finally begun to ravage Germany's industrial centers, but Hitler and his fascist allies still maintained an iron grip on nearly the entire continent. In the Soviet Union, the Red Army had just captured ninety-one thousand German troops in front of Stalingrad, but three hundred miles and two-thirds of the German army still stood between them and the German border. And the setbacks in the Soviet Union had not slowed the Germans as they busily expanded their empire of death that month. In Poland, the Nazis began liquidating the Jewish ghetto in Krakow, shooting thousands in the streets and sending thousands more to death camps. In the lovely port city of Thessaloniki, in northern Greece, they began filling freight cars with still more Jews, preparing to send an average of two thousand people every three days to Auschwitz-Birkenau, where mass gassings had begun in January 1942 and where four new, more efficient gas chambers, each capable of killing two thousand people at a time, were just now coming into use. Already, the Nazis had murdered well more than a million innocents.

Only in North Africa had the tide—despite a catastrophic American defeat at Kasserine Pass in February—turned decisively in the Allies' favor. There, American and British forces were poised to crush the entire German war effort in North Africa and to take a quarter million Axis troops prisoner. Now both they and the Germans had begun to shift the focus of their attention north, across the Mediterranean, to Italy.

ABOARD THE *LURLINE*, Kats immediately became violently seasick. He retreated to his bunk in his small, dark cabin, but with five cabin-mates the place soon reeked of sweaty clothes, diesel fumes, and vomit, all of which made him feel even sicker. He remained there, moaning and retching, for most of the next four and a half days as the ship followed the same zigzag course toward San Francisco that his father had taken the year before on his way to imprisonment on the mainland.

But for the boys who weren't seasick, the voyage was a lark. Most of them had never been on an ocean liner, never been beyond Hawai'i. Except for the fact that their destination was on the mainland, none of them had any clear idea where they were going, and for the most part they gave it little thought. This was an adventure. It was a change. It offered a chance for something far more exciting than what they had expected from their lives just a few months earlier, and they intended to enjoy it.

The Matson Company had kept its civilian crew on board, so the food—for those who could keep it down—was plentiful and relatively good. The boys pulled out guitars and ukuleles and they began to party. They sat in the ship's posh lounges and dining rooms—with their marble colonnades, mahogany paneling, and winding staircases—chatting, smoking cigarettes, eating everything they could get their hands on. They lounged in their cabins talking and telling jokes. They wrapped towels around their waists to serve as *'ilihau* skirts, climbed up on tables, and danced hula. And most of all they gambled. Many of them had been given traditional Japanese going-away cash—*senbetsu*—by their families. Others had been working on the plantations or in the pineapple canneries for months, saving up money. Now they laid it all on the line. With cigarettes dangling from their lips, they gathered in smoky cabins playing poker. They found bits of open deck, formed circles, and began shooting dice in wild craps games that went on all night, boys shouting, swearing, laughing, tossing down twenty-dollar bills as if they were dimes or nickels, encouraging each other with each toss of the dice to "go for broke!" Kats, who had never learned to gamble and considered twenty dollars a small fortune, occasionally staggered out of his cabin, watched the craps games with astonishment, and then retreated to his bunk. Another young man, Thomas Tanaka, also seasick, went for a walk on deck to get some fresh air but got pulled into three successive craps games. When he stumbled back into his cabin hours later, he had four thousand dollars in his pocket—enough to buy a modest house in Honolulu.

As the *Lurline* approached Northern California, the weather grew blustery, cold, and gray. With the ship rolling through rough seas, Kats sank even deeper into the misery of seasickness. But when they finally passed under the Golden Gate Bridge, he joined his brother and the other young men as they tumbled out onto the decks to gaze up at it in wonderment as California sea lions barked at them from the rocks at Fort Point. San Francisco was the biggest city most of them had ever seen, and even as they shivered in the fog, they tried to soak in all the sights—the notorious, windswept prison out on Alcatraz, elegant old Victorian homes along the waterfront in the Marina District, the grand old hotels atop Nob Hill, the Ferry Building. But what astonished Kats most was what he saw as the *Lurline* came to rest at a dock and stevedores began to unload cargo from its hold. Standing at the rail, one of the boys called out, "Eh, look at da haole buggah!"

Soldiers crowded the rail and stared at the men working down on the dock. Kats couldn't believe it. He had spent his life around stevedores in Kahaluʻu, but he'd never seen white stevedores. For that matter, neither he nor most of the boys gathered around him had ever seen white men doing manual labor of any sort.

A few days later, as they crossed California on a troop train, they gathered at the windows, taking in and talking about the landscape of an America most of them had never seen—the broad, muddy Sacramento River; the vast flat fields of the Central Valley, just greening now with spring crops; the red earth, manzanita chaparral, and tall pines of the Sierra Nevada's foothills; then the mountains themselves, majestic granite spires with patches of spring snow still clinging to them.

As the train rolled eastward, their officers circulated among them telling them, for the first time, where they were going—a place called Camp Shelby, near Hattiesburg, Mississippi. There they would go through basic training together as members of the Third Army, during which time they would be organized into at least two battalions and assigned to specific companies. After basic training, they would be sent into battle wherever and whenever the army saw fit. They weren't to concern themselves about where or when that might be. And they were henceforth to consider themselves members of the 442nd Regimental Combat Team, an all–Japanese American fighting unit.

The mention of Mississippi sent a ripple of anxiety up and down the length of the train. The one and only thing most of them knew about the Magnolia State was that it was a place where white people systematically mistreated, even murdered, "colored" people. Looking around the railroad coaches, looking at one another, they wondered what Mississippi would make of them.

IT COULDN'T BE put off any longer. A letter had just arrived, informing Fred Shiosaki that he was to report to Fort Douglas in Utah for induction into the U.S. Army. He was going to have to tell his parents what he had done.

He waited until he found his parents alone together in the kitchen upstairs over the laundry and then got straight to it. He sauntered into the room and said, as nonchalantly as he could, "I've got to report to Fort Douglas to join the army." His father stared silently at him for a moment, trying to comprehend it. Then he exploded in a torrent of Japanese curses that Fred couldn't understand. The tirade went on and on. Finally, Fred caught a familiar phrase—*Nante bakageta koto!* It wasn't the first time Fred had heard it, "What a stupid thing!" He was afraid his father was going to hit him. He'd never seen him so angry. But the more his father yelled, the more determined Fred grew. There was no way he was going to keep living through the humiliation of slinking around Spokane and the Gonzaga campus in civilian clothes. He was eighteen now, and he could make his own decisions. He didn't need anyone's approval, not even his parents', though he respected them above all others. This was something he had to do. His older brother, Roy, was in the army, serving in an integrated unit, the 324th Infantry's Forty-fourth Division. Now he was going. A few days later, his sister, Blanche, drove him down to the Great Northern depot in Spokane. His father refused to go, refused even to say goodbye.

Weeks later, Private First Class Shiosaki was back in Hillyard wear-

Private Fred Shiosaki

ing a crisp new khaki uniform. The army had conducted his physical, given him his inoculations, run some aptitude tests, and told him it would be a few more weeks before he'd get orders to report to basic training in Mississippi. To fill the interval, Fred went back to work in the laundry, spent some time strutting around town trying to see if he could impress any girls with the uniform, and hung around with his friend Gordon Yamaura, who had decided to join up, too.

Finally, the day came to leave for good. This time his father drove him downtown to the Great Northern depot on Havermale Island. There, standing on the platform in the shadow of the depot's great sandstone clock tower, Fred found Gordon waiting. When the train pulled in, Kisaburo Shiosaki took his son's hand, shook it, looked him in the eye, and said, simply, "Come back healthy." Then, without another word, he turned around, walked off the platform, drove back home, and began to do what millions of parents were doing that spring, enduring the long wait to see whether their sons would be among those who returned. Soon after that, a service flag with two blue stars appeared in the downstairs front window of the Hillyard Laundry.

TEN

=====

Hattiesburg is a good town if you don't know any better.

CHAPLAIN HIGUCHI TO HIS WIFE, HISAKO
NOVEMBER 11, 1943

On April 13, 1943, the Nisei boys from Hawai'i—now officially members of the 442nd Regimental Combat Team—climbed down from a train at Union Station in Hattiesburg, Mississippi. In the three-day ride across the country, they had been allowed off the train only twice, briefly in the middle of the night, in open countryside where no one would see them, to do calisthenics and stretch their legs. Now they were sore and stiff as they stood on the platform in olive-drab service uniforms looking warily around at their surroundings. Some of them had sooty faces from sitting next to open windows on the train.

Sitting at the confluence of the Leaf and Bouie rivers, Hattiesburg had a sleepy southern charm, with manicured neighborhoods of elegant old homes on tree-lined streets, two college campuses, a lively redbrick downtown, and a stately neoclassical courthouse guarded by an alabaster white statue of a Confederate soldier standing guard atop an equally white marble pillar. It was the kind of place where on warm summer evenings children played kick the can out in the streets while old men and women sat on wide verandas watching them and sipping lemonade, where fireflies drifted over broad front lawns, where the scent of magnolia infused the night air and it was easy to doze off in a rocking chair.

But the neat lawns and stately homes belied an ugly reality. Hattiesburg—and Mississippi more generally—could be cruel almost beyond reckoning. Since Reconstruction, more than five hundred Black Americans had been lynched in Mississippi. Seven of those murders had been in Hattiesburg itself, many others in the lush green surrounding countryside. In Laurel, a bit north of town, just a few months before the Nisei soldiers arrived, a mob had dragged two fourteen-year-old boys—Charlie Lang and Ernest Green—out of jail, tied ropes around the terrified boys' necks, and thrown them to their deaths from what locals had long quietly and confidentially called the Hanging Bridge. The bridge, on the Chickasawhay River, had earned its grim name in commemoration of an earlier lynching, in 1918, when two young men and two young women—both women pregnant, both begging for their lives—had been hanged there. Five days after Charlie Lang and Ernest Green were lynched, another mob removed yet another young man—Howard Wash—from the jail in Laurel and hanged him from a different bridge.

The lynchings were only the most brutal manifestations of an economic, social, and political order that white Mississippians had built on a foundation of intimidation and dehumanization. Forced to use inferior facilities, denied decent educations, exploited in their workplaces, barred from voting, called vile names to their faces, humiliated in front of their children, Black Americans in Mississippi and throughout the Jim Crow South lived and labored under a suffocating blanket of oppression. Beneath the scent of magnolia, there was always the smell of fear, the stench of degradation.

When Kats and Katsuaki headed into the depot to use the restrooms, they were immediately confronted by a dilemma. One of the men's rooms was marked WHITE, another COLORED. Drinking fountains nearby bore the same signs. The Miho brothers looked at each other, uncertain what to do. Kats asked a white officer which facility they should use. The officer scratched his head and looked around, equally baffled.

Finally, he growled, "Aw hell. You ain't colored, exactly. Use the white one." They did as they were told, but they weren't easy with it. How the heck, they wondered, had they suddenly become haoles?

At about the same hour that day—as the boys hoisted their overstuffed barrack bags, climbed into the backs of trucks, and headed out to Camp Shelby, just south of town—Lieutenant General John DeWitt, head of the Western Defense Command, was testifying before members of the House Committee on Naval Affairs' subcommittee in San Francisco. Arguing against allowing the return of any Japanese Americans to the West Coast, DeWitt declared, "A Jap's a Jap. It makes no difference whether he is an American citizen or not. . . . I don't want any of them."

At Camp Shelby, just south of Hattiesburg, the Nisei boys moved into hutments—long, narrow shedlike buildings set up off the ground on piers. With screens in place of windows, they looked like the commercial chicken coops the boys had seen while riding the train east. The spring weather had turned cold by Mississippi standards that week, downright frigid by Hawaiian standards. That night the Nisei boys huddled next to coal-burning potbellied stoves in the hutments and lay on metal cots, shivering under green wool army blankets. The water in the showers had only one temperature—cold. The roofs were leaky. The latrines were just open ditches outside the hutments, and they stank twenty-four hours a day. Boys who didn't ordinarily smoke took up the habit that week, just to mask the smell. The food in the mess halls—mutton, endless boiled potatoes, mushy peas, pork and beans, and creamed beef on toast, or "shit on a shingle" as American soldiers universally called it—was unfamiliar to them. Most of them found nearly all of it vile. Young men from Hawai'i, used to eating fresh fruits, fresh fish, and rice, pushed their plates away and went hungry. By the end of the first week, some of the Hawai'i boys could be found crouched behind the hutments, homesick and weeping.

But as they tried to settle into army life, the hardest problem the boys of the newly formed 442nd Regimental Combat Team faced wasn't the living conditions or the food or homesickness. It was one another.

. . .

RUDY TOKIWA, like many of the mainland recruits, arrived in Mississippi on his own. His journey to Camp Shelby had been long, circuitous, and full of surprises. When he'd turned eighteen, he'd eagerly reported to Fort Douglas in Utah, where he was sworn in and issued a uniform. He was excited about the uniform, but it came with a dose of humiliation. When a supply sergeant asked him what size shirt and trousers he wore, Rudy realized that he had no idea. "I don't know," he finally stammered. "My mother usually buys them for me." That had provoked a gale of laughter in the room and a crimson blush on Rudy's face.

After a quick farewell trip back to Poston, he caught a train east. To his surprise and consternation, his orders took him not south to Camp Shelby, where he knew his friends Lloyd Onoye and Harry Madokoro were waiting for him, but east to Fort Savage in Minnesota. When he got off the train, Rudy was confused, uncertain what was happening. A Nisei soldier approached him and tried to usher him to a jeep, but he would speak to Rudy only in Japanese. Rudy was fluent in Japanese, but this just annoyed him.

"What'd you say? Speak English, damn it. Aren't you in the American army?" he snapped. Another soldier who had gotten off the train with Rudy, a baby-faced kid from Glendale in Southern California—Sadao Munemori—began speaking to the soldier in Japanese, and it soon became clear what was happening. Both Munemori and Rudy, because they had lived for a while in Japan, had been assigned not to a regular army unit but to the Military Intelligence Service, the MIS. The purpose of the MIS was to train Japanese-speaking Nisei soldiers in intelligence gathering and then to send them to the Pacific theater of operations, primarily to act as interpreters, interrogators, translators, and propaganda writers. Rudy was shocked. He wanted no part of that. He wanted to fight. With a gun. And alongside his friends from Poston, who were already waiting at Shelby. Rudy decided he needed to find some way out of it.

It didn't take him long to arrive at a solution: when presented with Japanese-language tests, he quickly made a hash of it, affecting to be utterly inept with the language. Within a few days he was on his way to Shelby, with a stopover in New Orleans. On a one-day pass, he explored the city and discovered to his great delight that he could drink legally in Louisiana. He quickly decided that one day wasn't going to be enough time to enjoy that new privilege. So for the next four days, instead of getting on a train, he headed back down to the French Quarter.

Finally, nearly a week late, he arrived at Shelby tired and hungover. A corporal took him to his assigned hutment, showed him his bunk, and then left him standing in the doorway staring at it, his barracks bag slung over his shoulder. Someone had stacked four large footlockers atop the bed. It was a Sunday and there were only a few other soldiers in the building—some Nisei from Hawai'i lounging at one end playing cards, paying no attention to him.

Rudy called out to them, "Hey, do these boxes belong to anyone?" The Hawai'i boys looked up and glared at him, irritated at the interruption. One of them said, "Hey. Hear da kine buggah, yeah? He try and make us haul da boxes, yeah?"

Rudy stared back, trying to understand what they were saying.

"Well, this is my bunk and I gotta make my bed. If no one wants to move the boxes I guess I'll have to move 'em for you."

The boys smirked and said, "Tough buggah, yeah?"

Rudy picked up one of the footlockers and tossed it out the door. It landed with a loud thud in a cloud of red Mississippi dust.

For a long moment everyone just froze. Finally, one of the Hawai'i boys smiled and said, "Hey, da buggah right there, yeah?" He and the others got up and moved the footlockers. Rudy didn't yet know it, but he had just won a small skirmish in a war that was raging all around him.

THE CONFLICT UNFOLDING at Shelby revolved around language and ethnic identity. The 442nd recruits weren't the first Nisei troops to move

Private Rudy Tokiwa

into the hutments at Shelby. Immediately after the attack on Pearl Harbor, roughly fourteen hundred Japanese American men who had been serving in the National Guard in Hawai'i were pulled from their postings and confined to Schofield Barracks on O'ahu. Unlike the Territorial Guard in which Kats had served, these men were already considered to be in the U.S. military, and antidiscrimination laws prohibited the government from simply discharging them. So instead the army just hid them away at Schofield, keeping them in limbo, relegating them to menial tasks. Then, in June 1942, the army had a change of heart, secretly shipped them to Camp McCoy in Wisconsin, and designated them the 100th Infantry Battalion (Separate).* At McCoy—under wraps in deep secrecy—they underwent basic training. For the most part, it was the same standard training that countless other GIs across the country were

---

*"Separate" because they were an orphan unit, unattached to any division.

undergoing that year. But two dozen of them were sent quietly to Cat Island, a small, uninhabited speck of sand, brush, sloughs, and alligators, just two miles offshore from Gulfport, Mississippi. There they spent three months creeping through bushes and swamps, hunted by dogs being trained to detect what someone in the army brass thought was the unique scent of the Japanese. When a dog happened across one of the Nisei boys, a guard fired a shot in the air, the Nisei soldier dropped to the ground and played dead, and a piece of meat was thrown on the ground in front of him. The dogs inevitably ate the meat, licked the soldiers' faces, and wagged their tails enthusiastically. As one of the soldiers, Yasuo Takata, remembered, "We didn't smell Japanese. We were Americans. Even the dogs knew that." The following January the remainder of the 100th were sent to Mississippi, to be stationed at Camp Shelby while the government tried to figure out what else it could do with them.

By the time the 442nd recruits from Hawai'i arrived at Shelby, the 100th had come and gone and were now out in the swamps of Louisiana on field maneuvers. But another cadre of Japanese American soldiers—mostly draftees—was in place and waiting for the new guys from Hawai'i. They, too, had entered the service before Pearl Harbor, but they were from the mainland. Some of them, before entering the service, had been college students or on their way to becoming young professionals. Because they had previously gone through basic training elsewhere, these mainland Nisei already occupied nearly all the noncommissioned officer positions for the new 442nd. They were the corporals, sergeants, and staff sergeants. The upshot was that when the boys from Hawai'i arrived, they found themselves taking orders from boys who looked like them, who had surnames like theirs, whose ancestry was the same as theirs, but who spoke and acted as if they were from an entirely different world.

Then more young men like Rudy showed up, coming mostly from the concentration camps out west, and an already tense situation quickly spiraled downward. The mainlanders and the Hawaiians couldn't have a conversation without it devolving into a fight. The mainlanders just plain couldn't make sense of most of what the Hawaiians said. When one of the Hawaiians asked a mainlander to hand him a wrench, using "da kine," the Hawaiian pidgin term for "that thing"—"Hand me da kine"— the mainlander, confounded, asked, "What kind?" The boy from Hawai'i lashed out, "You stupid buggah. I asked you for a wrench." Another young man from Hawai'i told one of the mainlanders, "You go stay go," and was irritated when the mainlander didn't understand that he was being told to go ahead and leave.

George Goto, from Colorado, thought the Hawai'i boys just plain didn't speak or understand English. Chester Tanaka, from St. Louis, thought they were "savages." At first, many of the mainlanders, mistaking the dialect for ignorance, let their contempt show. Then they tried to laugh it off. But laughing was the worst thing they could do, almost guaranteed to set off a melee. By the end of the first few weeks at Shelby, fistfights were breaking out all over camp. The islanders started calling the mainlanders "kotonks" for the hollow sound a coconut makes when you hit it, claiming that's what the mainlanders' heads sounded like when they hit them. The kotonks started referring to the Hawaiians as Buddhaheads, though no one on either side was exactly sure what it meant.

Language wasn't the only problem. The mainlanders who had volunteered for the army out of concentration camps arrived angry, fueled by a grim, righteous determination to prove themselves as patriotic Americans. On the whole they were serious, reserved, clean-cut, earnest, well behaved, soft-spoken, conservative with their money, and prone to respect authority, as their parents had taught them to do. The Buddhaheads, on the other hand, were, for the most part, casual and happy-go-lucky. They approached life as an adventure, loved to drink, gamble, and spend their money freely. Many of them carried ukuleles and guitars everywhere they went, danced and sang whenever they could, were warmly open and affectionate with one another. As often as not, their families back in the islands knew one another. Their parents had immigrated together, their uncles did business with one another, their aunties worshipped at the same churches or temples, their cousins and calabash cousins had grown up as they had grown up, playing football barefoot, swimming at the same beaches, playing basketball at the same YMCAs.* They sang the same songs, relished the same foods, thought of one another as belonging, in a sense, to the same 'ohana, the same big family. And they tended to see authority—particularly any kind of authority that seemed designed to hold them down—as something to be defied at every turn.

THE ATTITUDE the Buddhaheads carried to Shelby with them came from a deep place—from their own and their Issei parents' lived experience in Hawai'i.

Between 1885 and 1894, fleeing economic depression and mass starvation in their native land, nearly thirty thousand Japanese contract laborers climbed into the bellies of ships bound for Hawai'i. As it was for millions of European immigrants coming to America in the late nineteenth century, getting there was a miserable affair for the Japanese. Most had never been on a ship before. Most, in fact, had never been more than a few miles from the villages in which they had grown up. Almost all began to vomit as soon as their ships set sail, and many remained sick for days. Meals, for those who could stand to eat, were monotonously the same day after day—black beans and chopped, dried turnip mixed with a few tablespoons of rice. Their bedding was infested with lice and fleas. Infectious diseases spread rapidly through the ships, sometimes with fatal results. The bodies of those who died were unceremoniously carted off to be kept in refrigerated rooms.

When they finally drew within sight of the Hawaiian Islands, those immigrants who had survived lined the rails and their spirits soared.

---

*In Hawaiian culture a calabash cousin is someone who, though not actually related to you, is so close to you as to be considered family.

The initial view was propitious—serene and beautiful. Buoyant white clouds drifted over lush, verdant mountains laced with cascading waterfalls. Coconut palms lined wide coral-sand beaches. As they came nearer, gentle, warm trade winds carried sweet scents—plumeria and ti and wild ginger. Hawai'i appeared to be everything that the recruiting agencies in Japan had promised—a veritable paradise.

But when they landed on Sand Island in Honolulu Harbor, they found a different Hawai'i. The place was bleak and sterile, a flat windswept expanse of dead coral, crushed shells, and mud dredged from the harbor, nearly devoid of vegetation, sun blasted and hot. Even as they disembarked, smoke billowed from the chimney of a small building as someone began burning the bodies of those who had died during the voyage. They were herded like cattle into a larger building for processing. Representatives of the sugar companies pushed contracts in front of them and told them they must sign them immediately. Written in both English and Japanese, the contracts often were not the same as the ones they had signed in Japan. These demanded more labor, obligated them for years, made it a crime to run away from the plantations, paid lower wages. When the immigrants complained about the changes, they were told they could refuse to sign, but they would have to leave immediately and pay their own way back to Japan. None had the means of doing that, so they signed, agreeing to work for, on average, nine dollars a month. Finally, they boarded interisland ships, and within a few hours they found themselves in the backs of horse-drawn wagons, bouncing up dusty cane roads, heading for whichever plantation their contracts now bound them to.

There, they quickly found that working in the cane fields was nasty, brutal work. Six days a week, screaming sirens awoke the immigrants at 4:30 a.m. To protect against the tropical sun, the lacerating edges of cane leaves, the enormous spiders, the centipedes, and the stinging yellow jackets that infested the fields, they swaddled their heads and arms with stiff, coarse fabric. Despite the tropical climate, they donned long underwear, button-up leggings, wide-brimmed hats, heavy gloves, and boots.

Armed with hoes and short, machete-like knives, they clambered onto the backs of wagons again to be transported along the dirt roads in the predawn darkness. As the sun rose, they trooped into the fields in gangs of up to two hundred and began to hoe weeds or cut cane, each gang methodically and relentlessly working its way forward like a machine. Foremen, *lunas*, carrying long black "snake whips," stood by, overseeing each gang, yelling at them, scolding them, belittling them, keeping them moving forward. Watching over the whole operation, a field boss, always a white man, sat on horseback a bit removed from the rest of them, a shotgun or a whip lying across his lap, keeping his eyes open for would-be runaways. Runaways were beaten, whipped, or jailed for breaking their contracts.

As the sun rose higher, the heat in the fields often became stifling, almost unbearable, as the twelve-foot-high cane cut the workers off from any possible breeze. In their heavy armor they sweated and stooped and grew dirty and exhausted. Dust infiltrated their throats and nostrils, the sharp-edged cane leaves sliced open any exposed skin, sweat stung their eyes. The women among them often carried infants on their backs, the infants swaddled in their own armor. From time to time, the women stood and swung their babies around to their fronts to nurse them briefly before stooping again and resuming their hoeing or cutting. Here and there children as young as eight worked alongside the adults, wading thigh-deep through the cut cane.

At the end of the ten-hour workday, they emerged from the fields, coughing up phlegm brown from the dust they had been breathing. They returned exhausted to their plantation camps, where they crowded silently around long tables to eat meager bowls of rice or beans with scraps of dried cod or shrimp. As often as not, weevils infested the rice. Then the majority of them, single men, trooped into rustic bunkhouses where they lay their weary bodies on rough wooden planks, twelve to fifteen inches wide, and tried to sleep.

The few married men and women among them retreated each night to small, single-walled houses with screen windows, rusty metal roofs,

and sinks with cold running water. The roofs leaked in Hawai'i's tor-
rential downpours, and the water in the sinks came directly from ditches
outside, so the immigrants had to tie Bull Durham tobacco bags over
their faucets to trap the tadpoles and insects that often emerged with
the water. Scattered through the camps were communal outhouses,
but the toilets were simply holes cut in boards placed over concrete
ditches in which constantly flowing water carried the waste away to unknown destinations.

But as hard as plantation life was, when their contracts expired—
typically after two or three years—many of them decided to stay rather
than return to even worse conditions in Japan. Then, in 1900, Hawai'i
became an American territory, and the contract system was abolished on
the grounds that it imposed conditions of involuntary servitude, prohibited by the U.S. Constitution. Thousands of Japanese immigrants flooded
off the plantations seeking other ways to make a living in Hawai'i. Thousands more continued to live and work on the plantations—still subject
to the harsh racial discrimination that governed life in the cane fields but
at least free to leave if they could find an alternative.

And as they decided to stay in Hawai'i, the young men among them
began to think about their futures. There were few Japanese women in
Hawai'i, though, roughly one for every four men. So the young men
began to write home to Japan, asking their parents to find appropriate
young women and arrange marriages for them. Under Japanese law, the
men did not need to be physically present at the marriage ceremony.
The parents of prospective brides and grooms met or corresponded to
negotiate terms. Parents on both sides studied family genealogies and
assessed social status. The young men sent statements about the work
they were doing in the new land, quantifying their earning potential.
They sent photographs of themselves, or purportedly of themselves. The
young women in Japan did the same. Both parties studied the photographs carefully before committing to marriage, though the women—
who would come to be called picture brides—were seldom given much
say in the matter. Eventually a wedding ceremony was held, sans the

groom, and apprehensive young women climbed onto boats bound for Hawai'i. When they filed off the boats on O'ahu, dazed, wearing simple, dark kimonos, they scanned the faces of hundreds of clamoring men shouting and waving at them from behind the barricades, trying to find a face that matched the photograph. Often, there was no such face. Many discovered too late that the photo they had received was a touched-up image of their new husband taken years earlier, or in some cases an entirely different man—a younger, healthier, or better-looking friend. But there was no way back, no way out, and so they followed their new husbands out of the immigration station and into their new lives together. For tens of thousands of them that meant a trip directly into the cane fields. By 1920, roughly 80 percent of the women in Hawai'i were working in the cane.

Soon after the women arrived, children—the Hawaiian Nisei—followed. And it was the boys among those children who now made up the bulk of the Buddhaheads at Camp Shelby. They knew well what their parents had endured at the hands of the powerful in Hawai'i. They knew what they had experienced themselves growing up in a racially and economically stratified society. And they weren't about to put up with a bunch of Japanese American boys their own age who sometimes seemed to mimic the language, the manners, and the attitudes of the haole bosses back home.

EXCEPT FOR SPORADIC and unenthusiastic visits to Japanese-language school at the Methodist church in Spokane when he was a kid, Fred Shiosaki had never really been around other Japanese Americans in large numbers before he arrived at Camp Shelby. That in itself proved a novelty and a bit unsettling as he tried to adjust to life in the hutments. But, as with other mainlanders, it was the boys from Hawai'i—the Buddhaheads—who presented Fred with his first and stiffest challenge. It took him less than a day to decide he didn't want to tangle with them. He wouldn't later remember what exactly he said to provoke it, but he never forgot the response of one of the Buddhaheads to something he had said that first day, "Eh, you, man. You one dumb kotonk, eh?"

These guys were an entirely different order of trouble from the boys Fred had scuffled with back home in Hillyard. There, he would have punched someone who called him dumb, just as he had many times punched white kids who called him a "Jap." But he'd already seen enough to know that the Buddhaheads almost never fought you one-on-one. They swarmed you, fighting not just for themselves but for one another, as if they were all brothers. For the first time in his life, Fred learned how to back down from a fight. He stayed clear of arguments. He kept a lid on his temper. And, like nearly all of the mainlanders, he set out to learn how to understand and speak the language of the guys from Hawai'i, if only to blend into the background and not draw attention to himself.

SHORTLY AFTER ARRIVING AT SHELBY, Kats Miho was detached from the infantry and—based on aptitude tests he'd aced while still at Schofield Barracks—assigned to the 442nd's dedicated artillery unit, the 522nd Field Artillery Battalion. Although he was to endure the same grueling basic training as infantrymen like Fred and Rudy, a lot of his time at Shelby was to be spent learning the complex geometry and calculus required to accurately fire the 522nd's big howitzers. That did nothing to insulate him from the ongoing war between the kotonks and the Buddhaheads, though.

Kats, not surprisingly, fell in with the Hawaiian contingent and laughingly called himself a Buddhahead. He already knew many of the plantation kids from Maui, and he was as comfortable speaking the Hawaiian pidgin as standard English. But Kats also occupied a kind of middle ground. He and the other boys from the University of Hawai'i tended to hang out with the other former university students, whether from the University of Hawai'i or from schools on the mainland. And Kats was also a natural politician, always ready to debate anything but much more likely to let fly with strong, logical arguments than with his fists.

One of the university boys he grew close to was a serious-minded twenty-one-year-old kid from Montana. George Oiye had been born on February 19, 1922, in a cabin in the woods, near a mining camp in Basin Creek, just east of the Idaho border. It was forty below zero. The nearest store was twelve hours away on snowshoes. He'd grown up, though, mostly in Trident, on the dry, dusty side of Montana. Trident was a company town, built for the employees of the cement factory where his father worked. Like most Montana boys, George grew up with a hunting rifle in one hand and a fishing rod in the other, devoting nearly all his free time to roaming the sagebrush-covered hills around Trident hunting with his friends or standing up to his waist in the Gallatin or Madison rivers, pulling sleek, iridescent-sided rainbow trout from the swift, clear, cold water. Like Kats, he'd been popular in high school in nearby Three Forks, playing quarterback on the football team and mingling easily with the nearly all-white student body.

Smart and sociable, he had moved on to Montana State College in Bozeman in 1941 and enrolled in ROTC, where he quickly rose to become a top cadet, and his hunting skills earned him a spot as captain on the marksmanship team. He began taking classes in aeronautical engineering, hoping to become an aviator in the army. But then came Pearl Harbor. After seventeen years at the cement factory, his father was peremptorily fired and reduced to eking out a living selling vegetables from his home garden. George's landlady in Bozeman let it be known that he wasn't really welcome as a lodger anymore. His pregnant sister and her husband, living in Los Angeles, were incarcerated at Santa Anita and then moved to the WRA concentration camp at Minidoka. Like nearly all of his friends, George tried to enlist in the service. But like Fred Shiosaki, he was told he was an "enemy alien," and soon he found himself going to ROTC classes every week embittered by the irony of the fact that he was wearing the uniform of an army he was not allowed to join.

George persisted, though, determined to get into the army and fly. He argued his case to some of the professors he had impressed in the classroom, and they went repeatedly to the adjutant general of Montana State's ROTC program, lobbying on George's behalf. Finally, one day in early 1943, his earnestness and his popularity on campus paid off. The adjutant general called George into his office and told him that if he could get five prominent white townspeople from Trident to vouch for his loyalty, he could enlist in the army and train as an aviator. Enormously popular in town, George quickly secured the recommendations. The town threw a going-away party for him, and soon he was on his way to Fort Douglas in Utah to be processed into the service. It was only after he was sworn in there that someone told him he wasn't actually going to be flying any planes. He was to report to a place called Camp Shelby for training as an infantryman. Shocked, angry, feeling betrayed, George boarded a train and headed for Mississippi.

Things only got worse when he got there. He had seldom been around other Japanese people or Japanese Americans other than his own family. He spoke no Japanese, had no interest in learning the language, did not in the least think of himself as Japanese. When he first encountered the other boys at Shelby, particularly the Hawai'i boys, his first thoughts were "Who are they? Why are they so short, dark, and talk funny?" Just emerging from a Montana winter, George was pale, particularly compared with the boys from Hawai'i. Almost immediately they started to call him Whitey, generally with an accompanying sneer. And that was just the beginning of what George would later describe as a "devastating" first few weeks at Shelby. His ROTC program had trained him to be a good soldier. He knew what uniform to wear, when to wear it, and how to wear it properly. He kept his shoes polished and his shirts buttoned to the collar. He snapped to attention when officers entered a room. He made up his bunk according to regulations. He did everything, in fact, according to regulations. He never addressed an officer without adding a "sir." The Buddhaheads—who by and large had a hard time remembering not to address their officers by their first names, who went barefoot as often as they could get away with it, and who on hot days wore their uniform shirts open to the waist—hated George's spit-and-polish ways.

More than almost anybody else in camp, George seemed like someone who, given a chance, would run a plantation back home. The Buddha-heads began to beat him up pretty much every chance they got.

Like Kats, George was assigned early to the 522nd Field Artillery Battalion, and there, almost immediately, he gravitated toward Kats. George was inquisitive, something of a philosopher, and, also like Kats, full of opinions. Both young men liked to talk about issues, to ponder the deeper significance of things, to understand the implications of what they were experiencing. And right now, one implication of George's new situation was that he needed friends, preferably friends who spoke like the Hawai'i boys. Kats liked him. He readily offered his friendship and his protection.

FOR THE FIRST MONTH at Shelby, the 442nd recruits were quarantined in their portion of the base. Army officials weren't at all sure how either the white soldiers at Shelby or the locals in Hattiesburg were going to take to having several thousand Japanese Americans suddenly dropped in their midst, and they wanted to give them time to get used to the idea. Not long before, across the river in Arkansas, a Japanese American soldier, Private Louis Furushiro, had walked into a café on his way to visit his sister, who was incarcerated at a new WRA camp just being constructed at nearby Rohwer. When William Wood, a white farmer with two sons in the military, got word that there was a "Jap" in town, he'd walked into the café, leveled a shotgun at Private Furushiro, and pulled the trigger. Furushiro ducked and escaped with only powder burns on his face, but the very next day M. C. Brown, a deer hunter, came across a pair of Japanese American men from the Rohwer camp working in the woods, decided they were escapees, and opened fire, hitting Shigeru Fu-kuchi in the hip and injuring him.

The Nisei soldiers at Shelby didn't have time for visits to town at any rate. They were plunged immediately into the same rigorous basic train-ing regimen that tens of thousands of young men were enduring all across the country that spring. As the weather warmed and dogwoods blossomed in the woods around them, they learned the fundamentals of soldiering. Wearing uniforms that were often too large for them and helmets that sometimes hung down below their ears, they drilled for endless hours on the parade grounds. They ran obstacle courses, dug foxholes, endured early morning bed inspections, disassembled and re-assembled their rifles, cleaned out latrines, pulled KP, and peeled vast numbers of the potatoes they loathed. Then it began to rain and the red Mississippi dust turned into red Mississippi mud, and they were made to get down on their bellies and crawl through it, clutching their rifles, wriggling their way under barbed wire as someone fired machine-gun rounds over their heads.

On June 15, the 100th Infantry Battalion—the Nisei soldiers from Hawai'i who had enlisted or been drafted before the war began—returned to Shelby from their maneuvers in the woods. For Kats Miho and many of the 442nd's Buddhaheads in particular it was a joyous occasion. Boys who had known one another in the islands renewed old friendships, exchanged family news, shared memories. They got out ukuleles and sat on the steps of their hutments singing island songs. They talked story. They gathered in circles on patches of red dusty ground, tossing dice, clutching fistfuls of dollar bills, going for broke again with every toss of the dice.

But the two groups weren't peers. The 100th soldiers were mostly a few years older. They had been in the service for at least a year and a half now. After months out in the field, they were lean and tough and hard-ened. They knew their jobs. They walked and talked with a certain amount of swagger and confidence. To the 442nd boys, they were like big brothers, somebody to look up to with respect and a measure of awe.

GORDON HIRABAYASHI, Esther Schmoe, and her father worked tire-lessly that spring, trying to ease the burden of Japanese American fami-lies in the Pacific Northwest, both those living in the camps and those who were now trying to settle in areas east of the exclusion zone. Almost from the beginning of the incarcerations, the WRA allowed selected Nisei whom they judged as loyal—but not Issei—to apply for leaves from the camps if they found employers willing to sponsor them or universities willing to enroll them. Although quite a few eastern and midwestern universities did open their doors to students from the camps, far fewer employers were willing to hire anyone of Japanese ancestry, a fact brought home to Esther forcefully one day as she tried to find jobs for some would-be relocators in Spokane. As Gordon waited in a car outside, Esther went into a laundry. All went well at first. The proprietor said he needed help badly. He had several positions. He was ready to hire—until he found out that Esther was there representing people from the camps. "Hell no! We don't want to take a chance hiring Japanese!" the man exploded. When Esther got back into the car, she wept for five minutes straight as Gordon comforted her. Until then she had not quite realized what she was up against. And he hadn't quite realized how different the world looked through her eyes.

For Gordon, of course, the treatment was nothing new. Just recently, he'd been traveling with a white friend in Idaho, when they had decided to stop at the Paramount Restaurant in the dusty little farm town of Caldwell. As they entered, they failed to notice the sign in the front window—NO JAPS. A waitress sauntered over and took their order, but half an hour went by and no food appeared. Finally, she edged back to the table and asked Gordon, "Are you Japanese?"

"No, I'm American. I'm of Japanese ancestry, but I'm American."

"Oh, well, if you're of Japanese ancestry, we can't serve you."

Gordon asked to speak to the manager. The man seemed nervous, almost apologetic.

"I'm forced to do it," he said. "If I don't, don't follow the line, I'll have people boycotting me, walking out."

Gordon didn't get angry, didn't argue. Instead, he proposed an experiment.

"Well, you have an empty table right near the entrance. Let me test whether you're correct or not . . . if anybody comes in, sees me, and leaves, I'll pay for an average meal so that you wouldn't lose, you wouldn't have lost that."

The man demurred. Gordon persisted, slowly, logically, patiently making his case: "I want to test this, whether you're correct or not. I'm curious myself."

Finally, the manager agreed warily to the deal, but only if Gordon sat at the counter, not at the table out front. Gordon and his friend ate as slowly as they could and managed to run another hour off the clock. Nothing happened. No one got up and left. No one even seemed to notice what was happening. Gordon paid and they left without further ado.

A few weeks later Gordon's friend wrote to him from Idaho. "Say, that guy took that sign off."

FOR WEEKS, Gordon had been growing more impatient to hear that his case had been resolved by the Supreme Court. He had no doubt that he would win. The racial rationale behind the curfew was so obvious, the lack of due process leading to the incarcerations so apparent, that neither could possibly fit within the framework of the Constitution.

When the Court did finally render its opinion in *Hirabayashi v. United States* on June 21, Gordon only learned of it when he happened to pick up a newspaper. And what he read was crushing. The justices, acting unanimously, had entirely sidestepped the issue of incarceration—the principal reason Gordon had taken his stand. Instead, they had addressed only the curfew order. Backing the government's assertion that wartime conditions justified the racial discrimination, the Court found, in Chief Justice Harlan Stone's words, that "in time of war residents having ethnic affiliations with an invading enemy may be a greater source of danger than those of a different ancestry." Gordon couldn't believe it. He later wrote, "I thought that the *raison d'être* for the Supreme Court was to uphold the Constitution. I didn't realize the extent to which World War II hysteria had swept up everyone."

Now all he could do, all Floyd and Esther Schmoe could do, was wait and see when and where someone would show up to take him back to jail.

WHEN THE YOUNG MEN of the 442nd were finally allowed to venture off base at Shelby and begin to explore Hattiesburg, it didn't take some of them long to get into trouble. With a sprawling army base right next door, Hattiesburg had long presented young servicemen with the usual array of treats and temptations on warm, sultry Mississippi nights. On Forrest Street, the 997-seat Saenger Theater movie palace, with chandeliers in the lobby and a 778-pipe organ, offered a rare modern luxury—air-conditioning—and Hollywood's latest picture shows. Glowing neon signs along Front Street and Pine Street—ICE-COLD DIXIE, JAX BEER, PINBALL—beckoned soldiers into bars and pool halls. There were back-alley doors and upstairs rooms, rooms a young man could enter as a virgin and leave a few sweaty minutes later no longer a virgin. On the outskirts of town, barbecue joints, steak houses, and cafés served up cheap eats for servicemen. One particularly popular place was the White Kitchen on Highway 49 South, run by Miss Mary White. There a soldier who was sick of army food could order up a quarter of a fried chicken, French fries, and some hot, buttered rolls, all for thirty cents, then top it off with a piece of pecan pie, an ice-cold beer, or a slice of watermelon for a few cents more. But the place was small and men had to crowd in and rub shoulders, and that didn't always go well. Miss Mary tended to favor the Nisei boys, especially the Hawai'i boys. They were fun to be around, drank a lot of beer, and were heavy tippers, so she often served them first. Almost every weekend, some white soldier, irritated, would sneer and refer to one of the 442nd boys as a "Jap." Punches would be thrown, crockery would be broken, and military police would be called.

It was up to Rudy Tokiwa, though, to get into the most spectacular trouble. Because Rudy was naturally inclined toward trouble, before he had left Poston his mother had asked his older friend Harry Madokoro to keep an eye on him at Shelby and, if he could, when they went off to war. "Please take care of him. He's our youngest son, you know," she'd implored Harry before they left Arizona. And Harry had done his best. He often accompanied Rudy into town, and if Rudy had a hangover the next morning, Harry was usually there to put an ice pack on his forehead. Rudy always waved him off.

"I'm old enough to go out and get drunk and get a headache, that's my problem."

"No, no, no," Harry would insist. "Your mother told me to treat you like my son, take care of you. I gotta take care of you. I told her I would."

But a Saturday night came when Harry wasn't around. Rudy and some friends wandered into a bar and ordered up some bottles of Jax. Most of the friends were Buddhaheads. From the day Rudy had walked into his hutment and thrown one of the Hawai'i boys' footlockers out the door, he'd earned their respect. In return, Rudy—who had always had an ear for language—had quickly picked up Hawaiian pidgin and could talk and swear as if he'd been brought up in Hilo himself. He was just fine with the Hawai'i boys, and they with him.

That night, Rudy noticed a young Black soldier sitting alone at a table at the back of the place. Rudy hated to see a man drinking by himself, so he called out to him, "Hey, Mac, how about comin' and join us?"

"Oh no, you don't want no trouble."

But Rudy encouraged him and finally the soldier came over, sat down, and began drinking and chatting with the Nisei soldiers. Pretty soon they were all feeling pretty good.

When the time came to catch a bus ride back to the base, they walked outside, and the young Black soldier headed for the bus's rear door.

"Hey, Mac, where you going?" Rudy said.

"Well, the coloreds all get in from the back," he replied.

"What the hell uniform are you wearing?" Rudy replied. "If I can walk in the front, you sure as hell can walk in the front."

"No, no, I don't want to cause trouble."

But Rudy was worked up now, angry. He began to usher the young man toward the front door. His buddies joined in. For weeks they'd been growing increasingly incensed at the way Black folk were treated in Mississippi—how they were obliged to look down at the pavement as they passed white folk, how grown men were called "boy," how they were made to use separate and inferior facilities, how impoverished they were, how squalid the shacks they lived in were. It all reminded the Nisei of how they—and especially their immigrant parents—had been treated. Now it boiled over. As Rudy and the others neared the door, the bus driver glared at them and growled, "The Black man either goes through the back door for the Blacks or this bus does not move."

Rudy and his buddies glanced at one another, then climbed onto the bus, dragged the driver out of his seat, deposited him roughly on the sidewalk, ushered the young Black soldier onto the bus, and drove away. By the time the bus reached the main gate at Shelby, there were red lights flashing in the rearview mirror. Rudy and his friends spent that night in the stockade, unapologetic and unbowed.

ELEVEN

They go home to the relocation camps on a furlough, see their folks behind wired fences and then come back wondering what it is all about.

CHAPLAIN HIGUCHI TO HIS WIFE, HISAKO
NOVEMBER 12, 1943

T he wet, suffocating blanket of a hot Mississippi summer descended on the 442nd. Their mornings started with four-mile hikes carrying full rucksacks, their weapons, and all their gear. They spent much of their afternoons marching in formation, back and forth across scorching, dusty parade grounds. At night they lay in pools of sweat on metal cots in stuffy hutments, listening to cicadas droning out in the night woods as moths the size of small birds bumped mindlessly against screen windows and mosquitoes whined invisibly around their heads.

But as that summer progressed, the new soldiers began to learn skills they'd never dreamed they would have need of. Young men who as boys had tinkered with old Fords and Chevys back home now learned how to repair tanks; men who had plinked at tin cans with .22s learned how to fire heavy machine guns; men who had a few months earlier been hoeing weeds in pineapple fields learned how to lay down and conceal land mines; men who'd done some construction learned how to blow up bridges and then rebuild them in hours, how to dig deadly tank traps, how to suspend 37-millimeter antitank guns on cables and winch them across rivers. Through it all, they heaved and grunted and pulled and pushed and sweated in the pine-pitch-scented air of Shelby's long, hot, soggy afternoons. And through it all those from Hawai'i and those from the mainland periodically went after one another with their fists.

Field maneuvers in Mississippi

But when they went into the woods, things got even harder. For weeks at a time, they left Shelby to conduct maneuvers in the wet low-lands of southern Mississippi and Louisiana, where Spanish moss hung in long beards from the branches of cypress and oak trees and alligators dozed, their mouths agape, on the banks of black bayous and fetid lakes. They stumbled through thickets of brush and fought their way through green tangles of kudzu. Laden with gear, they scrambled over fallen trees. Holding their rifles over their heads, they waded through muddy water up to their chests. New, unfamiliar dangers and miseries lurked everywhere. Clueless boys from Los Angeles camped in clumps of poison ivy. Boys from Hawai'i, who had never seen a snake in their lives, watched warily, and with genuine terror, for deadly coral snakes, cot-tonmouths, and rattlesnakes under every footfall. All of them quickly learned the relentlessness of mosquitoes, the tenacity of ticks. "Never let a tick get near your penis. It won't leave gracefully," they confided to one another and gave knowing looks. They ate out of tin cans, washed their faces and shaved with swamp water in their helmets, were awakened in the middle of the night by herds of marauding razorback hogs that ram-paged through their camps and trampled them in their pup tents. But the worst of it—the thing that all of them would remember most vividly years later as old men—were the chiggers.

The larval stage of tiny trombiculid mites, chiggers are creatures so small you can barely see them without the aid of a magnifying glass. They seek out and attack the most tender spots on the human body—places where the skin is thin and vulnerable, like the ankles, the backs of the knees, and the groin. There they drill microscopic holes in the skin and inject enzymes that quickly turn the underlying cells into what, for them, becomes a tasty mush that they can slurp up through tubelike mouth parts. Chiggers tend to occur in large, concentrated numbers, so bites usually come by the scores or hundreds at a time. The result is nasty red masses of swollen, painful, itchy tissue. Short of hot showers or chemical treatment, there is no easy way to get rid of chiggers and little one can do to relieve the pain they inflict.

And they were everywhere. The soldiers scratched and moaned and swore. They tried to burn them off by holding lit cigarettes close to their skin. They bathed in stagnant sloughs, preferring the company of alliga-tors and water moccasins to the company of chiggers, but it did no good. They rubbed salt into the bites to discourage the critters, but it only made the bites sting even more. Until they could get back to showers at Shelby, nothing really helped much. So mostly they just scratched and moaned and cursed.

Most of them had picked up army nicknames by now. Fred Shiosaki was called Rosie, for the pink blush that came to his cheeks when he was excited. One of his squad leaders, Harry Kanada, was Chowhound, because he was always first in line for food. George Oiye was still Whitey to the Buddhaheads but Montana to his kotonk friends. Kats stuck with "Kats," but among his comrades in the 522nd Field Artillery were Bulldog Nishizawa, Rocky Tanna, and Biggie Nakakura. Sometimes, the names arose when a white officer couldn't pronounce a Japanese name. That's how Rudy's friend Masao Noborikawa became, inexplicably, "Portagee." Other times, they hinted at a quirk of character or a physical trait, as with the diminutive Shortpants Hirashima and the somewhat corpulent Big Target Fujita. By the time they came out of the woods at the end of their first round of field maneuvers, most of them had earned names that would, in some cases, stick with them for life.

The artillery crews also named their guns—the 105-millimeter howitzers they would eventually take into battle. In B Battery, some of the guys on gun number two—Kats, his buddy Ted Tsukiyama from the University of Hawai'i, and their cannoneer Roy Fujii—got together and named their gun *Kuuipo*, Hawaiian for "sweetheart."

BY MIDSUMMER, some of them were heading off on their first furloughs. Many of the Buddhaheads had received large stashes of cash from their parents back in Hawai'i, eager for their sons to have a good time before they went off to war. Now they climbed onto trains or buses bound for New Orleans or New York City in high spirits and with wads of cash in their pockets. The kotonks, though, were not so flush. Most of them were sending allotments from their paychecks to their parents in the camps so that they could purchase small comforts and conveniences from the mail-order catalogs. And when the kotonks left on furlough, instead of setting out for the Big Apple, most of them headed for the camps to visit their families behind barbed wire.

They returned to Shelby, more often than not, in sour moods. Not everyone in the camps had been pleased to see Nisei in uniform. Some of their fathers and brothers and uncles took the newly minted soldiers aside and told them firmly that they were fools for enlisting, scolding them for becoming tools of an American government that was oppressing their people. For the most part, the young soldiers remained steadfast, convinced of the rightness of their actions. But virtually all of them headed back to Mississippi disturbed and angry after being reminded of what their families were enduring in the camps.

Back at Shelby, by the end of that summer, the two contingents again went at it in the hutments, at the PX, at bus stops, in the middle of base baseball games, in bars and eateries in Hattiesburg. The Buddhaheads—refreshed and gung ho after their furloughs—could not comprehend why the kotonks were always so serious, glum, hesitant to go all out for army life, to go for broke. The kotonks thought the Hawai'i boys frivolous, undisciplined, and clueless about what was going on in the country. As things continued to spiral downward, the senior officer corps at Shelby began to wonder whether the Japanese American boys would ever come together as an effective fighting unit and whether the whole thing had been a mistake. The question loomed: Should they just dissolve the regiment?

NEARLY ALL THE 442nd's commissioned officers were white, with only a smattering of Japanese Americans represented, mostly in the medical and chaplain corps, and none was higher than captain. To the Buddhaheads the army's racial hierarchy—the haoles at the top, everybody else working for them—seemed to mirror the paternalistic and racist way that the plantations back home were run. To the kotonks, it seemed to mirror the way the camps where their families were incarcerated were run.

Many of the white officers were perplexed by the Buddhaheads' language. One officer in Kats Miho's artillery unit, Lieutenant Bert Wydysh, in particular, often grew exasperated trying to figure out what the kids from Hawai'i were saying. It was only when he was assigned one night to the routine task of reading and censoring their letters home that he discovered they could all write perfectly good standard English.

The next day Wydysh, who hailed from New Jersey, pleaded with them to explain: "Why the hell don't youse guys speak like you write?"

But despite the racial disparities at Shelby, as training continued, both the kotonks and the Buddhaheads began to warm up to their officers. For Fred Shiosaki and Rudy Tokiwa, the first moment of reappraisal came one afternoon in the middle of a bayonet lesson. Their instructor, Captain Walter Lesinski, was reputed to be among the toughest basic training officers at Shelby. Lesinski put them through the same grueling drills over and over until he was sure everyone in the company had mastered each skill. Whenever he could, he scared the hell out of them, seeming to delight in gory descriptions of what various German weapons could do to their bodies.

During bayonet training that particular afternoon, Lesinski slipped and somehow managed to stab his own foot, the steel blade slicing through his boot and clean through the foot as well. The Nisei boys stared, wide-eyed, expecting a bloodcurdling scream or a torrent of curses. For a moment there was nothing. Then Lesinski, with his foot still pinned to the ground by the bayonet and blood oozing out of the boot, looked up, growled at them to stop standing around with their mouths hanging open, and ordered them to carry on with their practice. He withdrew the bayonet without a sound, hobbled away, and never made mention of it again. He seemed like someone you might want to follow into battle.

The fact was that most of the 442nd's white officers had made a deliberate choice to join the unit. Unlike many of the enlisted men from other units at Shelby, their officers specifically wanted to serve with them, to go into battle with them, to live in the mud and rubble of shattered villages with them, to fight and possibly die with them. This was something entirely new—almost incomprehensible to many of the Nisei soldiers, especially those from Hawai'i. Coming from a world in which they had seldom seen a white man bend his back to lift a heavy load, the notion that these haole officers would voluntarily share the hazards of war with them impressed them.

As summer went on—even as they fought among themselves—relations between the men and their officers continued to grow warmer. And it was clear that the respect and goodwill were reciprocal. Many of the white officers liked the casual exuberance of the Hawai'i boys in particular. When a reporter from Hawai'i visited Shelby, First Lieutenant Keith Stivers buttonholed him and gushed, "When this war's over, I'm going to take a vacation in Hawaii. I'm going to spend a week with each one of my men, and I'm going to have a *lū'au* every Sunday."

Among the officers whom the Nisei most came to respect and admire that summer was the man at the top, the overall commander of the 442nd. Colonel Charles Wilbur Pence was short, blunt-faced, and tough as a rooster. In college at DePauw University, he'd weighed only 140 pounds, but he'd still become the captain of the football team, a baseball star, and the president of the student body. When World War I broke out, he'd left DePauw early to enlist in the army, been injured in battle, and nevertheless decided to make the military his career.

Right from the day the boys had first arrived at Shelby, Pence had made it clear to them that they were in for a rough time. "We're going to get tough early and stay tough until the last shot is fired," he'd said, before turning them over to their basic training sergeants. But then he'd sat down and penned a heartfelt letter to be sent to each of their mothers: "You have given a soldier to the Army of the United States. He has arrived here safely and I am happy to have him in my command . . . we shall make a glorious record for the Japanese Americans in our country."

It was the "we" that mattered to the boys. It came through in everything Pence did and said. He—like most of the officers who served under him—made it clear that he would be personally leading them into battle, hazarding whatever they hazarded, putting his life on the line along with theirs. He did not put on airs around them, seldom resorted to pulling rank, welcomed their thoughts, played baseball on the camp diamond with them, enjoyed chatting with them in the mess hall. The fact was, he believed in them and what they were trying to do, and before long they began to believe in him.

By late summer, though, Pence was getting fed up with the endless bickering and fighting between the kotonks and the Buddhaheads. He decided to bring in the one force of nature that he knew would compel the attention of nearly all of them—girls. Although most of the concentration camps run by the War Relocation Authority were in the West, two happened to be nearby in Arkansas, not far from Shelby. Hundreds of young Nisei women were incarcerated there. Pence decided to invite them to a dance.

A couple of weeks later, several dozen young women—dressed for a party in full skirts and blouses with ruffles—climbed off buses at Shelby. With their hair curled and adorned with flowers and combs and barrettes, wearing touches of makeup, a bit of lipstick, and a hint of perfume, they entered a dance hall festooned with glowing red, yellow, and white Japanese paper lanterns. Pence and his wife led a parade of well-scrubbed, khaki-uniformed Nisei soldiers into the hall, gave each a lei to present to his dance partner, and made a brief speech welcoming the women. Someone brought in a mammoth cake with two American flags, a *V* for victory, and the 442nd's now official motto, derived from the shouts of boys shooting dice—"Go for Broke"—emblazoned across the top in red, white, and blue icing. A makeshift band—the Shelby Hawaiians—assembled onstage with steel guitars and ukuleles and began to play Hawaiian music. Private Harry Hamada came onstage and danced a hula to the great amusement and delight of the visiting women and hoots, whistles, and catcalls from the soldiers. Then an army band struck up dance tunes, and soldiers and young women nervously edged toward one another, paired off and stepped onto the dance floor. They waltzed and jitterbugged and Lindy Hopped under the glowing paper lanterns, the soldiers mesmerized by the curls, the scent of perfume, the feel of a woman's hand in theirs. From time to time, a young man and a young woman recognized each other from back home—from Los Angeles or Seattle or Honolulu or Hilo—and they went to the sidelines and perched on chairs, catching up on family news or old neighborhood gossip. At midnight, as fireflies danced in the dark gravel parking lot, the women and their chaperones climbed onto buses to take them to dormitories as the boys stood by in ranks and sang "Goodnight, Ladies."

Nisei women from Jerome join the 442nd for a dance

Pence was delighted. He ordered more dances. This time more young women showed up. But now a new problem emerged. To the kotonks, it seemed that the women were partial to the Buddhaheads. They seemed to gravitate to the island boys' spontaneity, their warm and transparent affection, their overt boldness, the way they'd cut in on a dance and sweep a woman away with a broad white smile, brimming over with confidence. The mainlanders felt they were losing out, and the infighting promptly resumed, the boys going at one another more furiously than ever.

IN AUGUST, the 100th Infantry Battalion—the 442nd's "big brothers"— quietly packed their duffel bags, said their alohas, and left Shelby, bound for North Africa, Italy, and the war.

The 442nd boys were sad to see them go. Most of the 442nd's various units had finished basic training and now faced batteries of testing and field trials to prove their competency in everything from marksmanship to physical fitness. The new Nisei soldiers had to demonstrate over and over that they were up to the mark—doing thirty-five chin-ups in rapid succession; marching four miles in fifty minutes with a full pack and rifle; sprinting three hundred yards in forty-five seconds, again with a full pack. Almost without exception, they excelled at all of the trials, with 98 percent of them earning passing scores, the highest average in the entire Third Army that summer. Another battery of tests indicated that the regiment also had the highest average IQs in the army. In early September, some of the army's top brass arrived at Shelby for a formal review of the 442nd. In full battle uniforms, amid the clashing of cymbals and the blaring of brass, as officers with stars on their shoulders stood watching sternly, the newly minted Nisei soldiers—infantrymen, engineers, medics, and artillerymen—unfurled the Stars and Stripes, hoisted their regimental colors, and then swung sharply down the parade grounds, marching in lockstep, in tight, crisp formations. As the last company of the "Go for Broke" 442nd stepped off the field, Pence turned to a reporter from the *Honolulu Star-Bulletin* and said, with a jut to his jaw and a glint in his eye, "I'll take these men into battle without hesitation."

The fact was, Pence was coming to love these young men. If only he could get them to stop battling one another.

WAITING IN SPOKANE for the FBI to take him back into custody, Gordon Hirabayashi continued to work that fall with his Quaker colleagues and to grow ever fonder of Esther Schmoe. When Esther was in Seattle, attending classes at the University of Washington, he and she kept up a steady stream of correspondence. When she could be in Spokane, the two of them played tennis, took drives out in the country, picnicked under ponderosa pines, sprawled in the sun on gravel bars alongside the tumbling white water of the Spokane River, and fell more deeply in love.

Gordon spent many of Spokane's hot, dry autumn afternoons mowing the lawn of a house that an Issei physician from Seattle—Dr. Paul Suzuki—and his wife, Nobu, had just purchased. Although people of Japanese ancestry could live in Spokane because it was east of the exclusion zone, there were only a few neighborhoods where racial covenants allowed them to purchase homes. This one was squarely in one such neighborhood. Nevertheless, the transaction had stirred controversy among white Spokanites. On August 21, a car pulled up and a neighbor, J. S. Burke, got out and approached Gordon as he was mowing.

"Japs purchased this place?" he spat out. "Well, they can't move in. . . . If they want to stay healthy, they'd better not move in." Gordon stared blankly at the man for a few moments, decided the comment didn't deserve a reply, and resumed mowing.

A week later, Burke returned as Gordon was watering the lawn. This time he handed Gordon a letter threatening legal action against the Suzukis. A week after that, someone threw a large rock through the window. Mrs. Suzuki was on the property at the time, cleaning the house and getting it ready for the day she moved in. Defiantly eyeing the rock, she picked it up and congratulated herself out loud on her good fortune. "I'm going to make use of that rock, because this is good as a weight for my barrel where I make my pickles." Soon much of Spokane was in an uproar as Floyd Schmoe at the American Friends Service Committee, attorneys for the Suzukis and the neighbors, the chief of police, real estate companies, and the ACLU fought over the fate of the property.

In the middle of all this, as Gordon was again mowing the Suzukis' lawn on a September afternoon, another car pulled up to the curb. This time it was a big black sedan. An FBI agent stepped out of the car, approached Gordon, and asked him if he knew where Gordon Hirabayashi was.

"I am he," Gordon replied. "What took you so long?"

When Gordon arrived downtown, though, there was a hitch. At his

sentencing hearing in Seattle, he had agreed to accept a longer sentence—
ninety days rather than sixty—so that he'd be eligible to do his time in
a federal work camp rather than sitting in another crowded jail. That
way, he figured, he'd at least be outdoors a lot and doing something
productive. Now, though, the agents in Spokane told him that wasn't
going to work. The closest such camp was at Fort Lewis, near Tacoma,
well within the exclusion zone, which Gordon could not legally enter.
The next closest was in Tucson, Arizona, and the government wasn't
about to pay to send him there.* He'd have to serve his time in the Spokane County Jail.

Gordon unleashed his customary firm, cool, implacable logic. The
government was violating its agreement with him, he pointed out. That
was their doing, not his. If the government couldn't afford to send him
to Tucson, that also wasn't his fault. But why not let him get himself to
Arizona? Supposing he just hitchhiked to Tucson? The agent in charge
was perplexed and surprised by the proposal, but Gordon wore him
down. Faced with Gordon's evident goodwill and his calm but relentless
manner of arguing, he finally shrugged and approved the idea.

So Gordon stuck out his thumb and set out for Arizona. Traveling first
to Idaho and then meandering down through eastern Oregon into Utah
and Nevada, he trudged for endless miles alongside remote highways as
black coupes and diesel trucks sped by, the drivers mostly disregarding
him. Heat waves shimmered over the black asphalt and mirages appeared
and disappeared over vast expanses of sagebrush off in the distance.

Sometimes drivers slowed down, saw that he was Asian, and sped up
again. In Mona, Utah, a car pulled over, and the driver asked Gordon
if he was Japanese. "Nope, American of Japanese ancestry." The driver
turned around and went the other way. Occasionally, though, someone
took him a few miles down the road. A Utah state patrolman picked
him up and asked him where he was going. When Gordon replied, "The

---

*In point of fact, Tucson was in the southern exclusion zone, though neither Gordon nor
the district attorney nor anyone else involved seems to have realized it at the time.

Tucson prison camp," the patrolman slammed on the brakes and skidded to a stop in the middle of the road. Gordon showed him a letter the agent in Spokane had signed explaining the situation, and the patrolman drove on.

Sometimes things took an unexpected turn. A farmer driving a pickup truck picked him up, studied Gordon for a while out of the corner of his eye as he drove, and finally said, "You're a Chinese, right?"

"No, I'm an American."

"I know that but you're a Chinese American, aren't you?"

"My parents came from Japan."

The farmer chewed on that for a few moments, then replied, "If I'd known that, I wouldn't have picked you up."

Gordon offered to get out of the truck but the man grudgingly kept driving. After a long silence, they began to chat, then to talk in earnest. Gordon explained why he was on his way to prison, what he believed in, how proud he was to be an American, what the Constitution meant to him. As the farmer neared his home, he pulled off the highway and into his driveway, invited Gordon inside, drew him a warm bath, fed him dinner, and drove him to a well-traveled road nearby so that he could continue on his way.

When Gordon finally got to Tucson, he'd been on the road two weeks. It was a typical, searing Tucson autumn afternoon. Gordon was hot, sweaty, and exhausted, but he walked downtown and into the office of the local federal marshal. The marshal was taken aback, perplexed by the sudden appearance of this strange young man. He tried to get rid of him.

"What's your name? We don't have any orders to take you in, so you might as well go home."

Gordon wasn't having any of that.

"It took me a couple of weeks to get down here, and I'd go home, but you'd probably find those papers and I would have to do this all again."

They jousted for a while. Finally, Gordon suggested the marshal make some phone calls to Spokane and Seattle.

Told to come back that evening, Gordon wandered outside into the blistering heat, found an air-conditioned movie theater, and settled in to watch a show and wait for whatever was coming next. By the time the show ended and he returned, the marshal had made the calls, decided Gordon was in fact a legitimate lawbreaker, and agreed to incarcerate him. A deputy drove him out into the foothills and delivered him to the Catalina Federal Honor Camp in a narrow side canyon in the Santa Catalina foothills, just east of Sabino Canyon. There, inside the gates, standing silently among scraggly pines, mesquite trees, and rock formations aglow in an Arizona sunset, stood a small contingent of inmates who had heard that the famous Gordon Hirabayashi was coming and wanted to welcome him personally.

AS THEY GRADUATED FROM basic training, some of the Nisei soldiers at Camp Shelby were sent to Alabama to guard German prisoners of war, remnants of General Erwin Rommel's Afrika Korps, defeated and captured in Tunisia the previous spring and now housed in camps throughout the American South. Largely to escape the boredom of sitting in stockades, hundreds of them had eagerly volunteered to dig peanuts on private farms that summer. With thousands of the Black farm laborers who ordinarily harvested the peanuts now off serving in the military, Alabama's peanut farmers were glad to have the help. And the locals seemed unperturbed at having German soldiers in the neighborhood. The editor of one local newspaper—the *Geneva County Reaper*—seemed almost bewitched by their appearance: "They are fine-looking, clean-cut young fellows in their late teens and early twenties, are blond, and are wonderful specimens of physical manhood." For the most part, Geneva County's white citizens appeared to be more at ease with the presence of the Germans in their midst than they were with American boys with Japanese faces, even though not long before these same Germans had been doing their best to kill Americans in North Africa.

And the tolerance shown the POWs in Alabama was not unique to that state. The presence of nearly 400,000 German POWs in America, in fact, led to some staggering ironies across the country. The camps in which they were held sometimes offered comforts and amenities that far exceeded those in the WRA camps for Japanese Americans. And in many rural communities, particularly in the South, they were not only tolerated but warmly welcomed, sometimes sharing Sunday dinner with local families or eating at lunch counters and drinking from water fountains where Black Americans were not allowed to sit or drink.

For the Nisei soldiers in Alabama, guarding the Germans proved to be exceptionally easy duty. By and large, they were friendly, easygoing, happy to be out of the war. They clearly hadn't the slightest interest in escaping, and the whole thing became a period of idyll for both the guards and the guarded. The Nisei sat in the shade under trees watching the Germans dig. Many didn't even bother to load their rifles. At least once, a soldier loaded his M1 rifle and handed it to a POW so he could shoot some crows that were gobbling up the peanuts as fast as they could dig them up.

KATS WAS ON maneuvers out in the woods on October 17 when he suddenly got word to return to Shelby right away. He rushed back to base confused and alarmed. There he found exactly what he feared he might, an army chaplain—Eugene West—waiting for him. A chill ran down Kats's spine.

"Son, I've got some bad news to tell you."

One of the boys guarding the Germans in Alabama was Kats's brother, Katsuaki. Late on the afternoon of September 16, after returning the POWs to their quarters, Katsuaki and roughly twenty more Nisei guards had climbed back into their two-and-a-half-ton army truck and driven a few miles to the tiny hamlet of Geneva, Alabama, to take in a picture show at the Avon Theater. The film—*A Night to Remember*—was light and amusing, a comedic murder mystery starring Loretta Young and

Brian Aherne.* As they emerged from the theater that night, they were in high spirits, Katsuaki especially so. Everything was working out better than he could have expected. At Shelby he'd been training as a medic, but he had just learned that he would be able to attend medical school at Tulane after all. The army needed more doctors. In just a week now, he'd be on his way to New Orleans to start his studies.

Katsuaki, Paul, and Kats Miho at Shelby

The air was silky that evening, the temperatures in the high seventies. A nearly full moon was high overhead. They climbed into the open back of the truck and headed out of town, but just east of the city limits the driver took a bend in the road a little too fast. He hit the brakes and the tires shrieked, but it was too late. The truck rolled over, and boys were catapulted from the back end, some landing in the grass alongside the road and some slamming into the asphalt roadway. More than a dozen were injured. Two were killed instantly—a twenty-year-old private, Shosei Kutaka, and Corporal Katsuaki Miho.

---

*Not to be confused with the much better-known 1958 film of the same title about the sinking of the *Titanic*.

Kats was devastated. No news could have been harder for him to bear. He was exceptionally close to Katsuaki and looked up to him as little brothers often look up to big brothers. He admired him for his intelligence and his commitment to service and was enormously proud of him for having gotten into medical school. When the two of them had tried to talk each other out of enlisting, it had been because each wanted to assure the other's safety. Now the worst had happened, and Kats was stunned. It was as if he'd been hollowed out. By the time he walked out of Chaplain West's office a few minutes after getting the news, he later realized, he'd already started to become someone different—harder-nosed, tougher, crouching in a more defensive stance against the world.

Kats used his furlough time to rush to Alabama, where his brother Paul, just out of divinity school at Yale, joined him. A few days later the brothers returned to Shelby with an urn containing their brother's cremated remains. At Shelby the entire regiment stood in silence as Paul spoke a few words about his brother. Then the regimental band played "Nearer My God to Thee" as the boys stood in ranks, many with tears in their eyes. Katsuaki and Shosei Kutaka—two Buddhaheads—had been the first of the 442nd to die, though they all knew they wouldn't be the last.

Then, on a dark, rainy day, the two Miho brothers climbed on a train, set the urn on a seat between them, and began a slow, painful journey north.

MONTHS BEFORE, their father had been moved from Fort Sill, Oklahoma, to Camp Livingston in Louisiana, just one in a series of transfers the Department of Justice and the army had made as they shuffled their Issei prisoners—along with smaller numbers of German and Italian nationals—from place to place. As the Issei were brought before hearing boards, their cases were disposed of in various ways, depending on the level of danger the boards thought they posed to the nation. Some were allowed to repatriate to Japan. Others were allowed to join their families in the WRA camps. The rest were moved from one facility to another as the government tried to figure out the most cost-effective way to keep them—along with increasing numbers of POWs—behind barbed wire.

When Katsuaki and Kats had enlisted in the 442nd, the Department of Justice had suggested that their father might be eligible to be released into the legal custody of his sons. But once again Katsuichi's principles dictated his actions. He refused to leave the prison camp in Louisiana unless roughly twenty other Maui Issei who had been incarcerated with him were also set free.

So instead of being released, he was moved to Fort Missoula, in Montana. The fort, a sprawling complex that was comprised of mostly low white buildings, had been established in 1877—just a year after George Custer met his fate at the Battle of Little Bighorn—as a base from which to wage war against the local Native Americans. Now it served as a detention facility for nonmilitary aliens, mostly Italian merchant marines who had been stranded in Great Britain and the United States at the outbreak of the war in Europe in 1939. Following the attack on Pearl Harbor, it was also used to incarcerate Issei men like Katsuichi Miho.

He had arrived there in June. He thought this new camp to be something of an improvement over the first two. The air in Montana was fresh and cool, redolent of the sweet scent of fresh-cut hay and clover from nearby farms. At night, brilliant sprays of stars lit up a vast and utterly black sky. By day, from almost anywhere in camp, there were spectacular views deep into the jagged Bitterroot Mountains.

Many of the Issei men he moved in with had already been imprisoned there for more than a year. They had developed a tight-knit society. When he arrived, practically all of them were afflicted by what they jokingly called "stone fever." With little else to do, they had collectively become obsessed with collecting and patiently hand polishing colorful stones—mostly agates and jasper and jadeite—they dug from the camp's soil, once the floor of the Ice Age Lake Missoula. With these treasures, they laboriously created various pieces of art and handicrafts—little figurines, ashtrays, jewelry, soap dishes. It passed the time and soothed the soul.

One of their number, Iwao Matsushita, serving as their spokesman, had successfully negotiated with the camp's administrator for some small privileges—better food, recreational opportunities, and social events, including opera performances put on by the Italian prisoners. Perhaps best of all, the men were allowed to venture down to the Bitterroot River, which flowed through a corner of the camp, to fish for trout and whitefish that they fried and ate fresh, or sliced up to make sashimi, or smoked and sent to relatives on the outside. To go with the fish, they contrived to make their own liquor. Katsuichi and a few friends began to divert a portion of the kitchen's allotment of rice to a small back room where—as the guards assiduously looked the other way—they lovingly brewed buckets of rice wine.

It had begun to feel to Kats's father that perhaps his fate was not quite so grim as he had thought when he was first incarcerated on Sand Island back in Honolulu or when Kanesaburo Oshima had been shot at Fort Sill. He missed his wife and children desperately. He missed the Miho Hotel and his busy social life in Kahului. He worried about his daughters living in Japan. He still thought of himself as Japanese, but he was nevertheless overwhelmingly proud that two of his sons had volunteered for the U.S. Army. He had never doubted that they should serve their country. That was the way of the samurai, after all, to faithfully serve those to whom one owed loyalty, even at the cost of one's life. So now, here in the mountains of Montana, he would wait out the war as patiently as he could, let younger men settle the dispute between nations, gather and polish colorful stones like the other old men, drink rice wine, and look forward to the day when his family would be reunited on Maui.

So it came as a crushing blow when late in September he got a telegram bearing the news of Katsuaki's death. A few days later, he was summoned to the reception room at the front gate of the compound and found Kats and Paul, grim-faced, holding an urn. Kats was wearing his uniform, but the guard at the gate would not let him any farther into the compound. All he could do was hand the urn to his father so that he could have some time with it and hold a private memorial service among his fellow Issei.

The even harder part for their father came the following day, when Kats returned to pick up the urn so it could be sent home to their mother in Hawai'i. This time, still grieving for one son, Katsuichi had to say goodbye to another, who he well knew might never come home from war.

TWELVE

_We had a group of musicians (professionals) come and give us
an hour and a half of home music. When the music ended
with "Aloha Oe," "Across the Sea," and "To You Sweetheart,
Aloha," you could hear a pin drop. I watched the boys from
the Islands—and was afraid most of them would break down
and cry._

CHAPLAIN HIGUCHI TO HIS WIFE, HISAKO
FEBRUARY 21, 1944

Kats returned to Shelby still shaken and despondent. The sense of
isolation and alienation he had felt on Maui after being kicked
out of the Territorial Guard returned. His family, his home, the
simple pleasures of his Hawaiian boyhood—all seemed further away
than ever. He was not at all sure now what he was doing in the army.
He'd never felt this alone.

But there was someone he could confide in. Two Japanese American
chaplains had arrived at Shelby to join Chaplain West. Both the Reverend Hiro Higuchi and the Reverend Masao Yamada were from Hawai'i.
Both had watched with admiration but also deep concern as thousands
of island boys signed up to serve. Both had eventually decided they
needed to accompany those boys to war, to watch out for them on the
battlefield. Both were among the 442nd's few commissioned officers of

Japanese ancestry. Both were Protestants but happy to minister to whoever came through their office doors or attended their services, including the many Buddhist boys in their charge. Both were married, had wives and children back in Hawai'i, and were significantly older than most of the Nisei soldiers. And most of all both cared deeply about the soldiers they had come to pray with, to console, to encourage, to advise, and in some cases, perhaps someday, to bury.

But the two men were different in many ways.

Hiro Higuchi was slender, introspective, and reflective, given to questioning everything, even as he strove to nurture the faith of his soldiers. Born in Hilo on the Big Island, the son of an itinerant plantation preacher, he, like Kats Miho, had been an academic star and president of his class at Hilo High School. He'd moved to the mainland to attend Oberlin College, started law school at the University of Southern California, then switched to USC's divinity school. While there, he'd met and fallen in love with a sociology graduate student, Hisako Watanabe. The two of them had married and, with the thirty dollars they had saved up between them, moved to Hawai'i, settled on O'ahu, and, with the birth of their son, Peter, begun a family. Now, in the fall of 1943 as he settled into life at Camp Shelby, Hisako was back home on O'ahu, pregnant with their second child.

Masao Yamada had grown up barefoot and speaking pidgin, the son of a carpenter in a plantation town on Kaua'i. He was notably short and round—a bouncing ball of perpetual optimism, rah-rah patriotism, and gung ho enthusiasm for military life. Nearsighted and a bit absentminded, he was also in the process of having every tooth in his mouth extracted that summer, so he featured a very gummy and comical smile. Before joining the 442nd, he had attended McKinley High School in Honolulu, studied theology in Newton, Massachusetts, and then returned to Kaua'i to settle in the dusty little town of Hanapēpē on the dry, western side of the island. There, before the outbreak of the war, he had been content to raise his children, pursue his hobby of hybridizing orchids with his wife, Ai, and preside over a small congregation at the Hanapēpē Japanese Christian Church. But when something seemed unjust to Masao Yamada, his instinct was to fight it with direct action and often with a fierce tenacity. Shortly after Pearl Harbor, seeing that Japanese Americans on Kaua'i were being stigmatized by some of the newly arrived mainland troops, he confronted the commander of a combat unit recently arrived on the island about it. The commander glared at him and grumbled, "I don't trust you."

That drew a rebuke that was typical of the often blunt Yamada: "If you cannot trust a Christian pastor, I wonder whom you can trust. I am not ashamed to tell you that I am Japanese. I was born on Kaua'i, educated in American schools, and I don't know anything but the American way of life. . . . If you cannot trust me, sir, I think you ought to be man enough to shoot me."

Like Higuchi, when Yamada learned that Japanese American boys from Hawai'i were to go off to war with only white mainland chaplains to minister to them, he had been deeply concerned. The cultural gap, he thought, would be too great. In the moments of their greatest spiritual needs, in life-and-death moments, his island boys would have nobody by their sides with whom they would be comfortable opening up, nobody who would know how to counsel and console them. So he had gone straight to army brass, insisted that the newly formed 442nd RCT include Japanese American clergy, won the argument, and offered himself up as a chaplain.

Kats had stopped in to talk to Yamada a few times even before his brother was killed, mostly just sharing news about families they both knew back in the islands. It was easy for both of them to just while away half an hour talking story. But now Kats came to Yamada more often, clearly anguished, trying to make sense of his brother's death. Following his father's lead, Kats had always focused his life on the idea of serving his fellow man, living by his principles, fulfilling his civic and human obligations, doing his duty. Now, Yamada told him, his brother's death imposed a new obligation on Kats—to renew that focus, to reinvigorate it, and to devote himself to a higher cause. In a sense, he suggested, Katsuaki's

Colonel Pence and Chaplain Yamada at Shelby

death had opened a door through which Kats must now walk. On this side, there was despair and desolation; on the other side, there was an opportunity. By living his life as well as he could—by reanimating the spirit of duty, enthusiastic participation, and leadership he had demonstrated at Maui High, by becoming the best soldier he could—he could help fill the void his brother's death left, not only in his own life, but in the world itself. He could become something powerful and potent, a force for good worthy of his brother's legacy. Kats listened and reflected, and in the weeks and months that followed he began to heal, to come back out of his shell, to engage with others as he had always done. But he knew he'd never again be the entirely carefree kid from Kahului. That person had died along with Katsuaki on a stretch of asphalt on a moonlit night in Alabama.

WHEN CHAPLAINS HIGUCHI and Yamada arrived at Shelby, the 442nd's commander, Colonel Pence, had given them an urgent task. The battles between Buddhaheads and kotonks continued unabated. Pence had assembled the whole regiment and chewed them out about it, more than once now. He'd demoted men for fighting. He'd ordered extra KP and latrine duty to the worst offenders. He'd thrown a few in the stockade. He'd threatened to disband the entire outfit. Nothing had worked.

It was Hiro Higuchi who found a path forward. As he talked to the men, it had become clear to him that those who had come out of the concentration camps were haunted by a particular specter. The boys from Hawai'i—the Buddhaheads—were always talking about what their homecoming would be like after the war: the parades, the lū'au, the leis hung around their necks by beautiful and grateful island girls, home-cooked meals, falling asleep in their own beds to the sound of pounding surf and rustling palms. But most of the mainland boys had nothing like that to look forward to. As one of them told Higuchi, with tears in his eyes, "I can't even imagine anyone even thinking of homecoming." For many of them, there would likely be no homes to return to. At best there would be a family patched back together, scrambling for land to lease, searching for a new house to rent in a segregated neighborhood, struggling to help their parents get a new business started, all amid the continued scorn of many of their neighbors. At worst, there would be barbed wire and more barracks.

Higuchi realized that the boys from Hawai'i largely had no idea what the mainlanders were contending with in regard to their homes, their families, and their futures. Some of the Buddhaheads had never even heard about the concentration camps. Others had laughed them off or refused to believe such places existed. Since July, some of the mainland boys had been making treks to the Jerome and Rohwer camps in Arkansas to visit family members incarcerated there. There was even a USO center at Jerome to serve visiting soldiers. Perhaps, Higuchi figured, if the Buddhaheads went, too, and saw the camps for themselves, they might begin to understand the mainlanders and ease up on them. Higuchi went to Pence and proposed a series of organized field trips to the two camps in Arkansas. Pence immediately agreed. Send as many Hawaiians as you can, he said, especially the noncommissioned officers, the leaders, the opinion formers.

Right from the beginning, Kats Miho had been widely admired at Shelby, just as he had been at Maui High, so he was selected to go on one of the first field trips. So was Corporal Daniel Inouye. They left early in the morning. By mid-morning, as they rolled through Jackson and Vicksburg, crossed the Mississippi, and started north up the river's rich wide bottomlands, traveling through a vast sea of white cotton, the ukuleles and guitars came out. The boys began to sing and to horse around, joshing one another and playing cards. Kats found the landscape deeply interesting—decrepit old plantation houses from before the Civil War, barefoot Black men walking behind mules in the fields, alligators basking in the sun on muddy riverbanks. Everyone was in high spirits, though they had no idea what was up, where exactly they were going.

Finally, they came around a bend in the road and saw what appeared to be some kind of military camp ahead, and to everyone's surprise they pulled up to the front gate and it opened. Kats piled off the bus with the others and found himself looking through tall fencing at row upon row of flimsy tar-paper-and-pinewood barracks. Guard towers stood above the entry gate and at all four corners of the compound. The people beyond the fence had Asian faces, and the reality suddenly dawned on the men. Kats was shocked. They were all shocked. The guns in the towers were aimed inward, toward people moving around inside. Although he had just visited his father, imprisoned at Fort Missoula, Kats couldn't quite believe what he was seeing here. These weren't Issei men—Japanese nationals—behind the wire. These were Americans. Like himself. He watched a group of little girls playing hopscotch. A boy bouncing a rubber ball against the wall of one of the barracks. A pregnant woman carrying a basket of laundry. Middle-aged men sitting idle on the steps of barracks smoking cigarettes and staring blankly back at them. As the Nisei soldiers, all in uniform, filed into the camp, they were patted down by white army soldiers searching for contraband, and their shock quickly turned to outrage.

They had arrived at the Jerome Relocation Center. This is where their dancing partners had come from. The camp had been built on five hundred acres of low, swampy ground adjoining Boggy Bayou, just three miles west of the Mississippi. The bayou was aptly named. When it rained, the camp flooded. When the sun came out and the water receded, the land steamed. Mud was everywhere. So were snakes, chiggers, mosquitoes, and disease. Malaria and typhoid fever had already made visits to the camp. Just now, an influenza epidemic was breaking out. The infirmary was full, and morale was at an all-time low. Kats could see it in people's eyes. Their expressions weren't frightened or angry or impatient so much as just dull, expressionless, as if the souls behind the eyes had given up, with nothing to look forward to. Chaplain Yamada, ordinarily a burbling font of good cheer, was shocked. He wrote sadly to his wife that night, "They are lost. They are not sure of anything in the future . . . many young people become careless and defeatist. . . . Life in a relocation center is not a real, free life."

Nevertheless, most of the families at Jerome did their best to welcome the Nisei soldiers. They had saved up their rations of food and used their communal kitchens to prepare small feasts for the boys. They presented gifts, mostly *kobu*, traditional wood carvings they had made from the twisted roots and knobs of oak and swamp cypress trees felled for construction of the camp. They arranged for another dance with the Nisei girls. They offered to sleep outside, so the boys could sleep in the barracks, but the boys said they'd do fine sleeping on the bus or in the mess hall. Kats came across his Japanese-language-school teacher from Kahului. Like Kats's father, he'd been picked up on December 7, 1941, and incarcerated in a Department of Justice camp but then allowed to join his family at Jerome. He and Kats spent much of the weekend reminiscing about life on Maui.

On the bus ride back to Mississippi, nobody pulled out musical instruments. For the most part, there was dead silence. People wanted time to think about what they had seen. Kats and the other young men from Hawai'i could not help but wonder, would they have volunteered for the army out of such a place?

Daniel Inouye returned to his hutment that night and said, "I got to tell you guys about these mainlanders. You won't believe what I'm going to tell you." Kats delivered the same message. All those who had gone had the same story. They told others to go see the camps for themselves. More buses full of island boys went to Jerome and Rohwer. With each busload that returned, more Buddhaheads began to ease up on more kotonks.

After visiting one of the camps, one of the Buddhaheads approached Rudy Tokiwa, eager to tell him about his visit.

"Hey, Rudy, all you mainland guys. Your families in places like that?"

"Well, majority of 'em, yes."

"Well, how much money these guys gettin' paid to be in there?"

"They don't get paid."

"Hey, you kotonk buggahs good up in the head, yeah? You be buddies with everybody?"

The war between the kotonks and the Buddhaheads was finally beginning to ease.

IN ARIZONA, Gordon Hirabayashi, now federal inmate 3751, spent his days that fall laboring under a broiling sun on a road crew, crushing rocks with a sledgehammer and shoveling gravel into dump trucks. It was brutal work. But again Gordon quickly made friends among his new companions. It was an eclectic group: Black Americans; Mexican nationals who had crossed the border illegally; Jehovah's Witnesses; white pacifists, mostly college students from Los Angeles; Mennonites; and a few run-of-the-mill bank robbers, embezzlers, and con men. Working and sweating alongside them, sitting in the shade of cottonwoods eating bologna sandwiches with them, he asked them about themselves, listened to their stories, and—whenever they gave him a chance—explained his philosophy of nonviolent resistance to them. The others listened to him intently, and as in the King County Jail he soon began to develop an ardent following in the camp. Noting this, the FBI began intercepting and making copies of letters he wrote to friends and acquaintances on the outside.

He also began, quietly but insistently, to question the rules and assumptions by which the camp was administered. The men were housed in wooden barracks, all segregated—white American citizens in one, Mexican nationals in another, and American citizens classified as "coloreds" (Black Americans, Hispanic Americans, and Native Americans) in a third. Gordon was put in with the whites. He figured that was intended as some kind of a privilege, but he wanted to know what the rationale was. Day after day, he buttonholed different camp administrators and wardens, interrogated them, and systematically poked holes not just in the policy of segregation itself but in the logic behind the particular scheme they had put in place. If he was subject to a curfew and incarcerated because he wasn't white, why was he white when it came to barracks assignments? "Why was I put in the white barracks when Spanish-looking Mexicans were put in the 'colored' barracks? What is your basis for barracks segregation? Why segregate at all?" Perplexed by the barrage of questions, one administrator stammered out that, yes, it seemed pretty dumb, but it had always been done that way, so that's the way it was going to be done. Pretty soon most of the "white" inmates were following Gordon's lead, demanding to be housed in the "colored" barracks as a means of protest.

Among the other inmates at Catalina were a group of young Hopi and Navajo men who had resisted the draft, some on religious grounds, others because they felt they should not serve in an army that had, in the nineteenth century, systematically deprived them and other Native Americans of their rights and their lands. They invited Gordon up onto a hillside above the barracks where they had built small huts. They poured water over hot rocks to give Gordon a ritually cleansing steam bath, then washed his hair with soap they had made from local weeds and herbs. They talked to him about their spiritual beliefs. Gordon talked to them about Quakerism. Soon, they, too, joined Gordon in actively agitating, vocally questioning the rules and assumptions by which the camp was governed. Eventually, one of the wardens, exasperated by the turmoil, approached Gordon and said wearily, "I want this war to end so I [can] settle down to the good old murderers and kidnappers. . . . They're not trying to change the system."

As THE FALL OF 1943 slid toward winter and the weather again cooled in Mississippi, the boys of the 442nd Regimental Combat Team spent little time garrisoned at Camp Shelby. Most of the time, they were out in the woods, living in pup tents or sleeping under the stars on beds of pine boughs or in dank foxholes. Practicing large-scale maneuvers now, they ranged all over Louisiana and Mississippi. Kats and George Oiye and the 522nd Field Artillery drove as far as the Sabine River in Texas, dragging howitzers behind their 6x6 trucks, piling up sandbags around gun emplacements, stretching camouflage nets over the big guns to make them invisible from the air. Infantry units like Fred Shiosaki's and Rudy Tokiwa's marched in columns down red-dirt roads or alongside paved highways, toting bazookas, mortars, and M1 rifles. Fred's feet hurt nearly all the time, but he was so fit now that he could march all day with fifty pounds of gear on his back and hardly break a sweat, even when his staff sergeant, Joe Hayashi, ordered his guys to double-time it. Rudy also slogged along uncomplaining, lean, lithe, and tougher than ever, grateful for the time he had spent on marches much like these as a boy in Japan.

Day and night, the Nisei soldiers, working in teams, practiced trying to outmaneuver one another, one slipping silently around the flank of another, a third leading a surprise bayonet charge through the woods to catch the other teams sitting down for a meal. At night, they crept through black swamps in the rain, bellying through red mud, trying to evade "enemy" patrols. They strung telephone wire through the woods to communicate with one another. They sent snipers climbing up into oak trees draped with Spanish moss. They lobbed dummy grenades into one another's dummy machine-gun nests. They repaired jeeps that had broken down. It was grueling, relentless, dirty, and exhausting. But more and more often they were comfortable and proficient at doing their individual jobs. And more and more often they were working together seamlessly now, moving through the woods not as individuals but as squads and platoons, as part of something larger than themselves. Though they didn't fully realize it yet, they were becoming one of the most proficient and deadly fighting forces in the Third Army.

John Terry, a reporter dispatched by the *Honolulu Star-Bulletin* to report on the 442nd, was mesmerized observing them on night maneuvers. "Moonlight flooded the meadows with a pale light and cast dark shadows through the pine woods. There were soldiers everywhere. . . . The woods were literally full of them. But you seldom saw them. . . . Their fatigue uniforms seemed a part of the grass, the trees, and the huckleberry bushes. The only persistent sound was the whirring of locusts in the treetops. . . . We noticed a group of men . . . walking Indian fashion. They moved out from a group of pines, filed across the meadow and slowly vanished into the dark woods beyond. . . . In the moonlight their soundless movement seemed ghostlike."

And for the first time, they began to have fun in the woods. In their free time, they foraged for wild persimmons sweetened by the first frosty nights of the season and filled bags with pecans and sat around campfires cracking them open with their trench-digging tools. They lay on their backs and smoked cigarettes and stared at the stars and talked story, conjuring up home, their mothers' cooking, girls they'd left behind. They played practical jokes on one another, and particularly on their officers, coiling up a dead water moccasin and putting it in a sergeant's bedroll or tying a tarantula to a thread and dangling it over the head of a sleeping captain. Boys who'd grown up in the American West surrounded by sagebrush—boys like George Oiye from Montana and Fred Shiosaki from Spokane—sounded now as if they'd grown up in Hilo or Lahaina surrounded by cane fields. Hawaiian creole, the pidgin

language that had at first divided them so sharply, was now beginning to knit the 442nd together, to define the contours of their unique
identity. As always, almost every night, the Hawai'i boys pulled out the
ukuleles and guitars and sang with sweet voices, their words floating
improbably through the night air over moonlit bayous. And now there
was something new. The kotonks were joining in.

Perhaps the best of it, though, was the great pig bonanza. It started
one afternoon when someone in Kats's artillery unit—the 522nd's B
Battery—spotted a hog rooting around the trunks of some shrubby oak
trees. One of the island boys, assuming it was a wild hog, though it
looked decidedly plump and pink, grabbed his M1 rifle, and shot it.
Excited at the prospect of a traditional *lū'au* treat, the boys decided to
make *kālua* pig. They tried to dig an *imu*—a pit in the ground in which
to roast the pig with hot rocks—but the water table in Louisiana was far
too high. The pit just kept filling with water. So they cooked it *huli huli*
style instead, roasting it whole over hot coals on an improvised rotating
spit. Before long, the woods were full of the scent of roasting pork and
the boys were leaning over the fire, greedily cutting slices of sweet,
moist meat from the flanks of the animal with their combat knives. Island boys and mainlanders alike, they feasted.

The next day, and the day after that, they came across more pigs,
and they soon realized that the country they were moving through
was abundant with pigs. It also became clear that these weren't wild
razorback hogs. These were somebody's domestic livestock. But the
boys had gotten the taste of roast pork in their mouths, and they weren't
about to give it up now. They learned to imitate the calls local farmers
used to summon their pigs, and soon they had the pigs trotting right
up to them, and to their demise. It wasn't long before Colonel Pence,
back at Shelby, began getting bills for livestock replacements. Pence
chose not to make an issue of it. A few pigs were a small price to pay
for the growing cohesion and effectiveness of the 442nd Regimental
Combat Team.

Hula at Shelby

BY THANKSGIVING, there was frost on the ground most mornings. As they sat around campfires on increasingly cold nights and mornings, they talked, Chaplain Yamada wrote home, about everything "from the sublime to the ridiculous, usually ending up with women." But they also began to talk tentatively about what was to come, what the war would be like once they finally got into it. They speculated about what it would feel like to be wounded or to die on the battlefield, what they would suffer or what their parents or siblings would suffer. But at the same time, they worried that the war might end before they got into battle. That would be the worst thing, they agreed. Worse than dying. They would lose forever the opportunity to prove their loyalty and earn Japanese Americans their rightful place in American society. "If we should only become part of an army of occupation, this whole thing is shot," one boy explained to a visiting reporter. "We've *got* to get into battle." They talked about their beliefs and values, about what was happening in Europe with Hitler and Mussolini, and about why it mattered in America. They came back again and again to the things they had learned in high school about the American Constitution, about the fundamental principles of democracy—personal liberty, equality, free speech. They debated whether those things really could be said to exist in the country that imprisoned their families. But they also talked about the things their Japanese parents had taught them. Fred Shiosaki talked about filial piety, about the expectation in his family that he and his siblings would always respect their parents' authority and uphold the family's honor. Kats Miho talked about watching samurai movies in the cane fields of Maui and learning from them the basics of the warrior's code, the eight virtues of Bushido: rectitude, courage, benevolence, politeness, honesty, honor, loyalty, and self-control. He talked about his father's emphasis on *giri*, social obligation, and balancing it with *ninjo*, human warmth and compassion. Rudy Tokiwa talked about the rigors of his boyhood military training in Japan, about the idea of *gaman*—enduring the seemingly unendurable quietly and with patience—and about the spirit of *Yamato damashii*, the virtue of sticking together no matter what, fighting for your group rather than for yourself. They talked about the last words they had received from their fathers when they left home. Almost always it had been some version of the same message: "Whatever you do, don't bring shame on the family." In Rudy's case the message had been explicit: "You chose your side. Now do it. If they tell you to go out and get shot, you go out and get shot."

As they talked things over and confided in one another, something solid and enduring began to take shape among them—a common identity that was both American and Japanese, but also unique, something formidable and unflinching yet warm and embracing, a unifying spirit, a silent but potent power that, in the not too distant future, would carry them through unimaginable hardships and terrors.

As CHRISTMAS 1943 APPROACHED, it got even colder as an unusual deep freeze settled over the Mississippi River delta. Ice encrusted the usual red mud and formed white margins around black pools of swamp water. Pine branches hung low, weighed down by icicles. When they got up in the morning and ran a comb through their hair, the young men of the 442nd found that it, too, was full of ice. Their socks were as stiff as leather; they could stand frozen towels on edge. At night they huddled in pup tents. Chaplain Yamada crawled into the back of a truck one night, hoping it would be warmer than a tent. The next morning he wrote to his wife, "Before I was asleep a plump Idaho boy came in, felt my belly, and placed his head neatly there and snored to sleep. An hour later another came in, pulling my leg, placing it to one side and laid on it. What a night."

When they weren't out on maneuvers, the boys spent much of their time in their hutments reading letters and Christmas cards from parents or siblings or girlfriends in Hawai'i or in the camps. Hiro Higuchi eagerly devoured a letter from Hisako in which she described their newly born first daughter, Jane. But other letters came from southern Italy, from boys they had grown up with in Hawai'i or come to know at Shelby and who were now fighting with the 100th Infantry Battalion. And there was nothing cheery about their letters. They were having a hell of a rough time.

After a brief time in North Africa, the 100th had landed in Salerno on September 22 and been attached to the Thirty-fourth "Red Bull" Division of General Mark Clark's Fifth Army in order to take part in the massive Allied invasion of Italy. The plan was for the Fifth Army to fight its way up the western side of the Italian peninsula, while the British Eighth Army, under General Bernard Montgomery, fought its way up the eastern side. The conquest of Italy, it was hoped, would open the Mediterranean to Allied shipping while simultaneously drawing German resources south, away from the site of the eventual and all-important Allied invasion of France.

Right from the beginning, the 100th had encountered fierce resistance from the Germans who were well dug into heavily fortified positions, and they had begun to take heavy casualties. For weeks that fall and early winter the 442nd boys back at Shelby had studied newspaper reports and casualty lists with a mixture of dread and admiration. The first Japanese Americans to step onto the battlefield were acquitting themselves with great distinction, but the price they were paying was heavy and—especially for the boys from Hawai'i—all too personal. By Christmas, almost all of them knew someone in the 100th who had fallen in Italy.

As the casualty reports came in, it often fell to the chaplains at Shelby to break the bad news to friends and family members in the 442nd. Hiro Higuchi spent one long night in the woods consoling two devastated young men, each of whom had lost a brother on the same day in Italy. One of them—one of three young men in his family who were serving—read Higuchi the letter he had received from his surviving brother in Italy: "Guess brother, it's just you and me now. You and I must live through this to go back to Hawaii. . . . I only pray your outfit won't have to come over. War is not like story books. It is terrible."

BUT FAR FROM shrinking from what was to come, the young men of the 442nd increasingly yearned to "go over," as they put it. The more newsreels they saw, the more they heard, the more letters from Italy they read, the more they wanted to do their part, to share with their brothers in the 100th the hazards of war.

By mid-February 1944, it was apparent that at least some of them were about to get their wish. Several hundred of them were abruptly culled from their ranks and vanished overnight, detached from the 442nd and shipped urgently overseas as replacement troops to rebuild the 100th.

There was a new level of tension in the air at Shelby now. Everyone was waiting. No one was sure when the call would come for the rest of them or where exactly they'd be going, but everyone had a pretty good guess. Chaplain Higuchi wrote to Hisako, back in Pearl City, "Expect I had better start learning to like spaghetti." Then, on March 5, an unmistakable sign. George C. Marshall—U.S. Army chief of staff—appeared at Shelby, walked in review past the 442nd as they stood row on row, and left a few hours later without making a public announcement beyond commenting that it was a "sharp looking outfit." But they all knew what the visit portended.

More weeks passed as the army finalized the logistics for moving men and matériel from Shelby to the East Coast. Enlisted men and officers alike sat down and began writing letters home, and for the first time their letters hinted at intimations of mortality. Letters to young wives reminded them to keep the life insurance up to date. Letters to siblings incarcerated in the camps pleaded with them to take care of the parents, no matter what. Letters to parents promised that their sons would not bring shame on the family, whatever the cost. Chaplain Higuchi wrote to Hisako, first assuring her that he would return from war unscathed, but then hedging his bets in the next paragraph instructing her on how he wanted his son, Peter, raised: "I would like to have him grow up with pride in himself and family. To be kind and understanding of other people's problems and to learn to sympathize with those in need." And he wrote separately to seven-year-old Peter so that his son would have something tangible to hang on to should the worst occur: "Daddy does not know how long he will be here, and sooner or later he will go to a war front somewhere. . . . You must be a gentleman always, like the children of our friends, very courteous to people and very unselfish in your needs. You must not hate anyone, for hates have caused this war and all the bad things in it. You must be kind to everyone. Remember these things and Daddy will feel so much better when he goes."

Finally, on April 22, the order came. They packed their duffel bags and climbed aboard northbound trains in Hattiesburg, heading for their staging area at Fort Patrick Henry in Virginia. There they were to remain for a few days, receiving inoculations, being issued new equipment, writing a few hurried last-minute letters home. Before they could set sail for Europe, though, they managed to get into one more big fight. And not surprisingly, Rudy Tokiwa was right in the thick of it.

A local USO club had arranged a farewell dance for the 442nd, busing some local Virginia women in to provide dance partners. As the dance got under way, some army aviators saw what was going on and decided they didn't take kindly to seeing Asian boys dancing with white women. They sidled over to Rudy and some of his friends and asked if a few of them could join the party. The Nisei boys glanced at one another. They were wary, but they figured a few haole guys wouldn't be a problem. After all, they were all in the same army, all heading into the same war, they'd better learn to get along, so Rudy said, "Sure, why not?" As the band started playing and couples headed out onto the dance floor, though, things went bad fast. "A few" turned quickly into a dozen, then several dozen. The aviators began to cut in on dances. Before long, the Nisei soldiers were nearly all standing against the wall watching the white boys dance. As Rudy and his friends eyed the spectacle unfolding on the dance floor, one of Rudy's buddies, a Buddhahead everyone called Bolo, edged up to him.

"I'm gonna go dance with da haole wahine. Da guy tap me on da shoulder . . . I'm gonna keep dancing. If he say anything I'm gonna bust someone."

Rudy started to work his way along the sidelines, whispering, passing word to the Nisei soldiers to keep their eyes on Bolo and to be ready to back him up. A few minutes later, one of the aviators tapped Bolo on the shoulder as he was dancing. Bolo wheeled around, fists cocked, and all hell broke loose. Nisei boys charged onto the dance floor, throwing punches. Outnumbered by men mostly much larger than themselves, at first the Nisei soldiers were in danger of getting driven out of the USO. But as word of what was happening spread through the surrounding area, every young man with a 442nd patch on his shoulder—scores of them—began to run full tilt toward the scene. They piled into the building, swarming the white soldiers. Many of them—like Rudy—had learned judo, kendo, or karate while studying in Japan or at the Japanese schools in their hometowns. Now they flipped men over their shoulders, leveled punishing kicks at midsections, delivered hard hand chops to carotid arteries, and dropped men to the floor like rag dolls. Before long the white soldiers were in retreat, desperately trying to fight their way to the front door, just to escape the mayhem.

By the time it was all over, an armored vehicle mounted with a machine gun had rolled up outside, half a dozen of the white soldiers were on their way to the base hospital, and dozens more were badly bruised and cut up. In the 442nd there were some split lips and black eyes, but also a quiet, steady, firm, and newfound pride. From now on, any talk of Buddhaheads and kotonks was mostly going to be for fun, and they all knew it. That night, more than anything they had been through until then, cemented it for them. They were all in this together now, whatever "this" turned out to be.

ON THE MORNING of May 1, a warm, breezy day on the Chesapeake Bay, dressed in olive-drab combat uniforms, boots, and helmets, the roughly forty-one hundred men and officers of the 442nd Regimental Combat Team arrived at their point of embarkation—ten long parallel docks at Hampton Roads and Newport News, Virginia. As a brass band played "Over There," Red Cross girls handed them doughnuts and a form letter from President Roosevelt, telling them that they bore with them "the hope, the gratitude, the confidence, and the prayers of your family, your fellow citizens, and your President." Then, clutching the letter and slinging their duffel bags over their shoulders, they stepped off American soil, filed up gangplanks, and worked their way down into the cargo holds of the gray-bellied Liberty ships waiting to receive them. The ships' cargo holds had been converted to primitive living spaces with canvas hammocks arranged in racks five high. They stowed their gear and selected hammocks—the wisest among them picking the top bunks, where no one could vomit on them from above. Then they settled in for what they were told would be a long, slow, crowded voyage.

As the first ships pulled out into the bay that afternoon, to lie at anchor while more ships were loaded, the boys with Chaplain Yamada realized that it was Lei Day back in the islands. In Hawai'i, since 1927, the first of

May has been celebrated by the making and sharing of leis. Schools hold lei-making contests, towns stage festivals, committees choose lei kings and queens, dancers perform hula, and people gather in parks and backyards for *lūʻau*.

With no flowers to be found on their ship, the Hawaiʻi boys made off with crates of oranges from the galley, used knives to carefully cut the peels in long continuous spirals, and hung them not just around one another's necks but around the necks of the mainland boys as well, wishing them and one another much aloha and feasting on the oranges. Proudly watching them, Chaplain Yamada wrote home to his wife that night, "Now we knew we could not do without each other . . . we were one happy family."

AT ABOUT THE SAME HOUR that day, forty-five hundred miles to the east of the Chesapeake Bay, the sun was setting over the Tyrrhenian Sea near the once lovely Italian seaside town of Anzio. There, as daylight faded, Nisei soldiers began to crawl from foxholes, dugouts, and improvised bunkers among the rubble of what had until recently been Italian homes.

Months before, in January, sometimes fighting in near-blizzard conditions and again taking enormous casualties, the 100th had seized a series of mountaintop strongholds as they approached the town of Cassino in southwestern Italy. Just west of the town—atop a steep, seventeen-hundred-foot-tall outcropping of brittle, badly fractured limestone called Monte Cassino—stood an ancient Benedictine monastery. The Germans had used the mountain as an observation post and then, following the destruction of the monastery by Allied bombing, turned the rubble of the monastery into a nearly impregnable fortress, key to a much larger series of fortifications they had named the Gustav Line. There, the 100th had joined in a series of ferocious Allied assaults on the mountain and its surrounding terrain. Over the course of several weeks, they waded through flooded fields in which the Germans had submerged thousands of land mines. They sent young men slithering forward on their bellies, feeling in the water and the mud with their bare hands for the mines. They forged across the wide-open Rapido River under relentless, merciless hailstorms of artillery shells, mortars, machine-gun fire, and the terrifying rockets they called screaming mee-mies. They climbed, hand over hand, the mountain's sheer, rocky slopes, advancing into the face of more machine-gun fire, finally seizing ground halfway to the top, desperately holding it until there were too few of them left alive or unwounded to sustain the attack, then pulling back, and doing it all again a few days later. One Nisei platoon entered the fray with 40 men and eventually retreated when only 5 remained uninjured. By the time the 100th was finally pulled off the line, only 521 of the 1,300 Nisei who had landed in Salerno were alive and still able-bodied enough to fight.

Their sacrifices did not go unnoticed back home. Accounts of their valor appeared in big-city and small-town newspapers, in popular magazines, and in movie-house newsreels across the United States. Some press accounts, noting that nearly all of them had suffered wounds in their first few months in Italy, began to call the 100th "the Purple Heart Battalion." It was the first time that most non-Asian Americans became aware that Nisei fighters were even on the battlefield. And the Germans, too, had taken note of their courage and fortitude and given them a nickname of their own—"the little iron men."

Then, in late March, even as the battle for Monte Cassino continued to rage, General Clark sent the survivors of the battered 100th north by sea, around the western end of the Gustav Line, and landed them on the narrow beaches of Anzio, just thirty miles south of Rome, where they joined other British and American forces clinging tenaciously to a small beachhead they had seized there back in January.

Recognizing that the force building at Anzio would give the Allies a direct and largely unimpeded route into Rome, the Germans had responded rapidly and furiously. They breached dikes and destroyed pumping stations to flood surrounding marshlands and make any advance out of the beachhead more difficult. Then, encircling the area with enormous amounts of artillery—including two massive rail-mounted guns the Germans called Robert and Leopold—they began pouring an unrelenting torrent of steel and high explosives into the town and its surroundings, even as the Allies continued landing more troops on the beach.* As civilians fled and their homes were reduced to heaps of smoldering wood and ancient stones, the newly arrived Nisei did as the Allied troops already there had done for months, going to earth, digging into mud and earth and sand like moles, hunkering down, trying to survive the daily onslaughts so that they could emerge each night to rebuild their fortifications. For weeks, it went on like that, death raining down on them with terrifying randomness.

But on that particular afternoon, May 1, 1944, the Nisei soldiers of the 100th Infantry Battalion had something other than the German shells on their minds. They hadn't forgotten what day it was. Cautiously, they emerged from the ground and began to search for flowers, walking among the corpses of dead horses splayed out in open fields, climbing over piles of broken masonry, circling around ragged shell craters, trying to ignore the stench of the dead bodies buried under the ruins, collecting the small, bloodred poppies of an Italian spring.

In the Chesapeake the next day, the ships bearing the 442nd weighed anchor, turned out into the Atlantic, and steamed east, carrying the Japanese American boys of the 442nd Regimental Combat Team to Italy, to Naples, and then on to Anzio.

---

*The Allied troops referred collectively to the two guns—capable of hurling five-hundred-pound shells twenty miles—as Anzio Annie.

PART FOUR

A THOUSAND
STITCHES

GIs landing at Anzio

THIRTEEN

===

*Please remember that whatever you do or wherever you are,
we are with you—and hope for the day when we can all be
together again in peace.*

HISAKO HIGUCHI TO HER HUSBAND, HIRO
JUNE 6, 1944

As the 442nd crossed the Atlantic, Gordon Hirabayashi was back in Spokane, waiting to be arrested again.

In December 1943, after serving his ninety-day sentence, he had been released from the Catalina Federal Honor Camp in Tucson, though not without causing more consternation for the authorities there on his way out the door. Just before he was released, some of the conscientious objectors in camp asked him to smuggle out a statement complaining about their treatment at Catalina. Gordon was hesitant. He didn't entirely agree with the statement they had drafted. It went beyond what he felt was reasonable. But in the end, he decided their point of view should at least be heard. It was too late to sew the paper into his clothes, so he simply taped it to the sole of his left shoe. As he was processed out of the facility, he got caught.

He spent the next nine nights in a dank, dirty jail cell in Tucson. The food was vile, and his only companions were the small herds of Arizona's notoriously large, dark cockroaches—some the size of small mice—

that scuttled noisily around his cell at night. Characteristically, he took a degree of comfort from their company, writing, "The cockroaches in whatever section of the country add atmosphere to the county jails and make me feel at home." On December 7, the second anniversary of Pearl Harbor, he was released and promptly sat down and rewrote the letter that had been plastered to his shoe and sent it on its way.

The papers the government had given him on release instructed him to report to the district attorney in Spokane immediately upon his arrival there. On his way home, sitting on a bus, watching the Sonoran Desert pass by outside, he decided he would ignore that. So far as he knew, no other prisoner released from federal custody was required to report to a local DA. Once again, the requirement seemed to have been imposed solely on account of his ancestry. Instead, he decided, he would stop in and visit Spokane County's assistant DA, Max Etter, who had become something of a friend, when he got around to it.

But the law wasn't finished with Gordon yet, nor Gordon with the law. When he got back to Spokane, he went right back to working with Esther and Floyd Schmoe at the American Friends Service Committee office, aiding displaced and incarcerated Japanese American families. Then, in February, he received a notification from his draft board in Seattle. After suspending the draft for Japanese Americans shortly after Pearl Harbor, the Selective Service had now decided to resume it. Although Gordon, as a Quaker, had been classified a conscientious objector, he, like all Nisei men of draft age, received Selective Service Form 304A. Titled "Statement of United States Citizens of Japanese Ancestry," the form required Gordon—under penalty of perjury—to disclose, among other things, any foreign languages he spoke, any clubs or associations he belonged to, his religion, and any magazines he subscribed to. It required him to provide five references from people unrelated to him. And, finally, it required him to answer the same two loyalty questions—questions 27 and 28—that some Nisei had already refused to answer on the grounds that as American citizens they should not be required to take oaths not required of other citizens. Gordon felt he, too, had no choice but to refuse to complete or sign the form. He returned it to the draft board blank, along with a statement pointing out that the very title of the form made it discriminatory. He went on: "This questionnaire, which I am returning to you unfilled, is an outright violation of both the Christian and the American principles of justice and democracy. . . . The form is based purely on ancestry. . . . I believe if I were to fill in this form I would be cooperating with a policy of race discrimination." This was familiar ground for Gordon, and he knew where it would lead. To save everyone time, he sent a copy of the blank form and his statement directly to the U.S. attorney J. Charles Dennis, along with his address in Spokane so that they would know where to find him when they came to make the arrest.

In the meantime, he and Esther Schmoe started talking in earnest about something that had been hanging in the air for months now— whether they should marry. It wasn't a simple question. There was no doubt that he loved her and she loved him. But in 1944 it was a radical— in many states an illegal—thing for a white person to marry a person of Asian descent. Neither Gordon nor Esther had qualms about violating a law such as that, and, in fact, interracial marriage was not illegal in Washington State.* But Gordon was on his way to national notoriety, and he knew the marriage would unleash a torrent of public scorn and hatred and that much of that hatred would be directed at Esther and her parents rather than at him. Esther professed not to care. Her parents adored Gordon, but they weren't sure the young couple was prepared for what would come at them in the wake of a wedding. A friend pointed out to Gordon that any children the couple might have would also likely be ostracized. And then there was the matter of whether they would start their marriage with Gordon in jail. The stated penalty for withholding information on Form 304A was ten thousand dollars or ten years in federal prison or both. Gordon could only guess what the penalty might

---

*In fact, mixed-race couples often came to Washington in order to marry after a series of anti-miscegenation laws failed to pass the state legislature in the 1930s.

be for refusing to put any information at all on it. But whatever it was, he was probably about to find out. He'd just been indicted by a federal grand jury.

Gordon was far from the only young Nisei man for whom the renewal of the draft and the required oaths of allegiance that attended it provoked a new crisis of conscience that spring. For hundreds of them, particularly those incarcerated in the WRA camps, the questions again arose: Why should they be compelled to fight for a nation that had removed them from their homes and denied them the rights and liberties afforded to other citizens? Why, if they were to serve, would they be relegated to a segregated unit? Why did the navy prohibit them from serving at all? In the camps a fierce debate erupted, just as it had when the Nisei were first permitted to enlist in the 442nd the previous year. In some of the camps, the debates were mostly private matters, fought out within the confines of individual families or groups of friends. In other camps, the arguments were far more public, carried out in camp newspapers, over meals in mess halls, and in organized meetings in high school auditoriums. The issues were essentially the same as they had been in regard to enlisting in the 442nd, but now there was no option of simply stepping aside and ignoring the matter. As orders to report for pre-induction physicals began to arrive in the camps, there was no escaping the fact that refusing to obey them constituted a federal crime, punishable by fines and prison time.

Nowhere was resistance to the draft stronger than at the Heart Mountain camp in Wyoming. Resistance to the incarcerations had run strong at Heart Mountain since the earliest days of the camp's existence, sparked in part by a series of clashes with the WRA, including one in which thirty-two children had been arrested for sledding outside the camp's boundaries. As the first draft notices began to appear in the mail at Heart Mountain, a group that called itself the Fair Play Committee had convened a public meeting at the camp's mess hall. Sixty young men gathered and laid out the the goals of the organization and the criteria for membership. In addition to paying a two-dollar fee, members were required to be U.S. citizens, be loyal to the U.S., and be willing to serve in the U.S. Army if their legal rights were first restored. If those rights were not restored, however, they were resolved to refuse to appear for pre-induction physicals.

As the spring of 1944 wore on, most young men in most of the camps ultimately complied with the orders to report. But others—like members of the Fair Play Committee at Heart Mountain—decided that they would refuse to serve so long as their families were incarcerated. As the orders to report arrived, they simply set them aside. Thirty-two refused at Minidoka, thirty-one at Amache, five at Topaz, one hundred and six at Poston, eighty-five at Heart Mountain, twenty-seven at Tule Lake. Federal marshals descended on the camps, charged the resisters with violating the Selective Service and Training Act of 1940, and hauled them off to local jails to await trial.

STANDING AT THE railing of his Liberty ship, looking out across the water, Fred Shiosaki thought the scene around him looked like a city afloat on the sea. The vessels carrying the 442nd had joined a much larger convoy, and now more than ninety other ships surrounded his, extending all the way to the horizon in every direction. The troop transports were clustered near the center of the convoy. Navy destroyers and cruisers protected the flanks, shepherding the rest of them across the sea, guarding them from the packs of German submarines that they all knew might be lurking anywhere below the waves. Barrage balloons flew from many of the ships, the steel cables tethering them to the ships designed to chop the wings off any German aircraft that might attempt to dive-bomb or strafe the convoy. By day, porpoises cruised alongside the ships, riding the bow wakes. From time to time, whales surfaced among them—exhaling long, sonorous plumes of spray. Enormous, undulating jellyfish, white and pink, floated by. At night, under vast black skies, the sea itself lit up beneath the ships as they slid over its surface, millions of phosphorescent organisms glowing green under the bows, each vessel etching its own faint trail of light across the sea. It was, Fred thought, one of the most beautiful things he had ever seen.

As the days went on, more young men joined Fred above decks, doing calisthenics, holding boxing matches, shooting dice, smoking cigarettes, resting against gray bulkheads discussing the twenty-five-cent detective novels the Red Cross had handed out. They speculated about where they were heading. The way the boats kept changing directions on a featureless sea, it was hard to tell. Most thought it was Europe, perhaps France for the long-rumored invasion, more likely Italy. With all the crazy course corrections, some thought it might even be Japan.

On the SS *Johns Hopkins*, Kats Miho and the 522nd's artillerymen spent much of their time mastering the intricacies of the new panoramic sights that their howitzers would be equipped with when they went into battle. On a different boat, Rudy Tokiwa had found some boxing gloves and passed his time sparring with anyone he could talk into it. By the time they were halfway across the Atlantic, he'd been pretty thoroughly worked over and picked up a new army nickname—Punch Drunk. Then he got into trouble again. On deck one night, he lit a cigarette without taking the precaution of cupping his hands around the flame, a brief flash of light that could have caught the eye of German submariners peering through periscopes. Instead, it caught the eye of an officer, and Rudy promptly "got gigged," as he later put it, condemned to spending the rest of the trip chipping old gray paint off the ship's steel superstructure.

All three chaplains—Yamada, Higuchi, and West—were on the same boat, along with a large contingent of the Hawai'i boys. Once again, the Buddhaheads pulled out ukuleles and filled every corner of the boat with Hawaiian music. After rehearsing for days, the 442nd's Cannon Company put on a performance for the whole ship. It opened with the Cannon Company boys rising and solemnly singing the soft, melodic Hawaiian anthem, "Hawai'i Pono'i." But then the party quickly grew raucous as they took turns standing on an improvised stage performing pantomimes, strumming guitars, singing popular tunes, telling bawdy jokes.

As the grand finale, a corpulent young man wearing lipstick, a silver wig, a coconut brassiere, and a grass skirt improvised from strands of shredded manila rope pranced out onto the stage and began to dance hula to a tune newly popular in the islands, "Princess Pupule," celebrating the many physical charms of an imagined island princess. The Hawai'i boys joined him in belting out the concluding lyrics:

> *Oh me-ya oh my-ya you really should try-a*
> *A little piece of Princess Pupule's papayas.*

Whereupon the dancer twirled around, bent over, parted the strands of his skirt, and unveiled his plump and utterly naked posterior. The boys exploded in laughter and thunderous applause. Even the chaplains Higuchi and Yamada found themselves standing and cheering. Only Chaplain West, a southern-born Protestant, sat silently still, sourly watching the spectacle.

BEFORE LEAVING SHELBY, the young men of the 442nd RCT had been assigned to the battalions and companies in which they would fight in Europe. Fred Shiosaki and Rudy Tokiwa were both placed in the Third Battalion's K Company. Fred wasn't particularly fond of Rudy. He preferred to keep his head down, stay quiet, tend to his own business, and fight only when he had to fight, and it irritated him that Rudy seemed always to be shooting off his mouth and getting into trouble. But he was delighted that his friend Gordon Yamaura, who had volunteered with him in Spokane, had wound up in K Company. And Rudy was thrilled that Harry Madokoro, one of his best buddies from Poston, was going to be with him in K Company. Rudy found the prospect of having the older Madokoro close by reassuring. Maybe Harry could—as he had promised Rudy's mom back in Poston—continue to keep Rudy out of trouble. Or at least keep him alive. His other best buddy from Poston, big Lloyd Onoye, was in I Company, so at least he'd be nearby in the Third Battalion.

In the 522nd Field Artillery Battalion, Kats Miho and George Oiye had fallen in with another young man who was, in many ways, a kindred spirit. Like Kats and George, Susumu "Sus" Ito was introspective and had a way with words. At twenty-four he was a shade older than Kats and George and had a measure of gravitas about him. He wore spectacles, spoke softly, liked to think things through, seemed possessed of both a warm heart and a keen mind. His start in life had been unpromising. He had grown up the son of poor, immigrant tenant farmers in California's Central Valley, moving constantly from farm to farm, sharecropping and living rough in a series of squalid, unpainted shacks set out in fields, with no running water, no toilet, no heating. When work on the farms allowed, he'd attended a rural grammar school. But even then, long before the war, barbed wire separated the classrooms of Asian students from those of white students, and the instruction offered to Asian students was cursory at best. He nearly failed to pass third grade. When his parents saved up enough money to buy a small bathhouse and settled in the town of Stockton, he was so far behind in school that he again almost flunked out, this time in the eighth grade. But by the time he got to high school, he had begun not just to survive but to flourish academically. In 1940, right out of high school, he'd been drafted into the army. Then, abruptly, following Pearl Harbor, his weapons were taken away, and he was shipped to Fort Sill, in Oklahoma—where Kats's father was then incarcerated—and put to work doing menial tasks in a motor pool. It was only when the 442nd RCT was formed that the army finally took a second look at him. When they did, they recognized his unusual aptitude for, among other things, quickly calculating numbers in his head, just exactly what artillerymen had to do. Before he knew it, he'd been made a sergeant and was on his way to Shelby, one of the advance cadre sent to Mississippi to train the newly inducted Nisei artillerymen like Kats and George Oiye. His family, meanwhile, had been removed from their home in Stockton and incarcerated in the Rohwer camp in Arkansas.

What drew both Kats and George to Sus Ito, though, what built a bond among them, wasn't just respect for his aptitude. It was his attitude. Sus carried with him wherever he went an ardently optimistic view of the world. In the hutments at Shelby, out on maneuvers, and now sitting in the hold of a Liberty ship on his way to war, he was a relentlessly positive presence, constantly encouraging the other fellows to keep their spirits up. "My outlook," he liked to say, "is, wherever you decide to go, if there are other people there or even if there are very few, there must be something pleasant or something, some positive aspect of this situation . . . look for the positive side, not the negative." That fit well with Kats's instincts for pulling people together and making things happen. And it meshed also with George Oiye's earnest determination to do well at whatever he attempted. They spent much of their time together, doing what they enjoyed most—talking about where they had come from, what they believed in, what they planned to do with their lives if they survived the war.

So in those first few days on the Liberty ships the boys of the 442nd RCT were mostly happy, at ease, pleased to finally be on their way, enjoying friendships that had been forged in foxholes in Mississippi, burning ticks off one another's backs, sharing tents, carrying equipment for each other on long forced marches down muddy lanes.

But as they approached Europe, as North America and home and family receded farther over the western horizon and the dark void of uncertainty that lay ahead of them to the east grew nearer, the mood on the ships began to shift. The Hawaiian music faded away. The practical jokes stopped. There were fewer games of craps belowdecks, more boys above decks, standing at the railing, staring out over the sea, looking eastward, wondering. By and large, they weren't afraid. They didn't yet know enough to be afraid. But they had been away from home for a long time already. They yearned for connection with the parents and siblings and friends they had left behind. So they sat propped up against bulkheads or hunched over tables in the mess hall, writing letters home.

And at night, in the dark, they lay in their berths and quietly reached out and laid hands on the things they had brought with them, things from home, things they hoped would carry them through the battles to come. Some reached for crucifixes, some for small Buddha figures. Some had slipped Bibles into their duffel bags, some love letters from girls back home. Some had rabbits' feet to bring good luck, some Saint Christopher medals. Hiro Higuchi had a new leather wallet with pictures of his wife, Hisako, his seven-year-old son, Peter, and Jane, the newborn daughter he had not yet met. Roy Fujii—one of the cannoneers in Kats's artillery battery and one of his closest friends—wore a Honolulu bus token on a chain around his neck. He planned to use it to get from the docks back to his parents' home in Honolulu after the war.

Sus Ito carried three things. One was a tiny pocket Bible his sister had given him. Another was an inexpensive Argus camera. The army forbade GIs to carry cameras, but one facet of Sus's relentless cheerfulness was that he sometimes took an impish delight in bending the rules, and the camera was small enough to keep concealed most of the time. But the third thing, the one that mattered most, the one that was precious to him, was a gift from his mother incarcerated at Rohwer—a white *senninbari*. A traditional Japanese warrior's sash emblazoned with the image of a tiger—a symbol of safe homecoming—the *senninbari* was embroidered with a thousand individual French-knot stitches. Each stitch had been made with red silk thread by a different woman to confer good luck, protection, and courage. It was meant to be worn around the waist in battle. Sus would, in fact, never wear his, and never show it to the other fellows in his unit, but when they got onto the battlefield, he kept it folded up in his pocket, close to his heart.

Rudy also had brought something that he preferred to keep concealed under his clothes. At Poston, his mother had plucked a single grain of brown rice out of a hundred-pound sack of white rice. Somehow, it had survived the rice-polishing machinery. Fusa Tokiwa sewed it into a pouch that Rudy now wore around his neck. When she'd sent it to him, she had said, "This rice kernel was real lucky. . . . It's the only one that lived through it and was able to keep this husk on. So I'm sending you this so that you'll come home to us."

Dust storm at Poston

AT POSTON, where Rudy's mother, father, and sister continued to live in Camp III's Block 213, another long Arizona summer was approaching, another summer of dust storms and searing heat and scorpions. For a year now, since the incarcerations had begun—not just at Poston but at Manzanar and Heart Mountain, at Minidoka and Rohwer, at all the relocation centers around the country—the stresses of confinement and regimentation had unraveled much of traditional family life. Long-held norms, values, and ways of living had suddenly been turned upside down. Families that had always sat together around the dinner table in the evening no longer did so as young people began going to the mess halls and taking their meals with gangs of their own friends. Kids who had grown up on remote farms observing and practicing their parents' traditional, conservative ways now began to mix with kids who had grown up in places like Los Angeles wearing the latest fashions, listening to the latest popular music, attending dances, driving cars, hanging out with friends at all hours. Moms worried about daughters who suddenly began ordering makeup or brassieres from mail-order catalogs and agitating to stay out in the evenings with their friends, sitting in the desert under the stars until all hours of the night. Fathers fretted about sons who roamed the camps in sometimes unruly packs and seemed less and less willing to show signs of the submission and filial piety they owed to their parents.

Many of the young adults now worked for the War Relocation Authority, helping to run the camps. Some, like Rudy, served as cooks. Others were nurses in the camp hospitals, lifeguards at the swimming pools, policemen, firefighters, teachers, hairdressers, mechanics, and farm laborers in the fields surrounding the camps. Still others worked within the camps on war-related endeavors. At Poston, dozens of Nisei—particularly young women—manufactured camouflage nets to cover artillery pieces like those the 522nd were using in Italy.

For the Issei, though, there were fewer opportunities within the camps. Men used to supporting their families sat idle and alone and despondent much of the time, feeling useless. Rudy's father did manage to secure a part-time job as a janitor at the camp's high school. It gave him something to do besides sitting on the steps of the barracks, smoking cigarettes, and staring at sagebrush. But it paid little and was menial work at best, and for a man now in his sixty-third year—a man who had fought in the American army, managed a large farm, raised a family, bought an automobile, and clawed his way toward the American middle class—it was humiliating to find himself pushing a broom down school corridors late at night, mopping out restrooms, picking up trash teenagers had thrown on the floor, peeling their chewing gum from the undersides of desks. Like many Issei men in the camps, he was increasingly bitter about the whole thing.

The Nisei women weaving camouflage nets at Poston were far from

Nisei women making camouflage nets at the Manzanar camp

the only Japanese American women contributing to the war effort, some of them very directly, by serving in the military. In February 1943, shortly after Nisei men were first allowed to serve, the Army Nursing Corps had begun accepting Japanese American women. Then, in September, the Women's Army Corps had begun to enlist Japanese American women. Many of those who wanted to enlist, particularly those hoping to serve as WACs, faced strong opposition from friends and family members. The very notion of women in military service flew in the face of the traditional gender norms expected of Japanese American women. Those who persisted and enlisted anyway were largely motivated by the same imperatives that had led Nisei men in the camps to enlist. Some had brothers in the army and wanted to support them. Some simply wanted to get out from behind the barbed wire of the camps. Some saw an opportunity to acquire job skills they could use after the war. But most simply wanted to show their loyalty to their country, to do what they could to serve it, and to help end the war as quickly as possible so they could all return home.

After five weeks of basic training, 142 Nisei women were assigned to active duty. For the most part, they found themselves doing clerical work, acting as typists, stenographers, and supply clerks. But 48 who had good Japanese language skills were assigned to the army's Military Intelligence Service Language School, where they were trained to act as translators of intercepted or captured Japanese communications before entering the MIS. Another 350 joined the Cadet Nurse Corps, a non-military program designed to rapidly replace the thousands of nurses who had left domestic hospitals to serve overseas. The program provided scholarships to cover thirty months of rigorous training at accredited nursing schools around the country. In return, the cadets were obligated to serve in federal or civilian hospitals until the end of the war. For the young women in the camps, the program offered the hope of a relatively rare opportunity for Japanese American women to pursue a real career outside the home. For many, though, that dream was cut short when they found that accredited nursing programs more often than not refused, on the basis of their race, to admit Japanese American students.

As THE FLOTILLA of Liberty ships carrying the young men of the 442nd to war approached the Mediterranean, the weather warmed, but an icy chill settled over the previously festive boat carrying the 442nd's three chaplains. Chaplain Eugene West had been acting increasingly dour, and at a meeting with some of his fellow officers belowdecks one day he got embroiled in an argument about religion and race. Things got heated. "America is a Protestant nation, and the Catholics have spoiled it," he growled. Then, agitated, he turned to Masao Yamada and spat out, "The Americans of Japanese ancestry are in the war to better their own future. America is for Anglo-Saxons and it is best for the AJAs to return to Japan." Yamada, taken aback, said he would pray that West had a change of heart. But Nisei soldiers who overheard the remark quickly spread it through the ranks, and by the time the boat passed into the Mediterranean, West was a pariah—not a soul on board, including the white officers, would so much as speak to him or even acknowledge his presence when he entered a room. His days with the 442nd were numbered.

On May 28, the SS *Johns Hopkins*, carrying Kats Miho, George Oiye, Sus Ito, and other members of the 522nd Field Artillery Battalion, docked in the port of Brindisi on the heel of the Italian boot. From here, and from the port town of Bari up the coast, where the remainder of the 522nd landed, they would have to travel by rail in rickety cattle cars northwest across Italy to rendezvous with one another and the 442nd's infantry units, most of which were just then disembarking from their own Liberty ships in Naples. The ride was long, slow, and jolting. The cars smelled of manure. At times, it felt as if the wheels were square rather than round. But, despite the discomfort of it all, Kats was fascinated by his first glimpses of Europe. He tried to absorb it all: the groves of gray-green olive trees dotting the coastal plains, some of them centuries old, their trunks black and gnarled; occasional spring showers slanting down onto sepia-colored hills; stone-and-mortar houses seemingly piled one atop another in ancient villages perched on the higher hilltops; the sun breaking through, illuminating the villages, lighting up wet red-tile roofs, painting church steeples gold. At first glance, it was lovely and bewitching. It seemed hard to believe that this was a country at war.

But a few hours into the trip, the train stopped abruptly in one of the larger towns along the route. In this part of liberated Italy, the British controlled the railroads, and it was teatime. As Kats climbed down from his boxcar to stretch his legs and look around, he quickly discovered that Italian towns in the aftermath of Mussolini and the German occupation were far more attractive from a distance. As they had in the Middle Ages, householders dumped buckets of their waste from upstairs windows into open sewers that ran through the streets. Parts of the town had been crumpled by artillery fire, razed by tanks, and scarred by street fighting, the rubble now pushed into heaps by army bulldozers. Throngs of people—desperate old men and women and children—approached Kats from all directions, their hands outstretched, asking for food, for chocolate, for cigarettes, for help.

Often their clothes belied their situation. Men in expensive silk suits and women wearing fashionable shoes picked through piles of garbage, looking for anything edible and scrambling to pick up cigarette butts that GIs threw on the street. But the worst of it was the children. There seemed to be no end of them. They roamed the streets in small bands, and, unlike the adults, they were not at all well dressed. Some wore cast-off German army jackets; others wore moth-eaten woolen trousers. Most were barefoot or wore tattered shoes. When they saw Kats's American uniform, they ran up to him and clustered around him, their faces begrimed, their hair matted, their eyes hollow. They pleaded with him, calling him Joe, as they did every GI in Italy. He could not turn a street corner without encountering more of them—"Joe, Joe, Joe, cigarette? Cigarette? Chocolate? No chocolate? . . . *Signorina, signorina,* my sister, young, young." The sight of boys not a great deal younger than himself, apparently half starved, trying to sell their sisters, tore at Kats. He dug into his kit, pulled out his rations of chocolate and fig bars and cigarettes, and tossed them to the boys. But around the next corner there were always more: "Joe, Joe . . ."

ON MAY 25, a bright blue Italian morning, Fred Shiosaki approached Naples from the sea. Like Kats, he was impressed by his first view of Italy. The Bay of Naples was placid, the water a deep, vibrant aquamarine. As his Liberty ship approached the dock, scores of boys paddling small boats approached it, smiling, calling out welcomes, throwing blood oranges up to the Nisei soldiers, asking for cigarettes in exchange. With Mount Vesuvius looming just beyond it, venting white plumes of steam, the city seemed lovely to Fred, as if it had been whitewashed, its buildings gleaming in the morning sun.

As with Kats, though, Fred's first impression of Italy darkened as he crossed the city on a truck. Much of Naples's waterfront had been reduced to rubble. The exterior walls of once elegant, seaside apartment buildings had collapsed into the streets, revealing bedrooms and kitchens and sitting rooms, much of the furniture still more or less in place, crucifixes still hanging on walls, beds still made up. Here, too, packs of children swarmed the arriving Nisei troops, offering services or begging for favors. Young women called out, "Joe, wash? Laundry, Joe." Younger children called out, "Hey, Joe, gimme candy." One boy approached Chaplain Yamada, eyed him critically, assessing his considerable girth, and then said in broken English and with some venom in his voice, "Italy no bread, America has plenty of bread. You are fat around the waist."

The 442nd RCT bivouacked that afternoon near Bagnoli, on the far northwestern reaches of the bay, where they moved into large pyramidal tents set in orchards among fruit and olive trees. The Second Battalion had not yet arrived, but in the Third Battalion's sector the boys in K Company began unpacking their equipment. Fred joined in, breaking into shipping crates, wiping Cosmoline from the big Browning automatic rifles the boys called BARs, assembling heavy machine guns. Medics sat down and painted white circles with red crosses on their helmets. Mechanics in the motor pool welded upright steel bars to the fronts of jeeps. Word was that the Germans were stringing piano wire across narrow Italian roads in order to decapitate unwary American jeep drivers and their passengers. That was the kind of thing that worked on your mind when you crawled into your tent at the end of the day. Almost everyone in the regiment was excited to be there. Almost everyone was raring to go, to take it to the Germans. But invisible wire, stretched across a road. A head suddenly lying by a roadside. It didn't matter how tough you were. The thought of it, the image it brought to mind, just made your stomach tighten up.

The weather was warm, verging on hot. The orchards were dry, and a fine film of dust clung perpetually to everything and everybody. For young Japanese American men from Hawai'i, used to regular baths in their *ofuros*, the dust was a constant irritant until Kats stumbled across a hot sulfur spring that had been used since ancient times for bathing. Soon they were enjoying long, luxurious soaks, Japanese style.

Chaplains Yamada and Higuchi ventured back into Naples and saw for the first time how utterly capricious war can be. They found lovely neighborhoods left largely untouched by the shelling and bombing. Here, stately pastel-colored homes, with ironwork balconies and tall, narrow windows bordered by forest-green shutters, stood behind arbors draped in fluorescent pink and orange bougainvillea. Expansive lawns, beds of blooming roses, and rows of date palms graced verdant parks. But no children played in the parks, no dogs romped, no parents pushed baby buggies, no old men sat on the benches idly reading newspapers. Instead, civilians peeked out from behind the shutters of nearby houses, watching the soldiers pass, some wondering how it could be that their allies, the Japanese, had invaded Italy wearing American uniforms.

Mostly, though, Naples was devastated and desperate. When they returned to their bivouacs at night, the soldiers who had ventured into town were dusted with DDT to kill the lice that afflicted nearly everyone in the city. And as they sat eating their evening chow, long lines of gaunt civilians—men, women, and children, many wearing oversized, cast-off Italian and German military coats or jackets—stood quietly in the background, holding buckets, waiting quietly and somberly for scraps.

A FEW DAYS LATER, on June 6, Fred Shiosaki found himself on his back in a flat-bottomed landing craft, staring up at a pale blue sky, vomiting again, as the boat rolled through undulating seas, heading north from Naples, hugging the Italian coastline. Nearly everyone in the boat was sick, as were many of the boys in a flotilla of similar landing craft bobbing all around Fred's. Miserable as he was, Fred took a quiet, grim satisfaction in watching one of the other fellows retch, one of K Company's cooks. On the long ride over from Hampton Roads, as Fred had lain moaning in his bunk on the Liberty ship during the first few days at sea, the cook—an open-sea fisherman in Los Angeles—had made fun of him, boasting endlessly about what a terrific seaman he was, how he had taken many Hollywood celebrities out fishing around Catalina Island, and how sick they had always gotten. Now he was the sickest of the lot, and that suited Fred just fine. He didn't much care for braggarts.

SINCE ANTIQUITY, when the area had been called Antium, Anzio and the adjoining town of Nettuno had been seaside resorts for well-heeled Romans. One of Rome's most infamous emperors, Nero, was born there. Relishing its cool sea air and its abundance of good seafood, he later built a sprawling, imperial villa on the beach—a terraced palace so opulent that succeeding emperors continued to occupy it for a century, up to the time of Hadrian. Much more recently—in the nineteenth and twentieth centuries—the area had remained popular with modern Romans, who motored down from the Eternal City to enjoy the area's posh hotels, pleasant beaches, and seafood, still excellent almost two thousand years after Nero's demise.

But there was nothing pleasant about the place when Fred Shiosaki—after twenty-four hours in the lurching boat—arrived at the Allied beachhead there. Devastated first by Allied and then by German artillery barrages and bombing raids, Anzio looked like something from World War I—a hellish landscape of rubble, extensive networks of trenches, dugouts, barbed wire, and improvised fortifications built by the 150,000 Allied troops that had stormed ashore since January under almost continual German fire. Led in part by the 442nd's "big brothers" in the 100th Infantry Battalion, the Allies had finally broken out of the beachhead just a few days before Fred's arrival. Pouring northward, they had quickly advanced on Rome as German troops retreated, streaming through the city, stealing cars, hobbling on foot, commandeering ambulances, riding motorbikes, driving horse-drawn carts, ignoring the pleas of desperate fascist Blackshirts trying to hitch rides. On June 4, Allied troops had crossed the city limits. By that evening, thousands of Romans had rushed into the streets to greet American troops entering

the city center, embracing them, offering them wine, kissing their recent enemies on both cheeks.

Now Fred, still weak in the knees from seasickness, walked down the
ramp from his landing craft. He glanced warily around him, hoisted his
gear, and began marching with the rest of K Company through the
shattered remains of Anzio's waterfront. They trudged past burned-out
tanks and half-tracks. Twisted steel girders lay in streets pockmarked
with craters and lined with uprooted palm trees. They passed the
splayed-out skeletons of horses and cows killed by the shelling. On the
outskirts of town, they trudged through open fields in which the Allies
had constructed enormous ammunition dumps surrounded by earthen
berms. They passed sprawling American and British tent hospitals with
underground operating theaters staffed by hundreds of army doctors
and nurses, "the Angels of Anzio," as the GIs called them.

Marching up gradually rising ground for five miles, K Company finally came to their assigned bivouac area on a grassy, wildflower-strewn
hillside east of Anzio. Exhausted, out of shape after nearly a month on
the Liberty ships, they threw down their gear in a weedy field, sat on the
ground, and began picking through their K ration boxes, trying to find
something palatable to serve as lunch. Hiking in, some of them had
bartered with locals, exchanging cigarettes for bunches of sweet, white
onions, baby carrots, and bags of string beans, so now they fired up little
Coleman stoves and cooked the vegetables to supplement their rations.
As they sat in the afternoon sun eating—surrounded by pale purple
rock roses, yellow lupine, and crimson poppies—looking out over Anzio
and the turquoise sea beyond, news began to filter through their ranks.
Word was that American tanks were now rolling through the streets
of Rome. Then still better news. Even as they had been boarding their
landing craft the previous morning, tens of thousands of young men like
them had been pouring off similar craft, plunging into the cold Atlantic, wading ashore into gales of machine-gun and artillery fire, storm-
ing the beaches of France in a place called Normandy. Neither piece of
news was entirely surprising or unanticipated; both had seemed inevi-

table for some days now. But hearing it gave them heart. Maybe this thing they were about to become part of would be short, glorious, and relatively easy.

In another field nearby, Kats was chatting with George Oiye and Sus Ito when one of their officers hustled up to them and told them to begin digging foxholes. Before long it became apparent why. Although the Germans were retreating north, they still apparently had some very big guns within range of Anzio. Shells suddenly came screaming and rattling over their heads. To Kats, they sounded enormous, like washing machines hurtling through the sky. His stomach tightened. He dove for his foxhole. They all did. But the shells weren't intended for them. They sailed over their heads and detonated far downslope, down by the waterfront, near the ammunition dumps. The barrage was short lived, but when it was over and Kats climbed out of his foxhole, he noticed he'd suddenly gone weak in the knees. The boys dusted themselves off and laughed about it. It was frightening, but at least now they'd been under fire—sort of. They went back to digging their foxholes, a little deeper now. One of the Buddhaheads called out. "Hey! I dug so deep I can hear Hawaiian music."

Just as twilight faded and a full moon rose above the dark hills behind the 442nd's bivouac area, the black forms of German bombers appeared overhead. Since the beginning of the Allied landing at Anzio, the Luftwaffe had periodically raided the beachhead at night. Now they came one last time, determined to destroy the massive ammunition dumps near the beach. As the Nisei soldiers again hunkered down in foxholes and slit trenches, antiaircraft guns around Anzio roared to life, belching flame. Searing red tracer rounds arced across the sky. Ack-ack shells burst overhead, bright flashes of white followed by black smoke drifting in the moonlight. The earth in which the boys were sheltering trembled with the concussions of German bombs hitting the ground. The night air rumbled. Occasionally there was a deeper roar and more violent trembling as a tower of flame and smoke rose from some part of the ammo dumps that had been hit.

When they realized that they were again not the real target, the boys peered over the edge of their burrows, mesmerized by the display, scared but exhilarated, equally and simultaneously. As the German planes finally peeled off and disappeared over the horizon and the ground fire died down, the moon rose higher over Anzio and they crawled out of their foxholes again, talking excitedly, their hearts thumping.

By the next afternoon, after making their way through a massive traffic jam of Allied military vehicles in Rome, they arrived at a new bivouac area in fields just northwest of the coastal town of Civitavecchia. And there they came across some old friends. For the Buddhaheads in particular, it was a joyous thing to meet up with the 100th Infantry Battalion. As they piled out of the backs of trucks, boys from the islands rushed to find friends they had grown up with. They sat in circles on the grass swapping news, talking story, showing one another photographs and letters from home. But it didn't take long for the 442nd boys to see that these weren't the same guys they had known back home, nor were they the swaggering recruits with whom they had been briefly reunited at Shelby. These guys had survived Monte Cassino and more, and it had taken a toll on them. Sometimes they just shut down suddenly in the middle of a conversation. Sometimes they looked right through you or stared off into space or got up and walked away while you were talking to them. They weren't unfriendly, but you could see at a glance that there was something new in them—something hard, something secret—and that they preferred to keep it that way.

The next day, the 100th was formally attached to the 442nd Regimental Combat Team. Ordinarily, they would have been re-designated as the 442nd's First Battalion, but in recognition of their extraordinary valor in southern Italy they were allowed to keep their original designation—the 100th Infantry Battalion (Separate). A few days later, the Second Battalion finally arrived and joined the rest of the regiment. Now, finally, the Nisei soldiers of the entire 442nd Regimental Combat Team were all together, a single all–Japanese American fighting force.

. . .

OVER THE NEXT TWO WEEKS, attached to the Fifth Army's Thirty-fourth Division, they moved north by truck again, pushing into western Tuscany, encamping first near the old walled city of Grosseto and then at Gavorrano. With each move north, their living conditions grew more spartan. There were no big pyramidal tents now, no tents of any kind. As they approached the front lines, they slept in the hay in barns, under grape arbors, or in foxholes out in the open under the Tuscan stars.

The civilians they encountered were, if anything, even poorer and more desperate here than those in Naples and Anzio. The faces of some were blackened with soot from living in caves, cooking over charcoal fires, eating whatever they could scavenge. And yet, as they passed some farmhouses—those that were still intact—old men and women ventured cautiously out to greet them. They had no food to share, but they almost always had wine, and they offered it freely. The boys were hot and thirsty, so they happily drank from bottles handed to them, then poured more into their canteens and kept marching. A captain in L Company purchased an entire wooden cask of wine to share with his men that night, "to ease their anxiety," he said. Sus Ito, traveling with the infantry to serve as a forward observer for the 522nd, soon found himself wobbling along a country lane surprisingly happy and, for the first time in his life, decidedly drunk.

The terrain before them began to change, the open coastal plain on which they had been traveling giving way first to rolling brown hills and then to forested ridgelines rising up toward mountains still farther on. In the distance, artillery rumbled. They passed long cypress-lined drives, at the ends of which stood red-roofed villas, many gutted by flames, some still smoldering. Then they began to see something most of them had never seen before—corpses, dead German soldiers, sprawled in fields or lying bootless in roadside ditches in the sun, their gray-uniformed bodies swollen by the mounting summer heat, flies crawling over their chalky-

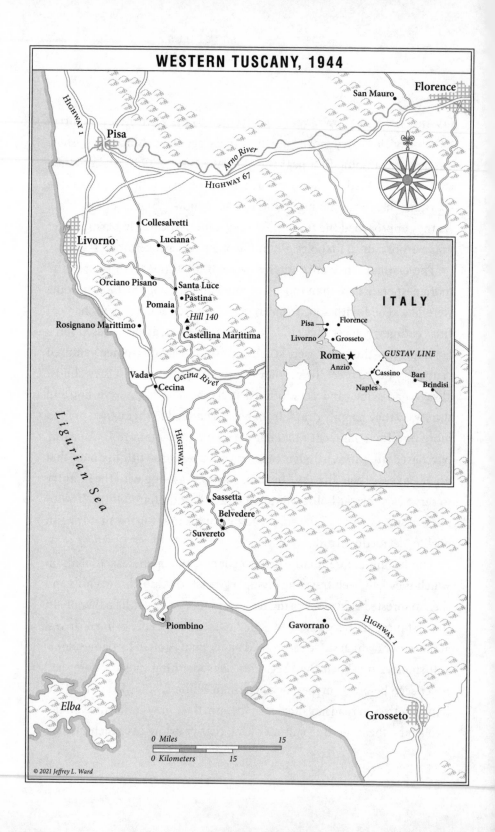

WESTERN TUSCANY, 1944

Florence

San Mauro

HIGHWAY 1

Pisa

Arno River

HIGHWAY 67

Collesalvetti

Livorno

Luciana

Orciano Pisano

Santa Luce

Pastina

Pomaia

Hill 140

Rosignano Marittimo

Castellina Marittima

Vada

Cecina River

Cecina

Liguria n Sea

HIGHWAY 1

ITALY

Pisa — Florence

Livorno — Grosseto

Rome ★

GUSTAV LINE

Anzio

Cassino

Bari

Naples

Brindisi

Sassetta

Belvedere

Suvereto

Piombino

Gavorrano

HIGHWAY 1

Elba

Grosseto

0 Miles   15

0 Kilometers   15

© 2021 Jeffrey L. Ward

white upturned faces. It stopped the 442nd boys short. As they rode past in their trucks, they stared silently at the corpses. But as they rolled on, Kats observed that the 100th guys didn't even seem to notice.

On June 25, they clambered out of their trucks and marched fifteen miles up narrow winding roads into the hills, closing in on the front lines. Artillery shells regularly whistled over their heads now, fired from somewhere in their rear, their divisional artillery trying to soften up whatever it was that lay in the hills just ahead of them. When they encamped that night, Chaplains Yamada and Higuchi gathered as many of their young men as they could together, and they formed circles and knelt in the dirt and prayed. Whether they were religious or not, whether they were Buddhist or Christian or Shinto or none of the above, whether they had ever prayed in their lives, they prayed now as the earth trembled and flashes of light lit up in the hills ahead. In the morning they were to attack.

Few of them slept that night, despite the long hike. Mostly, they lay on the cold ground, looking up into the stars and wondering what it would be like. But the wondering was fruitless. They couldn't really know. They couldn't know that they were about to see things and do things that would change them utterly, things they would regret, things that would sear their souls, and things they would cherish beyond all reckoning. They couldn't yet understand that they were about to step off the edge of the world.

FOURTEEN

It's not a pretty picture to see young kids who have not seen or begun to live life, all shot up or torn up by shrapnel, laying there, never to speak or laugh again. I only wish I could get those bigots, those hate mongers, those super patriots here to see them. Here in the front we're respected as fellow AMERICANS fighting for the same cause. We're proud as hell to be in there pitching, doing our share of the work.

HARRY MADOKORO, WRITING TO HIS
MOTHER AT POSTON
JULY 25, 1944

At 6:22 on the morning of June 26, just as the sun rose over western Tuscany, Cannoneer Roy Fujii in the 522nd's B Battery picked up a shell and tried to load it into the breech of the battery's number two gun, *Kuuipo*. Kats Miho crouched nearby, his fingers in his ears, just having set the deflection for what was about to be the 522nd's first shot of the war. Their target was a formation of German vehicles about to get under way perhaps two miles to the south of them. But as Roy shoved the shell into the breech, it jammed. He wrestled with the thirty-pound shell for a few moments. Swore at it. Wrestled with it some more. But with the enemy vehicles liable to move at any moment, there was no time to fool around. Roy picked up a sledgehammer, and—disregarding the distinct possibility that he would detonate the thing and kill them all—he frantically pounded on the shell until it finally popped into the breech. One of the other men pulled the lanyard, the shot was off, and the 442nd RCT was finally at war.

A LITTLE TO THE NORTH, Rudy Tokiwa and Fred Shiosaki had just crossed the line of departure on foot with K Company. The sky was beginning to lighten over the mountains to the east. Rudy was carrying his M1 rifle. Fred was lugging a mortar tube and carrying a lightweight carbine slung over his shoulder. Harry Madokoro and some of the other K Company guys near him were carrying the bigger, heavier BARs.

They spread out, walking ten feet apart through fields and olive groves on both sides of a narrow, winding road leading north. They weren't quite sure where they were going except that it was somewhere in the hills ahead of them and that they should expect to run into German resistance by mid-morning. The air was warm, dry, and dusty. The olive groves were full of rocks. From time to time one of the boys tripped, fell, cursed quietly, got up, and kept going. Enormous gray-white Chianina cattle—the largest breed in the world—stood in a field, silent and weirdly ghostlike, staring back at them as they passed in the thin morning light. Now and then there was the sharp, splitting sound of a cock crowing from the backyard of a villa or the soft, lilting cooing of wood pigeons hidden in dark copses of cork oaks. Occasionally, a cuckoo called from somewhere out in the bushes, sounding just like a cuckoo clock Fred remembered from back home. But mostly the world was silent and still except for the shuffling of their boots, the clanking of the gear they were carrying. It was silent enough that Fred could hear his pulse in his ears and still enough that he could feel his heart in his chest.

As they walked, Fred found to his surprise that he was not particularly afraid. More eager than afraid anyway. Anxious for it to start, if for no other reason than to know for sure that he wouldn't run when it did. Like the other boys in the company he felt reassured, to some extent, by the fact that their old training officer from Shelby, Captain Walter Lesinski, the one who had put a bayonet through his foot and then hobbled away without another word, was leading the company this morning. He was, by any measure, the toughest soldier any of them had ever met.

Directly ahead of them lay the town of Suvereto, one of those ancient Tuscan settlements that went back to Etruscan days, before emperors ruled these hills from Rome, though its architecture was more modern, which is to say medieval, roughly a thousand years old. The town—an attractive jumble of sepia-toned buildings and red-tile roofs—sat on a low rise looking out across the flat fields and orchards that the boys were making their way through. Beyond the town rose steeper hills clad in olive groves and vineyards on the lower slopes and mixed deciduous forests higher up. And at the summit of those hills was a tiny hamlet called Belvedere that the Germans were using as an observation post from which to direct artillery fire on a large swath of countryside below. It was those hills, and that small hamlet, more than the town of Suvereto itself, that the 442nd's commanders had their sights set on that day. If they could take it, they could clear the way for the Fifth Army to move men and supplies farther north through this sector of Italy. To accomplish that, though, they would have to take Suvereto first.

K Company's immediate mission—the mission of the entire Third Battalion—was to make a frontal attack on the town, clear it of the enemy, and then advance up into the hills. Somewhere off to their right, the Second Battalion was approaching the town from a slightly different angle with the same mission. For now, the 442nd's commanders had held the veteran 100th back in reserve. It was going to be up to the new guys, the 442nd, to pull this operation off.

As they neared the outskirts of Suvereto, Captain Lesinski called for a pause. Realizing that they'd crossed the same stream three times, he wasn't sure exactly where they were now in relation to the rest of the battalion. To compound things, the radioman, Calvin Saito, wasn't able to get through to the battalion's command post in the rear. As the rest of them crouched in place, Lesinski pulled out a set of Italian road maps—the only maps planners had managed to procure for the assault—and studied them. Still confused, he sent scouts forward. Cautiously creeping out ahead of the line, walking hunched over in drainage ditches alongside the road, the scouts moved up, trying to stay out of sight while reconnoitering the terrain ahead of them.

Back at regimental headquarters, Colonel Pence and Major General Charles Ryder were becoming increasingly concerned that they were unable to get in touch with some of the companies in both the Second and Third Battalions. They weren't entirely sure where some of them were, and other than what they could glean from the same Italian road maps Lesinski had, they didn't have a good sense of the terrain around Suvereto. Finally, trying to figure it out, they set out themselves in a jeep and an armored car to reconnoiter and better understand the disposition of their own and the enemy troops around the town.

And then everything went horribly wrong.

BY THE TIME the sun was well up, the morning had blossomed into a lovely, bright early summer day, the kind of day when you could see for miles if you had a good vantage point. And that's exactly what the Germans in the hills to the north and east had. All morning they had been patiently waiting and watching as the Nisei advanced on Suvereto. Now, as both battalions moved across the low, rolling hills below town, the Germans suddenly unleashed a torrent of shrieking steel.

The worst of it fell first on F Company over in the Second Battalion, off to the right of where K Company was advancing. F Company had gotten itself out ahead of the line and quickly been cut off. Mortar shells began to land among them with devastating effect, blowing men off their feet. Then Tiger tanks mounted with 88-millimeter guns rolled out from the cover of nearby woods and began to fire on them, more or less at point-blank range. The 88s—a particularly terrifying weapon—

were originally designed as antiaircraft guns, but the Germans had re-sorted to using them as antitank and antipersonnel weapons. With a muzzle velocity comparable to that of a rifle, the shells they fired—ripping across the terrain at half a mile per second, often just a few feet off the ground, like a bullet with an almost perfectly flat trajectory—produced an unearthly and unnerving screeching sound. You were lucky if you heard them at all, though. They came at you so fast that you never had a chance to hear the one that was going to kill you.

Lying prone on the ground, clutching their helmets to their heads, those F Company men who were still able to do so scrambled and crawled desperately for cover—any kind of cover they could find—a tree, a ditch, a stone wall, a ripple in the landscape. Each time another shell hit, dirt and fragments of rock sprayed over them. In the midst of the chaos, one young man stood up and moved forward. Twenty-two-year-old Private Kiyoshi Muranaga, although not a mortarman, dropped his rifle, shoved some mortar shells into his pack, grabbed a mortar tube, and scrambled to a position out in the middle of a field. From there he had a clear line of sight on one of the tanks mounted with an 88, and he began lobbing mortar shells at it. His third shot landed directly in front of the tank, but just slightly short. Before he could adjust the range and get off another shot, the German tank crew zeroed in on his position, fired, and killed him instantly. But then, apparently rattled by the mortar fire, they withdrew into the woods, and Muranaga's squad was finally able to scramble to safer ground.

In the confusion, three of the F Company boys had gotten cut off from the rest of the company. Huddled in a slit trench, they heard German voices nearby. When two Germans approached the trench, one of the boys abruptly stood up clutching a hand grenade in one hand, grabbed the safety pin with the other hand as if to pull it, and ordered the Germans to surrender. The Germans threw down their guns just as another barrage came hurtling in. All five men—Germans and Nisei alike—dove into the trench and huddled there together as the earth around them quaked. When it was over, there was a moment of awkward comradeship in having survived the barrage. But it didn't last long. Desperately thirsty, the Nisei snatched their German prisoners' canteens from them and eagerly guzzled their water.

By now K Company was also in trouble. Lesinski was still not quite sure where they were, but judging by the rattle of machine-gun fire to his rear, it was clear that they had gotten too far ahead of the rest of the Third Battalion. Out of position, caught on an exposed hillside, they began to come under direct fire from heavy machine guns on gradually rising ground immediately in front of them as well as from artillery pieces higher up in the hills beyond. They flung themselves on the ground and tried to dig in, frantically scraping the rocky, sunbaked earth with field shovels, bayonets, and even helmets.

Lying on his belly in a scraped-out depression, Fred Shiosaki watched in momentary confusion as a shower of leaves and twigs drifted down from an olive tree above him, then realized that the tree was being shredded by machine-gun fire ripping in just a few feet over his head. More shells came whistling in, each starting with a distant, whispering whine, then growing louder and louder until it was shrieking, sounding to Fred as if it were heading straight for the hole he was in. One hit somewhere nearby with a roar. The ground shook and plumes of dirt and stone and steel erupted from the earth. A shock wave pulsed through the air, and for a split second it pushed his eardrums in sharply, painfully.

A few soldiers broke and ran rearward, seeking better cover. One kid didn't stop running until he reached the battalion's command post in the rear, where Chaplain Yamada found him shaking uncontrollably, unable to speak. Yamada gave him some water, got him calm enough to talk, and sent him back toward the front. But the young man's sudden appearance at the command post alarmed everyone there. By now, communications with many of the units in the field had entirely broken down. Incoming shells were severing telephone wires the Nisei scouts had laid down as they advanced. To compound the problem, the hilly terrain was interfering with radio and walkie-talkie communications.

The officers directing the operation had a general sense of how the two battalions were deployed in relation to each other but still had little information on where specific companies were or what precisely they were encountering. Clearly, though, the assault was not going as planned, and a sense of unease was threatening to turn into a sense of panic.

At this juncture, General Ryder and Colonel Pence suddenly reappeared at the regimental command post, traveling on foot. Half an hour earlier, while reconnoitering in advance of the line, they had come under fire from one of the German 88s. Both officers had had to abandon their vehicles and flee under heavy covering fire from their entourage. By the time they arrived back at the command post, Ryder had lost his helmet and he was furious, decidedly unhappy with the 442nd's performance so far. With two entire battalions attacking Suvereto, the Nisei soldiers should have been working their way through the town and advancing into the hills beyond by now. Ryder and Pence hunched over maps again, trying to figure out what the hell was going on and what to do about it.

By late morning both battalions had been pinned down for hours, steadily taking casualties, unable either to advance on the town or to retreat to safer ground. The bulk of the Second Battalion was now perhaps half a mile east of the Third, but with smoke and dust from the relentless barrages of incoming artillery drifting across the battlefield, neither unit was able to maintain visual contact with the other. Some of the men had been trapped in their foxholes so long that they had to urinate in place, lying down, soaking their clothes. One soldier urinated into an unused condom he was carrying, filling it like a water balloon and tying the top closed. But as he tried to chuck it over the edge of his foxhole, it snagged on a root, burst open, and soaked him as well.

Still on his belly in his own hastily scratched-out foxhole, waiting for orders to advance or retreat amid the screaming and crashing of incoming shells, Fred Shiosaki focused for now on fighting fear rather than Germans. He clung desperately to the one thing he knew for sure: he couldn't afford to be scared. Scared would just get in the way of staying alive. But there was another thought that kept coming to him as well. It seemed to help, so he shifted his focus and locked onto it, trying to keep it at the front of his mind even as the shells kept falling around him, muttering it softly to himself, breathing it into the rocky ground: "I'm going to beat the shit out of these guys."

As the barrages continued, awareness of something else slowly washed over Fred. All the shells were flying in one direction—toward him. Nothing seemed to be heading toward the Germans. Where the hell was their artillery? Where was the 522nd? Why weren't they firing back, taking out some of the damned guns up in the hills?

IN FACT, all three batteries of the 522nd were sitting some miles away in their 6x6 trucks, slowly wending their way up narrow country roads, hauling their guns behind them, largely unaware of the disaster unfolding at Suvereto.

It wasn't really their fault. After firing their first shots at the concentration of German vehicles in the area of Grosseto, they'd been ordered to move north to take up positions closer to Suvereto, where they would be better able to support the beleaguered infantry. While they were on the road, the Thirty-fourth divisional artillery was supposed to fill in for them. But word of that hadn't gotten through to the division headquarters. It was just one part of a much broader breakdown of communications that morning, but it meant the infantry guys pinned down out in the fields were on their own for now.

WITH HIS MEN still dug in and taking heavy fire on the exposed hillside below Suvereto, K Company's Walter Lesinski was furious. Nobody seemed to know what the hell they were supposed to be doing, and he still wasn't getting any direction from the battalion's commanders. He scrambled over to where Rudy Tokiwa was hunkered in a foxhole. In addition to being a rifleman, Rudy was one of the Third Battalion's runners. As such, his principal job was to carry messages between head-quarters and company commanders out in the field when they couldn't be sent over the radio or field telephones. It was a notoriously dangerous job because it meant traveling across active battlefields, out in the open, often for miles at a time, without the protection of covering fire or support of any kind. In many ways it was the perfect job for Rudy. He was small, lithe, and athletic. Generally fearless, he liked to do things his own way and had a particular talent for being sneaky. It also helped that he had an ironclad memory. Part of a runner's job was to memorize—word for word—whatever message he had to deliver, to prevent written orders from falling into enemy hands if he were captured.

Now Lesinski bellowed at him over the din of the battle, "Go back to battalion and get us some help." Rudy took off at a lope, crouching as he ran, dodging shells, heading back downhill. For the next half hour, he traveled as inconspicuously as he could, moving across open fields when necessary but trying to stay in the brush or under the cover of trees as much as possible. Every now and then he had to dive into a ditch along-side the road as a shell came screaming in. Bursts of machine-gun fire rattled across fields nearby. From somewhere in an olive grove off to the left of him as he ran, someone screamed out in pain, a guttural sound so primal there was no way to tell if it was a German or an American scream. He couldn't stop to investigate at any rate. He had to keep going. Then he came around a bend in the road and froze in his tracks. In a split second he apprehended that he had to make a quick and conse-quential decision. A squad of 442nd guys was hustling up the road toward him. But between them and Rudy a single German soldier was kneeling behind a curved stone wall, holding a submachine gun, wait-ing to ambush the Nisei when they got close enough. Rudy hesitated, but only for a moment. The German's back was to him, but it had to be done. He took careful aim with the carbine and squeezed off a single shot. The man sagged to the ground.

Wanting to make sure he was dead, Rudy, his heart pounding, ap-proached him cautiously and turned the body over. It was the first time he'd looked a dead man in the face. The man's blue eyes were open, staring back at him blankly. Rudy averted his gaze, refocusing on the bloodied front of the gray uniform. Then he made a mistake. He pulled the soldier's wallet out of his coat pocket and rifled through it. Inside were three photographs—a little boy and two little girls. The children's ages appeared to range from about two to seven. Looking into their eyes, seeing the smiles they put on for the camera, Rudy felt his stomach lurch. It wasn't just a soldier he'd killed; it was a father. Back in basic training, they had told him never to go through the personal effects of enemy dead. Now he knew why. And it shook him. In the days and weeks ahead, he would kill other men. For the most part he would take little note of who they were, what they looked like. A hardness would grow in him, as it would grow in all of them. But this one was the one he would never be able to put out of his mind.

As Rudy resumed jogging downhill and finally drew near the Third Battalion's command post, an officer—none other than Major Emmet O'Connor, executive officer of the entire battalion—saw him approaching and began yelling at him. Then suddenly he raised an M1 and started firing over Rudy's head. Rudy dove for the ground. He realized the major was calling out for him to give the password of the day. For the life of him, Rudy couldn't remember the password, so he began calling out, "*Yon yon ni, yon yon ni*"—the numbers "442" in Japanese. The men had been using it as a kind of default password for weeks. But O'Connor had no idea what the words meant. He kept demanding the password and popping off rounds. Finally, Rudy rose to one knee, fired a single round of his own over O'Connor's head, and shouted, "You know, the next one could be right through you!" Finally O'Connor, realizing that Rudy was an American, lowered his rifle and motioned him to come forward.

But when Rudy delivered Captain Lesinski's message to O'Connor, he got a response that he didn't like at all: "Well, you go back and you tell your K Company captain that he's gotta get out of it himself." Rudy stared hard at him for a moment, then wheeled around and started jogging back toward the battlefield, trying to figure out how exactly he was going to break the news to Lesinski.

BY NOON, Colonel Pence, General Ryder, and Lieutenant Colonel Gordon Singles, commander of the 100th, had gathered enough information from runners like Rudy to come up with a plan. From what they could derive from the field reports and what maps they had, there appeared to be a gap between the Third Battalion, pinned down in wheat fields on the left, and the Second Battalion, pinned down in olive groves on the right. The gap was just a rocky slope covered with more olive trees and grapevines, perhaps two hundred yards wide, but it presented a possible path to the higher ground above Suvereto. Perhaps they could pull off the military equivalent of a quarterback sneak. They decided to bring some of the more experienced 100th men up to the line and send them through the gap as quickly as possible while the Germans were preoccupied with the two battalions on either side.

Orders went out, and within an hour A and B Companies of the 100th were racing uphill through the gap and beginning to circle around behind the Germans. Cutting telephone lines the Germans had laid down, they climbed rapidly into the hills above and beyond Suvereto before the Germans understood what was happening. From the high ground they seized there, they could see the German forces concentrated in and around Belvedere. Capitalizing on the element of surprise, they attacked Belvedere immediately, some of them charging the Germans from their flanks, others driving directly into the village from the rear. Within another hour, they had silenced most of the German artillery, destroyed their observation posts, overrun Belvedere in house-to-house fighting, and sent the astonished Germans fleeing on the road to Sassetta, the next town to the north. But the Nisei had also anticipated that retreat and sent more men farther north and then swung them west to cut off the route of the withdrawing Germans.

The road to Sassetta was a narrow, sinuous, spaghetti-like strand of pavement snaking its way through heavy vegetation for five tedious, though beautiful, miles along the top of a ridge. To the boys from Maui, it looked for all the world like the Hāna Highway back home. Now they lay hidden in the dense foliage alongside it, clutching their guns, waiting for the fleeing Germans to rush into their trap.

WITH THE GERMANS' ARTILLERY silenced and their infantry retreating north in the hills above them, the Second and Third Battalions of the 442nd were finally able to crawl out of their foxholes and start advancing uphill again toward Suvereto. As Lesinski led the way, Fred, Rudy, and the rest of K Company managed to slip around to the flank of the German machine-gun nests on the hillside above them and unleash rifle and mortar fire into their positions, gradually driving them off the hillside. Then they resumed their frontal attack, finally surging into Suvereto itself. By mid-afternoon they had cleared the town and begun climbing into the hills beyond to rendezvous with the rest of their battalion and the 100th. As they advanced, they drove more Germans up the forested hills toward the jaws of the 100th and the trap that they had set for them up on the Sassetta road.

The first of the retreating Germans to approach the ambush point arrived in a convoy of seventeen jeeps. The Nisei soldiers crouching in the roadside bushes held their fire until all the jeeps were nearly abreast of them; then they opened up with all they had, unleashing thundering volleys of fire. It was more or less a massacre. The few Germans who survived the initial barrage ran helter-skelter into the brush. A few minutes later, heavy trucks appeared, rumbling down the road, their back ends loaded with more German troops. As their drivers realized they were driving into an ambush, they accelerated, swerving this way and that, desperately trying to navigate their way around the abandoned jeeps littering the roadway. The Nisei opened fire again. Men in gray uniforms tumbled from the backs of trucks and tried to run or crawl away. And again, it was more or less a massacre.

By nightfall, the fighting had mostly died down, and the Nisei sat astride and firmly in control of the road and the ridge along which it ran, just south of Sassetta. What had started off as a massive American debacle had turned into a rout of veteran German troops.

But the 442nd's first day of combat had been brutal, their performance uneven. And they'd seen things they'd never dreamed of seeing. Rudy Tokiwa found a patch of ground to stretch out on and realized that though the evening had turned chilly, he was sweating. He felt sick. Sicker than he'd ever felt. A shaken Hiro Higuchi, after spending five hours squeezed into a small culvert as shells fell all around him, sat down and wrote to his wife about his first experience of war: "It's just hell—un-dreamable goriness and death. . . . The fear of those screaming, whining shells is indescribable and almost unbearable. . . . Someday I will tell you all about it, but now I don't want to think about it."

DAY ONE, though, turned out to be merely an overture for the 442nd.

That night, with almost no respite, Fred Shiosaki found himself on the move again, lugging his mortar up a steep mountain trail in the dark, hushed woods. Wanting to capitalize on the afternoon's momentum, Pence had sent the Third Battalion on a nighttime flanking move, swinging them west in a wide loop around Sassetta to seize the high ground north of the town. The terrain was steep, crisscrossed with ravines, and thick with tangled vegetation. A little after midnight, a crescent moon set over the sea to the west, and the already dark woods grew even darker. It was hard for Fred to see more than a few feet in any direction. All around him, men were grunting and panting but saying nothing, trying to maintain some degree of stealth.

Then a terrifying sound—deep, loud growling, coming at them out of the dark, in fits and starts, from multiple directions all at once. Fred knew immediately what it was. He had heard it described, though he had not experienced it himself. It was the sound of what GIs called

Hitler's buzz saw—the Germans' MG-42 machine guns. They belched fire at you in long ripping bursts, spitting out as many as 1,200 bullets per minute. Even the best American automatic weapons—Thompson submachine guns—fired at a much slower rate, their rounds rattling out of the barrel with discrete, individual sounds—*pop, pop, pop, pop, pop.* The MG-42 emitted a loud and continuous ripping sound and, Fred had heard, it could cut a man in half.

He dove for the ground. They all did. And now, as the guns again growled and belched fire at him, Fred was, for the first time, seriously and uncontrollably terrified. There was something so harrowing about the sound itself that it cut right through him. Somehow, it seemed more personal than the long-distance artillery barrages the day before. As he lay in the dark, his belly pressed to the rocks and twigs beneath him, it came to Fred for the first time with sudden crystal clarity that someone out there, some individual German soldier, wasn't just trying to win the war. He was actually trying to kill him, Private Fred Shiosaki of Hillyard, Washington, former vice president of the John R. Rogers High School photography club, sandlot baseball player, son of a laundryman, generally nice kid. And with equal clarity it came to Fred that if he was going to survive this thing, at some point he was most likely going to have kill someone himself.

Within a few minutes, the guns fell silent as the Nisei returned fire and the Germans they'd blundered into slipped away into the brush, wisely choosing not to take on an entire American battalion. Fred and the rest of K Company picked themselves up and resumed moving forward. The forest lightened as they climbed higher and the sun began to rise. By mid-morning, they had arrived at their objective for the day, a ridge overlooking Sassetta from the north. From here, Fred could make out German troops massed below him. Several Tiger tanks were rumbling through Sassetta's narrow streets, preparing to defend the southern entrance to the town. A mile or two farther south, out of sight, Fred knew, the 100th was also massing, getting ready to push their way up the road and directly into the village. If the Nisei soldiers could take Sassetta, the Allies would control four full miles of ridgeline overlooking the coastal plains and the roadways below.

The Germans appeared to be oblivious to the presence of the Third Battalion looming above their rear, looking over their shoulders. Fred's squad leader, Harry Kanada, found a good spot with a clear line of fire and put Fred and the rest of his five-man squad to work setting up their mortars and stockpiling shells. Sus Ito, serving as a forward observer for the 522nd Field Artillery, peered through binoculars and began selecting the best targets from the rich array laid out below him. One by one, he transmitted the targets' precise locations to the Fire Direction Center in the rear. There, in an abandoned farmhouse, men with protractors and slide rules hunched over tables on which they had spread out maps and reference tables and made the complex calculations required to produce accurate firing instructions to kill Germans and not their own troops.

A mile or two away, hidden behind another hill, Kats Miho crouched next to *Kuuipo*, waiting to receive targeting instructions relayed from the Fire Direction Center. All three of the 522nd's batteries, each with four 105-millimeter howitzers, were now finally in position and ready to open fire when given the order.

Just before noon, a number of the 442nd's officers—among them K Company's captain, Walter Lesinski—gathered at a new regimental command post they had established in a house on the Sassetta road, three miles south of town, preparing to supervise the upcoming attack. Rudy Tokiwa was there, too, ready to carry messages forward onto the battlefield if necessary.

Firing artillery at targets positioned just in front of your own advancing infantry was a tricky business. It required great precision and rapid reactions to changing situations as the battlefield evolved. Where the enemy was five minutes before, your own guys might be now. But as the Germans were about to learn, nobody in the U.S. Fifth Army was better at dropping their shells where and when they wanted than the 522nd

Field Artillery Battalion. At Shelby they had earned outstanding marks for their speed, accuracy, and adaptability. Now they had their first chance to prove that they could do equally well under battle conditions. As the 100th crept closer to the town, the 522nd's howitzers opened up on the German defensive positions in and around Sassetta.

With target coordinates flooding in over a field phone, Kats and his crew on *Kuuipo* leaped into action. It took as many as six men, each with a specific job, to fire just one of the battery's guns with maximum coordination and efficiency. Over the roar of other guns being fired, one man called out the targeting instructions as he received them from the Fire Direction Center, another adjusted the elevation of the gun, another set the deflection, another loaded the correct number of powder bags, another slid the shell into the breech of the gun, and another pulled the lanyard to fire it. Each had to do his job rapidly and perfectly each and every time if the shell they were about to fire was going to kill Germans and not Americans. Kats's job as a corporal gunner was to set the deflection—how far to the right or to the left to move the barrel of the howitzer in response to the coordinates being called in.

Flint Yonashiro calling out coordinates

As the artillerymen of the 522nd unleashed their first barrages of fire, the 100th started moving more rapidly up the Suvereto-Sassetta road, traveling on foot, advancing in fits and starts at first, pausing between the incoming barrages, then swarming into town, firing M1s and BARs. At the same time, the Third Battalion swept down from the ridge above town, advancing behind a curtain of mortar fire laid down by Fred Shiosaki and other mortarmen. The attack was precise, well coordinated, and overwhelming. By mid-afternoon the Germans were again in retreat, this time on the road leading north out of town.

But they sent the 442nd a parting gift. The house in which the regiment had set up headquarters south of Sassetta was a distinctive place, sitting on a curve in the road with a wide-open area in front of it. It was the kind of place that German observers in the hills would have taken note of and set coordinates for well in advance of a battle, in case it became a promising target for their artillery.

Men and officers had been milling about in front of the building throughout the battle. Now with Sassetta taken, K Company was regrouping there. Fred Shiosaki was just approaching the place when a single German artillery shell came screaming in, scoring a direct hit on the house. Windows shattered, fire erupted from the roof, men in front of the building were blown off their feet. Wounded men came stumbling out of the house veiled in smoke and dust, coughing, their faces white with plaster, some of them covered in blood. A sixteen-year-old Italian girl ran into another nearby house, pulled down some curtains, and started ripping them up and bandaging wounded GIs. Fred was uninjured but stunned. As men ran in and out of the building someone yelled that K Company's lieutenant Howard Burt had been killed. But what shocked Fred most was when he saw Walter Lesinski emerge from the building. Two men were holding him up, one on either side. Lesinski appeared uninjured, but his face was utterly blank, his eyes lifeless. When the men holding him up let go of him and stepped away, his arms remained outstretched on either side, as if the men were still there. He seemed glued to the ground, unable to take a step on his own. Moments before, he had been talking to a first sergeant. When the shell hit, the man had simply been torn apart, dismembered in an instant—one moment a face, a pair of earnest eyes looking into his, a voice, a human being, the next moment just bits of a body torn asunder, scattered around in the rubble. In that instant, apparently, Lesinski had cracked.

Fred didn't hold it against him. None of the K Company men did. Most of them feared the same thing happening to them, almost more than they feared being killed. After just a day and a half in combat, they already knew how fragile their own hold on sanity had suddenly become. Almost all of them had already—just in that short time—seen someone they knew killed or maimed in front of them. Each of them had been devastated by it. Earlier in the day, when Kats Miho approached a burned-out German tank, he'd found the bodies of two Nisei men lying under blankets. From the looks of things, they'd attacked the tank boldly, running up to within a few meters of it and then firing a bazooka. But they'd approached too close. The resulting explosion had destroyed the tank but killed them both. When someone lifted one of the blankets, Kats's stomach lurched. One of the dead boys was Grover Nagaji, his dorm mate back at Atherton House. That was hard enough. But there was something else. Just a day or two earlier, Kats happened to know, Grover had received a "Dear John" letter from his girl back in Hawai'i.

Fred also got a punch in the gut that afternoon. Among the bodies being pulled from the rubble of the house was that of the boy with whom he had climbed onto a train and left Spokane to go to war, Gordon Yamaura. Gordon had been a connection with home, an occasional reminder that somewhere back in Spokane life was going on as normal; his parents were brewing tea, folding laundry, stoking the boilers. But now, for Fred, Gordon's pale, crumpled body, covered with white plaster and splotches of black blood, seemed somehow to call into question whether that other world even still existed.

. . .

WITH ONLY BRIEF RESPITES, the 442nd fought on almost continuously—day and night—for the last few days of June and into July. Along with other elements of the Fifth Army farther to the east, they crept north through western Tuscany, slogging along mile by mile, sometimes yard by yard, facing stiff resistance from well-dug-in Germans. From nearly every hilltop and village they approached, they drew more artillery barrages. On a map taken from a dead enemy soldier, they found that well in advance of their arrival the Germans had plotted out artillery coordinates for every crossroad, farmhouse, or ravine where the Nisei might conceivably want to congregate. With the Germans always on the high ground, no place was entirely safe, so the Nisei soldiers began to move forward mostly at night when the Germans couldn't see them as they waded through wheat fields and trudged through olive groves in the wide-open valleys between the hills. The nighttime advances, though, greatly increased the chances that they would blunder into minefields. When they could, they worked with Italian partisans who guided them around potential hazards.

As the terrain grew hillier still, they brought in pack mules to carry their supplies up the winding, dusty trails the partisans showed them. But they themselves had to scale the hills under their own power, climbing through dry forests of cork oaks and chestnut trees on slopes so steep they sometimes had to get down on all fours and crawl up, grabbing at roots and rocks. It was grueling even when someone wasn't shooting at them. But usually someone was, and so they continued to take tremendous casualties. By early July, nearly four hundred of the roughly four thousand Nisei troops who had arrived in Anzio in May had already been killed or wounded as they advanced through Tuscany, adding to the already disproportionate number of casualties the 100th had previously racked up in the invasion of southern Italy.

But every time one of them went down, the others learned something new about surviving. Never linger in a crossroad; German artillery will have it zeroed in. Never pause in the shade under a single tree in the middle of an open field, for the same reason. Never wander into the bushes to relieve yourself without checking for trip wires and booby traps. Never use a trench latrine left behind by the Germans. It, too, will likely be booby-trapped, as will tempting "souvenirs" left behind, like German helmets. And never, ever kick a can in the road. One thing the Germans had figured out about American boys was that if they came across a coffee can lying on the ground, they were almost always going to kick it down the road, just for fun. But as the 442nd boys soon discovered, in Italy it was likely to be sitting on a land mine.

Rudy had to be particularly wary. As a runner, he spent much of his time out on his own, moving from company to company, carrying messages to and from the front lines, hustling from place to place without the benefit of backup, a second set of eyes, or advance reconnaissance. It was stinking hot now, the Tuscan hills brown and parched, the rivers in the valleys between them reduced to pools of green scum set here and there among beds of white sunbaked stones. Heat waves shimmered over fields of ripening wheat and rye. Rudy was tired and dirty all the time. His feet ached. His face was unshaven and perpetually caked in sweat and dust. His uniform was already torn and ragged, and it stank. At night he sometimes had to crawl into culverts or bushes alongside some dried-up stream, alone and unfed, to try to get some sleep.

But because Rudy was Rudy, he also found opportunities wherever he went as he roamed across the Italian countryside. When moving through villages that had been cleared of Germans, he hopped fences from one backyard to the next rather than walking through town on the streets. The backyards were where the good stuff was—a head of cauliflower, a handful of green onions, a nice fat cabbage, a fistful of baby carrots, half a dozen eggs, or better yet the hen sitting on the eggs. When he could, he left the owner a bar of chocolate or a pack of cigarettes as payment for whatever he took. When he couldn't, he declared the booty the spoils of war, the chickens POWs. He shoved it all in his pack and kept moving. He foraged in the open countryside between villages, too. There he collected sweet, plump figs growing on feral trees in the woods and harvested watercress thriving on the margins of ponds. He came across rabbits, too, almost every time he went out on a mission, but he always passed them by. As a kid in Salinas, he had had a pet rabbit that followed him around the farm and snuggled with him at night as he slept. He couldn't bring himself to kill a rabbit.

Still, he seldom returned without a pack full of fresh food for his guys in K Company, and he made a lot of friends that way. The Buddhaheads were particularly grateful for the bounty Rudy dragged in. Sometimes they would just prepare *okazu*—little side dishes of vegetables to go with their K rations or C rations. But when they had enough to work with, they made chicken *hekka*, a sort of Hawaiian stew. Made properly, it would include cut-up chicken, ginger, shoyu, Maui onions, carrots, mushrooms, and maybe some watercress. Now, here in Tuscany, with battles raging around them night and day, they had to improvise. Crouching around campfires, small Coleman stoves, or cans of Sterno, using whatever metal vessels they could lay their hands on, even their helmets if necessary, they cooked *hekka*. Substituting bouillon cubes from their rations for shoyu and avoiding wild mushrooms for fear of

The men of C Battery approaching Rosignano Marittimo

eating something poisonous, they loaded the pot or helmet with shredded chicken, carrots, onions, green beans, peas, watercress—whatever vegetables they had—and set the concoction to simmer. And when they tasted it, spooning it from their stainless-steel mess kits—even as artillery boomed and machine guns rattled in the hills around them—they smiled, often for the first time in days, savoring the taste of home.

IN THE FIRST FEW DAYS of July, the 442nd crossed the Cecina River and advanced toward a defensive line the Germans had established roughly six miles to the north on high ground around and between two towns—Castellina Marittima in the east and Rosignano Marittimo in the west. Here they would meet the most ferocious German resistance they had yet encountered.

FIFTEEN

At 7:30 a.m. on the Fourth of July, as a Black American bugle corps struck up "The Star-Spangled Banner," a large American flag crept slowly up a flagstaff and unfurled over the Piazza Venezia in Rome, where Mussolini had declared war on France and Great Britain in 1940. The same flag had flown over the U.S. Capitol on December 11, 1941, the day on which Congress declared war on the Axis powers. As the ceremony in Rome concluded, Major General Henry Johnson proclaimed that in due time the flag would be removed so that it could later be flown over Berlin and Tokyo. A few hours later, precisely at noon, hundreds of American artillery guns all along the Normandy front each fired a single shot simultaneously at whatever German targets happened to be handy. A few minutes later, many of them fired more shells, these containing pamphlets informing the Germans that this was how Americans celebrated Independence Day and asking how they liked it.

The war was, by any measure, finally going well for the Allies that Independence Day. In France, despite horrendous weather and muddy roads, the United States was advancing east along a forty-mile-wide front, fighting their way off the Cherbourg Peninsula. The Soviet Red Army was rolling westward into Minsk, the last German-occupied city on Soviet soil, bringing the Soviets to within 140 miles of Poland. In the South Pacific, U.S. forces observed the holiday by bombing Japanese forces on Iwo Jima, sinking three destroyers, and occupying what little remained of Garapan, the capital of Saipan, the first Japanese town to fall to the Americans. In Italy, the young Nisei men of the 442nd laid wagers on when the war would be over. Some optimists said it would be by the end of the summer, some said Thanksgiving, a few pessimists said Christmas.

In the States, people celebrated the holiday quietly. The production of fireworks had been overtaken by war needs, and they had largely been banned throughout the country for the duration of the war at any rate, but around the country people celebrated in other ways. There were still parades on Main Street, picnics in parks, band concerts in gazebos, baseball games in sandlots, horse races and pie-eating contests at county fairs. In New York City, where temperatures were in the mid-eighties, 1.2 million people crowded the beaches at Coney Island and another 1.1 million lay on the sand at Rockaway, feasting on burgers and hot dogs and cotton candy and corn on the cob and guzzling untold gallons of Coca-Cola and lemonade.

Japanese American families incarcerated in the War Relocation Authority camps made an effort to celebrate the day as well. At Poston there were baseball games, swim meets, and diving competitions. More than two years after opening, the camp had more amenities than when the To-kiwa family had first arrived. Now, in observance of the holiday, the mess halls offered barbecued chicken, hot dogs, and—to replicate Hawaiian shave ice—snow cones. Camp administrators used the occasion to dedicate a new USO club for visiting Nisei servicemen. A special tea was served for the mothers and sisters of the boys in Italy. That evening, at Poston II camp's new amphitheater, the Cottonwood Bowl, there was a Hawaiian-themed talent show and a separate Japanese-language program for the Issei. At the high school, there was a dance to which Nisei servicemen on leave were admitted free. In a front-page editorial in the *Poston Chronicle*, under the image of an enormous American eagle, Poston's project director, Duncan Mills, wrote about the bravery of the Nisei boys fighting overseas and asked the camp's residents to contribute to the war effort: "They're coming home some day in the not too distant future. What can we tell them about OUR activities when they return?"

It was a nice holiday, and almost everyone at Poston enjoyed the break from the usual monotony of camp life. But two and a half years into the war, Poston was a deeply divided community, fractured over questions of loyalty and identity, conflicted over issues of duty and principle. On page 6 of that same Fourth of July issue of the *Poston Chronicle*, the editors published a bitter letter they had received from a Nisei soldier in Italy, furious after hearing about the refusal of some of the young men in camp to be inducted into the service: "The guys ought to get shot for refusing to show up." On the same page, the editors also printed the names of those who had refused to appear for induction and announced that if they were on the project's payroll, they would lose their jobs.

Tensions had been simmering inside Poston since the earliest days of the incarcerations, as they had at all the camps. Even before Rudy had left, in the fall of 1942, a general strike had paralyzed Poston's I camp for ten days when two men were arrested for assaulting a third who they felt had been sharing too much information with the camp's administrators. For a week, Nisei and Issei employees working for the WRA provided the camp with only the most essential services such as cooking and medical treatment. Some of the tension was generational—between Issei parents, on the one hand, who had lost their homes and businesses and whose attachments to Japan were still strong, and, on the other hand, their Nisei offspring, most of whom felt little attachment to Japan and simply wanted to be accepted as entirely American.

But there were schisms among the Nisei in the camps as well, or at least a wide divergence of attitudes and opinions.

Many Nisei believed ardently that the best course for all of them was just to remain quiet, placate the public and the authorities, put the best face possible on the situation, and embrace incarceration as their contribution to the war effort. This was particularly true for those who belonged to the Japanese American Citizens League, the JACL. The JACL had been formed in 1929 as a national organization devoted to fostering political awareness among American citizens of Japanese ancestry and to lobbying for laws favorable to their interests. At the outbreak of World War II, the organization undertook to actively improve the public image of the Nisei and cooperate with the FBI and other federal agencies to identify potentially "disloyal" Issei. In their publications and conversations, they tended to idealize camp life as normal, healthy, and even enjoyable. But others, at Poston as at other camps—particularly the Kibei, those Nisei who had lived and been educated partially in Japan—tended to harbor much more bitterness about the incarcerations and often agitated to resist the camp authorities and their rules.

It was the resumption of the draft, though, that continued to rip the camp communities apart. By late spring 1944, dozens of young Nisei men, just at Poston alone, had refused on principle to register with the Selective Service or, if registered, to report for induction so long as their families were incarcerated.* This put them at odds not only with the law but also with the families of boys who had enlisted and were by then fighting and dying in Italy. It also put them at odds, very conspicuously, with the JACL, which harshly criticized their actions. Many of the resisters were by now out of jail on bond and back in camp awaiting trial and eventual imprisonment, further heightening tensions. Meanwhile, the no-no boys, who had refused to answer "yes" and "yes" to questions

---

*Poston, in fact, would ultimately have the largest number of resisters among all ten WRA camps, more than a third of the total.

27 and 28 on the loyalty questionnaire, had been hauled off to the Tule Lake camp in Northern California, where they joined thousands of "disloyals" like themselves from other camps.

SINCE GORDON HIRABAYASHI'S PARENTS had been sent to Tule Lake in 1942, the camp had undergone massive changes. In late 1943, in the face of internal strife, food shortages, and harsh conditions, mass protests and strikes had broken out. Between November 1943 and January 1944 things had gotten so bad that the authorities had imposed martial law in the camp. Then, as they prepared to turn the camp into a segregation center to incarcerate those deemed disloyal, they had added extra barbed-wire fencing, expanded the number of guard towers from six to twenty-eight, and brought in a thousand military police equipped with armored cars to control the newcomers, who soon made up the bulk of the camp's population. Many of the families incarcerated there early had been transferred to other camps to make room for the new arrivals, but roughly 40 percent of the original population remained. Many of them, like many of those at Poston, did not necessarily agree with the stance the no-no boys had taken, and that further heightened tensions behind the barbed wire. By the spring of 1944 the Tule Lake camp had been transformed into, for all practical purposes, a military prison. Then, as the Liberty ships carrying the 442nd RCT neared Italy, there was a homicide at Tule Lake.

Shoichi James Okamoto was, by all accounts, an affable young man. He'd grown up in Garden Grove, California, playing football and helping out on his parents' farm. But his father—to whom he was deeply devoted—had died while incarcerated at the Heart Mountain camp in Wyoming, and the younger Okamoto was angry and sick of the whole thing. He'd decided he could not sign the loyalty oath. That had landed him at Tule Lake.

A little after 2:00 on the afternoon of May 24, 1944, Okamoto, carrying out his usual duties, drove his Dodge cargo truck up to Gate Four at

Tule Lake in order to deliver a load of lumber for a construction project. Riding with him was twenty-five-year-old Henry Shiohama. Both young men had passes authorizing them to enter and leave the camp in performance of their jobs.

A new military sentry—Private Bernard Goe—had just come on duty at Gate Four that morning, and he seemed to witnesses to be, for unknown reasons, in a foul mood. As Okamoto and Shiohama approached the gate in their truck, Goe raised his hand to stop the vehicle, approached the passenger side, and demanded to see the occupants' passes. Goe, apparently believing Okamoto was being impudent in the casual way he waved the pass, yelled at him, "Don't get fresh with me!" and walked around to the driver's side of the truck, cocking his gun as he went. He ordered Okamoto out of the truck and told Shiohama to get into the driver's seat and drive on. Shiohama shook his head and protested that he didn't have a driver's license. This apparently outraged Goe, who started cussing at both of them: "All you Japs and your WRA friends are trying to run the whole camp." Goe again told Okamoto to get out of the truck. Okamoto hesitated for a moment, then climbed down. Goe, cussing again, ordered him to walk to the rear of the truck, just outside the camp gate. As Okamoto started in that direction, he hesitated, apparently not wanting to step outside the boundaries of the camp. Goe clubbed him on his side with the butt of his rifle, and Okamoto fell backward, raising his left arm slightly to ward off another blow. But Goe didn't hit him again. Instead, he took a step back, leveled his rifle, and shot Okamoto point-blank in the stomach. As Okamoto crumpled to the ground groaning, Goe swung his rifle in the direction of some teenage boys standing nearby and yelled, "Get the hell out of here!" Okamoto died shortly after midnight in the camp hospital.

Goe was arrested and charged with manslaughter. Six weeks later, on July 6, at a military court-martial proceeding, a panel of eight officers—disregarding the testimony of more than a dozen Japanese American eyewitnesses—acquitted him.

. . .

THAT SAME DAY, Fred Shiosaki and Rudy Tokiwa were down on their bellies, crawling through a hellscape in Tuscany. For two days and nights, since about noon on the Fourth of July, when they had moved up to relieve the 100th, the Third Battalion had been under nearly continual shelling from the German defensive positions spread out between Castellina Marittima and Rosignano Marittimo. Able to move forward only yards at a time, they'd been pummeled relentlessly by the German 88s, conventional artillery, and heavy machine-gun fire. They'd tried to move mostly at night, but with a nearly full moon rising shortly after sunset each evening, they might as well have had a spotlight shining down on them as they waded through wide-open fields of waist-high wheat and rye.

The key to the problem they faced was a ridgeline designated on their maps as Hill 140. As had been the case with so many hills they had approached, the Germans atop the hill could spot and bring a deluge of fire down on anything that moved across the open plains below. As they got closer to the base of the hill, they came within range of dozens of machine-gun nests arranged in such a way that they produced interlocking fire—the trajectories of bullets fired from each position crossing those of bullets fired from another. The net effect was that whenever they tried to advance on one nest, they exposed their flanks to fire from at least one other.

Attempting to relieve the pressure on the slowly advancing infantry, in just twenty-four hours the 522nd had fired 4,544 rounds, pounding German positions on the hill. Kats Miho's crew in B Battery was rotating shifts—five hours on, five hours off—the exhausted men sleeping just feet from roaring guns, while others aimed, loaded, and fired so rapidly and efficiently that at times the barrels of their guns had overheated and they'd had to stop, pour water over them, and let them cool down as other batteries took over. But they were getting good at what they did now—so good that any one gun crew could put as many as three shells in the air at one time. From the vantage point of the Germans entrenched near the top of the hill, the artillery fire was coming at them so fast and furious that they were convinced that the Americans had invented some kind of automatic artillery gun. The Germans had had months to dig in and prepare for this, though, and despite the relentless barrages their positions at the top of the hill remained mostly intact and entirely functional.

By the morning of July 6, the Third Battalion had taken dozens of casualties crossing the lowlands, but they'd finally reached the base of the western side of Hill 140. There, as they bunched up in the lee of the hill, it was harder for the German observers at the top of the hill to see them and harder for the big artillery guns to target them. But now they faced a new problem. In addition to the maelstrom of interlocking machine-gun fire, a relentless rain of mortar shells began to fall on them from the slopes just above them. It was clear they couldn't linger there, but to move forward seemed suicidal. Nevertheless, a stark, unambiguous order came crackling in over the radio. K Company was to immediately lead a frontal assault on the west side of the hill, take a ridge running toward the summit, and destroy the German strongholds there.

As K Company started up the ridge, a squad of riflemen moved out in front, led by Harry Madokoro. Rudy, following his older friend's lead, ran forward a few yards. Streams of bullets hissed past overhead and on both sides of him, smacking into trees, ricocheting off rocks, kicking up little clouds of dust in front of him. He dove back to earth. This was by far the most intense fire he—or any of them—had experienced so far. As he lay prostrate on the rocky ground, all Rudy could think was "Oh God, don't let one of those hit me."

Slightly behind him, Fred Shiosaki and his mortar squad began lobbing shells over the line, trying to take out the German machine-gun nests upslope from them. But the nests were well camouflaged, and through all the smoke and dust they couldn't really see what they were shooting at. And even as they fired, they were taking as much incoming mortar fire as they were putting out. With rounds dropping all around them, they constantly had to scramble for cover between shots. Sometimes there just wasn't any cover to find. In the middle of one barrage, Fred watched in horror as a German mortar landed right beside his friend Johnny Matsudaira from Seattle. When the dust cleared, he saw that Johnny had crumpled to the ground, his body bloodied and maimed. James Okubo, K Company's medic, crawled forward, hunched over Johnny for a moment, peering into his face, then began to drag him back down the hill. Fred figured that meant Johnny was at least still alive. Okubo was quickly becoming something of a hero to Fred, to everyone in K Company, in fact. The medic seemed to be everywhere on the battlefield, pushing forward after every artillery barrage, carrying no weapon at all, lugging an aid kit, trying to get to the wounded, seemingly heedless of the consequences for himself.

One of the guys farthest out front was Calvin Saito, K Company's radioman, a quiet, good-natured kid from L.A. Calvin was just one of three brothers serving in the army. His older brother Shozo had been drafted before Pearl Harbor, but Calvin and his brother George had volunteered for the 442nd while incarcerated at Amache, a WRA camp in Colorado. Now Calvin had a thirty-six-pound radio strapped on his back. The pack was cumbersome, and it slowed him down as he scrambled over boulders and hummocks on the hill. But he maneuvered into a position where he could see for the first time a network of trenches and caves the Germans had excavated deep into the stony ridge above them. He could also see that they were starting to emerge en masse from those fortifications, apparently preparing for some kind of downhill counterattack. With as little as twenty-five yards of ground separating the Nisei from the Germans in places, it was risky business to call in artillery fire. Ordinarily it would be the job of an officer or one of the designated forward observers to make such a call. But Calvin, calculating that K Company could easily be overrun if he didn't act quickly, grabbed the handset on his radio and called the Fire Direction Center asking for an artillery strike on the hillside just above him. A few minutes later, a barrage of shells from the 522nd began to fall among the Germans up the slope, and they scurried back into their trenches and caves.

Throughout the rest of the day and deep into the following night, under withering fire, K Company crawled up the hill, yard by yard, through tall grass painted silver by an entirely full moon. At times, they and the Germans blundered into face-to-face confrontations, both sides surprised by the immediate presence of the other, each side firing point-blank at the other from as little as five yards' distance, then withdrawing hastily. In the middle of the night, the Germans did finally mount a furious downhill counterattack. The Nisei repelled it but only after being pushed partway back down the hill. As dawn broke on the morning of July 7, little had changed except that more of them were lying dead on the hillside.

For now, the dead got scant attention. At best, someone pulled a coat over their face, stuck their rifle in the ground, set their helmet atop the rifle to mark their position, and moved on. There wasn't time to stop and mourn. That was left to Chaplain Yamada, the medics, and the graves registration team, who worked their way forward between firefights and dragged the bodies left behind downhill as the rest of them began to work their way back up again. Lying prone behind a rock outcropping, Rudy Tokiwa realized it was his nineteenth birthday. He wondered whether he'd live to see another. Under the circumstances, it seemed unlikely.

By mid-morning, it was clear to all of them now that the only way out of this was to get up the damned hill. So, finally, they just stood up and they went. One by one, and then all together, they switched off what was left of thinking, smothered any anxiety or hope or pity. Hunched over again, running in fits and starts, dodging exploding mortars, scanning the ground before them, looking for positions of advantage, they surged up the hill into a torrent of hissing bullets and shrieking shells.

Again, Harry Madokoro charged out front, leading the way, with Rudy right behind him, trying to keep up. But even clutching a Thompson submachine gun, Madokoro quickly moved well out in advance of the others and clambered up onto a rocky ledge from which he could scan the terrain ahead of him. There he was partially exposed to enemy fire, but seeing that he'd outflanked a German machine-gun nest, he pivoted and poured fire directly into the nest. Gray-clad men scrambled out of it, scurrying for shelter, abandoning their gun. Moments later, Madokoro came under fire from another machine gun, still higher up the hill. With bullets ricocheting off the rocks all around him, he hunkered down and began to return fire, engaging the Germans in an extended firefight, giving the rest of K Company cover to advance.

Fred Shiosaki's squad leader, Big John Oroku, screamed orders for his mortar crew to move uphill through the gap Madokoro had opened. Fred stood up and started forward, not sure what they were getting into. In the din of battle all he really *could* know was what the guy to his right and the guy to his left were doing. This high on the hill there was nothing to hide behind, just dry grass and rocks. It was firecracker hot, and he was desperately thirsty. But something in him had shifted again. In the last twenty-four hours he'd seen too many of his guys carried down this damned hill on litters, screaming in pain, or dragged down, dead. Now it didn't make him scared. It made him mad. So he stumbled uphill with bullets whipping around him, glad to finally be taking it straight to the enemy, focused now on one thing: keeping them from killing any more of his guys, to hell with everything else.

Up ahead of him Technical Sergeant Ted Tanouye spotted five German infantrymen trying to set up a machine gun off to his left. Moving quickly, in a running crouch, clutching a Thompson submachine gun, he closed in on them. Before they could get their gun operational, Tanouye opened fire, killing or wounding three of them while the others fled. But he'd drawn attention to himself. Immediately, more Germans opened up on him, firing machine pistols spitting out five hundred rounds per minute. Tanouye—now out on a wide-open exposed hillside—hit the ground behind some rocks. A grenade exploded nearby, and shards of hot metal shattered his left arm. Out of ammunition, he crab-crawled twenty yards to his left, dragging his bloodied arm through the dry grass, got a fresh clip from one of his men, slammed it into his gun, then worked his way back out onto the exposed hillside. By now he was above and behind some of the German positions. Below him another German had pinned some Nisei down with a machine pistol. This time, Tanouye hurled a hand grenade with his good arm and took the man out. With much of the fire directed at them suddenly suppressed, the rest of K Company surged up the hill to where Tanouye was now sprawled out on the ground at the top of a ridge, bleeding into the dry grass.

Tanouye's actions had created enough separation between the Nisei and the Germans that there was now finally an opportunity to get on the radio and call in some more artillery support from the 522nd. Looking around, though, nobody could find Calvin Saito and his radio. Then someone spotted him lying prostrate out on the hillside below. Clambering up the hill, struggling under the weight of his radio, he'd been hit and killed instantly by a German mortar shell.

Behind the lines, at the 522nd's Fire Direction Center, Lieutenant Colonel Baya Harrison wrestled with a tough decision. While the Third Battalion had been fighting its way up the west side of Hill 140, the Second Battalion had been doing the same on the east side. Like the Third, they had been taking heavy casualties. Now they'd called in a startling request. Lieutenant Edgar Langsdorf wanted the 522nd to unleash a barrage of "time fire" on the German positions atop the hill. It would be an enormously risky move. The 522nd had never attempted to use time fire in combat before. It required setting timing fuses on the shells so that they would detonate not on impact but, if set correctly, about twenty yards overhead, directly above the enemy positions. If the shells detonated at the right moment, they would send a deadly shower of hot steel shrapnel down on the Germans, decimating them even if they were hunkered down in trenches and foxholes. But it was dangerous stuff. If the fuse was set just a second or two off and shells detonated too early, they might well decimate their own men.

Harrison called Langsdorf back to make sure he understood the request correctly. Langsdorf was adamant. His men were being slaughtered on the hillside, he said. Still Harrison hesitated. But finally he approved it, and the Fire Direction Center went into action, the men with the slide rules and reference tables quickly but carefully calculating the distances, the coordinates, and the timing for the fuses. Out in the field, Kats Miho and the other artillerymen manning the howitzers received the orders, grabbed wrenches, and nervously turned the timing mechanisms on the fuses, dialing in the necessary settings. Then they loaded the shells and pulled the lanyards, and the big guns roared. For several long minutes after the barrage began, Harrison heard nothing from the Second Battalion. Finally, convinced that he'd killed his own men, he radioed the Second Battalion's forward observer asking for a report. The observer apologized for not reporting more quickly. They'd all simply been stunned into silence, he said, by the sheer devastation rained down on the Germans. At least an entire company of Germans had simply been obliterated. On a ridge nearby, forward observers saw the Second Battalion's commander, Lieutenant Colonel James Hanley, and some of his senior officers jumping up and down in jubilation. On the western side of the hill, nobody had to tell Fred and Rudy and the rest of the Third Battalion how devastating the strike had been. Even over the thunder of the shells exploding, they'd all heard the Germans at the top of the hill screaming.

By the end of the day, the surviving Germans had withdrawn, and the 442nd was in firm control of Hill 140. As the Third Battalion hooked up with the Second Battalion on the upper reaches of the hill, Rudy and some of the other K Company men wanted to climb up to the German fortifications to see the results of the artillery barrage for themselves. But on the way up they ran into men coming back down the hill who had just been there. They stopped the K Company guys, looked them in the eyes, shook their heads, and told them soberly, no joking, not to go up. They'd regret it.

· · ·

ONE OF THE marvels of the massive logistical operation that supported the Allied invasion of Europe was the speed and reliability with which troops in the field were able to stay in touch with loved ones back home in America. V-mail facilitated correspondence back and forth on small, standardized blue sheets. The military censored those written in combat zones, photographed them, stored the images on rolls of microfilm, and shipped them overseas, where they were printed on paper and delivered, saving much-needed cargo space on ships. As a result, a letter written from a battlefield in Italy or France could arrive—more or less miraculously—in a mailbox in Iowa in as little as a week or two.

Late on July 7, the same day that K Company's radioman, Calvin Saito, fell in the battle for Hill 140, his brother George, in H Company, not yet aware of his brother's death, sat down somewhere on the same hill to write a V-mail letter to his father, Kiichi.

July 7, 1944

Dear Dad,

We've just come out of another battle. . . . From the number of casualties that we suffered I have certainly plenty to thank the good Lord for. My only wish now is that Calvin shall be just as fortunate—By the way, I did see him a few days ago—He was moving up at the head of his company as his battalion was moving into position for an attack. He had his carbine slung over one shoulder, his radio over the other, sending a report to his company commander. The old boy is really doing all right.

George

That same afternoon, Kiichi sat down in the kitchen of the white woman for whom he was working as a houseboy in Belmont, Massachusetts, and wrote to Calvin.

July 7, 1944

Dear Calvin,

*How are you getting along? In spite of the weather lately
we are in best health. Mary, her friend, and I went to . . . a
historical place where Longfellow used to stay and wrote a
famous poem—and the place where George Washington stopped
on his way to Cambridge—and the scenery, surroundings are
beautiful. . . . I wished you were with us—perhaps some other
day. My thought always with you.*

> *Love,*
> *Your father*

The next day, July 8, the 442nd resumed moving north, seeking to
capitalize on the confusion and disorder they had wrought in the German ranks at Hill 140. The entire Thirty-fourth Division, in fact, kept
moving north, starting to close in on the Fifth Army's next major objective in western Italy, the vitally important port city of Livorno. As the
rest of his company moved forward with the Third Battalion, Rudy was
sent to the rear to pick up a new commanding officer—Lieutenant Colonel Alfred A. Pursall.

When Rudy arrived at battalion headquarters to escort Pursall to
the front, he quickly sized up the new man. His first impression wasn't
positive. Standing six feet five inches tall and weighing in at about 250
pounds, Pursall towered over Rudy and the other Nisei soldiers gathered around him. But as big as he was, Rudy was skeptical. The guy just
didn't look like a leader. Although he was only thirty-nine, to Rudy's
nineteen-year-old eyes, Pursall looked downright old. His hair was thin-
ning at the temples, he had a bit of a paunch at the waist, he peered at
Rudy from behind thick, wire-rimmed glasses, and his pleasant, rounded
face seemed to bespeak a mild-mannered affability, not resolve and fortitude. Rudy wondered if the man was fit enough to get around on the

battlefield and tough enough to lead them into harm's way. "What the hell kind of replacement have we got?" he thought. "Man, how in the hell's he going to take it?"

Hiking up toward the line, Pursall turned to Rudy and said, "I hear they call you 'Punch Drunk.'"

"Yeah, I guess they do."

"But they tell me you're the smartest man in the group."

"No, I'm the dumb one. I wouldn't be here if I was smart."

"Well, you show me how to be dumb. . . . I hear your outfit's one of the best fighting outfits around. You think they'll listen to me?"

"Sure, they'll listen to you, but you should ask. The guys up there know what they're up against. They know what has to be done. Talk to 'em."

Pursall nodded. Rudy couldn't believe that a lieutenant colonel was talking to him this way, soliciting a mere private's advice. He decided to take Pursall to K Company first, to give his boys a good look at their new commander so they could compare notes later. But as they approached the line, a German shell came shrieking in. Rudy ran for a nearby foxhole and dove in. But he landed squarely on top of Pursall. Horrified, Rudy cringed, figuring he was about to get chewed out by the top man in the whole damned battalion. Instead, Pursall chuckled and said, "Yeah. See, soldier. You thought I was all gray haired. But you get me scared and I'll move faster than you any time."

As Rudy crawled out of the hole, he thought, "I like this guy. I think he's going to do us good."

OVER THE NEXT FEW DAYS, the Nisei, facing sporadic resistance from the slowly retreating Germans, and always, it seemed, fighting their way up some slope, took a series of hill towns—Pomaia, Pastina, and the village of Santa Luce—as the Thirty-fourth Division advanced toward Livorno. With its deepwater harbor, an oil refinery, shipyards, and a massive railroad yard, Livorno was easily the most important Tuscan city still in German hands.

As they drew nearer to that city, German resistance stiffened again, but the 442nd just kept fighting their way forward, night and day.* They fought crouched behind stone walls. They fought climbing up brushy hillsides. They fought running across wide-open fields of rye and creeping down narrow cobblestone streets. And as they advanced across the Italian countryside, something surprising began to happen to Rudy. At some point almost every day, usually early in the morning, Colonel Pursall sought him out and said, "All right, Punch Drunk. Let's go."

"Where are we going, sir?"

"Let's go see what's happening."

And the two of them would head out on patrol. Pursall was clearly good at what he was doing. Probing the enemy's defenses, he began to teach Rudy to pay attention to little things, things out of the ordinary, things that you might otherwise walk right past but that might mean something important—some trampled-down grass, cigarette butts tossed on the side of the road, the smell of diesel fuel lingering in the morning air. Even a pile of human excrement was something to stop and look at, to examine, to prod, to poke. Was it fresh? How long had it been there? Could any of their guys have been there? Did it mean Germans were close at hand? And time and again Pursall didn't just tell Rudy what he thought about something. Instead, he asked Rudy, "All right, Punch Drunk, what's this mean?" It forced Rudy to think in a way he wasn't used to. As self-reliant and sometimes cocky as Rudy generally was, he found that Pursall could teach him new tricks, new ways of thinking creatively, of operating on his own, of being where he wasn't supposed to be and taking advantage of it.

---

*During the battle for Hill 140, a number of Germans the 442nd had taken prisoner reported that their orders were to fight a rearguard action, slowing down and delaying the Allied advance for as long as possible while their comrades to the north reinforced defensive positions along the Arno River between Pisa and Florence.

. . .

As the Thirty-fourth Division closed in on Livorno, the 442nd swung to the northwest and entered an area of low rolling golden hills covered with the stubble of recently harvested wheat and rye surrounding the village of Orciano Pisano. Just to the north lay the last important bit of high ground from which the Germans were attempting to defend Livorno. Before tackling it, Pence, Pursall, and the rest of the 442nd's senior officer corps wanted to figure out where exactly the enemy troops were dug in and how heavily armed they were. The quickest way to do that would be to capture and interrogate some German officers. Pursall went straight to Rudy Tokiwa. Did he think he could sneak behind the enemy lines and capture some officers? Rudy didn't hesitate. This was a chance to show Pursall what he could do on his own.

That night he grabbed a few days' rations, a pair of binoculars, a canteen, and an M1 rifle and slipped out of camp into the dark, grassy hills beyond the front line. For the next several days, moving mostly at night, he crawled through the grass, hid behind bushes, burrowed into haystacks to sleep, and gradually maneuvered himself to within earshot of the German positions, even as they slowly retreated northward. It was hot, dirty work. Daytime temperatures were well above ninety, the sun was unrelenting, heat waves were wavering over crackling dry and dusty fields. When his canteen ran dry, he had to fill it with dirty ditch water, drop some halazone tablets in, and hope that they would kill whatever was living in the water before it got into his gut. With almost no cover on the hillsides, he had to spend much of his time down on his belly, slithering. And because he was entirely alone in enemy territory, he knew that if he were caught, he'd be considered a spy and shot.

After three days and nights of this, he noticed that a group of four German officers kept bringing a small squad of enlisted men out into a particular field at a particular time each morning for what seemed to be some kind of training. The next morning, he lay in wait for them, hiding in some scrubby bushes. As they passed, he simply stepped out and whacked the trailing man across the back of the head with the butt of his rifle, dropping him to his knees. By the time the others had turned around to see what had happened, Rudy had already leveled his rifle at them. He had eight bullets in his clip, just enough, he figured. As the Germans dropped their weapons and raised their hands, Rudy hissed the one word of German he knew, "*Raus*," and waved the rifle barrel toward the American lines. When someone spotted Rudy bringing some Germans up to the line, Second Lieutenant Richard Hayashi ordered his men to hold their fire and sent an army photographer out to record the moment.

Rudy Tokiwa bringing in captured German soldiers in Italy

THE NEXT DAY, acting on information they had gathered from the captured Germans, the Third Battalion focused their attention on another hilltop village, Luciana. Snaking along a ridgeline, the long, narrow town sat above a network of roads leading into and around Livorno, and the Germans, it soon became clear, were determined to hold it. Again, they had dug trenches along the stony crest of the hill. But here they had also positioned their much-feared 88-millimeter artillery guns and Tiger tanks at all points of entry into the village, laid "Bouncing Betty" mines—designed to spring up to waist height and spray steel balls in all directions—on the approaches, built barricades in the town's narrow streets, booby-trapped doorways, set up machine guns in windows, and deployed snipers in church steeples. The place was a fortress.

As the 442nd's Engineer Combat Company went to work using bangalore torpedoes filled with TNT to blast paths through the minefields, they began to come under heavy artillery and sniper fire. When they got near the base of the hill, Fred's mortar company set up their tubes in a backyard grape arbor, and before they could even begin to fire it, they, too, began to draw fire from a sniper in a church steeple. Fred's squad leader, Harry Kanada, got on the radio, trying to get some fire directed at the steeple. Not wanting to give instructions over the airwaves in English, he did what the 442nd guys were doing more and more often, speaking in either Hawaiian pidgin or rudimentary Japanese or a combination of both to thwart Germans who might be listening in. The problem was he couldn't remember the damned Japanese word for church. Finally, he threw together some words he did know—"*Oinori suru toko*"—roughly, "Place do prayer." It seemed to work. A few minutes later Fred could hear bullets clanging on church bells and the sniper's fire stopped abruptly.

It fell to K Company to lead the assault on the town. As he had at Hill 140, Harry Madokoro quickly moved ahead of the rest of the company as they began to pick their way through the minefields and start up the hill, trying to stick to gullies and more protected areas. Again, though, the Germans had set up machine-gun nests in such a way as to produce interlocking fire. And now they opened up with everything they had— with the machine guns, with mortars, and with the weapons the Nisei most feared, the 88s that shot artillery shells at the speed of bullets. Steel and fire rained down on K Company. As Rudy followed Harry up the hill, men began to fall all around him—here a man with his leg blown away, there a man lying prone in the grass, decapitated by one of the

88 shells. Streams of machine-gun fire cut down men running directly into them. Dirt, dust, and smoke filled the air. So did the shrieking of shells, the screaming of men, the rattle of guns, the smell of blood. Fred Shiosaki dove headlong into a ditch and found to his horror and disgust that it was an open sewer. He crawled out of the stinking ditch but remained prone, hugging the ground. The entire company was simply going to be wiped out if they kept advancing in this way. An officer up front started waving the men back. Madokoro, still out in front, rose to one knee, laying down bursts of heavy fire with his Browning automatic rifle, swiveling this way and that to fire at one German position after another, covering his guys as they slowly retreated to safer ground.

K Company wasn't backing down, though. As night fell, they consolidated their forces and began to advance again, fighting their way back uphill toward the fringes of town. In the dark, Italian partisans, who had over the last few days watched the Germans lay down mines and rig booby traps, guided the Nisei up ravines and along paths and routes they knew to be relatively safe. By morning K Company had gained a small foothold in one end of the town itself. But it had come at a heavy cost. A good portion of the company's officers were dead or incapacitated, leaving Lieutenant Hayashi in command. And now they faced a kind of fighting that was new to them—the ugliest kind of fighting, street fighting, house to house, sometimes hand to hand.

As they worked their way down ancient, twisting cobblestone streets, death lurked in every dark window, every doorway. Bullets ricocheted off stone walls. Mortars dropped suddenly, silently, unexpectedly from the sky, exploding on rooftops, in open piazzas and narrow lanes, showering the men with shards of hot steel and cold stone. Machine-gun fire erupted from cellars. The door of each and every house and shop had to be breached, and every time a door flew open someone had to decide whether to throw a grenade in and possibly kill civilians or to enter with his rifle leveled, not knowing who or what might be waiting within.

Lieutenant Hayashi set up a command post in one house on the outskirts of town, but it quickly came under such intense artillery shelling that they had to abandon it almost immediately. Within minutes of their leaving it, a shell scored a direct hit and brought the entire building down. Several hundred yards ahead of K Company, a Tiger tank crouched next to a house blocking the main street through town. So far, Hayashi had refrained from calling in artillery fire from the 522nd, figuring that there must still be many civilians sheltering in buildings. But the tank had to go, so Hayashi, speaking in Japanese, radioed the coordinates to the Fire Direction Center. A few minutes later a single shell plunged into the house, detonated, collapsed a corner of the building, and buried the tank in tons of rubble.

As they moved deeper into town, Harry Madokoro went out in front, yet again, hurling grenades through second-story windows, trying to take out the German machine guns that were firing down on his guys. As he followed Madokoro, creeping slowly down rubble-strewn streets, clutching a BAR, Rudy noticed that there didn't seem to be any civilians, either dead or alive, in the buildings they were entering.

Slowly, building by building, K Company began wresting control of the town from the enemy. Fred Shiosaki's squad raced up stairways and seized rooftops where they set up mortars and machine guns with command of the surrounding streets. By late afternoon, most of the remaining German fire seemed to be coming from one building in particular. Hayashi ordered a bazooka team forward. As they blasted the windows in the upper stories, more of his men sidled up to the building and began hurling grenades through the ground-floor windows. Within a few minutes a white flag emerged from one of the windows. Hayashi ordered his men to hold their fire, and twenty-two German soldiers wearing camouflage fatigues emerged with their hands up. Nearby, someone broke down a door and found almost the entire civilian population of the town huddled in an enormous dark cellar into which the Germans had forced them at gunpoint, intending to hold them hostage if necessary.

The Nisei marched their German prisoners out of town in a column, their hands held behind their heads. When they arrived at battalion headquarters, Chaplain Yamada, curious, began to question them about their backgrounds and beliefs. Some of them seemed not to be much more than perhaps seventeen years old. Mostly tall, slender, and good-looking, they struck Yamada as fiercely defiant. They were, they said, from the Sixteenth SS Panzer Grenadier Regiment. And even in defeat, they clung tenaciously to illusions about their place in the world. When a Nisei private ordered a German sergeant to keep moving along, prodding him with his rifle, the German turned and snarled at him in English, "We are of a master race!" The guard, cracking a smile, glanced at his buddies and said, "Eh, tough buggah, yeah?"

WHEN THE 442ND MOVED OUT of Luciana early the following day, the town they left behind had largely been reduced to piles of rubble in which lay the remains of dozens of Germans like those who had been taken prisoner. As the boys drove out of town, a scruffy but spirited little white dog they had adopted and named Lucy after the name of the town trotted along behind one of their jeeps until someone stopped and picked her up.

That afternoon, they and Lucy raced north, quickly seizing the last high ground south of the Arno River at Collesalvetti, due east of Livorno. That same day, with the 442nd protecting their right flank, elements of the Fifth Army, including the 100th, swept into Livorno and seized the city. Making their way down to Livorno's deepwater harbor, the third largest in Italy, they found that the Germans had slipped away during the night. But before they left, they had blown up most of the port's facilities, sunk ships to block the harbor entrance, and laid thousands of mines and booby traps throughout the city to maim and kill the newly arrived Allies.

Over the next few days, the 442nd spread out laterally just south of Highway 67 running east to west, roughly parallel to and a bit south of the Arno River between Pisa and Florence. Then, finally, after a month of nearly continual combat they came to rest. As the din of battle in their sector died down, an exhausted Fred Shiosaki and Rudy Tokiwa dug in with the rest of K Company and waited to see what was next. George Oiye and Sus Ito climbed high into the hills above the river and established artillery observation posts. To the north, with their binoculars, they could make out the Leaning Tower of Pisa and the dome of the adjoining Cathedral of Santa Maria Assunta, both rising white and gleaming above a sea of red-tile roofs. From time to time, they called in coordinates, and Kats Miho and his crew on the 522nd's B Battery lobbed a few shells at the German defenses around Pisa. But the firing was desultory and intermittent.

Chaplains Yamada and Higuchi drove jeeps south, back across the battlefields they had left behind, probing into dark woods, getting out and climbing down into irrigation ditches, peering into culverts, looking for the bodies of Nisei GIs so that they could see to it that they received proper burials. When they were done with that grim work, they began to do the same for the bodies of German boys left out on the field, many of them now badly decomposed after weeks of lying out under the hot Italian sun. Next to the bodies, they often found photographs and other personal effects scattered around. The photographs, in particular, deeply affected Hiro Higuchi.

Recently, Higuchi had begun to hear about German atrocities in some of the villages they had passed—reports of men, women, and even children being lined up and shot in cold blood. Now, looking at a batch of photographs he found in the pocket of a German soldier's field jacket, he was filled with a righteous rage. On July 25, he wrote to Hisako in Honolulu about a letter he imagined sending to a German mother:

> Dear Mother of a German soldier,
>
> I saw your son's body today. He was lying in a hot sun, face black and unrecognizable except the golden lock of hair that must have pulled away from his scalp. There were pictures of himself in uniform, of a lady sitting by a window smiling, which

I presumed must have been you, and several pictures of a blond little feller like my own boy—so very fair and happy looking— who must have been his brother.

The boys tell me that when he fell, he cried "Mama," like all the German boys do. I expected them to cry "Heil Hitler" but, no they always cry for mama. It was one of those boys, still little over fifteen, who must have led some sixty Italian civilians and shot them—men and boys in cold-blooded murder—and left them screaming in one of the towns we passed. It may have been your boy that a paesan lady told me raped her daughter and murdered the father. And yet he looked so young and sweet your boy. Instead of bringing him up yourself you gave him to Hitler. He became a fiend—and yet when he died he did not cry "Hitler," he cried "Mama." He really did not want Hitler—he wanted his mother from his childhood. But no, you sent him to the SS group and felt proud. He cried for his mother.*

---

*German troops, mostly SS men, and Italian fascist forces committed a series of atrocities that summer as the Allied troops pushed them relentlessly up the Italian peninsula. In dozens of separate incidents, they murdered approximately seventy-five hundred civilians, including hundreds of children.

SIXTEEN

═══════

I can picture myself coming home to Peter and Jane and you.
Bet you'll cry—wanna bet? Wonder if I will. Peter maybe will
act nonchalant and just say "Hi, Dad" as he always does, but
know that I'll feel his little heart pounding within. Jane will
probably scream with fright to see my mug. Bye dear—
optimism reigns today—perhaps tomorrow I'll be blue as all H
so I'd better close before I get that way. My kisses to the kids
and tonight when Janie is asleep kind of give her a little peck
right on her forehead for me and ask Peter to include me in
his prayer.

CHAPLAIN HIGUCHI TO HIS WIFE, HISAKO
AUGUST 27, 1944

Waiting.

For tens of millions of Americans and their allies around the world in 1944, it seemed as if the waiting would never end. They were always waiting for something. Waiting for letters, waiting for Christmas cards, waiting for photographs, waiting for phone calls. Waiting for any sign that a loved one overseas was still alive. Waiting for a sweetheart to return with an engagement ring in his pocket. Waiting for a husband to come home and meet his son or daughter for the first time. Waiting with dread for the sudden arrival of a Western

Union telegram. Waiting behind curtains, watching a pair of army officers walking down the street, hoping against hope that they are on their way to someone else's front door.

In Belmont, Massachusetts, Calvin Saito's father was having a hard time waiting. On July 22, he sat down again at the kitchen table in his employer's stately home and wrote to his youngest son:

> Dear Calvin,
>
> I have not heard from you in over a month. How are you getting along? . . . I know you are well but perhaps you have no time to write. I am anxious and praying for your safety—please do write even a few lines. I am waiting to hear from you every day. . . . Take care. Let me hear from you. Your loving father.

But two days later, the Western Union telegram boy showed up at the front door.

> THE SECRETARY OF WAR DESIRES ME TO EXPRESS HIS DEEPEST REGRETS THAT YOUR SON PRIVATE FIRST-CLASS CALVIN T. SAITO WAS KILLED IN ACTION ON SEVEN JULY IN ITALY. LETTER FOLLOWS.

A few days later he received a letter that Calvin's brother George had written from the battlefield on July 11:

> Dear Dad,
>
> I believe the War Dept. has notified you of our loss of Calvin. I've just learned of his passing. . . . Dad—this is no time to be preaching to you but I have something on my chest which I want you to hear. In spite of Cal's supreme sacrifice, don't let anyone tell you that he was foolish or made a mistake to volunteer. Of what I've seen in my travels on our mission I am more than convinced that we've done the right thing in spite of what's

happened in the past. America is a damned good country and
don't let anyone tell you otherwise. Well, Dad, the Germans are
beginning to throw a few shells our way now so maybe I'd better
get down in my hole. . . . Chin up, Dad, and do take care of
yourself. Regards to all, your loving son, George.

In Honolulu, Ayano Miho waited, too. With no family left on Maui to help her, she had sold the Miho Hotel and moved in with her oldest son, Katsuro, the attorney in Honolulu. With little else to do except mourn for Katsuaki, she waited daily for letters from Kats, letters from her husband incarcerated on the mainland, and letters from her daughters in Japan, Fumiye and Tsukie. When letters from Kats and her girls did finally come, they usually arrived weeks after they had been sent and were heavily censored. It was hard to learn much from them, beyond the fact that all three of them—as of late that summer—were still alive. For that, at least, she could be glad.

In Tokyo, Fumiye waited for life simply to become tolerable again. She was bone weary, weary of the war, weary of life in Japan, weary of deprivation. After four years of living in Japan, she had long since found that it was not what she had thought it would be when she had arrived in 1940. For her, as for millions of Japanese, daily life had become spartan, drab, pinched, regimented, and filled with suspicion. Even the most basic foodstuffs were increasingly difficult to get. Industry was collapsing. The war effort was failing. Overt hostility hung in the air, directed in particular at anybody who might embrace Western ways or seem at all sympathetic to the American view of the world.

The extent of that hostility had been driven home for her some while back. She had stepped off a train in Tokyo wearing a conservative black suit, rust-colored shoes, and a hat bedecked with a veil and feathers. She felt someone touch her from behind and turned around smiling, expecting to see her brother-in-law. Instead, it was a stout, middle-aged man, angry, red in the face, glaring at her. He snatched the hat from her head, threw it on the station floor, and began cussing, hurling coarse

Japanese epithets at her, disgusted by what he called her degenerate Western apparel. Fumiye froze, humiliated, realizing that seen through Japanese eyes, she was still conspicuously American, not Japanese. Now she just wanted it all to end and to know that her family was all right.

Her father was waiting, too, in a new prison camp. As the federal government continued reviewing the cases of the Issei it had arrested after Pearl Harbor, paroling some to the WRA camps, expatriating others back to Japan, consolidating facilities for the rest, Katsuichi Miho had been moved to yet another Department of Justice detention center. This one was located on eighty acres of scrub pines just two miles west of downtown Santa Fe, New Mexico. To Katsuichi's eyes, the camp was a step down from the one at Fort Missoula. This one felt more like a military prison, with twelve-foot fences and eleven guard towers equipped with heavy machine guns. Recently, there had been more sporadic outbreaks of violence at the Tule Lake camp, and some of the "troublemakers" from that camp had been transferred to Santa Fe, causing political, personal, and ideological conflicts to break out among some of the men crowded into the barracks. Still, Katsuichi resolved to make the most of his situation. Stone fever had spread here from the camp in Montana, and like the other older men he spent much of his time patiently searching for and laboriously polishing colorful stones to craft into works of art. Inspired by the kindness of volunteers from the Red Cross and the American Friends Service Committee who visited the camp and brought packages of Japanese commodities like shoyu and miso, Katsuichi had also begun volunteering at the camp hospital. He participated enthusiastically in the camp's art exhibitions. And day after day, when he awoke, he committed himself again to using this experience as an opportunity to refocus on a central tenet of his philosophy, *gaman*, living patiently through a hard time, waiting until he could go home to his wife.

Tori and Kisaburo Shiosaki waited in Spokane, doing as they had always done, rising before dawn, washing, drying, ironing, and folding mountains of laundry; cooking modest meals in the apartment above

Katsuichi Miho at the Santa Fe Detention Center, back row, far right

the laundry; and praying that neither of the two blue stars in the front window would ever need to be changed out for a gold star.

At Poston, Nisei women pinned photographs of brothers and fiancés on the walls of their barracks and waited. At the camp's pinewood-and-tar-paper Buddhist temples and Christian churches, their Issei parents prayed for the safe return of sons serving overseas. For some of them, though, the waiting was over. Army officers had already appeared a number of times at the camp gates with long, sorrowful faces requesting that a parent or pair of parents be summoned to the administration building for some important news. In room 13-G in Block 213, Harry Mado-koro's sixty-six-year-old widowed mother, Netsu, waited alone.

IN SPOKANE, Gordon Hirabayashi waited again to be taken into custody. But he and Esther Schmoe decided to wait no longer to get married. For months Gordon had wrestled with the question of whether he should entangle Esther and any potential children in what was bound to ensue. Even though Washington had no anti-miscegenation laws, he knew that there would be years of public scorn and derision over their interracial marriage. But time was running out if they were to be married before Gordon was taken away again.

So, on Saturday, July 29, Gordon—wearing a gray suit and a white carnation boutonniere—and Esther—in a simple white dress and holding an orchid corsage—entered a redbrick church in Spokane. There, nearly two hundred of their friends, family members, and fellow Quakers joined them. A Quaker leader from the University Friends Meeting in Seattle, Frederick Elkington, read a statement. Then, after a period of silent worship, when Gordon and Esther felt the moment was right, they rose, held hands, put rings on each other's fingers, and declared their commitment to each other, to the Holy Spirit, and to the community assembled with them in the church. When they had finished, they signed a wedding certificate, sat down again, and resumed silent worship, listening as members of the congregation occasionally rose to say a few spontaneous, heartfelt words of support for the couple.

As they walked out of the church to have some photographs taken, a reporter approached them. This was something Gordon had been worried about. He had hoped to keep the marriage as low-key as possible and out of the news. But now, pressed, Esther and Gordon had little choice but to answer the reporter's questions. Esther asserted, as she had many times, that Gordon's race was irrelevant to her, "I love him. . . . He is a sweet and loving character. . . . Gordon is as American as I am." On Gordon's arrest and impending incarceration, she said, "He simply refused to fill out the form because it was sent only to Japanese-Americans and is discriminatory." The reporter seemed sympathetic, and his lede cast the news in a favorable light: "The barriers of race, national enmity, and criminal charges went down before love and Quaker brotherhood with the marriage here of an attractive young white girl to a Japanese-American youth." But the news was also picked up by the Associated Press, and a shorter, sparer account emphasizing that Esther was an "attractive white girl" spread quickly across the country and around the world.

Esther and Gordon
Hirabayashi's
wedding photograph

Within a few days, hate began to fill the newlyweds' mailbox. Most of the letters were anonymous, and most of the venom was directed at Esther, whom the writers repeatedly labeled a "traitor to her race." There were crude drawings of Gordon with absurdly slanted eyes, accompanied by vicious racial epithets. There were clippings of magazine ads selling household items, with colorful images of happy white couples admiring their newborn babies, a message scrawled beneath, "A picture like this will never be yours." There were anonymous phone calls, too, always for Esther, voices hissing at her in the dark. Sometimes she argued with the callers. Occasionally they came away chastened or with a new perspective, but usually she just had to hang up on them and sit down and try to compose herself again.

But one letter of a very different sort arrived in their mailbox. This one was addressed to both of them, and it was signed by the sender. It came from an American GI fighting the Japanese in the jungles of the

Philippines. "I'm risking my life out here for the rights—you know, the values of our American citizenship and way of life. And that includes your safety and enjoyment. And I'm contributing this to your future." Enclosed was fifty dollars.

THE MEN OF the 442nd were waiting as well. As summer wore on, with the German and American armies staring each other in the face along the Arno River, the 442nd's officer corps wanted to know exactly what they would encounter if the order came to cross the river. Sus Ito, George Oiye, and the other observers in the hills behind them could see German forces maneuvering on the flatlands in front of Pisa, but it was difficult to reliably discern how many there were, how they were armed, or how they were situated. Someone needed to get into the city itself, make contact with Italian partisans, and report back on their assessment of the strength and disposition of the German defenses. Lieutenant Colonel Pursall asked for volunteers. It was clearly an enormously dangerous mission, but Rudy Tokiwa readily said he'd go. This was just the kind of thing he excelled at.

A twelve-man patrol, composed mostly of men from L Company, set out a little before midnight on July 20, a moonless night, heavily armed with grenades, Browning automatic rifles, and M1s. They moved as silently as they could, trying to stay off roadways, crossing fields of recently cut grain, wading through muddy creeks, struggling through tangles of brush. It was harrowing work. They could hardly see one another, let alone whatever might be lurking behind a stone wall or in a nearby barn. As they neared the southern outskirts of the city, they were forced to advance down narrow streets among darkened buildings. Occasionally a vehicle came rumbling down a roadway, and they had to scramble into ditches or crouch behind garden walls to avoid being caught in its headlights. As the sun began to rise, they could begin to make out German fortifications scattered at key road junctures, though many of them seemed not to be manned. They paused and rested in a culvert, consulting maps, trying to locate the house where they were supposed to meet the partisans. The city, or at least this part of it, seemed to be largely deserted, most of the civilians having fled into the hills south of the river. They advanced cautiously from street to street. From time to time, they peeked around a corner and saw a German tank or a cluster of gray-uniformed men squatting in a piazza smoking cigarettes.

Finally, they found the house. Once they were safely inside, the partisans handed them exactly what their commanders had hoped for—a detailed sketch of the German defenses around Pisa, showing the location of major minefields, gun emplacements, and river crossings. Now they just had to get it back to the regimental command post.

They waited through the day, until well after nightfall, and then stepped out of the house and began working their way down darkened streets again, weapons at the ready. They were nearly out of town when they ran head-on into a German patrol, much larger than their own. Men on both sides yelled in alarm, hit the ground, crawled for cover, and began firing and tossing grenades. All Rudy could make out in the chaos were dark forms moving this way and that, muzzle flashes, and the bright orange bursts of grenades exploding. It was nearly impossible to tell who was who. Rudy darted across a street seeking better cover in a doorway, but something, a bullet or a grenade fragment, nicked him in the heel, and he crashed awkwardly into a heavy wooden door and slumped to the ground with a bloody foot and a wrenched back. Moments later, the door opened and a pair of arms pulled him inside. A woman bent over him and began talking excitedly in Italian; then someone else pulled him to his feet and pushed him up a flight of stairs into an attic. He wasn't quite sure whether he was being helped or being taken prisoner, but it soon became clear that these people were trying to hide him. Rudy crept into a darkened corner, sat down, aimed his M1 at the doorway, and waited to see what would happen.

Downstairs, Germans entered the building. Rudy felt his gut tightening. A loud conversation erupted, the Germans speaking broken Italian and occasional bits of German and English, the rest of the household speaking nothing but rapid-fire Italian. Rudy could make neither head nor tail of it, but eventually the Germans left. An hour later, when the family finally beckoned him to come back downstairs, they studied him closely while talking softly but excitedly among themselves. They suddenly seemed exceptionally wary and kept glancing at Rudy's rifle and the name patch on his uniform—TOKIWA. Finally, Rudy realized they couldn't understand why an apparently Japanese soldier was wearing an American uniform. They seemed to think they had somehow inadvertently intervened in some kind of dispute among Axis troops, that Rudy was Japanese, perhaps some kind of spy, that he might betray them to the Germans. Rudy tried to explain that he was American, but he made little headway. "No, no, no, no, Hitler and Japan same side," they insisted. Finally, they seemed to relax. Once the streets were clear of German troops, they sent Rudy on his way. By sunup, he had located and rejoined his patrol outside the city, and by noon that day they had all safely reached their command post, carrying with them the invaluable sketch of German defenses.

TWO DAYS LATER, instead of crossing the Arno to move on Pisa as they had expected, the Nisei soldiers climbed into trucks heading south for a much-needed period of rest and recuperation as other elements of Mark Clark's Fifth Army moved up to relieve them.

They encamped in and around the seaside village of Vada, just south of Rosignano Solvay. If there was a place in Italy that looked like Hawai'i, it was the spectacular mile-long stretch of white-sand beach that lay between the two towns. There were even palm trees interspersed with the stone pines scattered along the shoreline. The Buddhaheads lost no time in fashioning crude WAIKĪKĪ BEACH signs and affixing them to the palms, then stripping down to their skivvies and wading eagerly into the bathwater-warm aquamarine water. The water was teeming with marine life. Fred Shiosaki and some of the K Company boys commandeered a skiff, rowed a safe distance from the swimmers, and threw hand grenades into the water. As white columns of water erupted from the surface, a bounty of seafood floated up from the bottom—white-fleshed sea bass called branzino, octopus, sea bream, squid, a pink and silver fish with huge yellow eyes called *parago*—all stunned, easy to grab, and ready to grill on the beach or slice up for sashimi.

Kats Miho headed straight for the shower tents. Each man was allowed five minutes under hot water lathering up, five minutes rinsing off, and then a freshly laundered uniform. For Kats—for most of the guys from Hawai'i especially—after weeks without any way to bathe except for splashing cold, fetid creek water out of a helmet, this was a luxury beyond dreaming.

For the first time in weeks, hot meals were readily available in mess tents, but like everyone in K Company, Rudy Tokiwa was sick of army food. He resumed foraging for alternatives, and he wasn't alone. Nisei soldiers fanned out across the Tuscan countryside, looking for provender. They quickly found that the retreating Germans had looted most of the local farms and villages, making off with everything of value, from women's jewelry to clothing to oxen with which to pull their artillery guns. At one villa after another, they came across families who were subsisting only on produce from their backyards, but they were so angry and disgusted with what their former allies had done to them that they freely offered to share with the American soldiers whatever they still had.

And now, in late summer, backyard produce, at least, was still abundant. Almost every house had a grape arbor laden with sweet purple fruit, or a fig tree, or tomato vines. Italian housewives were more than happy to exchange a chicken or a handful of eggs for a bar of chocolate or a bit of ground coffee, and fishermen eagerly swapped lobsters and buckets of fresh sardines for packs of American cigarettes. Sus Ito pried open a wooden box his father had mailed from California and found it stuffed with Japanese essentials and delicacies—canned abalone, rice, squid, and shoyu. Now and then a pig the Germans had overlooked wandered in front of a boy with a rifle just as he happened to accidentally discharge it.

In the evenings Rudy, Fred, Kats, Sus Ito, and George Oiye—like all the Nisei soldiers, in different pairings and combinations—spent their evenings barefoot, hanging out on the beach, cooking up pots of chicken *hekka*, feasting on *kālua* pig, reading pocket cowboy novels, playing their guitars and ukuleles, talking story, all of them—kotonks and Buddhaheads alike, speaking mostly Hawaiian pidgin now—smoking cigarettes, shooting dice, trying desperately to push out of their minds what they had just been through. When there was nothing else to do, they found radios and listened to "Axis Sally" broadcasting propaganda from Berlin, laughing at her crude attempts to sway them from their loyalty but happy to listen to the American music she used as bait.* Lying on the beach at night, listening to the music and the lapping of waves on the shore, staring up into dark, star-strewn Italian skies, Kats sometimes felt almost as if he were back on the beach at Kīhei with his Boy Scout friends.

Many of the officers took up quarters in Italian households, sharing the families' meals with them, drinking a great deal of good wine, getting to know them. Chaplain Yamada moved in with a family of professional entertainers. When they found out that he was from Hawai'i, they pulled some cellophane grass skirts out of a trunk and began to perform one of their regular acts, shimmying and swaying in a rough approximation of a hula, much to Yamada's thigh-slapping delight. By day, Yamada and Higuchi spent most of their time together sitting in a favorite haystack, watching Italian farmers thresh wheat, and working on their correspondence. Balancing typewriters on their laps, the two

---

*Two American-born women—Mildred Gillars in Berlin and Rita Zucca in Milan—broadcast fascist propaganda to American troops, who knew both women as Axis Sally. In northern Italy, the 442nd was most likely listening to Zucca, who sometimes addressed the Nisei troops directly, calling them "you little iron men" and "America's secret weapon."

chaplains labored over condolence letters to the families of boys who had been killed during the preceding few weeks.

Now that they were off the battlefield, letters from home had a chance to catch up with the 442nd. Every bit of news they brought was precious, something to be pondered and marveled at, to be grateful for or worried about. Each time Higuchi received a letter from Hisako, she duly informed him of how much taller Peter had grown since the previous letter. Higuchi, enormously proud of each new inch, had begun carrying a walking stick with him just so that he could carefully measure out the length and cut a new notch on the stick, keeping with him wherever he went a reminder of the little boy waiting at home for his return.

When they weren't writing to grieving parents and their own families, both chaplains spent much of their time visiting wounded Nisei soldiers in field hospitals, conducting memorial services for those who had died, and leading groups of their boys to visit freshly dug graves in one of the new American military cemeteries now appearing all over Italy so that they could pay their last respects to friends they had lost on the battlefield, friends to whom they had never had a chance to say goodbye. That's how George Saito was able to kneel at his brother Calvin's grave, how Kats was able to say goodbye to his old dorm mate from Atherton House, Grover Nagaji. On August 14, after leading one young man from Hawai'i to the grave of his best buddy, Hiro Higuchi wrote home to his wife, "[He] brought along with him a little flower plant—a beautiful little thing which he got somewhere and carried so carefully to the cemetery. He laid the plant carefully over the mound and then came and asked me to read a passage of scripture and say a prayer over the grave of his pal. It was so touching, so sad. . . . I left there with a lump in my throat, for many of these boys grew up with me."

During their stay at Vada, the Nisei troops were given generous leaves, and many of them took the opportunity to travel as far south as Rome and Naples to do some sightseeing. Because the Germans had declared Rome an open city and given it up without a fight, it showed little damage, few outward signs of the war except for the huge number

Service for fallen comrades in Italy

of Allied troops now coursing up and down its cobbled streets. The boys joined the weekly throngs in St. Peter's Square to hear Pope Pius XII speak at the Vatican, bought souvenirs for wives and girlfriends and sisters, visited the Colosseum, wandered among marble ruins in the Forum, climbed onto the Palatine Hill for the view, and sat in sidewalk cafés on warm sultry evenings, drinking coffee from tiny cups. But as they watched people pass in the busy, narrow streets, many of them grappled for the first time with something new, something unexpected that gnawed at them. They struggled to understand what was before their eyes. They wrestled inwardly with the utter incongruity of life here and life on the front, trying to comprehend how it could be that the woman across the street was pushing a baby carriage down a cobbled street so casually, that a young couple could be standing hand in hand looking into a storefront window as if contemplating a purchase, that the yeasty smell of bread baking and the sound of a man singing could be emanating from the basement of a nearby bakery, that life here was simply going on as if, at that moment, not far to the north of them, lives were not being snuffed out among the shrieking of men and artillery shells. They were profoundly grateful to be out of that, but the normalcy of it all somehow irritated them, made them sullen, put them on edge at the very moments when they most wanted to relax.

Perhaps nowhere was the incongruity more startling than where Hiro Higuchi found himself one evening, not in Rome, but in Naples, sitting in a red plush velvet seat, listening in hushed awe as the voices of some of the finest operatic singers in the world rose in soaring arias into the ornate, gilded interior of the Teatro di San Carlo, Naples's spectacular eighteenth-century opera house. To Higuchi, who had, in recent weeks, written so many sorrowful letters to grieving parents, who had buried the mangled bodies of so many good-hearted young men, it did not seem plausible that such extraordinary beauty and such horror could exist in such proximity to each other. For the first time doubt had begun to fray the edges of his faith.

WHEN THEY LEFT the rest area at Vada and moved north again to take up positions along the Arno west of Florence, the young men of the 442nd were not the same boys who had landed in Italy four months before. Having seen combat, having watched friends die, having smelled death, having been both more afraid and more courageous than they knew they could be, they stepped back into the war transformed. They had come to Italy determined to prove their loyalty, determined not to bring shame on themselves or their families, determined to prevail for the sake of their country and its ideals. And they had come united by their shared ethnic identity, comradeship, and friendships developed on the beaches in Hawai'i or in the mud at Camp Shelby. But now there was something more. Now they were bound together by something invisible but inviolable, born out of their shared experience in battle, by the certain knowledge that before this was over, more of them would die, that it was up to each of them now to watch out for the others, to take any risk, bear any burden for one another. In many ways it was irrational. It would cost some of them their lives. But it was also holy and sacrosanct, and it would last for the rest of their years.

NORTH OF THE ARNO, the Apennine Mountains, running up the spine of the Italian peninsula, swing to the northwest, extending in a long curve all the way to the western coast, raising a natural barrier that for centuries protected the fertile Po valley and the industrial city of Milan from invasions from the south. In the flatlands below these mountains, and in the mountains themselves, the Germans, using slave labor, had prepared another series of defensive positions, the most formidable in Italy, and named it the Gothic Line.*

From observation posts in the hills south of the Arno, George Oiye and Sus Ito again studied the movements of German troops along this line beyond the river. Kats Miho and the artillerymen of the 522nd built sandbag barricades around their howitzers, strung camouflage nets—some of them likely woven by Nisei women back at Poston—over the guns, and prepared to unleash tons of steel and explosives on targets called in from the Fire Direction Center.

At the center, the men with slide rules and maps and protractors had a new challenge. Increasingly the various artillery units in the Fifth Army had begun working in concert as they faced more concentrated German targets along dug-in defensive lines. The tactic was called time on target, and the 522nd's Nisei artillerymen soon proved particularly adept at it. Rather than bringing the guns of individual batteries to bear on a single target, they would bring the fire of many batteries—not just of the 522nd but of other Fifth Army batteries as well—to bear on the same target at the same time. This meant that shells fired from one battery had to arrive at the target at the same moment as shells from other batteries scattered over miles of terrain. It called for extremely complicated calculations in the Fire Direction Center and equally precise exe-

---

*Later renamed the Green Line.

cution by each and every crew on each and every gun. But when it was done properly, the effect on the enemy was utterly devastating. When all went as planned, with an avalanche of shells descending on them all at once, entire German positions could be obliterated.

As the 522nd started to employ this new tactic, the 442nd's infantry launched another series of nighttime patrols and raids across the river, probing the German defenses and attempting to capture Germans from whom they could extract intelligence about what they were facing along the Gothic Line to the north, beyond Pisa. In the first few forays, they repeatedly ran into German patrols, got into sporadic firefights, and came under artillery barrages. But most of the casualties came from mines. The Germans had laid thousands of them along both banks of the river, and they were nearly impossible to detect unless you got down on your hands and knees and crawled, and even then you could easily fail to see them.

On August 24, Pursall went to K Company to ask for volunteers for a riverside patrol to assess the feasibility of building pontoon bridges when the time came for a full-scale assault across the Arno. He could not have been surprised that once again among the first to step forward were Rudy Tokiwa and Harry Madokoro. That night, shortly after a thin crescent moon set at 10:53, they slipped down to the riverbank under cover of darkness. As when Rudy had joined the patrol into Pisa a month earlier, this was a nerve-rattling mission. Again, they could hardly see each other, let alone see whatever might be lurking in the tall grasses growing along the riverbank or what might be buried in the mud. Every footfall presented a hazard to be survived.

They encountered no German patrols that night, but prowling the dark tangles of vegetation and probing every farm shed or culvert they came across, they scouted the terrain effectively and gathered much useful information for the 442nd's engineers. By the time they were walking back to their command post in the early hours of August 25, they were exhausted, their nerves were nearly shot, their attention was flagging.

Then, in an instant, thirty-two-year-old Harry Madokoro from Salinas, California—Harry who had been the former chief of police at the Poston War Relocation Camp, who had encouraged Rudy and a dozen other young men at Poston to enlist, who had promised Rudy's mother he would take care of him, who nursed him when he was hungover, who had always gone out at the front of K Company when danger lurked, who was the only son and sole living relative of his mother waiting for him in room 13-G, Block 213, in the barracks at Poston, Arizona—stepped on a mine and simply disappeared in a shower of mud, metal, blood, and bone. There was nothing Rudy could do, nothing any of them could do, but stare silently at the crumpled form lying in the dark void where he had once been.

ON THE NIGHT of August 30, U.S. forces all along the Arno could hear explosions as German demolition teams destroyed bridges up and down the river. A patrol from K Company brought in four POWs who reported that their comrades were preparing to withdraw behind the Gothic Line. Two days later the Fifth Army surged across the Arno and began to advance. In its sector, the 442nd moved forward on a front six miles wide. Almost immediately, they encountered hidden hazards everywhere—trip wires, antipersonnel mines rigged in trees, heavy-duty antitank Teller mines buried on roadways and in fields, Bouncing Betty mines, booby-trapped houses, piano wires strung across roads at neck level.

By the end of the day on September 1, K Company had advanced only about fifteen hundred yards beyond the river, into the little village of San Mauro and the fields surrounding it. For much of that day, as shells whistled over his head, Fred Shiosaki found himself down on his belly again, having to crawl as much as walk, probing the earth in front of him with his bayonet, hoping to avoid touching the pressure plate on the top of any mines ahead of him, before creeping forward a few more yards.

But no matter how carefully one probed, or how lightly one walked, no one could be sure that his next move wouldn't be his last. And the war didn't grant you immunity for wounds already suffered or heroics already performed. Just days after being released from the hospital for the wounds he had received at Hill 140—where he had charged one machine-gun nest after another with a shattered arm—K Company's Ted Tanouye stepped on a mine and was mortally wounded.

Hiro Higuchi and Masao Yamada were right there with their men, crawling through the minefields to retrieve mangled bodies, crouching in culverts and ditches, sheltering briefly in stone barns, conducting hasty five-minute services in which the men got down on their knees, prayed quickly, then got up and moved forward again, yelling over their shoulders, urging the chaplains to get the hell back to safer ground. But more often than not, they didn't. On September 1, after writing some condolence letters, Yamada accompanied Lieutenant Clarence Lang and medic Takezo Kanda on a dangerous mission well beyond the front lines to retrieve a body. With an enlisted man, K Company's Wendell Fujioka, driving their jeep, they had secured the body and were trying to maneuver their way back to safety when they hit one of the antitank Teller mines. In an instant of flame and smoke and dirt and terror the rear end of the jeep was shattered. Lang and Kanda were hurled twenty yards and killed instantly. Fujioka was mortally wounded. Yamada landed perhaps ten yards from the jeep, with nine pieces of shrapnel in his left arm, left leg, chest, abdomen, and buttocks. Dazed and bleeding, he staggered his way across the minefield, back toward the U.S. lines. When he came across a bicycle, Yamada climbed aboard and, despite the injuries to his posterior, cycled wobblily another two hundred yards to a K Company aid station. Once there, though, he refused to be treated, demanding instead that Rudy and a few more K Company guys drive him, along with some medics, back into the minefield to see if they could help the others. But Fujioka had already been taken away, and Lang and Kanda were well beyond help. A few hours later Yamada was safely in a field hospital, then on his way to a general hospital in Naples.

. . .

OVER THE NEXT FEW DAYS, in the face of ferocious resistance, the Fifth Army began to hurl itself in earnest against the southernmost defenses of the Gothic Line. Then, suddenly, almost as soon as the offensive had started, the 442nd was suddenly out of it, abruptly recalled from the front. On September 6, they boarded trucks and began moving south toward the port city of Piombino. From there they sailed farther south to Naples.

Three weeks earlier, one element of the 442nd—the Antitank Company—had been quietly separated from the regiment and whisked away for special training. After a quick, secretive course in glider warfare, they had climbed into glider aircraft on August 15 and been towed from Italy to positions just off the southern coast of France. There, silently swooping down out of the sky with their guns secured in the backs of the gliders, they had participated in Operation Dragoon, the Allied invasion of southern France.

Over the summer the 442nd's reputation had spread far and wide. Their battle record was outstanding. The Germans had come to respect and fear what they continued to refer to as "the little iron men." American newspapers and newsreels back home had brought their accomplishments into movie theaters from Maine to Honolulu. Stirring accounts of their exploits had appeared in *The Stars and Stripes,* drawing the attention of American servicemen around the world, from common dogfaces to general officers. Suddenly the Nisei soldiers were in high demand. Mark Clark had wanted to keep them in Italy with his Fifth Army in order to assault the Gothic Line. But Alexander Patch wanted them in his Seventh Army in France, for a drive up the Rhône valley, and Patch was backed up by Generals Patton and Eisenhower. So by noon on September 27, the 442nd was again boarding Liberty ships, this time bound for Marseille to hook up with the glider troops, their numbers boosted by the addition of 672 Nisei replacement troops, freshly arrived from the States.

Fred and Rudy and Kats were all glad to be leaving Italy. They'd seen enough of the place. They'd seen enough of their own friends killed or maimed by Germans. They'd heard by now of enough German atrocities. Now it was beginning to look as if Berlin might fall before Christmas, and they wanted to be in on the kill, to pay the Germans back personally, face-to-face, on their home turf. They dreamed of tearing Nazi flags from public buildings, of marching through the streets of the German capital, of seeing Hitler in chains, and most of all of going home victorious. And they dared to think that it might happen sooner rather than later. George Saito, still grieving for Calvin, could feel it in the air. He wrote to his friend Miyoko Hayashi in New York, "I can hardly wait to get back home. Get ready for the big-time reunion. When I get home, I'm really gonna celebrate."

But it wasn't going to be anywhere near that easy. They still had not seen the full magnitude of the evil that lay in their path. Nor had they yet discovered the true extent of their own resolve and courage.

PART FIVE

TO THE GATES
OF HELL

Advancing toward the Lost Battalion in the Vosges

SEVENTEEN

Oh Lord when will this horror end. Whenever I pass one of our men so still in the road with their body covered—I think of some family in the islands—think of the bright future the young lad might have had—all because a couple of mad men in the world wanted everything for themselves.

CHAPLAIN HIGUCHI TO HIS WIFE, HISAKO
OCTOBER 20, 1944

On September 29, 1944—a cool gray breezy day on France's Mediterranean coast—three Liberty ships arrived off the port of Marseille carrying the 442nd Regimental Combat Team. The old city was a sad sight to behold. Just a month before, the Allies, led by the Free French Forces, had liberated it. But during the fighting the port and the town had been heavily damaged. As they retreated, the Germans had dynamited buildings, sunk ships in the harbor entrance, and hidden thousands of mines both on the land surrounding the city and in the waters of the port itself.

Given the devastation, simply getting the troops and their equipment ashore presented a logistical challenge. With the ships rolling in heavy seas about a mile from shore, the men had to climb overboard, clamber down rope ladders, and drop the last seven or eight feet onto landing craft heaving up and down alongside the ship's hulls. Moving the 522nd's guns and vehicles ashore proved even more challenging. In the hold of one of the boats, George Oiye packed a jeep with radios and combat gear and climbed into the driver's seat. Then, with the jeep suspended from a crane by steel cables, a French operator lifted the vehicle from the hold, swung it out over the sea, and tried to lower it onto one of the plunging landing craft. Partway through the maneuver, a heavy swell caught the ship broadside, one of the cables slipped, and the jeep flipped over in midair, dumping most of its contents into the sea and leaving George dangling from the upside-down vehicle, clinging desperately to the steering wheel, yelling and cussing. The crane operator hastily reeled the jeep in, swung it over an open hatch, and gingerly lowered man and machine back into the cargo hold.

By that evening, all the 442nd troops had made it ashore, and Kats was struggling to pitch a pup tent in an expanse of stunted, windblown pines outside Septèmes, about eight miles north of Marseille. A cold breeze blowing in off the Mediterranean earlier in the day had become a biting gale, and Kats fought to keep his tent from flying away, wrestling with canvas and piling limestone rocks on the outside corners. Then it began to rain, a miserable, wind-driven rain, slanting down out of the leaden sky. Kats crawled into the tent in a wet uniform, wrapped himself in what was soon a wet blanket, and tried, without much success, to sleep. Nearby, Chaplain Yamada—released from the hospital in Naples just in time to board a ship to France with his boys—also lay shivering under a single blanket. It wasn't long, though, before other men appeared, crouching at the front flap of his tent, offering him their blankets. Since Yamada had been wounded, the young men of the Third Battalion had become increasingly solicitous of their short, rotund chaplain, determined to keep him from further harm, appreciating him more than ever for the role he played on the battlefield and off, salving their emotional wounds, consoling them in moments of grief, offering them hope, or at least understanding, in the middle of gut-ripping losses.

. . .

ON OCTOBER 5, Esther Schmoe Hirabayashi walked into the federal building in downtown Spokane, opened her purse, pulled out two one-thousand-dollar bills and one five-hundred-dollar bill, laid them on a counter in a clerk's office, and announced that she wished to post bail for Gordon. Two days before, he had finally been arrested and charged with violating the Selective Service Act by refusing to fill out the loyalty questionnaire and refusing induction. Now he was awaiting his trial before a federal jury, scheduled for December. The bail money would afford the couple a few more precious weeks together before they were to be separated for what might turn out to be years if Gordon was convicted.

THAT SAME EVENING, at Poston, as the last desert twilight faded away and a few bats flitted through a purple sky overhead, someone helped Harry Madokoro's sixty-six-year-old mother, Netsu, onto the stage at the Cottonwood Bowl. Originally just a circle of dust scraped out of the sagebrush, the Cottonwood Bowl had become one of the most pleasant places in the camp. With a stage built of timber and stucco in the style of a Japanese theater and sitting in the cooling shadow of several large cottonwood trees, it was a place where people could come together for community events. It had dressing rooms, a large raisable curtain, and basic stage lighting. What the Cottonwood Bowl lacked, though, was seating. If they didn't want to stand, audiences had to bring chairs, stools, and benches they had cobbled together out of scrap lumber. Over the past two years it had been the site of Japanese dramatic performances called *shibai*, graduation ceremonies, Christmas pageants, band concerts, variety shows called *engei-kai*, and sundry other community gatherings. Lately, though, it had been used more and more often for memorial services for fallen Nisei soldiers.

As Mrs. Madokoro sat watching somberly, a bugler summoned forth a color guard. The camp's Boy Scout troop led a salute to the American flag. Priests from all three of the camp's churches gave readings from Buddhist and Christian texts. Friends approached Mrs. Madokoro and laid flowers at her feet and read her telegrams sent from Harry's friends, among them some of the boys now in France. A choir sang. The camp's MPs fired a salute with their rifles. Then, finally, the bugler played "Taps," and as the long sad, lingering notes drifted out beyond the circle of lights, into the absolute darkness of a desert night, friends helped Mrs. Madokoro back to her now solitary quarters, room 13-G in Block 213.

FRED SHIOSAKI AND the rest of K Company threw their gear into old World War I–era boxcars, climbed in, and began to travel by rail from Marseille up the Rhône valley on October 10. At the same time, Kats and the 522nd artillerymen boarded trucks and began driving along a parallel route, hauling their howitzers behind them.

Their destination lay four hundred miles to the north. Since landing on the beaches of Normandy in June, more than two million Allied troops had fought their way through Belgium and northern France, sweeping across the old battlefields at Verdun, closing in on places the names of which would soon be etched in history—Bastogne and Aachen and the Hürtgen Forest. By September the German frontier lay in front of them. Beyond that lay the Rhine, and beyond that lay the Ruhr, Germany's industrial heartland. Now great armies, led by the likes of General Omar Bradley, Field Marshal Bernard Montgomery, and General George Patton were crouched, facing the beast, preparing to assault Germany's last best defensive line—the Siegfried Line, or *Westwall*, a vast network of pillboxes and bunkers, tank traps, barbed wire, and earthworks stretching nearly four hundred miles from the Dutch border all the way south to the Swiss border. Near the southern end of the Allied line, Alexander Patch's Seventh Army—after fighting their way up the Rhône valley from the Mediterranean, had turned east to face Germany southwest of Strasbourg, and it was there that the 442nd was now headed.

Fred, loaded down with all his combat gear, crowded into a boxcar with about twenty other men, knew none of this. All he knew was that the trip was a miserable affair. His uniform was still damp and muddy from the boggy encampment at Septèmes. There was little room to lie down, so he spent most of each day on his feet, wobbling back and forth as the train rocked, looking out an open door at the French countryside as the rain continued to drizzle down out of somber skies. In some ways it was beautiful despite the rain; it was harvesttime in the Rhône valley, and men were at work in the vineyards harvesting grapes, heaping them in baskets, and then loading baskets onto wooden carts pulled by donkeys. There were quaint stone villages, turreted castles perched on hills, stately châteaus with gray slate roofs. The leaves on chestnut, sycamore, and poplar trees had begun to turn color. For many of the men from Hawai'i it was the first time they had seen the vermillion-and-gold splendor of fall foliage.

But the trip seemed to take forever. Because of the danger of German mines, and because sections of the track had been damaged by recent fighting, the train could travel only in daylight and even then only very slowly as the French engineers peered up the line looking for trouble on the tracks ahead. Each night the men had to pitch tents in soggy fields and forests, then reload all their gear onto the train the next morning. And the farther north they traveled, the grayer and bleaker the countryside became. All the way from Lyon to Dijon, there was stark evidence of the mayhem that had just unfolded here. Factories and farmhouses had been reduced to piles of blackened rubble. Bomb craters pockmarked major roads. Scores of burned-out German tanks, half-tracks, jeeps, and trucks—gray hulks with black swastikas emblazoned on their sides— lined the highways paralleling the railroad tracks. Studying the wreckage as they rolled past it, Fred wondered if there would even be a German army to fight by the time they got to wherever they were going.

· · ·

BECAUSE THEY WERE DRIVING their own trucks, the 522nd took a different route and had an easier trip, stopping from time to time to stretch their legs, take in the local sights, meet and chat with local people. Kats and Sus and George hung out together most of the way, venturing into cafés and restaurants, sampling French cuisine, much of which they found odd and sometimes disquieting—platters of quivering raw liver, a creamy fish soup in which the fish's eyeballs swam, staring back at them.

Ever curious, Kats in particular seized on the trip as an opportunity to learn as much as he could about French life. In Dijon, he decided to take in a local circus. The train carrying the 442nd's infantry had arrived in the city the same day, so the circus tent was packed with uniformed Americans that night. As Kats sat happily listening to the shrieks and whistles of an old-fashioned steam calliope and watching the antics of white-faced clowns wearing pointy hats and harlequin suits, a little bit of home materialized. Wading through the crowd, calling out Kats's name, one of his friends from Maui, Dan "Balloon" Aoki, suddenly appeared at his side. Aoki grabbed him by the shoulders, shouted over the crowd noise, "Hey, Kats, come, come, I want you to meet someone," and dragged him through the crowd. The young man Aoki introduced Kats to was someone Kats already knew by reputation. Everyone in the 442nd had heard of Daniel Inouye by now. He'd already developed a reputation within the regiment for his uncommon courage, his intellect, his baritone voice, and his command of seemingly every situation he found himself in. Kats was thrilled just to meet him. Like Sus Ito and George Oiye, Inouye seemed like someone who liked to ponder things. He was exceptionally eloquent. And, like Kats, he was both diplomatic and socially gregarious, a natural politician. The two of them hit it off immediately, and a lifelong friendship was born that night, one that would, in time, help shape the destiny of Hawai'i.

. . .

By October 13, all three battalions of the 442nd had arrived at an assembly point near Charmois-Devant-Bruyères, a village roughly forty miles west of the German border. There they were formally attached to the Seventh Army's Thirty-sixth Infantry Division and brought under the immediate command of General John E. Dahlquist. The Thirty-sixth Division—sometimes called the Texas Army—had been built around a core of the Texas and Oklahoma National Guards and was composed mostly, though not entirely, of young men from the Lone Star State. Now they and the Nisei soldiers stood together facing the Vosges—the region of heavily forested mountains that lay between them and Germany.

The Vosges was a dark and forbidding place—a place that conjured up visions of wolves and werewolves, a place where armies had clashed and men had died in battle since well before Roman times. Studded with medieval castles, its forested hilltops had long commanded control of access to the Rhineland beyond. Now, in 1944, Hitler was determined to defend it and the fatherland to the east of it as he desperately tried to buy time, preparing for the titanic clash that would, in a matter of weeks, come to be called the Battle of the Bulge.

As the Nisei contemplated what new horrors might now lie in store for them, their stomachs tightened. After weeks of relative relaxation, of being out of daily mortal danger, their mood soured quickly. They grew quiet and serious. They knew now what combat was like, and they dreaded it. But there was an added dimension to their apprehension this time. The place they were approaching looked downright sinister. Heavy, brooding clouds hung over hulking, dark mountains. Ghostly mists wreathed the crowns of the higher peaks. Muddy torrents of water cascaded down from unseen heights. Daniel Inouye took one look at the Vosges and declared that it looked like a nightmare.

One of the young men who was struggling the most to master his emotions as he prepared to go back into battle was H Company's George

Saito. For weeks, in the wake of Calvin's death on Hill 140, he had been sending his father a steady stream of optimistic, upbeat letters, hoping to ameliorate Kiichi's grief. But as they approached the Vosges in the relentless rain, George had fallen silent, increasingly depressed himself. On October 14, he finally mustered the will to scrawl a brief note home:

> Dear Dad,
>
> It has been quite some time since I last wrote, I know but please pardon me. We're up at the "front" now somewhere in France and the weather has been really miserable—Why I haven't seen the sun for the past ten days or so—With all this movement, our "dampened" spirits, and the fact that our mail is not coming through, put me in no mood to write.

That same afternoon, in Massachusetts, his father, heartened by George's earlier, cheerier letters, and just as eager to keep the other's morale up, sat down and wrote to him:

> I'm glad to hear that you are pepped up again.

At 3:15, also that same afternoon, Kats Miho and his gun crew—now located near the village of Viménil—slipped a round into the breech of the howitzer they had named *Kuuipo* and fired the first shot of the new campaign, commencing the battle for the Vosges. Then they settled into almost continual firing through the night, working in shifts, starting to soften up German defenses, pounding the dark mountains two or three miles to the east of them.

As the 522nd's guns rumbled behind them and white flashes lit up the gray underbellies of the clouds ahead of them, the 442nd began to move up to the line, slogging through muddy fields of wheat stubble and wet country roads.

At dawn the next morning, Sunday, October 15, Hiro Higuchi held a service in a clearing among some pines. Standing in a circle in a

Kats Miho firing a howitzer at a high angle in France

cold, drizzling rain, with water dripping from their helmets, the Nisei sang "America the Beautiful" and "The Battle Hymn of the Republic." Then Higuchi stood and spoke: "You are already good Americans, and you don't have to prove it. But if you are here because you don't like Hitler, Tojo, tyranny, and the kinds of murderous dictatorships and supernationalism they represent, then that cause is the right one." The men nodded and knelt in the mud and murmured the Twenty-third Psalm—Christians and Buddhists and atheists alike saying words in unison as Higuchi led them—"Yea, though I walk through the valley of the shadow of death." Then the 100th and the Second Battalion stood up, hoisted their weapons, and threw themselves into combat.

Their first objective was to secure the high ground around the small town of Bruyères, where several roads and a railway line converged at the entrance to the Vosges. Four forested and oddly conical hills—designated by military planners as Hills A, B, C, and D—surrounded the town. The 442nd was going to have to take each of them in order to liberate the town and move into the mountains beyond.

As the Nisei advanced through heavily forested terrain and battled

Chaplain Higuchi conducting a service in the field

their way up the first of the hills that morning, the Germans stood and fought as they had never done in Italy, at least not since Monte Cassino. With their backs to their own border, just thirty miles to the east, they threw everything they had at the regiment, counterattacking every forward movement the men attempted, contesting every yard of territory, hurling barrages of mortars and artillery shells at them, directing streams of machine-gun fire into their lines, sniping at them from adjacent hilltops and church spires, unleashing their terrifying 88-millimeter guns, the shells of which shattered the trunks of trees almost as easily as they shattered men.

In the dark pine forests, the sounds of battle—the screaming of shells, the howling of men, the shattering of steel—was even more terrifying than it had been in the dry, rolling hills of Italy. And now a new terror descended on them—"tree bursts." Because the canopy of the pine forest was so thick, German artillery shells almost always exploded when they hit the tops of the trees, sending lethal showers of both steel and splintered wood down on the men's heads. There was no way to hide from them. All you could do was hunker down and hope for the best or move forward through a curtain of shrapnel, still hoping for the best. Either way, survival was a crapshoot.

Meanwhile, behind the lines, Kats Miho and the 522nd artillerymen were doing their best to inflict the same degree of suffering on the Germans, still firing around the clock, attempting again to deliver what they had begun to perfect in Italy—their devastating time-on-target barrages, plastering the summits of the four conical hills and the ridges beyond the town with thundering salvos of shells, shattering whole forests, denuding whole mountaintops.

OVER THE NEXT THREE DAYS, as the rain continued to fall and the four thousand residents of Bruyères huddled in their basements, the two battalions of Nisei soldiers fought furiously for every yard they could gain against the Germans. As they came closer to the town itself, the terrain opened up and flattened out, but they still had to take the hills before they could move through the flats. Occasionally American P-47 Thunderbolt fighters roared in overhead, strafing German positions with their .50-caliber machine guns, but with the cloud cover so low and the surrounding terrain so rough, aircraft were mostly unable to operate in the area.

German artillery had long since zeroed in on every crossroads in and around Bruyères, and their shells fell on these junctures frequently and with seeming randomness. Anyone who happened to find himself in the middle of one at the wrong moment was likely to be hit. Such was the fate of one H Company man who entered a crossroads at the same moment as an 88-millimeter shell. When a graves registration team brought his body in that afternoon, a horrified Hiro Higuchi had to check the dog tags to see who he was. Broken with grief, Higuchi wrote to his wife that night, "A boy came in without a face. It's horrible, I know—it nearly finished me." He'd known the boy back when he and Hisako had been students in Los Angeles. It was George Saito.

A few days later George's last letter to his father arrived in Massachusetts. Kiichi was heartened to receive it. Then, as parents all over America were doing, he began to wait for the next one. But it never came. When he could stand the silence no longer, he wrote again:

> *Dear George,*
>
> *Three weeks passed since I heard from France. I am a bit anxious from not hearing as often as I did before. I presume you must be very busy . . . please do write me. At home everything is well so don't worry. Do let me hear from you.*
>
> *Your loving father*

But two days later, another Western Union telegraph boy appeared at the front door of the house in Massachusetts, bearing grim news from the secretary of war. And not long after that, Kiichi's final letter to George showed up back in the mailbox, returned with the word "Deceased" scrawled across the front of the envelope. Two of Kiichi Saito's sons had now fallen in the ranks of the 442nd.

JUST BEFORE DAWN on the morning of October 18, Fred Shiosaki crawled out of a dank pup tent, strapped a mortar tube on his back, grabbed his rifle, and began to walk toward the battle. With the other two battalions still fighting for control of the hills around town, Colonel Pence had ordered the Third Battalion to make a frontal attack on the German forces in Bruyères, liberate the town, and then advance toward the village of Belmont to the northeast. George "Montana" Oiye hoisted a carbine and fell in alongside Fred. He'd been temporarily assigned to K Company to serve as their forward observer in the event that they needed artillery support from the 522nd while making their assault.

As K Company spread out, moving through dense stands of pine, the sounds of the battle ahead of them were oddly muffled. A thick gray fog made it hard to see more than a dozen yards in any direction. Fred's breath issued forth in small white clouds. His footfall was nearly inaudible, softened by thick piles of wet moss on the forest floor. The moss worried Fred. He had been warned that the Germans had hidden hundreds of Bouncing Betty mines in the stuff, and he feared those almost as much as he feared the deadly 88-millimeter shells that he knew might come shrieking at them out of the fog at any minute.

But when K Company finally emerged from the woods and entered the flatter, more open terrain immediately in front of the town, everything around them seemed to explode. The roar of the battle engulfed them. Fred stumbled forward over muddy furrows in an open field. Bullets whipped by on both sides of him. Incoming shells whistled over his head. Columns of black earth and fractured yellow stone erupted in front of him and behind him. Wounded horses in a nearby barn screamed. Searing-hot shards of shrapnel flew in all directions, making weird fluttering sounds. The smell of explosives and diesel and mud and blood filled the air.

Fred and the men near him dropped and began to crawl forward on their bellies as streams of machine-gun fire poured from the windows of nearby farmhouses and machine-gun nests hidden behind stone garden walls. But returning the fire, lobbing mortars at the buildings, firing bazookas, and throwing hand grenades, K Company kept moving forward, assaulting each machine-gun nest in turn, concentrating their fire on it until it was silenced, then moving on to the next.

On the outskirts of town, they came across a wide bend in a road. Sergeant George Iwamoto, squad leader and one of Fred's closest friends—a kotonk through and through, a kindred spirit from the eastern side of Washington State—raised his hand to pause his men and get their attention. He didn't like the looks of the place. He wanted them out of there as quickly as possible. He stood up, started waving his hands, bellowing, "Come on, you guys, come on!" urging them to cross the road quickly. Fred hunched over and ran for it. He made it across. They all did—except one. Just as Iwamoto began to follow the last of his men across, a shell landed right behind him, hurling him forward a dozen

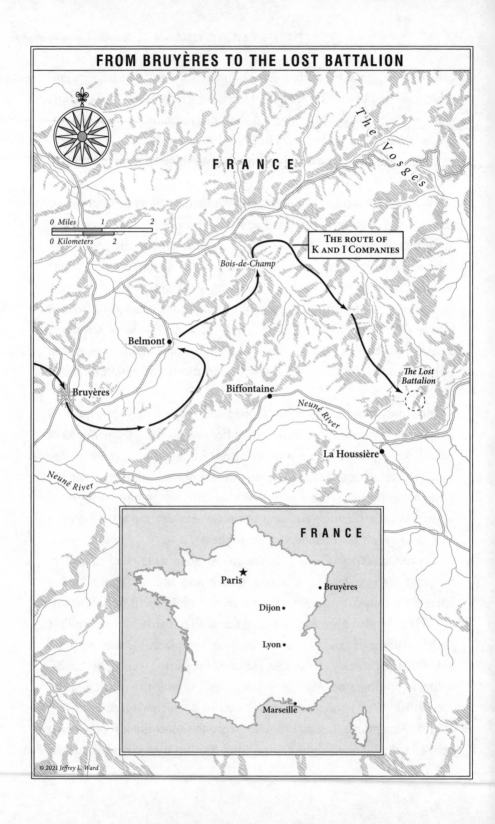

FROM BRUYÈRES TO THE LOST BATTALION

The Vosges

FRANCE

0 Miles   1   2
0 Kilometers   2

THE ROUTE OF
K AND I COMPANIES

Bois-de-Champ

Belmont

Biffontaine

Bruyères

Neuné River

The Lost
Battalion

La Houssière

Neuné River

FRANCE

Paris ★

Bruyères •

Dijon •

Lyon •

Marseille •

© 2021 Jeffrey L. Ward

feet, shattering his spine, paralyzing him from the waist down. Seeing his friend there, sprawled out on the road in the rain, bloodied, desperately trying to crawl forward, dragging his legs, helpless, Fred felt suddenly and overwhelmingly sick to his stomach. For a moment, he closed his eyes and slumped against a stone wall. Like everyone else, he wanted to turn and run from this place, from the horror. Like everyone else, he didn't. A medic dragged Iwamoto off the road. The rest of them got up and moved on.

AT THE ENTRANCE to the town itself, they faced a barricade—a roadblock built of enormous logs, timbers, and boulders that the Germans had chained together and intertwined with land mines and booby traps in order to block one of Bruyères's main streets. George Oiye got on a field phone and called up the Fire Direction Center. A few minutes later the 522nd, still several miles to the east, dropped a shell precisely onto the barricade. Gravel and dirt flew in all directions, but the effect was mostly to rearrange the tangle of obstacles into an even more imposing jumble of wood, stone, and explosives. Finally, with German snipers firing on them from nearby houses, engineers from the 442nd's Combat Engineer Company crept forward, wrapped explosive Primacord around the larger obstacles, and blew them far enough apart to allow men, jeeps, and half-tracks to start snaking their way into the center of the town.

Fred advanced cautiously, crouching, running from one doorway to the next as K Company worked its way down a narrow street. Lobbing grenades, knocking down doors, racing to rooftops, clearing houses, the Nisei gradually drove the Germans out of town. By early evening, most of Bruyères was theirs, though occasional German shells and mortar rounds continued to fall in the streets as a furious battle for the high ground raged on just to the east. The streets were littered with the detritus of war—slate roof tiles, bricks, piles of stone and mortar, burned-out vehicles, here and there a dead German in a bloodied gray uniform lying in the street or a charred, contorted corpse sitting in a burned-out half-track. The smell of powder lingered in the air, along with a whiff of singed flesh and death.

But then, one by one, Fred noticed flags emerging from upstairs windows—French flags and the Croix de Lorraine, the emblem of the French resistance. The people of Bruyères, peering out from their hiding places, seeing American jeeps and tanks entering the village, began pouring out into the rainy and rubble-strewn streets. Confused at first, seeing Asian faces, they exclaimed, "*Chinois! Chinois!*" The Nisei, pointing to their uniforms, tried to explain. "No, no, Americans. Japanese Americans!" "*Japonais!*" The French looked at one another, clearly baffled, but nobody really cared. Young women, old men, children, utter strangers, ran to the men, embraced them, kissed them on both cheeks. Old men brought out bottles of wine and strings of sausages and offered them to their liberators, patting them on the back. Children flocked around the Americans cheering, shouting things in French the men mostly could not understand except for the one word, over and over, "*Merci, merci, merci!*" Fred dug a chocolate bar out of his kit, broke it into bits, and handed them to the kids.

Then he moved on, making his way toward the southwestern side of town, bullets from a sniper up in the hills still occasionally whipping by, ricocheting off stone walls. But the civilians kept coming out. Fred rounded a corner and came upon an old lady grinning, standing in a pile of rubble next to a collapsed soda-pop warehouse, handing bottles of pop to the men as they hurried past. Around another corner a middle-aged woman waved at them and began vigorously sweeping battle debris from the street, even as artillery shells whistled overhead. She swept with such cheerful enthusiasm that to George Oiye it seemed as if she were trying to sweep away the war itself.

As evening settled in and the town darkened, the Nisei consolidated their hold on Bruyères, and the mood of the civilians seemed to shift. Fred heard loud, shrill voices. The French began dragging certain people out into the street, mostly women who had consorted with German soldiers, but men, too—anyone who had been too helpful to the Germans. Crowds gathered around. They beat the men, pummeling them with fists and broomsticks. They stripped the women naked, shaved their heads, and then ran them through the streets in the rain, jeering, spitting at them, hurling insults and trash at them—potato peels and rotten vegetables and offal—as the women ducked and dodged and tried desperately to hide their nakedness. Fred watched impassively. This wasn't for him to judge, he figured.

OVER THE NEXT FEW DAYS, K Company left Bruyères behind them and slowly inched deeper into the Vosges itself. At the same time, slightly to the rear of K Company, in the midst of a bloody battle raging on Hill D, F Company's technical sergeant, Abraham Ohama, walked forward under a white flag, attempting to recover a wounded comrade. German forces, disregarding the flag, opened fire and wounded Ohama. When Nisei litter bearers tried to remove the two wounded men from the field, the Germans opened fire on them as well, killing Ohama as he lay helpless on a stretcher. Seeing this, and infuriated, the men of F Company, nearly two hundred of them, rose spontaneously and charged. They plunged into the German lines so suddenly and unexpectedly that many of the Germans didn't even have time to return fire. As the Nisei overwhelmed their position, dozens of German boys—some just sixteen or seventeen—cowered in their foxholes, throwing their arms in the air, so scared that the Nisei had to reach down and drag them out in order to take them prisoner. Others fell to their knees, crying, begging for their lives. When it was over, eighty-seven German troops were dead, dozens more wounded.

At a railway embankment east of town, K Company and much of the Third Battalion got bogged down for hours, until the 522nd laid down a long, sustained, thundering barrage that went on for twenty straight minutes, pounding the embankment and the ground immediately behind

The 442nd going into battle in the Vosges

it. For a few moments after the last shell fell, there was dead silence but for the hissing of rainfall. The smells of powder and wet earth drifted over the men. Fred, crouching in a foxhole, peered through the rain and drifting smoke and saw the Germans finally falling away to the east beyond the tracks. K Company rose to their feet and scrambled across what was left of the railroad embankment.

Beyond the twisted rails and craters and mounds of scattered gravel, they moved cautiously forward across muddy and heavily mined fields. Approaching some densely wooded hills, K Company's sergeant James Oura spotted what appeared to be a high-ranking German officer emerging from a line of trees ahead, walking toward them, apparently unaware of their presence. Motioning his men down, holding his fire until the man was well within range, Oura rose and dropped him with a burst of fire from his BAR. When they got to his body, K Company found maps indicating the disposition of enemy troops throughout the hills in front of them. This was an unexpected windfall, and they needed to capitalize on it quickly. Rudy Tokiwa headed back to the regimental command post at a lope, clutching the maps.

Within an hour, Major Emmet O'Connor had studied the captured maps and launched a special task force to take advantage of the intelligence it represented. That night, as the rest of the regiment continued crawling forward, O'Connor and his task force slipped through enemy lines and made their way along a forested ridge well ahead of the Third Battalion's position. By dawn on October 21, they had outflanked the enemy, circled back, and occupied a vantage point from which they could see a large concentration of German forces in and around a cluster of houses in a clearing, just where the maps had indicated they would be. Crouching in the woods, Lieutenant Al Biondi and George Oiye began quietly calling in coordinates. A few minutes later, the 522nd unleashed their howitzers—the shells again timed to arrive all at the same moment—and the houses disappeared in an eruption of fire, earth, and smoke. Eighty Germans were killed outright, another sixty wounded. O'Connor's task force swept down on the astonished survivors from their rear as K and I Companies surged forward from their front. By noon the Nisei had seized the entire sector, taking fifty-four prisoners, the only Germans left alive in the vicinity.

As Rudy made his way back to the battalion's command post to report the successful completion of the maneuver to Pursall, K Company's medic, James Okubo, stopped him.

"Hey, Punch Drunk, when you came through, you see . . . dead Germans out there."

"Yeah."

"You see any of 'em alive?"

Rudy shrugged and said, "I don't know. I never look."

Okubo had been up all night tending to the wounded, but now he wanted to see if there were wounded Germans still out on the field.

"Aw, you know I can't carry a rifle. Will you go with me?"

Rudy shrugged again, but he picked up a Thompson submachine gun and led Okubo into the hills. The two men began to sort through a pile of German dead and eventually found one boy who was still alive. Okubo patched him up as best he could, and the two of them carried him back to an American aid station. There, Okubo turned to Rudy and said, "I hope you don't get mad at me now."

Rudy replied that he was glad they'd helped the boy. But the truth was, it seemed odd to him, after he and his guys had spent so much time trying to kill Germans, to be trying to save one. It wasn't really that he objected. He just didn't particularly care one way or another. But it got him to thinking about something he'd pondered more and more, something that had been eating at him ever since he'd shot that German soldier carrying photos of his children his first day in battle. "I wonder," he thought, "when I get out of this, if I do, whether I'll be a human being."

THAT NIGHT, exhausted, the young men of K Company tried to hunker down and finally catch some sleep, sliding into slit trenches the Germans had dug or craters left by their own artillery shells. By now both the trenches and the craters were half-full of cold, muddy water, but many of the men were beyond caring about that. They just lay against muddy walls, closed their eyes, and let their feet and legs soak. A few chose to lie out in the open instead, despite the possibility that shells might at any moment begin dropping among them again. Fred lay in one of the trenches, his eyeglasses smeared with mud, his teeth chattering uncontrollably. The worst of it, though, was that his feet ached terribly. He lifted a foot out of the water, pulled off one of his boots and a soggy sock, and noted that the foot was turning an odd shade of purple, the beginnings of trench foot, the slow, agonizing death of the nerves and tissues in his feet.*

Nobody really slept that night. When morning finally came, gray

---

*Trench foot often precedes gangrene and was an old, familiar enemy of soldiers everywhere. It had caused an estimated two thousand American and seventy-five thousand British casualties in World War I.

and wet and cold, they got up and pushed on to the northeast. They were entering increasingly rugged terrain now, steeper hills cloaked in dark forests, advancing into the face of periodic artillery barrages, blistering fire from German tanks mounted with 88s, the howling Nebelwerfer rockets they called screaming meemies, and the growling of German burp guns. For two more days and two more nights, they just kept moving forward, yard by yard, under fire almost continuously, with nothing to eat but cold K rations, nowhere to sleep but in the mud. And still the rain kept falling.

By late on October 24, the 442nd had taken control of the villages of Belmont and Biffontaine and pushed the Germans deeper into the Vosges. K Company had now been on the battlefield for seven days and nights. Some units had been out eight days. Finally, that afternoon, as the sun finally broke through, two Texas units—the 141st and 143rd Infantry Regiments—began moving up through the 442nd's lines to relieve them.

Fred and Rudy and the rest of K Company, their uniforms stiff, caked in mud, their faces pale and drawn, their eyes blank and all but unseeing, crawled out of slit trenches, marshaled themselves into a semblance of a column, and stumbled back down out of the mountains into the shattered remains of the village of Belmont. There they collapsed in whatever shelter they could find—old stone barns, half-demolished homes, burned-out shops, horse stalls, any place they could find a dry corner or a pile of hay or some feed sacks or just a cold slate floor to stretch out on—and fell asleep. A few of them, still amped up on adrenaline and fear and rage, couldn't sleep. They wanted something hot to eat first. Officers told them just to relax. Hot food was on the way, and after what they had been through, they would have plenty of time to rest now.

BUT A LITTLE MORE THAN forty-eight hours later, at 3:00 on the morning of October 27, as Fred slept soundly on the floor of an ancient stone tavern, Rudy Tokiwa began to shake him awake. Fred wasn't sure what was happening. He fumbled for his eyeglasses. Around him, other K Company guys were grumbling in the dark.

"Hey! What the hell? Why you wakin' me up?"

"No argue. Just get your gear. . . . We're moving back up."

"Oh, Christ!"

Cussing, angry, in disbelief, the men began to crawl around on the floor groping for rifles and helmets, pulling on still-wet boots, stuffing things into packs. An hour later, Fred and Rudy stepped out onto a street in Belmont, hunched their shoulders, and began to walk. More men emerged from other buildings and fell in with K Company. George Oiye, still assigned to K Company as a forward observer, joined in. Right beside him was his friend and now superior officer, Lieutenant Sus Ito, just recently given a battlefield commission.

A ragged column of men formed, shuffling east on wet, cobbled streets. From what he could see in the scattered lights of the village, it looked to Fred as if both the Third Battalion and the 100th were assembling, with K and I Companies out front, taking the lead. Leaving the village, still wondering where they were going and why, they turned down a narrow, paved road leading roughly northeast and uphill. Behind them, Fred could hear tanks starting to move, too, and more men marching—masses of them. Whatever this was all about, it was big.

Ahead of them, up in the mountains, rain was again slashing down through tangles of pine and brush. On one of the higher ridges, where the rain was now threatening to turn to snow, more than two hundred young men, mostly from Texas, were desperately trying to stay alive.

EIGHTEEN

_I am spiritually low for once. . . . When we complete this
mission . . . we will have written with our own blood another
chapter in the story of our adventures in Democracy._

CHAPLAIN YAMADA TO COLONEL SHERWOOD DIXON
OCTOBER 30, 1944

G eneral John E. Dahlquist was physically courageous. No one disputed that. That wasn't the issue, or why so many of the Nisei soldiers he commanded came to loathe him.

The thing you noticed first about the man was his notably square jaw, a jaw that seemed to bespeak resolve, determination, forthrightness. When he talked, you got the same impression. He spoke brusquely, curtly, authoritatively—just as you would expect from a hulking general with a square jaw. The package looked good.

Born in 1896, the son of Swedish immigrants, he'd grown up in Minnesota, joined the military in 1917, served as a second lieutenant in occupied Germany following World War I, and then gone on to advance rapidly through the ranks, serving in the Philippines and holding a series of desk jobs, rising to the level of brigadier general in 1942 and major general in 1943, and most recently serving as Dwight Eisenhower's deputy chief of staff. Along the way, he had been something of a scholar of infantry tactics, enrolling in formal studies of the subject and writing a manual on the effective use of machine guns. But until the summer of 1944, he had never actually led men in combat, and by the time the campaign in the Vosges was under way, that had become all too evident to both those who served under him and those to whom he reported.

Earlier that summer, during the Allied invasion of southern France, Dahlquist had been taken to task and nearly removed from command when his division failed to advance aggressively and effectively on the hill town of Montélimar. Perhaps because of that, when the 442nd had begun to assault Bruyères and the surrounding terrain, he had taken to striding onto the battlefield, blustering, scowling, berating any perceived slackers, personally taking command of individual units, peremptorily issuing orders to particular infantrymen, countermanding the orders of officers in the field, disregarding intelligence they had gathered, and ordering advances into uncertain terrain with no regard for plans worked out by staff officers. The result was to alienate many of those who served under him—both officers and men. At one point during the battle for Bruyères and the surrounding terrain, the 100th's brilliant Korean American captain, Young Oak Kim, had yanked the wire from his field telephone when he learned that Dahlquist was about to get on the line. That way his men wouldn't have to follow what he knew would be wrongheaded and possibly suicidal orders.

But it was Dahlquist's behavior following the liberation of Bruyères that the Nisei who fought under him would never forgive. On October 23, despite warnings of heavy concentrations of Germans ahead, he ordered the 141st Infantry Regiment of his Texas Division to push as rapidly as possible along a series of ridges north of the village of Biffontaine. By late the next day, Companies A, B, and C of the regiment's First Battalion had worked their way along a muddy logging road nearly to the end of a narrow ridge above the little village of La Houssière, a crossroads still in German hands in the valley below. Initially, they met only light resistance, and as evening approached, all was surprisingly calm. Then suddenly, as darkness enveloped them, the forest behind them erupted with gunfire. German forces lying in wait in the forest had intentionally let them pass unmolested. And now they opened fire.

The Texans formed a perimeter and hastily dug in for the night, unsure what exactly they had wandered into, but already wishing they had brought more than a single day's rations. The next morning, when some of them tried to retrace their steps, they came under withering fire and suffered heavy casualties. Those who survived stumbled back into camp to report that during the night the Germans had felled pine trees and built a fortified blockade on the logging road. There was no doubting it now. The battalion had been lured into a trap, and the trap had been sprung. Stuck on a rounded hilltop near the end of the ridge, they had become a stationary target six kilometers behind enemy lines. With no avenue of escape, they began to come under nearly continuous artillery fire and repeated ground attacks from the German infantry now arrayed all around them.

For the next several days, communicating with them over their one operating radio, Dahlquist repeatedly ordered the stranded men to fight their way out of their predicament. When those attempts failed, he ordered other elements of the 141st to break through and relieve them, all to no avail. On the hilltop, a first lieutenant named Marty Higgins found himself in command of more than two hundred men enduring rapidly deteriorating conditions. Within a roughly circular defensive perimeter, in a bitter cold and still unrelenting rain, with virtually no provisions or medical supplies, his men, lying in flooded trenches, were hungry, dirty, tired, and demoralized. Half a dozen of them were grievously wounded, and Higgins had little in the way of medicine with which to treat them. Several had already died of blood loss or gangrene, and their bodies were now splayed out in the mud near his foxhole. More, it appeared, would die soon.

Dahlquist, growing increasingly desperate with each passing hour, gave the order to start waking up the battle-weary men of the 442nd and send them up the mountain. If none of his regular guys could get the Texans out, maybe the Nisei could. He started with the 442nd's Second

Battalion, ordering them onto the mountain on the night of October 26. But the Second Battalion ground to a halt, bogged down several miles short of the Texans' position. Now Dahlquist had decided to throw the rest of the 442nd into the effort as well.

FRED SHIOSAKI, his fingers already going numb, grasped the pack of the man walking in front of him, a man he could not really see. The blackness around him was so nearly absolute that Fred felt as if he'd been blindfolded in a darkened room. Nearby, Sus Ito paused to tie a white handkerchief to his pack, trying to guide the man behind him.

They walked thus for a mile or two in the dark and the driving rain, like a human accordion, pulling apart, then bumping into one another, working their way along a logging road the engineers had corduroyed with sapling logs. Then the French resistance fighters, acting as their guides, led them off the road onto a rutted dirt track and up a steep incline into a wet forest the locals called the Bois-de-Champ. As the track grew steeper, their boots sank into ankle-deep mud, and they began to slip and slide backward, grasping at one another, struggling to stay on their feet, trying to keep moving forward.

At first all Fred could hear was the wet sucking sound of boots pulling out of mud, the hiss of the rain in the treetops, the soft cussing of the men around him. But as dawn approached and the patches of sky showing through the canopies of the trees above shifted from absolute black to slate gray, he began to hear the sound of a firefight up ahead of them. Then, rumbling down a logging road, came a U.S. Army Graves Registration Service truck. In the back were bodies—half a dozen contorted corpses, their American uniforms bloodied, their blank faces gray like the dawn.

Half an hour later, as they advanced through thick fog and dense forest, the sounds of battle—the rattle of machine guns, the cracking of rifle fire, the concussions of grenades, the growling of tanks—began to close in all around them. Fred still couldn't see more than a few dozen yards in any direction through the trees and the fog. He still had no idea where they were going, what their objective was, or what they were up against. Nobody had told him or anyone in his squad about any trapped Texans. All he knew was that they had come to an abrupt halt and their officers were suddenly screaming at them to spread out and take cover.

Kneeling behind a tree with an M1 in his hands and a mortar tube strapped on his back, he tried to make sense of the situation. The sounds of battle extended off to both the left and right of him. Through the forest ahead, he could see what appeared to be a couple of Nisei soldiers slumped in foxholes, dead. Fred didn't recognize them, but they had to be Second Battalion guys. Beyond that it was impossible to make much out through the trees. Judging from the amount of fire coming at them, though, there seemed to be a sizable enemy force somewhere ahead in the wet gray murk.

K Company started to advance. Fred tried to move up, tree by tree, toward the still mostly invisible Germans ahead as periodic bursts of machine-gun fire ripped through the forest around him. Dirt and stones and bits of bark flew in all directions. Then 105-millimeter howitzer shells began to whistle overhead.

George Oiye and Sus Ito had crept out in advance of the line with their forward observer teams. Using a forested ravine for concealment, they'd spotted some German tanks about a hundred yards in front of K Company and called in their coordinates. With their guns now located down in Bruyères, at the base of the mountains, Kats Miho and the 522nd guys had begun firing on the reported position of the tanks, but they were having a hard time with accuracy. The terrain before them was so steep that they had to elevate the barrels of the howitzers to an unusually high angle, above forty-five degrees. That meant the shells necessarily took high, looping trajectories, keeping them in the air much longer than usual so that the slightest gust of wind tended to deflect them from their intended targets. The barrage was having little effect on the tanks.

By early afternoon, K and I Companies, still out ahead of the rest of the Third Battalion, had advanced only a matter of yards in the face of the relentless, interlocking machine-gun fire and the devastating, howling 88-millimeter shells fired by the tanks. Just behind the front line, K Company's James Okubo and the other medics had excavated a large dugout among the roots of some trees and covered it with logs, stones, and earth to serve as an emergency aid center. Already, it was overflowing with maimed young men needing to be taken down the mountain.

Medics tending to the wounded at an aid station in the Vosges

ROUGHLY THREE MILES to the southeast, on top of the ridge overlooking La Houssière, in breaks between the attacks the Germans kept throwing at them, the surrounded Texans tried to bury their dead. Things were continuing to deteriorate within their perimeter. They were almost entirely out of rations now. They had run out of medical supplies. And they were fast running out of hope. The only source of drinking water was what rain they could catch in helmets and one shallow muddy pool sitting in a low, boggy no-man's-land right on the edge of the perimeter. But the Germans, too, were taking water from the pool, so every attempt to get more came with the potential for a deadly face-to-face confrontation. At any rate, they had also run out of halazone tablets to purify the putrid stuff.

Huddled in a foxhole he had covered with logs, his feet swollen and aching with trench foot, the Texans' radioman, Erwin Blonder, a gangly twenty-three-year-old Jewish kid from Cleveland, switched on his radio. He hated to do it. He knew that the radio's batteries would soon be depleted and then their only means of communication with the outside world would end abruptly. But he and Marty Higgins were increasingly worried that the cries of their wounded men were giving German artillery forward observers too good a fix on their exact location within the perimeter. They desperately needed morphine. Blonder had repeatedly asked for an airdrop of emergency supplies, but so far the dense fog enveloping the mountaintops had made it impossible for pilots even to locate the men, let alone approach close enough to make an accurate drop. Now he asked again when the desperately needed supplies would arrive. The response that crackled over the radio was short, simple, and demoralizing: "Not yet."

AT ABOUT 3:30 P.M., the Germans launched a full-scale counterattack on the Third Battalion, and the brunt of it fell on K and I Companies. As Fred and his squad frantically dug in wherever they happened to be, someone shouted, "Tank! Tank!" A German Panzer IV tank rumbled out of the foggy woods ahead of them, firing point-blank into K Company's positions. Shells slammed into stout trees, shattering their trunks, toppling them over on men on the ground. Alongside and behind the tank, German infantrymen advanced steadily, firing machine guns. Within minutes they had come to within fifty yards of where Fred lay in the shallow depression he had hastily hollowed out of the forest's soggy floor. As they closed in, the Germans began throwing grenades. The Nisei lobbed grenades back at them. But they just kept coming. So did the tank. It was clear that the enemy was about to overwhelm them. Fred tossed aside his mortar tube, grabbed his M1, and began shooting at anything that moved out in front of him, firing reflexively, on instinct. He was beyond thinking now, except for one overwhelming thought, an absolute conviction: he had to kill these bastards before they could kill him. Nothing else mattered. Everything had suddenly become extraordinarily sharp—every pebble that flew by, every pine branch that broke overhead, every distant cry, every minute rustling of his mud-caked uniform. He took it all in instantaneously, apprehended it fully, even as he kept firing, reaching for new clips, slamming them into the gun, and firing again.

Out of the corner of his eye, he saw Matsuichi Yogi stand up. Yogi—one of the Buddhaheads who'd given Fred a hard time when he first got to Shelby—had since become a friend. Fred had originally been a bazooka man, but when he'd been shifted to a mortar unit, it was Yogi who had replaced him on K Company's bazooka team. Now Yogi had the weapon up on his shoulder, and he was running full tilt toward the tank. Fred sucked in some cold, wet air and held his breath. Out in the open now, right in front of the tank, Yogi stopped and knelt. With bullets smacking into the trunks of the trees all around him, he fired and scored a direct hit. Flames erupted from the underside of the machine, black smoke poured out of its hatch, and it ground to a dead stop. When no Germans emerged from the tank, Yogi pivoted, saw a German bazooka man, and fired his own bazooka again, obliterating the other man. As another German moved toward him through the woods with yet another bazooka, Yogi unslung his carbine and dropped the man in his tracks. By the time Yogi made it back to K Company's lines, the German attack was tapering off, it was twilight, and the gray-suited enemy were ghosting back into the trees and the fog.

. . .

As DARKNESS FELL, George Oiye came stumbling out of the woods, rejoining K Company after his reconnoitering mission. "Start digging in. The enemy is all around us," someone told him. Grabbing a trenching tool, George and his radioman, John Nishimura, crept a short distance into the now utterly black forest, found a bare patch of soggy soil, and began to scrape out foxholes, trying not to make too much noise. They hadn't gotten far into their task when something or someone touched George on the back. Alarmed, George hissed, "John, is that you?" But before Nishimura could answer, a voice behind George rasped out, "*Kamerade! Kamerade!*" Terrified, his pulse pounding, George wheeled around, hands outstretched in the dark, trying to figure out who or what had crept up on him. He made contact with human flesh, then saw something white held in a hand, then a pallid face. It was a German infantryman, waving a handkerchief. With his rifle leaning against a tree somewhere in the dark, George had no weapon, but he stood the man up, turned him around, and began to push him in the direction of K Company's command post, hoping this wasn't a trap, that other Germans weren't about to ambush him. As they approached the command center, a guard called out, "Halt! Password!" George hesitated. He'd forgotten the password.

"I'm 522. A forward observer."

"Halt! Password!"

"I've got a prisoner for you!"

Finally, the guard approached, materializing slowly out of the dark, his rifle leveled at George's belly. When he saw that it was a Nisei soldier with a German prisoner, the guard smiled, relaxed, and marched the German away.

AN ERUPTION OF EXPLOSIONS and the sound of tree branches shattering overhead startled Rudy awake the next morning, October 28.

German artillery had opened up on K Company from positions to the south and east of La Houssière. Shards of hot steel and jagged splinters of pinewood sliced down from the treetops, quickly killing or maiming anyone who wasn't under cover. Rudy, like most of the men, had covered his foxhole with logs and mounds of earth the night before for just this reason. But a few hadn't been as careful, and within minutes men were shrieking in pain in the cold morning rain. Someone bellowed for medics to come forward. James Okubo raced among the trees, heedless of the deadly shower, dragging writhing, wounded, cussing men into dugouts, leaning over them, trying to patch up those who still had a pulse, peering down into their upturned pale rain-splattered faces, watching their eyes, trying to keep their lives from flickering out.

George Oiye and Sus Ito scrambled from one foxhole to the next, trying to find someone with a radio so they could call on the 522nd for countervailing fire. Fred Shiosaki huddled in his dugout peering out at the mayhem through mud-smeared eyeglasses as the earth around him shuddered. With each new tree burst a wave of superheated air washed over him. Fragments of wood and sharp shrapnel flew by. The air reeked of sulfur and pine pitch.

With their position now obviously and accurately zeroed in on by the German forward observers, K and I Companies had to get out of there, fast, and it wasn't going to be easy. Just crawling out of their burrows wasn't going to be easy. Overnight, the temperature had continued to drop; the intermittent rain was again verging on snow. Their hands ached, their fingers were numb, their uniforms were saturated, everything they touched was cold and wet. Many of them were showing signs of trench foot now, their feet throbbing, turning purple, blue, and black, swelling up in their boots after long immersion in flooded foxholes and slit trenches. Fred, for one, was having a hard time just walking.

The much larger problem, though, was the continued fierce resistance of the forces arrayed in front of them. As the artillery barrage finally subsided, the men crawled out of their improvised bunkers, grabbed their weapons, and advanced, crouching low, sometimes running, sometimes crawling from tree to tree in the face of almost unrelenting fire from riflemen and machine gunners they could not even see in the dense woods ahead. Still they kept moving forward.

By mid-morning, though, they came to a place that was simply impassable. In a clearing where several logging roads converged, the Germans had felled dozens of trees, constructed another massive roadblock, surrounded it with mines, and set up a water-cooled machine gun they had captured from the Texans. In the adjoining woods they had placed snipers with clear lines of sight on anyone who approached the barrier. K Company's advance ground to a halt as the machine gun began to rake their ranks.

ON THE HILLTOP ABOVE La Houssière, Marty Higgins ordered his men to scrounge up anything white or light colored they could find in their packs and lay out a twenty-five-foot-long arrow on the ground, pointing to a clearing where he figured U.S. Thunderbolts might—if the weather cleared—finally be able to drop the ammunition and medical supplies he'd been requesting from Dahlquist for days.

A little after 9:00 a.m., the Texans finally heard the welcome rumble of aircraft approaching and the unwelcome *ack-ack* of German antiaircraft batteries down in La Houssière firing at them. Then, suddenly, six-foot auxiliary fuel tanks stuffed with food, water, medical supplies, and radio batteries began crashing through upper branches of the pine forest, trailing half-open parachutes. The Thunderbolts had come in low, under the clouds, dodging the German fire and swerving around the higher ridges. Higgins and his men rose to their feet and cheered.

But the cheers died in their throats. Most of the tanks slammed too hard into the edge of the ridge, bounced off, and rolled downhill, directly into the German lines. Within a few minutes the Texans could see German soldiers on the slopes below them, gleefully scooping up biscuits, C rations, cans of meat, candy bars, canisters of freshwater, cartons of cigarettes, tin boxes of medicine. Everything a hungry, thirsty, or wounded man could want. Furious, the Texans opened fire on the Germans, who scampered away with most of the loot.

BY LATE AFTERNOON, after struggling with the problem of shooting at such high angles, Kats and the other 522nd artillerymen had mostly reduced the roadblock and the minefields where K and I Companies had been bogged down. The infantry began to creep forward again, forcing their way through the breach, advancing into the darkening woods beyond the clearing. Moving cautiously from tree to tree, Fred was gratified to see dead Germans slumped over their weapons in foxholes and machine-gun nests as they entered the woods. Apparently, the 522nd's barrage had done more than move logs out of the way.

Rudy had strapped a radio on his back in order to stay in touch with Pursall, and it was slowing him down. As he approached a gully in the woods, he glanced down, saw a German lying on his back, looking up at him. Without hesitating or thinking, Rudy raised his rifle and shot him four or five times in the chest, point-blank. Blood blossomed on the man's gray jacket. He stared at Rudy with astonishment, took one sharp breath, exhaled, and died with his eyes wide open. As Rudy stood staring at the body, an ice-cold jab of doubt stabbed at him. It suddenly occurred to him that perhaps the man had simply been trying to surrender. The possibility burbled up in Rudy's mind unbidden and unwelcome. But it lasted only a moment. He shrugged and walked on. He wasn't in the mood for entertaining scruples.

In Bruyères, as daylight waned, Kats Miho and his cannoneer, Roy Fujii, packed the hollow ends of 105-millimeter artillery shells with chocolate bars, rations, and medications instead of explosives and began firing them toward the mountaintop where the Texans were stranded. Almost all of the shells, though, simply slammed into the mountainside and disappeared neatly and irretrievably into the mud.

. . .

DARKNESS FELL OVER K Company like a nightmare. It began to rain again, hard. Up to their knees in cold, muddy water again, their teeth chattering, their feet aching, the men hunkered in slit trenches. The rain pelted their faces, dripped from their helmets, saturated their now ragged uniforms, penetrated them to the skin. By midnight, the rain was turning to stinging sleet.

But the mud was the worst of it. It clung to their hands and faces. It was in their hair. It was in their mouths, gritty and foul tasting. It worked its way under their shirts and up their trousers, a cold, clinging, relentless mire. Fred Shiosaki's feet were now so swollen in the tattered remains of his boots that he thought the boots might split open. The last time he had seen his feet, several days before, they were turning purple and smelled like carrion, like a dead deer he had once come across in the woods back in Spokane. He wasn't sure he would be able to stand and walk, let alone run, when the order came to advance in the morning.

Rudy hunkered down in a trench, struggling, having to work at not thinking about certain things—the kid he'd shot earlier that day, the friends he'd lost in the last few days. They were all trying not to think about that—about the boys with whom a few days before they had sat around campfires or sprawled in haylofts in French barns, talking, playing ukuleles, smoking cigarettes, sharing letters from home, trying to ignore the relentless boom and crash of artillery in the hills above them.

Now they were dead. So many of them.

It was impossible to see more than a few feet in any direction. Here and there a match flickered in the rain, and the tip of a cigarette glowed briefly before someone ducked back down into his hole. Somewhere out there in the dark, George Oiye and Sus Ito were down on their bellies in the mud again, trying to slither close enough to the German positions to be able to call in more strikes from Kats Miho and the artillerymen in the morning.

Exhausted as they all were, nobody slept much that night. Nobody said much of anything either. Not a good idea to speak too loudly with the Germans so close. And there wasn't really much to say, anyway. When the sun finally came up, more of them were probably going to die. No wishful thinking. More of them were certainly going to die, and they all knew it. So they tried to imagine they were somewhere else. They closed their eyes against the horror of here and now and tried to conjure up there and then. Home, maybe. A warm bedroom. Family laughing downstairs. Pots and pans rattling in the kitchen. The smell of ginger being grated, tea being brewed, bread being toasted. Anywhere but here, any time but now.

But here and now would not relent. Up ahead, above them, they could hear the metallic clatter and clank of German tanks maneuvering into position in the cold, wet dark. And then, toward dawn, something worse, a boy somewhere out in the woods, one of their own, someone the medics had not been able to get to, dying, calling plaintively for his mother in Japanese, "*Okaasan, okaasan, okaasan.*"

Billeted in a French farmhouse near the town of Biffontaine, rising each gray morning to help unload more mangled bodies from the backs of the trucks that rumbled down off the mountain, Chaplains Yamada and Higuchi were shocked and horrified by what was happening to their boys. The almost always optimistic Yamada had grown sullen and downcast. But it was Hiro Higuchi for whom the relentless horror was becoming a moral crisis. Just recently he had written to his wife, saying that after seeing what he had seen, he might have to give up the ministry: "Going back to the pulpit to speak on love and hope and faith and living a soft minister's life is [going to be] a difficult adjustment."

Then, during the battle for Bruyères, one of the Second Battalion's young men had come to him, troubled by the fact that he had killed German boys. What was he to make of the commandment "Thou shalt not kill"? Was he now to be punished by God? Higuchi had reassured him: "It's either you kill or get killed. Your cause is the right one. God won't punish you." But his own answer didn't sit well with Higuchi. It felt pallid and limp. And just before they had started up into the mountains again, another young man had come to him and asked Higuchi more questions: Did God only care for causes? Did he really care for individuals, for men like himself? After seeing so many of his friends killed, he thought it didn't make sense. "What is God to me? What am I to God?" the soldier had asked plaintively. For that Higuchi had had no answer at all, just stunned silence, and the soldier had set out for battle ill at ease.

Now Higuchi learned that he had been killed up on the mountain, and the chaplain couldn't get it out of his mind, couldn't forget that he'd had no answer, no solace to provide. And the more he pondered the question, the more he recognized the fragility of his own faith.

AT DAWN ON OCTOBER 29, the Third Battalion continued to push southeast through the mountains toward the stranded Texans. The 100th Battalion remained just to the right and slightly behind the Third. The only realistic option for reaching the stranded men, though, still lay with the Third and specifically with K and I Companies, both of which remained out front, working their way along the narrow ridge that led directly to the hill where the Texans were trapped.

The narrowness of the ridge presented Pursall with a nearly insoluble problem. It provided a near-perfect defensive position for the Germans. The terrain fell away so steeply on both sides that it would be impossible to outflank the enemy. The Nisei were going to have to go straight down the middle of the ridge, through a series of heavily fortified positions while under constant fire from the higher ground near the far end. The whole setup looked like a death trap.

As Pursall talked things through with Pence, trying to work out a plan of attack, the two of them also found themselves fighting an increasingly fractious battle with their commander. That morning Dahlquist

repeatedly bellowed at them on the radio, demanding to know why prog-
ress was so slow, why the hell their regiment wasn't breaking through to
his Texans. Pence finally decided to go up to the front line to check on the
situation for himself. Almost as soon as he arrived, though, his jeep came
under attack, he suffered severe leg wounds, and he was hastily evacuated
from the battlefield. For the young men of K Company who had witnessed the incident, it was tough to see the diminutive but rooster-tough
Pence go down. He had seen them through the kotonk-Buddhahead wars.
He had played baseball with them in swirling clouds of red Mississippi
dust. He had toughened them up, taught them soldiering, and then
brought them young women to dance with.

But he was gone now, and so it fell to Pursall alone to make Dahlquist
understand the near impossibility of what he was asking for. Again, he
tried to explain that the extreme terrain and the enemy's command of it
dictated prudence. The smart thing was to wait until more resources
could be brought up to the front and the weather cleared to allow for air
support. But the general was more adamant than ever. "Let's keep them
moving. Even against opposition. Get through to them." With each passing hour, it seemed to Pursall, Dahlquist was edging closer to panic
about the whole situation, which was hardly surprising. It was he who
had ordered the Texas unit to advance too swiftly into unreconnoitered
territory in the first place. If the entire bunch of them were to be killed
or captured now, the Germans would score an enormous propaganda
coup and Dahlquist's military career would likely come to an abrupt
and inglorious end here in the Vosges.

But if he was going to stand up to Dahlquist, Pursall decided he, like
Pence, needed to see the situation on the ground himself. Once again,
he turned to Rudy and said exactly what he always said, "Come on,
Punch Drunk, let's go." And so, with automatic fire ripping through the
trees above them, Pursall and Rudy slowly worked their way forward a
few dozen yards, out past the line, crawling on their bellies through wet
moss and mud and rotting leaves, reconnoitering, trying to get a better
view of what exactly was throwing so much fire at them. What they saw

was chilling. The entire sloping hillside above them bristled with German machine-gun nests and dug-in infantry armed with heavy weapons. Higher upslope, they could hear tanks and half-tracks moving. Pursall asked Rudy what he thought about trying to take the hill. Rudy didn't really want to answer the question—didn't care for the weight it put on his shoulders—but he answered honestly and bluntly. It would be insane. They needed to wait, needed to bring up more firepower first. Pursall nodded.

By the time they had worked their way back downslope, Dahlquist himself had appeared just behind the line, riding in a jeep. Dahlquist's personal aide-de-camp, Wells Lewis, was sitting behind the wheel. Lewis, the son of the Nobel Prize–winning novelist Sinclair Lewis, was an extraordinary young man by any measure. Tall and handsome, with wavy blond hair, he'd published a well-regarded novel of his own, graduated from Harvard magna cum laude, and then, forsaking the many privileged paths that lay before him, enlisted in the army as a buck private a year before Pearl Harbor. Since then, he had fought in heavy combat in North Africa, Italy, and France, earned a Bronze Star and a Silver Star, risen to the rank of first lieutenant, and become Dahlquist's right-hand man. It was a plum assignment for him and a distinct honor for Dahlquist to have the dashing young man—wildly popular back in the States—at his side.

Now he and Dahlquist climbed out of the jeep. The general looked around and saw just what he didn't want to see—men down on the ground, dug in on all sides of him. Immediately he laid into Pursall.

"I want you guys to charge," Dahlquist yelled at Pursall. "Charge, charge, charge!"

Pursall planted himself squarely in front of the general, standing closer than was comfortable for either man. Speaking slowly but firmly, in measured phrases, he tried to explain the situation, that he'd talked to his men, that a charge now would be suicidal, that they needed to bring other units up first.

"Look, if my men said that's the only way they can do it, that's the only way it can be done."

But Dahlquist, getting red in the face now, didn't want to hear it. They argued some more. Dahlquist wasn't budging. Finally, Pursall wheeled around, spotted Rudy, and said again, "Okay, Punch Drunk, let's go."

This time Rudy hesitated. The last thing he wanted was to start back up that hill again.

"Where're we going, sir?"

"We've got to take the general up, to show him what we are up against."

Rudy and Pursall began leading Dahlquist and Lewis uphill into the woods ahead as bullets again began snapping into trees all around them. Pursall leaned over and whispered to Rudy, "Okay, Punch Drunk, I don't want you to hit the ground. . . . I'm six foot and you won't see me hitting the ground."

Now Rudy was horrified. This was crazy shit. But he wasn't going to be the first one to dive for cover, so he kept walking into the fire. When they got within viewing distance, Pursall began pointing out the German positions uphill from them—here a machine-gun nest, there what looked to be most of a rifle company dug in, to the right more machine guns, farther up those tanks—all in all, an impenetrable wall of resistance. Dahlquist seemed unimpressed. Pursall was adamant. Rudy slid behind a tree. He couldn't believe what he was seeing—two hulking senior haole officers and an aide standing there in full view of the Germans, arguing with each other as bullets whipped by them. Dahlquist told Lewis to fetch a map, but as the young man spread it out, a bullet slammed into the back of his head. Lewis slumped into Dahlquist's arms, dead. Dahlquist, stunned, his uniform bloodied, sank to the ground holding Lewis's body. He stared into the young man's face, murmuring over and over, "Lewis is dead." Then he looked up and said to no one in particular, "They were shooting at me and killed this fine young man."

When Dahlquist finally arose, his face ashen, he began to jog downhill toward his jeep. He was even more enraged now, bellowing at individual soldiers he passed, pausing occasionally to kick at them where they lay, ordering them to get up, fix bayonets, and charge. Pursall pursued the general downhill, with Rudy trailing just behind. Pursall was enraged himself, furious that Dahlquist was now issuing direct orders to his men. The two men came face-to-face. nose-to-nose, in a pouring rain.

"I'm ordering you, you will attack! I want you to fix bayonets and attack. That's an order!" Dahlquist spat at Pursall. Pursall, risking a court-martial now, grabbed Dahlquist by the lapels of his bloodied shirt and leaned into him: "Those are my boys you're trying to kill. Nobody kills my boys like that. Nobody."

The two men stood seething at each other silently for a long moment. Finally, Dahlquist wheeled and walked away, shouting again over his shoulder, "That's an order!"

WITHIN A FEW MINUTES Rudy and Pursall were back up on the line, crouching behind some logs. The older man seemed deeply perplexed. He turned to Rudy and asked, "What do you think, Punch Drunk?"

Rudy hesitated. There was no good answer to the question. "I don't know. I'm not the boss. You're the boss. You're the one that wears that leaf on your shoulders," he said.

Pursall nodded silently, staring grimly up the hill in front of him. Then, abruptly, he pulled a pearl-handled pistol from a holster on his hip, stood up, and yelled, "Come on, you guys! Let's go! Let's go!"

For Rudy, for all of them watching him, time suddenly slowed to a crawl. Pursall stepped over a log and started up the hill, firing the pistol, and bellowing again, "Let's go! Artillery, too! You charge, too!"

K Company's sergeant Chester Tanaka looked up, saw him, and thought, "My God! If that dumb son of a bitch is going to walk up into that fire, I guess we'd better, too." He stood up and motioned for his men to follow him. Fred Shiosaki stared, disbelieving for a moment, at Pursall. He had the same reaction as Tanaka. "You crazy bastard," he thought. "You're going to get shot!" But like Tanaka he rose to his feet and started hobbling forward, his swollen feet throbbing with pain. George Oiye heard someone next to him clicking his bayonet onto his rifle. Getting bayoneted was George's greatest fear. He hesitated, wondered whether anyone would notice if he just crawled behind a nearby rock. But just to his right, his radioman, Yuki Minaga, got up and took a few steps forward. Pursall, looking back again, saw Minaga, pointed at him, and shouted, "There's the man!" Scared to death, armed with only a pistol, George got up and started running up the hill, too, following Minaga. So did Sus Ito. So did Rudy. They all did. With their fathers' words echoing in their minds, their mothers' love beating in their hearts, the men of K Company, one by one, then en masse, rose and began to charge up the hill, shooting from their hips, shooting blind through the tangle of trees looming above them.

Down the line, in I Company, Private Barney Hajiro saw K Company go. Without a word, he stood, too, and began moving steadily uphill, carrying his BAR at his hip in a sling, spraying the terrain ahead of him with automatic fire. The rest of I Company rose and followed him. Some

Charging uphill into enemy fire in the Vosges

of them screamed obscenities at the Germans. Sergeant Joe Shimamura began yelling, "*Make! Make! Make!*"—"death" in Hawaiian. Others yelled insults in Japanese or Hawaiian pidgin. Most, though, just gritted their teeth and ran silently, slipping and sliding in the mud, tripping over roots, falling on their faces, getting up, running again, expecting to die at any moment. A torrent of steel and lead descended on them. Mortar shells plunged down among them with terrifying randomness. Machine-gun fire ripped them apart as they ran. Matsuichi Yogi, the bazooka man who had single-handedly taken out a tank two days before, crumpled to the ground, mortally wounded. A bullet smacked into the head of the man running next to Fred, and he pitched forward into the mud, dead in an instant. Howling 88-millimeter shells slammed into trees, shattering them, toppling them over onto men. Enemy artillery shells burst in the treetops again. A 155-millimeter shell exploded a few yards in front of George Oiye. The blast blew him thirty feet downhill. As he staggered back onto his feet, he realized the world had gone silent. He'd been deafened. He started up the hill again. Another shell, an armor-piercing tank round, hit a tree next to him and fell right at his feet, spinning maniacally in the mud, but this one didn't go off. He stepped over it and kept going. Yet another shell slammed into a tree directly ahead of Fred. This one did explode. Something hard and hot sliced into Fred's side. "God, I'm hit," he muttered to himself as he went down. He rolled over onto his back, pulled up his shirt, and found a jagged piece of steel shrapnel embedded in his abdomen. But not much blood. James Okubo crawled over to him, pulled the shrapnel out, hastily bandaged the wound, and told Fred he was okay, to get up and go. He did.

As they climbed higher, the slope steepened. Grabbing at tree roots and rocks, and hoisting themselves higher, they drew closer to the German tanks, the noses of which were pointing directly downhill, firing point-blank at them now. Bazooka men crouched and fired back at the machines' treads, trying to knock them out, but the tanks kept swiveling and maneuvering, their cannons booming, the shells screaming through the woods, shattering trees and dismembering men as they ran. The hillside itself seemed to explode: columns of earth and rock erupted, men screamed, machine guns growled. Dust and smoke mixed with the fog in a dense yellow-gray soup that made it hard to discern friend from foe. The men crawled over logs, stepped over dead bodies, hurled grenades uphill. And still they kept going.

As Fred neared the crest of the hill, he heard someone sobbing. In a ditch, a very young German soldier lay curled up in the fetal position. He seemed to be calling out for his mother. Fred raised his rifle and thought, "Well, say goodbye to your mother." But he hesitated. The kid was about the age of his little brother, Floyd. He lowered the rifle. "All right, you lucky son of a gun," he hissed, and kept climbing the hill. But a moment later, just behind him, he heard a single rifle shot. Then, just as he reached the top, the sounds of battle simply ceased, almost in an instant. One moment there was a cacophony of explosions and shrieks and wailing and bellowing, the next near silence. Nothing but the crack of occasional rifle shots and the whumping sound of artillery off in the distance and the moaning of wounded men. In the woods ahead of him Fred saw something he had never seen before, Germans running full tilt away from him. "My God," he muttered to himself. "It's done." But then he looked around and thought, "But there's hardly anybody left."

As the Germans withdrew behind a large roadblock seven hundred yards up a logging road, K Company's survivors dug in for the night. Pursall went looking for Rudy as he often did after a battle and was relieved to find him already securely in a foxhole. Rudy looked up and said, "Hey, Colonel, you coulda got shot runnin' up here like that!"

"Well, I'm still kickin'. You all right?"

"Yeah, I'm fine."

"Okay. We're happy."

But Alfred Pursall had never been less happy in his life. Darkness was again enveloping the Vosges. On the slopes below him, more than a

A horrified soldier during the rescue of the Lost Battalion

hundred Germans lay dead, sprawled in the mud. Only perhaps a quarter of a mile and the one remaining roadblock now separated the Nisei from the trapped Texans. But the gains had come at a staggering cost. K and I Companies had both been devastated. Of the hundreds of men who had started up into the Vosges with the two companies three days before, fewer than two dozen in K Company were still alive and able to walk out of the woods; in I Company there were even fewer.

AT DAYLIGHT on the morning of October 30, the remnants of K Company moved forward again. All the company's commissioned officers were now dead or wounded, so command fell to Sergeant Chester Tanaka. During the night, the 522nd's artillerymen had pounded the final roadblock standing between the Nisei and the Texans, largely reducing it to splinters, but it quickly became clear that the Germans had regrouped in the woods beyond. German artillery and mortar shells again began to rain down on them. Rudy hadn't gone far when a shell slammed into a tree above him. Jagged bits of shrapnel sliced into his hand, mangling two of his fingers. He was going to have to head down to an aid station in the rear to get them bandaged. He found one of the new replacement troops and told him he'd have to serve as battalion runner until he could get back. The kid was green. He'd been raised in Japan, hardly spoke English, and didn't really know what he was doing most of the time. But Rudy figured it would be okay. His wound wasn't that serious; he wouldn't be at the aid station long.

By the time Rudy got back up to the line an hour later, K Company had moved up and dug in about four hundred yards from the knoll on the end of the ridge where the Texans were trapped. Rudy asked Tanaka where the kid he'd left behind as a replacement runner was. Tanaka jerked his thumb over his shoulder. "Oh yeah. Look in the foxhole over there." Rudy walked over and looked in. The kid was dead in the foxhole, his head a bloody mess.

AT THE END of the ridge, Marty Higgins and his men were again enduring a full-on assault. As the Nisei approached the knoll slowly from the northwest, the Germans charged the Texans from all directions, closing to within thirty yards in a matter of minutes, pouring fire into their positions. It seemed clear to Higgins that the intent was to kill them all before the Nisei could reach them. His men, fighting from foxholes and dugouts, threw everything they had back at the oncoming enemy, hurling grenades and unleashing furious automatic weapons fire with their BARs and M1s. But they all knew they wouldn't be able to sustain it for long. If the Germans kept coming at them in this way, they'd quickly run out of ammunition and be at their mercy. And there was no reason to believe the Germans had any mercy to give.

As impending disaster seemed to loom, General Dahlquist issued another confounding order. Despite being far removed from the scene of the action, and bypassing the chain of command again, he took it upon himself to call in specific coordinates for an artillery barrage. The

Fire Direction Center relayed the coordinates to the batteries in the field, and Kats Miho began to dial in the settings on *Kuuipo*. But then, almost immediately, the Fire Direction Center called B Battery's commander, Captain Billy Taylor, back. They had just realized that the coordinates Dahlquist wanted to hit were precisely those where the Texans were and way too close to those where they believed K and I Companies must now be. If they followed the orders, they would likely wipe out most of the Texas unit and perhaps some of their own guys as well. Under continual sniper and mortar fire, Taylor headed off through the woods to Third Battalion headquarters, where he was able to find maps, get a fix on the Germans' true location, adjust the coordinates, and call in accurate fire. No one was about to tell Dahlquist what had happened, though.

For the next hour, working their way southeast along the ridgeline toward the knob on which the Texans were surrounded, K and I Companies crept slowly toward them while the Texans fought furiously to repulse the Germans assaulting them from all sides. It seemed an even bet whether the Germans or the Nisei would break through to the Texans first. But then, in the midst of the chaos—mingled with the smells of high explosives, shattered wood, and mud—both the Nisei and the Texans suddenly began to smell smoke. A few minutes later they saw it—white billows rising from the German-held valley beyond the southern end of the ridge. As the smoke spread out, filtering through the woods, the Germans slowly pulled back, moving south, down off the end of the ridge as both they and the forest itself gradually disappeared, fading into the white clouds of a smoke screen.

SINCE EARLY THAT MORNING, a small patrol from I Company had been cautiously advancing out ahead of the main force, the men down on their hands and knees much of the time, following a thin black telephone wire through the woods, a wire they thought might lead them straight to the Texans.

Now, at about 2:00 p.m., as the Germans' smoke screen spread through the woods, one of them, Mutt Sakamoto, scanning the terrain ahead, saw a pale face peering around a tree. The face disappeared, then reappeared, then disappeared again. Eventually, a figure stepped cautiously out from behind the tree, clutching a rifle and staring hard at the approaching Nisei.

Twenty-one-year-old technical sergeant Edward Guy wasn't quite sure what he was looking at, who it was approaching out of the smoke. He waited warily as Sakamoto drew closer. Then, finally, he could be sure. On the shoulder of the approaching figure's uniform he could make out the brilliant blue and red of the 442nd's patch. He threw down his rifle and ran downhill toward Sakamoto, shouting, whooping, laughing. As the two of them came face-to-face, Guy embraced Sakamoto in a bear hug. Sakamoto didn't know quite what to say. He hesitated, then smiled and said simply, "Do you need any cigarettes?"

At about the same moment, Rudy Tokiwa and Chester Tanaka, approaching from a different direction, saw a helmeted head moving in a foxhole. They froze. Tanaka leveled his rifle, drawing a bead on the head, preparing to shoot, but then he hesitated. Even through the smoke he was sure. It was an American helmet. Tanaka lowered the rifle, and Sergeant Bill Hull scrambled out of the hole. Someone unseen in the woods called out, "Hey, the 442 guys are here!" More Texans began rising out of the earth, emerging from camouflaged foxholes all around the Nisei soldiers like prairie dogs, their faces gaunt, begrimed, and overgrown with stubble, their eyes hollow. They looked around warily. Then, starting to believe that it was finally over, they began hugging one another, some of them laughing, some blinking away tears. As the men of K Company came closer, one of the Texans croaked out, "God, thank you, thank you, thank you." Erwin Blonder grabbed the handset on his radio and sent one last transmission, this one for the 442nd's command post: "Tell them we love them."

Watching the Nisei approach, Marty Higgins felt chills run down his spine. These guys were nearly as dirty and grimy and beat-up-looking as his boys. They were generally small and wearing uniforms made for much larger men. The legs of their pants were bunched up around their ankles, their helmets hanging down well over their ears. But as he later said, "Honestly, they looked like giants to us."

Just-rescued members of the Lost Battalion

As the Texans began to filter down out of the woods and onto a muddy logging road, passing through the 442nd's lines, a newsreel cameraman arrived by jeep and began to film the scene. The rescued GIs shook the Nisei's hands and patted them on the back. The Nisei handed them cigarettes and candy bars and canteens full of water. The Texans, mostly, smiled wearily and said thank you. They took swigs of the water and lit the cigarettes, but then walked quickly on. None of them wanted to linger. They wanted to get off the damned mountain. As they passed Rudy and some of the K Company guys, one of them nodded and, with a cigarette dangling from his lips, said simply, "Hey, kids. Some balls you got. We thought we was all dead and gone."

NINETEEN

*A merry Christmas to you. . . . I love you so much and need
you so much. Today when the boys were playing the carols a
thought came to me—"Hisako plays the piano too and
wonderfully"—and a great longing to hear you play the carols
once and sing as when we were so happy around the house. . . .
Tonight more than ever I miss you.*

CHAPLAIN HIGUCHI TO HIS WIFE, HISAKO
DECEMBER 24, 1944

On November 9, in Parker, Arizona, the little railroad town just
north of the Poston concentration camp, a Nisei soldier—Private
Raymond Matsuda—wandered into a barbershop to get a haircut. He was on crutches. Back on July 22, as the 442nd approached the
Arno, he had been shot in the knee. Now, recently released from a hospital in California, he was on his way to visit friends incarcerated at
Poston. He figured he should get spruced up before heading down to the
camp. So, wearing a uniform emblazoned with the 442nd patch and six
or seven other army ribbons and badges, including the combat infantryman's badge and a Purple Heart, he hobbled through the barbershop's double swinging doors. He did not see, or chose to ignore, a sign
on one of the doors, JAPS KEEP OUT, YOU RATS. The proprietor, Andy

Hale, took one look at Matsuda, strode over to him, cussing, and shoved him right back out through the doors and into Parker's single dusty street, crutches and all. Asked about it later, Hale was unapologetic. "I don't want none of their business. . . . I sure as hell won't work on a Jap." When someone pointed out that Matsuda was both an American citizen and a wounded U.S. Army soldier, Hale just snarled, "They all look alike to me."

Two days later, on November 11, Rudy Tokiwa's mother arose early, before the dawn began to lighten the desert sky to the east of Poston, before the mourning doves began to coo in the mesquite trees down by the river. She slipped on a robe and a pair of slippers, checking each carefully to make sure no scorpions had moved in during the night. As quietly as she could, she stepped out of her room into the chill desert air and padded her way across a stretch of cool sand to the women's shower room. There she switched on a bare electric lightbulb hanging from the ceiling, slipped out of her things, and turned the cold water tap on. When she stepped into the frigid stream, she gasped and shut her eyes tight, struggling to endure the pain of it without calling out. Instead, as she had done every morning since Rudy had left for the army, she stood still under the punishing stream, praying silently for Rudy, imploring God to let her pain suffice, to let it be enough, enough that he would allow her son to come home safe.

A little later that day, the *Poston Chronicle* reprinted parts of an Associated Press story, the first brief telling of what happened in the Vosges. The article—"442nd Unit Saves 'Lost Battalion'"—quoted one of the rescued Texans, Private Walter Yattaw, expressing his gratitude. "It really was ironical that we were so glad to see the Japanese, but boy, they are real Americans." But the piece bore little specific news about what Fusa Tokiwa and everyone in camp most wanted to know about—the casualties. That news would soon begin to arrive in dribs and drabs, brought by blunt telegrams or by military officers arriving unexpectedly in full dress uniforms.

. . .

ON NOVEMBER 12, after an additional week of fighting in the Vosges and a few days' rest, the surviving members of the 442nd assembled in a snowy field near Bruyères so that General Dahlquist could formally acknowledge their role in rescuing what by now everyone was calling the Lost Battalion.

The surviving Nisei soldiers had only just come down out of the mountains. Even after they'd accomplished the rescue, General Dahlquist had ordered them to remain in the Vosges and press deeper into the forest, despite their severely depleted numbers. For seven more days the survivors had fought on, limping on swollen feet, sleeping again in flooded foxholes, enduring relentless artillery barrages, and taking still more casualties in thick stands of pines now laden with snow. By the time they were finally relieved, K Company's roughly 180 men had been reduced to 17 riflemen still alive and able to fight. I Company had been reduced from approximately the same strength to only 4 riflemen and a handful of machine gunners.

Now Fred Shiosaki, one of the seventeen, stood more or less at attention in a black frozen furrow with what was left of K Company, his rifle over his shoulder, watching wearily as Dahlquist and a cluster of officers approached them in a jeep for the ceremony. Fred, like all the men around him, was tired in his bones and tired in his soul. His face was pinched and pale, his cheeks devoid of their usual rosiness, his eyes downcast, cold, black, and blank. Like the others, he wore new combat boots and an oversized, heavy winter coat. A dusting of snow clung to his shoulders and sleeves, and his feet still throbbed from the ravages of trench foot. In another snowy field nearby, black crows had assembled in their own ranks. As the officers drove up, the birds cawed raucously. A few snowflakes drifted down out of a leaden sky. Nearby, newsreel cameramen worked to set up cameras on tripods. Chaplains Yamada and Higuchi stood stamping their feet to keep warm and chatting with each other. Finally, the ceremony got under way. A color guard paraded past the Nisei, led by the 442nd's regimental band.* Dahlquist and Lieutenant Colonel Virgil Miller clambered out of their jeep and stood at attention. Miller—a forty-four-year-old native of Puerto Rico—had taken over command of the 442nd when Pence was wounded. Stationed at Schofield Barracks in Hawai'i before Pearl Harbor, he had been with the 442nd from the very beginning. Good-natured, jovial, generous, always watching out for the least among his men, he was widely liked and respected throughout the regiment—especially by the Buddhaheads who had known him longest. Now he and Dahlquist stepped forward. But instead of addressing the men, Dahlquist paused, looked out at the paltry number of men arrayed before him, and scowled. He turned to Miller and, clearly agitated, snarled, scolding him, loudly, in front of his men.

Stunned survivors of the Lost Battalion rescue
standing in review for General Dahlquist

---

*Band members often served as litter bearers when the 442nd was in combat.

"Colonel, I told you to have the whole regiment out here. When I order everyone to pass in review, I mean the cooks and *everybody* will pass in review!"

Yamada, standing nearby, watched Miller's face tighten, his jaw clench. Dahlquist glowered at him. A long, awkward silence ensued. Finally, Miller, standing ramrod straight, pivoted slowly, looked the general in the eye, and, his voice wavering, croaked, "General, this *is* the regiment. This is all I have left."

Yamada, transfixed, studied Miller's face. The man's eyes had filled with tears. Dahlquist fell silent. Apparently, this was the first time he fully realized the magnitude of the price the Nisei had paid to rescue the Texans. He stuttered out a few words of congratulations, then silently made his way down the lines of soldiers, pinning on the chest of each a ribbon representing a Presidential Unit Citation. As he passed and shook their hands, the men simply stared past him, looking over his shoulder at the mountains beyond.

As Thanksgiving 1944 approached at Poston, lists of casualties and stories of the Nisei's battles in France began to crowd out the usual news of social events and sports scores in the *Poston Chronicle*. Nearly nine hundred of Poston's young men and women were now in the armed services, and even as the casualty lists from France grew, more were signing up. Almost every week now, friends and well-wishers gathered for farewell ceremonies in which color guards paraded the American flag, a band played "The Star-Spangled Banner," and camp administrators made patriotic speeches as more young men climbed onto buses and headed off for Fort Douglas to begin active duty. And every week the stage at the Cottonwood Bowl became the scene of more frequent memorial services.

Many of the new recruits left with a particular sense of pride. They had a keen awareness of their mission—of who and what they were leaving behind, and why. After three years of incarceration, for all the harshness of the climate, despite the heat, the dust storms, the rattlesnakes, the communal showers, the monotony of mess-hall meals, and the degradation of confinement, the people incarcerated at Poston, like those at the other camps, had created extraordinary communities under trying conditions, and they were justly proud of them. By the fall of 1944, they had dug irrigation canals from the Colorado River to the camp. Land that had been nothing but sagebrush and sand was green. Vegetable patches now flourished; tea gardens now surrounded ponds full of goldfish. Carefully transplanted cottonwood trees offered at least a bit of shade over barracks and walkways.

Thousands of people who had lost their homes, jobs, businesses, control over their own lives, found some solace in exercising their creative impulses—writing haiku, practicing calligraphy, carving ironwood and mesquite sculptures, and polishing local stones and assembling them into exquisite objects of art. From salvaged scraps of wood, they carved tiny, lovely, hand-painted bird pins, using photographs in old issues of *National Geographic* as their models. They painted evocative watercolor landscapes, often—at Poston and at almost all the camps—of distant mountains, rising purple and serene and eternal, beyond the confines of the barbed wire, beyond the dreary reality of here and now. Women tore out the colorful pages of mail-order catalogs and saved colored tissue paper from the lining of apple and orange crates and fashioned them into artificial chrysanthemums and irises and gardenias. Some people unraveled strands of burlap from gunnysacks and wove them into rugs and place mats. Others searched in the desert for seedpods and vines and twigs and used them and the paper flowers to create ikebana arrangements. *Bon-kei* artists gathered sand and pebbles and bits of wood to create miniature landscapes in trays. When it wasn't being used for memorial services, the Cottonwood Bowl was the scene of almost daily theatrical performances, ranging from kindergarten holiday pageants to formal Kabuki productions. Young women—often for the first time—began working for wages in everything from nursing to manufacturing camouflage nets for the men overseas. Buddhist priests and Christian ministers tended to their flocks. Doctors, lawyers, architects, farmers, carpenters, truck drivers, florists, and electricians all brought their specialized skills to bear on improving the quality of camp life. And increasingly, there was a sense of pride arising out of their shared experience. In the face of cold injustice and profound humiliation, they had stood tall. They had nourished their spiritual lives, educated their children, found a refuge in creativity and productivity.

THEN, ON DECEMBER 17 A front-page article in the *Poston Chronicle* sent shock waves through the camp. For months, the Roosevelt administration had been quietly wrestling with the question of whether to do away with the exclusion zone and end the incarcerations. Secretary of the Interior Harold Ickes—under whom the WRA had been placed—and First Lady Eleanor Roosevelt had been urging the president to agree to a plan for resettling the "evacuees" back on the West Coast. Even the army had concluded that there was no longer any pretense of military necessity for keeping people in the camps. But through the summer and early fall, with his campaign for reelection under way, Roosevelt was wary of giving the impression that he was "coddling" the Nisei and their parents. Three days after his reelection, however, he relented. And now the news was out. The government was terminating both the mandatory exclusion zone and the "evacuation" orders. The incarcerations were to end. The camps, in time, were to close. In just weeks, the vast majority of people of Japanese ancestry would suddenly be allowed to travel and live anywhere in the United States, including on the Pacific coast. Only a relatively small number of people whose loyalty the government still questioned would continue to be denied the right to return to their old communities in the former exclusion zone along the West Coast.

At Poston, as at all the camps, the news was met with a profound sense of relief mixed with an equally profound sense of anxiety. In the preceding weeks, small numbers of prescreened individuals and families had already been allowed to travel back to the coast. Though some had been met cordially and treated civilly, others had not been. Many, in fact, had been met with scorn and abuse. For weeks that fall, new rounds of virulently racist editorials had been popping up in West Coast newspapers, arguing vehemently against allowing the return of the Japanese Americans, citizens or not.

As at the other camps, the makeup of Poston's population had shifted over the years of incarceration. As more young people had entered the service or been granted leaves by the WRA to attend college in the east or to take jobs outside the exclusion zone, it had become a camp mostly of old people, young mothers, and children. Now, as news of violent rhetoric on the West Coast reached them, there was growing anxiety about what might happen to them if they did indeed try to return home. And for many of them, there was an even bigger problem, a stark question that loomed large before them. For them, there were no longer homes to return to. Where were they to go?

BY THE TIME they finally came back down out of the Vosges, many of the Nisei soldiers were broken in every way that war can break young men. The battle for Bruyères and the rescue of the Lost Battalion, followed immediately by the subsequent operation to drive the Germans out of their sector, had proven every bit the nightmare that Daniel Inouye expected when he first looked at the Vosges back on October 13. By the end of that month alone, the Nisei soldiers had taken 790 casualties, the largest number of those in the process of rescuing just over 200 members of the Texas unit. Hundreds of them now lay in hospitals all over France, many of them grievously maimed. Many of those still able to walk and talk were shattered emotionally. They needed rest and succor. They needed to grieve, to bury their faces in pillows and sob, to drink, to smoke cigarettes, to swear and stare into the far distance, to wrestle inwardly with what had just happened. Or, if possible, to forget it.

On November 19, the 442nd boarded trucks and headed south, slogging their way through a snowstorm, en route to the Maritime Alps in southern France to take up defensive positions along a mountainous, eighteen-mile-long front on the French-Italian border, overlooking the Riviera and a world few of them even knew existed. Their official mission there was to block any potential German movement from northern Italy back into France, but nobody really expected the Germans to make such a move, so there was little likelihood that they would see significant combat. The army intended it to provide the Nisei with a bit of a break, and for many of them it would come just in time to keep their souls intact.

To KATS MIHO it didn't look, at first, as if it were going to be much of a rest period. The last week of November found him and the artillerymen hauling their howitzers behind their trucks, grinding their way laboriously up impossibly twisting roads into the mountains toward a village called Sospel, about eight miles inland from Menton on the French Riviera. The bends in the roads were so tight that every few hundred meters or so they had to climb down out of their trucks, unhitch the guns, and—grunting and heaving—push them by hand around the curves and up the steep grades. One particularly tortuous stretch, snaking its way about a thousand feet up a mountainside, took them half a day to manage. When they finally got to Sospel, though, it turned out to be a lovely village, nestled in a deep green mountain valley and bisected by a shallow, stony river, the Bévéra. There they met up with the Third Battalion, which had just moved in and made the town their new headquarters. Kats and his crew set up *Kuuipo* in a strategic location nearby, stretched camouflage nets over its position, piled sandbags around it, and settled in to see what was next.

For George Oiye, Sus Ito, and the various forward observer teams, the journey wasn't over. They loaded pack mules with supplies, preparing to take them still higher into the Maritime Alps, where they were to occupy massive French fortifications and tunnels, the Alpine extension of the Maginot Line, and establish observation posts overlooking the Mediterranean. But mule skinning, they soon found, was not in their skill set. Once loaded, the animals bucked and brayed and refused to budge. The men yelled at them in English, then tried Japanese and then, getting frustrated, wild bursts of pidgin. But it did no good. Figuring they were French mules, they tried borrowed bits of that language and got no further. They stood behind the animals and pushed and found that mules knew how to kick. They slapped them across the hindquarters and the mules just laid back their ears and stared at them. They attached halters and ropes and tried to pull the animals. The mules dug in their heels and began braying loudly. Finally, Sus Ito made a more or less miraculous discovery. Whispering in the animals' ears, soothing them, gingerly offering them various treats from his pack, he found, to his astonishment, that the mules had a passion for C ration biscuits. He soon had them calmed down and following him wherever he wanted them to go.

By the time they approached their assigned posts among craggy

A Nisei soldier arguing with a
mule in the Maritime Alps

mountaintops devoid of trees, it had begun to snow and several of the mules had slipped on icy trails and plunged screaming down sheer cliff faces, carrying with them precious provisions. But as they unloaded the surviving mules, the weather cleared, and from the mountaintops they now occupied, they had staggering vistas of a bright blue Mediterranean and the improbably beautiful coastline stretched out below them. At sunset they sat smoking cigarettes, watching the sea turn purple, the sky blossom orange and violet. They built campfires and heated up cans of beans and hash and chowed down, then attached the empty cans to wire and strung them around the perimeter of their positions to serve as alarm systems lest any Germans attempt to creep up on them in the night. Inside the hulking concrete fortifications, they felt safer than they had in a long while, and they slept that night as they had not slept in months.

"THIS IS THE kind of war we dream about," Hiro Higuchi wrote to his wife on December 12.

As all three battalions of the 442nd settled into their new assignments, they realized that, at least in part, it was going to be a bit of a lark. At times their accommodations were nothing more than primitive earthen dugouts on snowy mountaintops, but at other times they were palatial private homes and posh hotels down along the semitropical Côte d'Azur. Given generous allowances of leave, they spent their free time roaming up and down the sun-drenched Riviera coast. In Cannes, they drove jeeps along the palm-lined Boulevard de la Croisette. They sat at sidewalk cafés, as they had in Italy, but now they drank cognac instead of wine. They ate at restaurants with white linen tablecloths. They sipped champagne on sunny hotel terraces. In Menton, they strolled through the Jardins Biovès, with its elaborate formal flower beds—white chrysanthemums, orange zinnias, red roses all blooming side by side, even now in winter. They picked plump, ripe oranges from trees overhanging shady lanes. Seized by what they called "perfume fever," they bought scores of bottles for girlfriends and wives back home and visited perfume factories, emerging from them smelling of lavender and rose and jasmine. In Nice, they checked into opulent seaside hotels where months before black-booted SS officers had partied. In their rooms, they stared at bidets, uncomprehending, figuring they must be intended for washing one's feet and set about using them for just that purpose. At night they luxuriated, sleeping on real beds with silky sheets and plush duvets.

Kats wandered into a photography studio in Nice to get a snapshot to send home to his mother, not knowing that the studio catered primarily to movie stars. And the resulting photo, in fact, made him look like one of the movie stars the girls back at the University of Hawai'i had compared him to. When the other artillerymen saw it, they all headed to Studio Erpé. So did Rudy. When he found out that the French word for bar was *bar* and that no MPs patrolled Nice, Rudy also dove headfirst into the city's nightlife, dancing with French shopgirls and British and American nurses, testing how many ways he could get drunk—on champagne, on red wine, on cheap cognac—sitting in smoky bars late into the night, sometimes conversing with German speakers who professed to be Swiss but whom he half suspected were really German soldiers just enjoying their leave like him. Although it was officially off limits, some of the Buddhaheads slipped into the palatial Beaux Arts Casino de Monte-Carlo, where stern-faced croupiers in dark, well-tailored suits quickly made it apparent that the stakes at the gaming tables were far too high for GIs, even for the Go for Broke boys from Hawai'i.

The French civilians they met in the streets were warm and gracious and, as always, seemed to be dressed impeccably. But beneath the glitter and glamour of the Riviera, despite the fashionable clothes, chic restaurants, and posh hotels, the Nisei soldiers soon found that the reality of everyday life for most of the French was much harsher than appearances suggested. After years of occupation, first by the exploiters and collaborators of the Vichy government, then by the rapacious black-shirted

Italian fascists, and finally by the Germans, the Riviera, like all of France, had been sucked dry of many resources. French families eagerly invited the GIs into their homes for dinner, but apologetically asked the soldiers to show up with most of the actual food. Here, as in Italy the preceding spring, and even in the shadow of the grand hotels and casinos, long lines of civilians formed each day near the mess tents at U.S. Army rest centers, the well-dressed French clutching tin pails waiting for the GIs to scrape their leftover roast beef or pancakes or bacon and eggs into them. A few cigarettes, a cup of ground American coffee, or a chocolate bar could buy a GI almost anything. A bit of fresh meat could pay for a five-star hotel room for a night. Brothels that had recently served Germans, largely staffed by women with no other options for feeding their families, still flourished.

The Nisei soldiers sat in darkened movie theaters, watching American-made films with French subtitles. And then, to their surprise, they were watching themselves. In the weeks since they had arrived on the Riviera, French movie theaters had begun showing newsreels featuring the rescue of the Lost Battalion. Watching them, it seemed to Hiro Higuchi that the newsreels almost gave the Lost Battalion more credit for getting lost than the 442nd for rescuing them. But at each showing the audiences burst into applause and then patted the men on the back and shook their hands as they filed out of the theaters. The Nisei were fast becoming celebrities in France.

And it wasn't only in France that newsreels featuring the 442nd were having an impact. While Fred Shiosaki was on patrol duty up in Sospel one afternoon, a runner approached him and said, "Hey, Rosie, Captain wants to see you."

Fred's first thought was "Oh God, now what did I do?" He found the captain—one of many new officers just arriving to replace those killed in the Vosges—looking irritated and clutching a letter forwarded from the American Red Cross.

"Your sister says she hasn't heard from you in umpteen months and she wants to know what happened to you," the captain growled. "You go back and you write a letter to your sister!"

Chagrined, Fred took the letter back to his quarters and read it. Blanche's fear and pain came through in every line. She had seen the Lost Battalion newsreels in Spokane and read in the papers about the catastrophic casualties. The *Hillyard News* had even published an article about Fred. It made him sound like Eisenhower's number one man, Blanche said, as if he were winning the war almost single-handedly, but it offered no clue as to whether he was even still alive. Fred felt like a dog. He had been meaning to write to the family since arriving in Marseille back at the end of September, but amid the horrors of the battle in the Vosges and the struggle simply to survive, home had become such an abstract and improbable concept that it had almost vanished. Now, though, seeing Blanche's words, it all came flooding back. That evening, he borrowed a typewriter and began to peck out a long, reassuring letter home to the family living above the laundry in Hillyard.

DECEMBER BROUGHT SNOW AGAIN, on and off, at the observation posts up in the Maritime Alps and occasionally lower down in Sospel. The men—especially the Hawaiians—began to grow excited about the prospect of a white Christmas, a first for most of them. As anticipation grew, they staged epic snowball battles and spent hours lovingly sculpting voluptuous snow pinup girls instead of snowmen. They hunted in the woods for chestnuts and then sat around smoky campfires roasting them in the ashes. They read Christmas cards to one another, cards that had made it all the way from Waikīkī or Hilo or San Francisco or Los Angeles to their snowy mountaintops.

Chaplains Yamada and Higuchi set about preparing holiday festivities. They recruited soldiers to drag a large fir tree down out of the mountains, set it up at Sospel's town hall, and help the townspeople decorate it with homemade garlands and ornaments cut from tin cans and other odds and ends. Planning a series of parties, the chaplains decided that perhaps the best Christmas treat they could offer the men was simply a chance to be in the presence of young women, so they set about recruiting young Frenchwomen to sing Christmas carols for the troops. The single women of Sospel, eager to meet some GIs, eager to have some fun, and eager most of all to perhaps get a decent meal out of the deal, flocked to the chaplains' tents to sign up. Before they knew it, Higuchi and Yamada had eighty enthusiastic French girls holding practice sessions—lilting through beautiful French carols, stuttering and giggling through attempts at "White Christmas" and "Silent Night" in English.

The first big event, though, didn't involve the French girls. It was a Christmas program the Nisei themselves put together for the children of Sospel. On December 18, two hundred kids and their parents packed into the town hall. The men handed out the candy they had saved up from their rations. The regimental cooks served up hot cocoa, cakes, and sandwiches with sliced meat and cheese fillings. Parents and wide-eyed children crowded up to the tables eager to partake of the bounty. The mayor and the town's ancient priest, the curé, stood up and with great ceremony made speeches in halting English. A quartet of GIs sang "Hark! the Herald Angels Sing" and "O Little Town of Bethlehem" to the accompaniment of guitars and ukuleles. Some of the children assembled nervously at one end of the room and sang French folk songs. As the regimental band played American jazz tunes, Colonel Miller strode into the hall in a full dress uniform. Seeing him, the curé insisted that the band play the American national anthem in his honor. Someone tried to explain to him that that wasn't really necessary. But the priest insisted. While Higuchi went searching for the sheet music for "The Star-Spangled Banner," the band began playing "Sweet Georgia Brown" to fill the time. The curé, mistaking it for the American anthem, leaped to his feet and commanded the townspeople to rise and stand solemnly at attention as the raucous, brassy, swinging strains of the jazz standard lit up the room. When it was over, the curé nodded solemnly, and the French applauded wildly. Finally, to conclude, an elderly villager rose and began to sing, a cappella, "La Marseillaise," his lone, wavering voice—"*Allons, enfants de la patrie, / Le jour de gloire est arrivé*"—at first stunning the crowd, young and old, French and American, into silence. But then the French, one by one, began to stand, joining in until they were all roaring in unison, "*Aux armes, citoyens! Formez vos bataillons!*"

By December 23, the young women of Sospel had sufficiently mastered their carols that Yamada and Higuchi brought them to the Third Battalion's headquarters, where the Nisei soldiers had decorated the mess tent in order to host them. Eagerly anticipating their arrival, K Company's men had carefully set up tables in their area, each with a tablecloth and four place settings, enough for two couples. They'd slicked back their hair, shaved, put on fresh uniforms, and practiced bits of French on one another. When the young women arrived on Red Cross buses, Yamada ushered them into the tent and arranged them in rows by height, and they began to sing the English carols they'd been taught. The performances were halting and rough and a bit discordant, but the effort was earnest, and at the conclusion the Nisei stood and cheered and whistled and applauded wildly. The fact was, the girls could have brayed like donkeys and the boys would have applauded. These were the first women some of them had seen in any kind of social setting since the Nisei girls had come to their dances back at Shelby.

When the singing was over, each soldier approached a young woman and presented her with a Christmas gift package that the army quartermasters had prepared—two GI chocolate bars, a bar of Lux soap, a toothbrush, a tube of Colgate toothpaste, and a pack of cigarettes—treasures beyond value in war-ravaged France. The women opened their gifts eagerly and stared disbelieving at the contents. Then the boys brought out grilled steaks, opened bottles of red wine, and invited them to sit down. The women, eyes widened, exclaimed again, "*Mon Dieu! Merci!*," sat down, and fell to consuming the meat, as Chaplain Higuchi noted, "like wolves."

As the wine flowed, the conversations intensified and grew louder—

staccato bursts of Hawaiian pidgin and English and French punctuated by quizzical looks and wide smiles and self-conscious laughter. Young men and young women talked about the war, about their parents, about their homes, about the Germans, about food, about American movie stars, about Hawai'i, about what they would do after the war. Some of the boys, buoyant with alcohol, intoxicated by perfume, announced loudly that most certainly the very first thing they would do was return to Sospel and marry the girls to whom they were talking. The girls laughed and pushed them away and eyed the remainders of the boys' steaks.

ON CHRISTMAS EVE, Hiro Higuchi, riding in a jeep, made the rounds of the observation posts higher up in the mountains, where the temperature had dropped well below freezing. In an old stone cellar on a windblown mountainside, he gathered as many of the frontline men as he could and conducted a candlelight service. Someone banged out carols on a battered upright piano while the others, wearing heavy woolen winter coats, their breath forming small white clouds, gathered around a crackling fire and sang. When they got to "Silent Night," Higuchi began to weep silently. Glancing around the room, he saw that many of the men were doing the same. They had all come through so much together, and so much that was unknown still lay in store for them. But in this place, for at least this moment, they were safe and at peace and together.

TWENTY

───────

One often wonders why this has to happen to fellers so young.
Millions of lives lost in this war and unless we build up a better
world after this—all for naught.

CHAPLAIN HIGUCHI TO HIS WIFE, HISAKO
FEBRUARY 14, 1945

On Christmas Day, seventeen-year-old Solly Ganor stood in the snow, staring into a bright blue sky, praying. In the near distance, he could hear the Nazi guards singing Christmas carols. They sounded drunk. That was good. It meant the morning's reprieve from the usual round of beatings and torment might last through the day. But Solly was focused on his praying. He did not expect his prayers would end his misery. All he wanted, he told God, was that the dream that had just awakened his father had been only that, a dream and not a premonition.

Solly was only sixteen when the Nazis made a slave of him. But by then he'd already become well acquainted with unfathomable evil. When he was thirteen, hiding in bushes near Ukmerge, Lithuania, not far from his home in Kaunas, he had watched as two German officers and about a dozen right-wing Lithuanian militiamen forced more than thirty men, women, and children out of a barn where they had been hiding and ordered the adults to begin digging a trench. Men and women—all of them Jewish like Solly, their faces etched with terror, their eyes darting this way and that, looking for something, anything that might change what was about to happen—dug until the Germans supervising the operation judged the trench to be deep enough. Then the Germans ordered the Jews to strip to their underwear. Some of the Lithuanian soldiers began laughing. They wanted to see the women fully naked. They grabbed at them, the young, pretty ones, and began to strip off their underwear, but a German officer stopped them.

"No. They will stay in their underwear!" he barked.

A Lithuanian officer persisted, smiling and speaking in German. "Let the men have their fun!"

But the Germans were in command, here and throughout Lithuania.

"I said no!" the Nazi officer snapped. Naked the Jews would seem human, he said. In their underwear they looked ridiculous. Better to shoot them that way, so as not to feel any remorse later.

Then it was simple and straightforward and brutal. Soldiers forced the people into the trench and began shooting. It took only a few moments. When they were done, the nearly naked and bloodied bodies of almost twenty children lay interspersed among those of the adults. The Germans ordered the owner of the land, a Lithuanian farmer, to fill the trench. As the man picked up a shovel and looked into the grave, he vomited. Solly, watching from the bushes just six or seven feet away, his heart pounding, heard the sound of a baby wailing in the grave as the man began to shovel the dirt. It was then that he fully understood for the first time that in the eyes of the Germans who had come to Lithuania, and the Lithuanian nationalists who had joined forces with them, he was, at best, an animal to be hunted. It was as if someone had, at that moment, applied a hot branding iron to his young flesh.

A few days later, forced from their home in Kaunas, Solly, his parents, and his sister, Fanny, were herded—along with about twenty-nine thousand other Jews—into the miserable confines of the Kovno ghetto, a jumble of small, mostly primitive houses with no running water in an area called Slobodka. There for more than two years they somehow managed to survive mass starvation, periodic outbreaks of disease, and the regular mass executions that the Germans called *Aktions*. In one of these, the *Kinder Aktion* of March 27 and 28, 1944, the SS systematically murdered twelve hundred children as police cars drove through the ghetto blaring music to mask the sound of mothers and fathers screaming.

In July 1944, as the Russians approached Kovno, the SS "liquidated" the ghetto, deporting much of its remaining population to its vast slave-labor camp at Dachau in Germany or the Stutthof camp near Danzig. When they had rounded up as many Jews as they could capture, they set fire to the ghetto, where thousands, including Solly's family, remained in hiding. As the ghetto burned, perhaps two thousand people perished, either burned alive or shot down as they tried to escape the flames. Solly and his family huddled in the smoldering cellar of a burned-out building, where they smeared their faces with ashes, hoping to avoid discovery. But they were found out, loaded into a cattle car, and sent to Stutthof. There, SS guards with snarling dogs marched them under a sign—*ARBEIT MACHT FREI* (WORK MAKES YOU FREE)—just like the one under which so many had already marched to their deaths at Auschwitz. Immediately, the guards separated Solly's mother and sister from his father and him. As she was led away, his mother turned and tossed Solly a sweet, confident smile over her shoulder. Then other prisoners stripped, shaved, and deloused Solly and his father and handed them purple-striped prison uniforms that were little more than flimsy pajamas.

Solly and his father did not stay long at Stutthof. Both were relatively sturdy men, even after the horrors they had endured in the ghetto. In the short term, they were more valuable to the Germans as living slaves than as another pair of corpses among the millions they were already struggling to dispose of. So, as others were deported to Auschwitz to be murdered, they were sent instead to a slave-labor camp in southern Bavaria, just outside the picturesque village of Utting am Ammersee. The camp—Lager Ten—was just one of a network of labor camps collectively called Kaufering, all of them subcamps of Dachau, where the SS worked Jews, Poles, and political prisoners to death instead of shooting or gassing them. At Lager Ten, most of the work involved hauling 110-pound sacks of cement from place to place or shoveling sand to make more of the stuff for the production of nearby bombproof aircraft factories. It was brutal work, killing work, and most of those enslaved there died within weeks of arriving.

Solly and his father survived through the fall of 1944 only by employing all their wits. Solly's father made himself valuable as a storyteller, entertaining one of the head *Kapos* in the camp, a florid-faced man named Burgin. Like other *Kapos*, Burgin abused his fellow prisoners in order to curry favor with the Germans and thus remain alive a little longer. By keeping him entertained, Solly's father avoided being beaten and occasionally won small favors. Solly talked Burgin into putting him to work as a human donkey, pulling wagons full of provisions from Utting am Ammersee to the kitchens that fed the German engineers building the bombproof factories. Pulling the wagon was hard and degrading work, the work of brute animals, but it gave Solly an opportunity to occasionally steal a loaf of bread or a bit of sausage to share with his father. Eventually, though, that job gave way to another donkey job—pulling carts filled with the emaciated corpses of his fellow prisoners to a mass grave in ever larger numbers. By December, Solly was weakening, his thin, striped pajamas were perpetually infested with lice, and his father, now fifty-two, was failing fast. It seemed impossible that either of them could last much longer.

So when, on Christmas Day, his father had abruptly awakened and called out his wife's name—Rebecca!—and then begun weeping, wailing to Solly, "Your mother just died!" Solly thought he could bear no more. He tried to tell his father that it was just a dream, but his father insisted that no, it was real, that he had seen it happen before his very eyes. He had seen Solly's sister, Fanny, bending over her mother, and in that moment his wife had died. He was sure of it. In the dark and fetid stink of the barracks, Solly's father had begun to recite the kaddish.

Now Solly—standing outside in the snow at Lager Ten as the Nazis sang Christmas carols nearby—looked up into the sky and prayed that it wasn't true.

TWO DAYS AFTER spending Christmas with Esther—now newly pregnant with twins—Gordon Hirabayashi was put on a bus in Spokane with perhaps twenty other inmates and sent over the Cascade Mountains to the federal prison at McNeil Island, a windswept dot of land in the southern reaches of Puget Sound.* There prison wardens stripped him, issued him a stiff denim prison uniform, and placed him in a temporary holding facility—"the fish tank"—until he could be assigned to one of the three dormitories on the prison's work farm. Noting that two of the dormitories were designated for "white" inmates and a third for everyone else, what prison authorities termed "mixed" inmates, Gordon bristled. But with his young family waiting for him on the outside, and knowing that he might earn an earlier release with good behavior, Gordon decided that he wasn't there to reform the prison system. He was there to underscore a different set of principles: as a Quaker, his religious opposition to conscription and, as an American, his objection to conscription of men whose families had been removed from their homes and incarcerated. He resolved to serve out his time quietly and hold his peace. That resolution, it turned out, would not last for long.

GORDON WAS NOT THE only Nisei confined at McNeil Island that December. Through the spring, summer, and fall of that year, nearly three hundred draft resisters from the WRA camps had gone to trial in various federal courtrooms on charges of violating the Selective Service Act. Their trials unfolded in a number of disparate ways but concluded

---

*Other notable inmates who at times were held at McNeil included a two-bit forger and future murderer named Charles Manson, the Los Angeles mob boss Mickey Cohen, and Robert Stroud, later known as the Birdman of Alcatraz.

almost universally with convictions. Sixty-three Nisei resisters from Heart Mountain—members of the Fair Play Committee—were tried en masse in Cheyenne, Wyoming. After addressing them dismissively as "You Jap boys" on the opening day of the trial and summarily rejecting their constitutional arguments, Judge T. Blake Kennedy made short work of convicting all of them and sentencing them to three-year terms at either McNeil Island or the federal penitentiary in Leavenworth, Kansas. In Boise, Idaho, Judge Chase Clark—formerly the state's governor— presided over the trial of the resisters from Minidoka. This was the same Chase Clark who in 1942 had opposed relocating any Japanese Americans to Idaho, advocating instead that the United States should "send them all back to Japan and then sink the island" and comparing Japanese people to rats. Now, after declining to recuse himself in light of those comments, he set up a kind of assembly line for the rapid disposition of the cases, impaneling juries and conscripting often unwilling local attorneys to represent the defendants, presiding over as many as four trials per day, and convicting thirty-three of the Nisei in eleven days—all those who had been brought before him except for several who had pleaded guilty and one who was acquitted on a technicality but then subsequently convicted at a later trial.

Trials in Arkansas, Colorado, and Utah produced similar results, resulting in sentences ranging from six months to three years and three months in federal prison. And yet the point these young defendants were trying to make—the fundamental injustice of their situation—did not always go entirely unheeded. Many of the trials were held in communities in which the citizenry was overwhelmingly hostile to anyone of Japanese ancestry. One of these communities was the foggy logging town of Eureka, in the redwoods of far Northern California, where there was a long and often vicious history of anti-Asian sentiment. There, Judge Louis E. Goodman presided over the trial of twenty-seven Nisei draft resisters from Tule Lake. For six of the defendants who were marched through the town from the county jail to the courthouse in front of hostile, gawking locals on the first day of the trial, the initial portents all seemed bad. But Judge Goodman was a very different man from Chase Clark of Idaho or T. Blake Kennedy of Wyoming. Before the trial even began, Goodman was troubled by the fact that the defense attorneys assigned to represent the Nisei seemed to show little genuine interest in winning their cases. But he was even more troubled by the very notion of trying young American citizens who had been transported to his courtroom from what he termed a "concentration center." How, he wondered, could they be considered free agents over their own affairs when their fundamental rights as citizens had already been stripped from them? How could he say that due process had been carried out in his courtroom if due process had already been abrogated by the defendants' incarceration at Tule Lake? Goodman waited until the last moments of the trial to reveal his thinking, but when he did it was a stinging rebuke to the prosecution: "It is shocking to the conscience that an American citizen be confined on the ground of disloyalty, and then, while so under duress and restraint, be compelled to serve in the armed forces, or be prosecuted for not yielding to such compulsion." And with that, in front of a stunned courtroom, he dismissed the charges against all of the Nisei resisters standing in front of him. They were free, but free only to return to confinement behind barbed wire at Tule Lake until such time as the camp was closed.

By DECEMBER, the closure of some of the WRA camps was drawing near. In those camps, fear, hope, and indecision continued to mount as families incarcerated there contemplated the prospect of returning to the West Coast. A fiery, often vicious debate over their return still raged in communities up and down the coast, playing out in small-town newspapers, in barbershops, in bars and coffee shops and church socials. Much of the public discussion centered on an incident in Hood River, Oregon. As in many American towns, the local American Legion post in Hood River had put up a monument to honor local boys serving overseas. But on the evening of November 29, the legionnaires had blacked out sixteen names—all of Hood River's active-duty Japanese American servicemen. Lest there be any doubt about the intended message, the post's commander, Jess Edington, stated it bluntly: "We simply want to let them know that we don't want them back here." Eight other American Legion posts promptly followed the Hood River post and removed the names of Japanese American servicemen from their honor rolls for no other reason than their ancestry.

As news of the Hood River incident spread across the country, it provoked a backlash of indignation. *The New York Times* called it "Hood River's blunder." *Collier's* slammed the "dirty work at Hood River." The *Chicago Sun-Times* called the Hood River American Legion "not so American." An American Legion post in New York went out of its way to invite sixteen Nisei soldiers to become members of its post. But in Oregon, and in much of the West, the reaction was very different. There, despite the increasingly well-publicized heroics of the 442nd in Europe, millions of Americans still seethed when they heard a Japanese name or saw a face that might be Japanese. An Oregon state senator spat out his contempt: "Get your heart in America and the Japs out!"

Then news reached Hood River about another local Nisei soldier. This one wasn't a member of the 442nd. At the same time that the 442nd was fighting in Europe, nearly six thousand additional Nisei soldiers were now serving in the Military Intelligence Service, most of them in the Pacific theater of operation, fighting the Japanese imperial forces. Trained as translators, interrogators, propaganda writers, and radio announcers, many of them served behind the front lines, on relatively safe ships and in listening posts. Others, though, were embedded with active combat units in the jungles and on the beaches of the Philippines, Burma, New Guinea, and every other combat zone where U.S. troops fought in the Pacific. There, because of their ethnicity, they faced unique risks, particularly the danger of being captured by Japanese forces, labeled traitors, and subjected to barbaric tortures and execution. Another risk was simply being mistaken for the enemy.

That winter, while his family was incarcerated in the bitter cold of the Minidoka concentration camp, twenty-four-year-old Frank Hachiya was serving in the MIS alongside other U.S. forces in the steaming jungles of Leyte Island in the Philippines. For weeks, he had been slipping behind enemy lines on Leyte in order to reconnoiter and map Japanese positions. On December 30, when forward elements of the invasion force captured one of the enemy, Hachiya volunteered to cross an open valley to interrogate the prisoner. As he worked his way back across the valley, returning from his mission, a volley of gunfire dropped him in his tracks. It was not clear whether he'd been shot by concealed Japanese snipers or by U.S. forces who mistook him for one of the enemy, but either way he was mortally wounded. He died in a field hospital on January 3, 1945.

Because he had enlisted from an address in Portland, Hachiya's name had never been on the honor roll in Hood River, and so wasn't stricken from it. But he was very much a local boy, and when news of his death worked its way across the Pacific and up the Columbia River to Hood River, it hit the community like a bomb, reigniting outrage over the removal of the names from the honor roll but provoking ever more virulent defensiveness from the local American Legion and many others in the community. And as the rhetoric in Oregon and up and down the coast grew more heated, some of it began to grow violent.

WHEN THE 442ND HAD finally come down out of the mountains following the rescue of the Lost Battalion, one of the few survivors of I Company able to walk under his own power was a twenty-three-year-old technical sergeant named Shig Doi. Like all the others, Doi was beat up, downcast, and sick with grief for his lost buddies.

Early in January, Shig's parents, Masuru and Satoru, his brother, Sumio, and his sister, Lily, were among the first to leave the Amache camp in Granada, Colorado. When they arrived back at their eighty-five-acre fruit farm outside Auburn, California, in the foothills of the Sierra Nevada, they found portions of the place in disrepair, largely neglected by the tenants who had lived there rent free during the Dois' incarceration. After the thirty years it had taken the Dois to build the place up, seeing it look like this was hard to take. Many of the trees had not been pruned properly or pruned at all, and many of the buildings were deteriorating. But as the new year began, they set to work to re-open the business and restore the home that Shig had grown up in so that he would at least have that to return to when the war finally ended.

The Dois' return had been front-page news in the local paper, the *Auburn Journal*, though, and some of their neighbors were not happy to hear of it. Late on the evening of January 17, Claude Watson, an AWOL soldier, approached a bartender in Auburn and asked if he wanted to have some fun. He did. They, the soldier's brother, also a soldier AWOL from his base, the bartender's brother, and some girlfriends drove around town for a while, drinking, picking up a rifle, and buying gaso-line. Then they headed out to the Doi farm.

In the early morning hours on January 18, Sumio Doi became con-cerned when he heard voices and cars out in the farmyard. He rushed to his front door, flung it open, and found that flames were erupting from their packing shed across the yard. He and his father rushed outside and managed to put out the fire as several cars roared away, tires squealing in the night.

Not wanting to cause trouble in the community, the Dois did not report the incident. But the following night, Sumio again heard cars out in the yard. Again, he and his father went to the door. This time a bar-rage of gunshots slammed into the front of the house. The Dois dove back into the house, scrambled across the floor to the telephone, and called the police. Huddling in their house, they could hear young men and women laughing and shouting at one another out in the dark farm-yard. As a squad car pulled into the farmyard, the intruders' vehicles again sped away in the dark. But before leaving, they had stuck sticks of dynamite under the shed and lit the fuses. The fuses had all burned out before reaching the dynamite, but their goal had been accomplished nonetheless. The Doi family would not sleep peacefully in their home for years to come, even after Shig came safely home from the war with medals on his chest.

The four male raiders were apprehended and promptly confessed. At trial, the defense attorneys did not try to deny the facts or even present a factual case. Instead, one of them simply rose and argued that the young men couldn't be held accountable: "These boys like thousands of others have been trained by the army to destroy Japs. That fact, plus their intoxication, makes them not responsible for their acts." Another attorney pinned the blame on the War Relocation Authority for allowing the Dois and other Japanese Americans to return to the coast, and then went on to raise the specter of Pearl Harbor, saying, "The Japanese infiltrated into this country . . . we accepted them, never dreaming they would stab us in the back." He concluded by imploring the jury to keep this part of California "a white man's country." The jury was given the case at 11:30 a.m. They promptly took a lunch break and then came back less than two hours later to find the defendants not guilty.

As winter began to verge into spring in France, snow still clung to the higher peaks in the Maritime Alps, but a bit lower in the mountains purple and white narcissi began to spangle green alpine meadows. Down along the Riviera, bougainvilleas and roses and chrysanthemums bloomed. More and more of the Nisei soldiers' wounded comrades began returning from hospitals farther north in France, and hundreds of new troops—many of them draftees from the concentration camps back home—began to arrive to fill the ranks of those who would never return.

Veterans and newcomers alike, the men of the 442nd continued to alternate between periods of rough living at far-flung observation posts and much softer stints, living in luxurious quarters down along the coast. Even when up in the mountains, they worked to contrive simple pleasures, staging epic snowball fights and strumming ukuleles as they sat around campfires. Kats cut an oil drum in half, filled it with steaming-hot water heated over a fire, and used it as an *ofuro*, sitting for hours on end, buck naked, happily soaking in the tub while looking over the blue Mediterranean spread out below him.

The war along the Riviera continued, though. The Nisei spent much of their time on reconnaissance patrols, climbing up and down rocky hillsides or huddled with radios and binoculars in natural caves and concrete fortifications studying German movements across the border in Italy. Occasionally, Nisei patrols wearing white parkas ran into similarly clad German patrols, and fierce, deadly firefights erupted on snowy, windswept mountainsides. Now and then artillery duels broke out, with hundreds of shells flying in both directions. In January alone, six Nisei soldiers were killed and twenty-four were wounded.

George Oiye scored what he considered perhaps his greatest accomplishment of the war one cold, clear morning when he spotted an enormous, 320-millimeter German artillery gun mounted on a railroad car on a distant Italian hillside. German gunners had been using it for weeks, randomly lobbing shells into Nice, terrorizing civilians there. Because the Germans ordinarily pulled it quickly back into a protective tunnel before anyone could get a fix on it, American forces had been frustrated in their efforts to neutralize it. But George spotted a bright white smoke ring moments after the gun fired and before it could be withdrawn into the tunnel. He also noticed that two U.S. Navy cruisers were plying the waters directly off the coast below him. Acting swiftly, he radioed the gun's location to the divisional Fire Direction Center, which relayed it to the two ships. Within moments, both ships swung about and unleashed broadsides with their eight-inch guns. To George's great satisfaction and pride he watched in fascination as the massive German gun tumbled end over end down a rocky slope and plunged into the Mediterranean.

BY THE END OF FEBRUARY, it was becoming clear that what the Nisei had begun calling the "Champagne Campaign" was about to end. Despite the optimism they had all felt the preceding fall—and even as the Allies crept closer to the German border from the west and the Red Army pressed in from the east—Germany still remained stubbornly defiant. In northern Italy, tens of thousands of hardened German troops still held the nearly impenetrable Gothic Line. In Germany, even larger numbers lay in wait between the advancing Allies and the Rhine. No one was getting a ticket home anytime soon. Sooner or later, the Nisei soldiers were going to have to go back into heavy combat somewhere, and now, even more than when they had left the rest area in Vada in August, they dreaded it. A year before, they couldn't wait to get into the war. Now they just wanted to get it over with and go home.

In early March, the artillerymen of the 522nd learned that they were to be detached from the 442nd and sent back to eastern France to rejoin the Seventh Army in its assault on the German heartland. Kats, like Sus and George and most of his artillery buddies, was loath to part from this place of relative ease and his many infantry friends. But he didn't really regret the new orders. More even than when he had entered the army, he was committed to a personal sense of ethics, to doing what had to be done for the greater good. For him, it was still about maintaining a delicate balance between *giri* and *ninjo*, between his formal obligations and his natural, personal feelings. He had not heard from his father, still incarcerated in Santa Fe, for a long while, but even in his imprisonment he knew he would say the same thing. And then there was what Chaplain Yamada had told Kats when Katsuaki died in Alabama, that his mission in life now was to honor his brother's legacy by being the best soldier he could be. If going into Germany would hasten the crushing of the Nazi state that had cost so many of his friends' their lives and prevent more of them from dying, Kats still wanted to be in on it.

He and his crew on *Kuuipo* began to pack up their gear. On March 9, they bivouacked at Antibes, then formed a convoy and began to drive north, retracing their route from the previous November, starting to imagine what Berlin would look like when they got there.

But a curious air of secrecy seemed to hang over the infantry's future, even as they were told to begin preparing to move out. The senior officers appeared as uncertain as the enlisted men as to what was up, where they were going next. Some feared they might be on their way to the South Pacific to participate in the eventual invasion of Japan. A few dared to think they might be going home. Most just resigned themselves yet again to enduring another cycle of uncertainty in their lives as GIs.

On March 17, they boarded trucks bound for Marseille. It was a lovely spring morning, and they were determined to extract the last ounce of pleasure from their Riviera sojourn. As many of them as could fit climbed onto the roofs of the cabs, and as the vehicles wended their way through the old city, they sat dangling their legs over the edges, strumming guitars and ukuleles, throwing lemon drops to children running alongside, calling out in English and mangled French and Japanese to every young Frenchwoman they passed. The women, understanding the sentiment if not the words, waved and smiled and shouted back, "*Bon voyage!*" "*Bonne chance!*"

But the mood changed abruptly as the trucks pulled in to an assembly area on the waterfront, where enormous gray landing craft awaited them with their ramps down, their great jaws agape. Strange things began to happen. They were told to strip all unit-identifying marks from their uniforms and obscure the markings on their equipment—their 442nd and 100th shoulder patches, insignias on their helmets, lettering painted on their trucks and jeeps. Something was afoot, and they couldn't make sense of it. Whatever was in store for them, it was apparently not something the army wanted the world to know about. Wherever they were going, they were to go incognito.

TWENTY-ONE

Our boys accomplished what was considered an impossible feat.

CHAPLAIN YAMADA TO HIS WIFE, AI
APRIL 10, 1945

A t Poston that spring, Rudy Tokiwa's mother continued to rise before dawn every day and step under a stream of icy water, praying for her son's safe return. In Spokane, Kisaburo and Tori Shiosaki also arose before dawn each day, brewed some tea, and ate a bit of toast before heading downstairs to heat up the laundry's boilers and raise the shades where two blue stars hung in the front window. At the prison camp in Santa Fe, Katsuichi Miho sat on the steps of his barracks most mornings, watching the sun rise over the mountains to the east, sipping coffee from a metal mug, trying to warm up, preparing to walk over to the camp infirmary, where he served as an aide. And very far away, in Tokyo, Fumiye Miho awoke well before dawn each morning, straining to hear any rumbling in the distance that might portend American B-29 Superfortresses, coming again to resume the firebombing that had on the night of March 10 incinerated as many as a hundred thousand people and injured another million.

By dawn most mornings, at the federal prison camp on McNeil Island in Puget Sound, Gordon Hirabayashi was already dressed in his stiff denim prison uniform and on a bus, on his way to work in the soggy fields of the prison's farm. Gordon worked diligently at whatever task he was assigned. He had resolved not to rock the boat at McNeil, to finish his sentence without incident and rejoin Esther and his newborn twin daughters as quickly as possible. But when the time came for Gordon to be moved from the general holding facility to a dormitory on the work farm, he felt his principles again required him to act. At the Catalina work farm in Tucson, Gordon had started a protest movement among the inmates when he had been assigned to a "whites only" dormitory. Now, at McNeil, he was assigned to barracks housing only non-white inmates. The assignment was precisely the opposite of what it had been in Tucson, but for Gordon the issue was the same. The prison authorities were practicing racial discrimination. Ordered to gather his things and report to the non-white barracks, Gordon simply stayed where he was, refusing to move. A night guard, his face reddening, bellowed at him, "Get your stuff and move!"

"Well, no. I'll move when I get clarification."

"You're moving right now. That's an order!"

Gordon looked at the man, unmoved and unmoving, his expression once again implacable.

"Well, okay. You did your part, you gave me the order, so what I do is up to me. If I do something that you want to punish me for, you can punish me. But don't get upset. You did your part."

The guard, wide-eyed, incredulous, spluttered, "You're going to defy my order?"

Gordon, fearing that things might get violent, got up and moved, not in the direction indicated by the guard but simply to another room. He fully expected to be thrown into what inmates at McNeil called "the black hole" and put on a diet of bread and water. If that happened, he figured, he would go on a fast, drinking the water but not eating the food. That would be a good way to underscore his point without resorting to any kind of physical resistance, but it might mean a longer delay before he could be reunited with his wife and daughters.

But, to Gordon's great surprise, the guard left and nothing at all happened. Two weeks later, the prison's superintendent finally called Gordon into his office. Gordon explained what he had done and why. The superintendent insisted that the prison didn't discriminate but finished by saying, "Let me study this. I'll call you in later." He never did call Gordon back in, but within a week or so, the prison slowly began to integrate the previously all-white barracks, and Gordon never saw the inside of the black hole.

NEAR MIDNIGHT, on the cold, rainy night of March 12, the 522nd Field Artillery Battalion crossed the Saar River and entered Nazi Germany near the town of Kleinblittersdorf, just south of Saarbrücken. Attached now to the Sixty-third Infantry Division in General Alexander Patch's Seventh Army, the Nisei artillerymen met no opposition. By 11:30 the next morning, they had dug in on German soil for the first time and begun firing on targets along the Siegfried Line just to the east, where the Germans hoped to make a stand and prevent the Allies from crossing the Rhine and threatening major cities like Mannheim, Frankfurt, and, to the south, Munich.

That night, as the Nisei continued lobbing shells over their heads, the Sixty-third Infantry probed deeper into Germany on foot. Moving with them were forward observers from the 522nd, including Sus Ito and George Oiye. It was an utterly black night. Somewhere above a heavy cloud cover, a new moon hung dark and useless in the sky. The men couldn't see what lay on the ground even a few feet ahead of them, and their first task was to cross fields that the Germans had salted with hundreds of Schu-mines, simple wooden boxes topped with pressure plates, each filled with a quarter pound of TNT, just enough to blow a man's legs off at the hips.

As he set out across what seemed, by the feel of it under his boots, to be a field of fresh close-cropped grass, George Oiye didn't like the situation at all. In the darkness, nothing but luck seemed to stand between him and the loss of his legs or perhaps his life. But then, suddenly, an odd buzzing sound hummed behind him, and the world grew noticeably lighter. The Army Signal Corps had switched on huge thirty-inch searchlights, aiming them at the sky and bouncing the light off the clouds to create an eerie green wavering, artificial moonlight out in the fields. It wasn't much, but it was enough at least to see where your next step was going to take you, and that in itself was an enormous relief to George.

As they moved on, George found himself walking perhaps ten feet behind a tall blond infantryman. He figured that if he stayed in the man's tracks, it would cut down his chances of stepping on a mine. No sooner had George made that decision than the man stepped on a mine. Both he and George were blown off their feet in a shower of sod and earth and gravel. George climbed to his feet unhurt, but the GI was on the ground, bloody from the waist down. After a moment of stunned silence, he began to scream. George called for a medic but nobody came, so he leaned over the fallen soldier, trying to comfort him. The man fixed a wild, wide-eyed gaze on George and begged him to shoot him. He was nearly incoherent but utterly convinced that his private parts had been shot off. "Shoot me! Just shoot me!" he bellowed. "I can't do that," George said softly. He did a quick assessment. The man's groin area seemed to be fine, but one of his feet was almost entirely blown off, dangling from his leg by a single tendon. George took out his knife and cut the tendon and the foot fell to the ground. The man didn't even seem to notice. George again called for a medic, or for a litter bearer, but still nobody came. Realizing the man was going into shock, George crawled under him and somehow rose to his feet with the man draped over his shoulders. The guy was at least half a foot taller than George and outweighed him by perhaps fifty pounds, but George began staggering back across the field toward the rear, heedless now of whatever mines lay in his path. When he could carry the man no farther, he laid him down on the grass, took him by both arms, and dragged him until he finally found a medic. Then, his uniform bloodied, he turned around and resumed walking into Germany.

KATS MIHO WAS perplexed by what he was seeing from the moment he entered Germany. As the 522nd rolled eastward in their trucks, approaching the Siegfried Line and the Rhineland beyond, pausing from time to time to set up their guns and pounding targets out ahead of them, Kats couldn't help but notice the landscape. On any given March day a few years earlier, this would have seemed a lovely place, the Germany he had read about since childhood, a land of fairy tales, of tidy villages, of whitewashed cottages, of signposts with heavy Gothic script pointing the way to nearly unpronounceable places—Bliesransbach, Neumuhlerhof, Oberscheckenbach. And it was in fact a country of elegant soaring steeples rising from simple Lutheran churches, of ruined medieval castles perched, crumbling, on hilltops overlooking lush river valleys. Between the villages lay miles of low, rolling hills, emerald green, flecked with drifts of bright yellow buttercups.

But this March, in 1945, it was hard to see loveliness in the German countryside. The landscape, bright and green and blue as it might be to the eyes of an innocent, seemed to the American troops now entering it to be overhung by a gray pall. It wasn't just the buildings crumpled by Allied bombing, the burned-out wreckage of German tanks and half-tracks strewn alongside the roadways, the black pillars of smoke rising from the remains of factories and railroad depots. It was more diffuse than that—a general sense that something dreadful lay in the land's immediate past or the immediate future, one couldn't be sure which. Kats could see it in the eyes of the civilians they passed, standing in barn doors, peering out from behind shutters as they rode through villages in their trucks. Kats had seen war-shocked civilians in Italy and France, but this was different. The eyes into which he now looked seemed to suggest that something even beyond the horrors of war, something profoundly dark, lay just over the horizon ahead of them.

. . .

ON MARCH 25, Fred Shiosaki, apparently doomed to be seasick every time the army put him on a boat, found himself once again retching in a berth in a heaving landing craft wending its way into the war-ravaged harbor of Livorno.

When the craft finally stopped moving and the enormous doors at the bow opened, Fred discovered that the rumors he'd heard on board were true. He and the rest of the 442nd were in northwestern Italy, right back where they'd left off when they'd departed for France seven months before.

He and Rudy and the rest of K Company climbed onto trucks and were hauled to a staging area outside Pisa, where they moved into large tents. There they were issued some new equipment and told that under no circumstances were they to leave the base. The brass, apparently, did not want anyone—certainly not any spies circulating among the Italian civilians in Pisa—to know that the Nisei troops had returned to Italy.

General Mark Clark had been mightily impressed when the 442nd had fought for him the preceding spring and summer. He'd told Pence then, "The courage and determination which the men of the 442nd RCT have displayed during their short time in combat is an inspiration to all." In the seven months since then, after learning of their exploits in the Vosges, Clark had been lobbying hard to get the Nisei back to Italy. And now that they were back under his command, he had a plan for them.

Throughout the preceding fall and winter, the Allied armies had hurled themselves repeatedly at the Gothic Line, the Germans' formidable fortifications stretching all the way across Italy, from the Apuan Alps north of Pisa in the west to the Adriatic Sea in the east But they had made little headway, and now large parts of the Fifth Army remained bogged down just north of the Arno River, not far from where it had been when the 442nd left the line on their way to the Vosges. So long as the Germans remained entrenched in their mountain caves and concrete bunkers overlooking the roadways along the Ligurian coast, the Fifth Army could not move up the coast, seize Genoa, turn northeast to enter the Po valley, and advance toward Milan.

Now Clark wanted to send the Nisei troops against the Gothic Line. And he wanted their presence in Italy to be a surprise to the Germans, who he knew feared them. He did not necessarily expect that the 442nd would be able to break through the rugged terrain on the western end of the line; nobody had been able to do that. But if they pressed the line hard enough and fought as they had in the Vosges, the Germans would have to shift troops west, and that would greatly aid the main Allied effort to push up the east coast of Italy, seize Bologna and Milan, and end the war in Italy.

Neither Fred nor Rudy nor any of the 442nd's men knew any of this. All they knew, all they were told, was that they were now back in Italy, back in the Fifth Army, attached to the Ninety-second Division—the Black "Buffalo" Division—and about to go back into combat in another jumble of jagged mountains arrayed in front of them.

Over the next several days and nights, hiding in barns by day and riding in the backs of trucks with blacked-out headlights at night, Rudy tried to decide whether he was glad to be back in Italy. He dreaded what was to come, but there was a kind of familiarity to the place. There were things he had missed without knowing it when they were in France—the sound of a phonograph playing a scratchy aria behind shuttered windows, the musty smell of wine cellars, the homey smell of someone frying fish in olive oil, the clattering of wooden wheels on cobbled streets, old women scolding old men.

At the beautiful little town of Pietrasanta, nestled in the foothills of the Apuan Alps, they climbed down from their trucks. Fred peered around him. He couldn't make out much in the dark, but it was a clear night and he could see the black mass of the mountains looming above him, silhouetted against a starry sky. He likely did not know it, but several months before, in those mountains, just two miles from where he stood, the Nazis had slaughtered as many as 560 Italian civilians, among

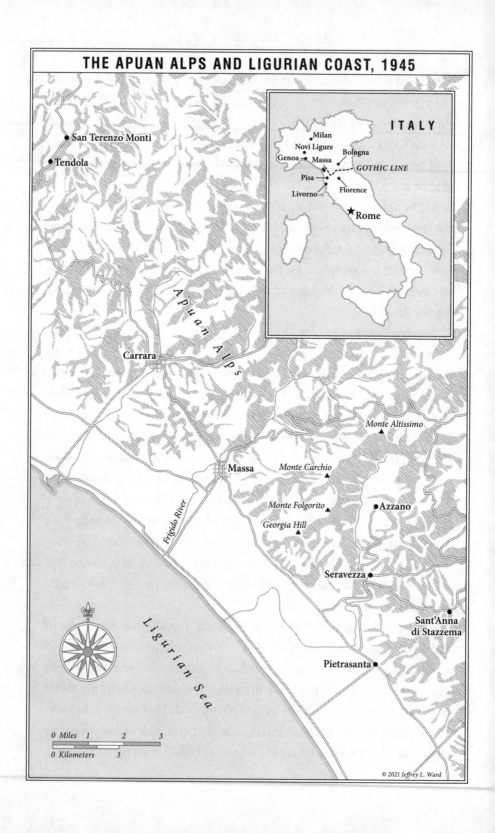

THE APUAN ALPS AND LIGURIAN COAST, 1945

San Terenzo Monti

Tendola

Apuan Alps

Carrara

ITALY

Milan
Novi Ligure
Genoa Massa Bologna
GOTHIC LINE
Pisa
Livorno Florence

★ Rome

Monte Altissimo ▲

Massa

Monte Carchio ▲

Frigido River

Monte Folgorito ▲ ●Azzano

Georgia Hill ▲

Seravezza ●

Sant'Anna
di Stazzema ●

Ligurian Sea

Pietrasanta ●

0 Miles   1   2   3
0 Kilometers   3

© 2021 Jeffrey L. Ward

them dozens of children and eight pregnant women in the village of Sant'Anna di Stazzema.

Fred hoisted his gear and fell into a column of K Company men shuffling up another narrow road heading northeast. The guys in the 100th Fred noticed, headed off in a different direction, disappearing in the darkness off to the northwest. Someone hissed that the road might be mined and to stay off to one side or the other. When they came to a darkened village called Seravezza, the road steepened dramatically and began to wind through a series of switchbacks. Fred began to struggle, huffing and puffing, his legs aching. It had been months since they'd been on a real march like this. Every now and then an officer told them to pipe down, to be as quiet as they could, not to light any cigarettes. The road narrowed further. A little before 4:00 a.m., after five hours of trudging uphill, they arrived in another darkened village, Azzano, hugging the side of a ridge. As the men, exhausted, squatted on their haunches in the town's one street, their officers began quietly rapping on doors, awakening townspeople, telling them to keep their lights turned off, informing them that they had unexpected houseguests arriving. Then in small groups the Nisei soldiers arose and shuffled silently into cellars and barns and stone kitchens, anywhere they could be kept out of sight.

In the gray predawn light, Fred could make out another, much larger mountain rising just on the other side of a deep, narrow valley below them. And something he could not account for. The river at the bottom of the valley appeared to be white. It wasn't the water but the stones along the shoreline and beneath the water, so white they almost glowed in the faint light. Later in the day, he would learn that the very hearts of the mountains into which they had hiked that night were white, composed of the finest marble in the world—Carrara marble. Since ancient times, men had come into these mountains to quarry it. Pietrasanta, the lovely little Tuscan town where they had climbed down from trucks the night before, had, for a time, been home to Michelangelo, who wanted to live near the marble quarries in order to select the finest stone for his sculptures. Since then, quarrying had been carried out on an industrial scale. And, most recently, the Germans had turned some of the enormous white scars in the mountains into formidable stone redoubts.

At dawn, the Nisei soldiers remained hidden away behind closed shutters and heavy doors in homes and sheds throughout Azzano, out of sight of German observers and gun crews on the mountain just across the valley. Sprawled out in hay and on earthen floors, they tried to get some sleep. But as more of the Italian villagers awoke to find that they had unexpected guests, they did as Italians have always done and began to ply their visitors with whatever food they could find in their meager pantries—eggs and cheese and olives and something some of the men would remember for the rest of their lives, pancakes made from freshly milled chestnut flour, drizzled with mountain honey.

THE SECOND AND Third Battalions spent the remainder of that day in their hiding places in Azzano. As darkness fell, they cleaned their weapons one more time, tied their dog tags together so they wouldn't clank in the dark, and rubbed soot on their faces to darken them.

A little before midnight, I and L Companies slipped quietly out into the main street and followed a dark path down through a forest of chestnut trees into the narrow valley below. As they crossed the white-stone river at the bottom of the hill, two German snipers spotted them and a brief firefight erupted, but the Germans were quickly dispatched. Then, walking single file, each man holding on to the pack of the man in front of him as they had in the Vosges, the Nisei followed an Italian partisan as he guided them along a rocky and sinuous footpath on the other side of the valley, winding up the steep mass of a peak called Monte Folgorito now towering above them. Their mission was audacious—to make what seemed an impossible ascent up the back side of the mountain, surprise the Germans from behind, and capture the high ground between the summits of Folgorito and nearby Monte Carchio before the dawn light revealed their presence to German observers on nearby peaks.

As the Nisei started up the mountain, Colonel Pursall hissed an ominous command in the darkness: "If you fall, don't call out." The footpath soon became little more than a game trail, and the grade steepened sharply until it was perhaps sixty degrees in places. Laboring under their heavy combat gear, the men soon found themselves without a trail of any kind, down on their hands and knees scrambling over loose shale, grabbing at roots and shrubs and each other, trying to keep from sliding into the canyon below. Some did fall. One, Mamoru Shirota, was hit by a boulder dislodged by someone above him. Knocked unconscious, he tumbled sixty feet downslope into the dark, his fall finally broken by a tree stump. Chaplain Yamada slid down the slope to his aid. But nobody made a sound. Not a single curse or scream. They just kept climbing silently, foot by tortuous foot, gasping for breath.

Well before dawn, after ascending nearly three thousand feet, the first of them hauled themselves over a final rock ledge and crawled out onto a narrow saddle of land running between the summits of Folgorito, just to their left, and Monte Carchio, off to their right. It was a cold clear night. A half-moon was now high in the sky, but no Germans were in sight in its silvery light. L Company swung quietly to the left and scrambled the last few dozen meters toward the top of Folgorito. I Company swung right and headed for the more distant peak of Carchio. Both groups promptly came across and captured German sentries asleep at their positions. As they started up a stony knob atop Folgorito, wading through patches of yellow thorny broom, L Company passed a cave with machine guns pointed at the saddle they had just crossed, but the guns were unmanned, their crew apparently asleep deeper in the black cave. Private Arthur Yamashita fired a burst from a BAR at the entrance of the cave, and after a tense few minutes seven sleepy Germans crawled out waving strips of white cloth.

Now Germans in distant observation posts on nearby Monte Altissimo were alerted to what was unfolding. German and Italian artillery opened up on the ridge. American artillery returned fire, and soon the mountains were thundering. Chaplain Yamada, who had returned to Azzano, stood in a doorway, marveling at what was unfolding in the marble mountains above him, writing to his wife later in the day, "At ten to five the guns, big and small, opened up. It was a beautiful sight. So many rounds were fired that the whole hillside was aflame with light and shell burst."

The Nisei hunkered down in defensive positions. But by the time the sun rose at 8:00 a.m., the battle for the high ground had already been won, and the 442nd had forced open a crack in the Gothic Line.

THEN IT WAS K Company's turn to assault the mountain. To Fred and Rudy, the flames and smoke blossoming among the crags above them did not seem the least bit beautiful. But following in the footsteps of I and L Companies, they—along with a mortar platoon from M Company—worked their way down toward the white-stone river in the narrow valley below them. By now, with the sun well up, the Germans could see every move they made. As they reached the bottom of the valley, Germans concealed in a nearby marble quarry unleashed a massive barrage of mortars at them. Shells from artillery on a nearby hillside began to whistle in as well. Trapped at the bottom of the draw, Fred and Rudy dove for cover, but the shells and mortar rounds fell relentlessly, pounding them like hail in a thunderstorm. There was no place to hide and no place to run to. All they could do was dig in, hunker down, and call for artillery strikes on the marble quarry and the German guns. Some of the new replacement troops did try to run, though, leaping to their feet and sprinting upstream or downstream. Fred bellowed at them, "Get down! Get down!" but panic had set in, and several of them ran directly into a maelstrom of flying shrapnel and shattered white stone. Within minutes, three men were dead and twenty-three wounded. Even with shells continuing to fall, litter bearers began hauling the dead and wounded back up the hill toward Azzano. Fred, Rudy, and the other surviving members of K Company knew they had to get out of there one way or the other. Retreat wasn't an option. The only real option lay directly before them.

They rushed forward and began to scale Monte Folgorito. And as they started up the steep slope, waves of Nisei soldiers—the entire Third Battalion—began to follow them up the mountain, determined to flood into the breach opened by the initial assault.

AT ABOUT THE SAME TIME that the first Nisei troops reached the top of Monte Folgorito from the east, the 100th Battalion attacked the same mass of mountains from the southwest. Their first major objective was a rocky ridge that military planners had dubbed Georgia Hill, which was bristling with German gun emplacements. Over the course of more than five months, Allied units had repeatedly pounded it with artillery and launched assaults on the German positions there, but each time they had failed to reduce it. Now, in the dark, the men of the 100th started up it. As they approached the German perimeter, stumbling over the rugged terrain in the dark, Company A blundered into a minefield. When the first mine exploded, the men, many of them green recent replacement troops, scattered in all directions, promptly detonating seven more mines and killing many of them. The Germans, alerted by the explosions and screams, began raking the confused mass of men below them with machine-gun fire and tossing clusters of grenades they had tied together to form particularly lethal bundles. Seeing a disaster in the making, some of Company A's more experienced men ran forward, plunging into the melee in the dark.

One of those running forward was Rudy's buddy twenty-two-year-old Sadao Munemori, the baby-faced kid from Glendale whom Rudy had first met at Camp Savage when both of them had been pegged for service in the Military Intelligence Service. Like Rudy, Munemori had been incarcerated in one of the concentration camps—Manzanar in California. Like Rudy he had rejected service in the MIS in favor of the infantry and had joined the 100th as a replacement at Anzio a year before. Since then he and Rudy had grown close. Both spoke fluent Japanese, were from California, and spent a lot of time talking about their families back in the camps. Munemori was perhaps the only man in the 442nd who preferred potatoes to rice, so Rudy, like all his buddies, called him Spud.

Now, seeing his squad leader go down, Munemori realized he was in charge of his unit. With his men in disarray, and with rounds whistling past him in the dark, he launched himself forward, rallying his men and leading them through the minefield, quickly closing to within thirty yards of several entrenched machine-gun nests. As they neared the German gunners, his men dove for cover in shallow shell craters, but Munemori charged directly at the Germans, hurling grenades, coming within fifteen yards, and taking out two of the nests before beginning to work his way back toward his men under heavy direct fire. He had nearly made it to a crater where two of his men—Akira Shishido and Jimi Oda—were sheltering when an unexploded grenade bounced off his helmet and rolled toward the crater. Without hesitating, Munemori dove for the grenade, arched his upper body over it, and smothered it just as it exploded, killing him instantly but sparing the lives of Shishido and Oda.

The battle was fierce but brief. As more Nisei poured up the hill in waves, they quickly overran the German positions, and thirty-two minutes later they stood triumphant atop Georgia Hill. Then they pushed on. Four American attack aircraft joined the fray, strafing and bombing German positions. Over the next forty hours—fighting by day and by night—the 100th climbed higher along the ridgeline leading northeast up to Folgorito, taking, in turn, a series of successively higher peaks before finally linking up with elements of the Third Battalion at 7:00 p.m. on April 6.

The operation had cost thirty-two Nisei soldiers their lives. Dozens more had been wounded. But in a little less than two days the 442nd had again done what no other unit had done, and what nobody had thought possible. They had opened a gaping hole in the western end of the Gothic Line, effectively flanking the last major German defensive positions in western Italy. What Mark Clark had intended primarily as a diversion had turned into a major breakthrough, and while the fighting in the Apuan Alps was far from over, Allied forces could now move men and matériel up the Ligurian coast toward Genoa with its massive shipyards and easy access to the Po valley. The German army in Italy was now all but doomed.

That didn't keep them from trying to kill as many Americans as they could. As they withdrew north, the Germans continued to defend a series of mountaintop positions, raining artillery fire down on the advancing Americans as the Ninety-second Division's artillerymen pounded them in return. On the ground somewhere between the two—he was not later able to say exactly where—Rudy Tokiwa got caught in the cross fire. Whether it was a German shell or an American round that fell short he never knew, but Rudy was too close when it hit. Perhaps a dozen jagged pieces of shrapnel sliced into his lower body. The wounds weren't mortal, at least not immediately so, but for Rudy the war was over.

TWENTY-TWO

The fact our men can be acclaimed as good fighters is because they are believers in what they do. They have an understanding heart, a purpose driven by the long nights of challenge after December 7 to prove themselves.

CHAPLAIN YAMADA TO HIS WIFE, AI
APRIL 11, 1945

B y March 27, the 522nd had penetrated 170 miles into Germany, passing through the Siegfried Line and crossing the Rhine on a pontoon bridge just south of Worms. The German defenses in front of them were beginning to crumble in the face of the massive Allied invasion that stretched from the North Sea all the way south to the Swiss border, pushing relentlessly eastward. The Nisei artillerymen now found themselves firing in support of different divisions almost every day—sometimes more than one division in a single day—as a dizzying array of new targets of opportunity opened before them. They quickly fell into a regular routine, setting up and firing their guns for a few hours, then moving on to richer pickings. They often found themselves out ahead of the main Allied forces now, still formally attached to Alexander Patch's Seventh Army but frequently following close on the heels of armored units from George Patton's Third Army as they spear-pointed the drive in their sector. As the armor found pockets of resistance, the 522nd moved up to pound them into submission, while Patton's tanks moved on and the infantry filled in behind to mop up. The whole effort functioned as an efficient, effective, ruthless machine of war, and it was now beginning to utterly crush German resistance.

WEST OF NUREMBERG, the 522nd turned south and advanced toward Munich, often traveling now on something new in the world, freeways, complete with cloverleaf interchanges. The autobahn—a point of pride for German engineering—now provided a great convenience for the invading Americans.

By mid-April, sometimes riding on tanks, sometimes walking, sometimes driving their own trucks and jeeps, they were pursuing a German military in full collapse. Whenever they had a break, Kats and his buddy Flint Yonashiro foraged for food, scouring the countryside for chickens and vegetables to supplement their K rations and C rations as they had in Italy and France. On one occasion, they returned with more than twenty squawking chickens stuffed into sacks and served up a barbecue for all the B Battery guys. But the biggest prize came when they stumbled across an abandoned warehouse full of luxury provisions, apparently meant for German officers. The place was stacked to the rafters with all manner of delights—enormous wheels of Dutch cheese, crates of canned Portuguese sardines, cases of schnapps and cognac, cartons of cigarettes, boxes of cigars. There were even some brand-new Hohner accordions still in their boxes. That night and for days to come—whenever they had some downtime and their guns were under wraps—the men attacked their newfound bounty, passing around bottles of schnapps, slicing up wedges of cheese, cooking an oily concoction they called "sardine soup," gagging and choking on cigars, making hilarious attempts to play Hawaiian music on the accordions, wearing top hats and coats with tails that they had found in a house nearby.

B Battery's chicken barbecue

But the breaks from the war were always fleeting, the cold reality always just around the next bend in the road. And that reality was increasingly difficult to grasp. As they entered southern Bavaria, Kats continued to struggle, trying to process all that he was seeing. There were things that were hard to comprehend: a whole town that had been reduced to rubble by Allied bombing, but with an elegant church steeple rising from the ruins; the bodies of young German soldiers in gray uniforms, dangling from the lampposts where older SS men had hanged them for desertion or cowardice; dead horses sprawled in front of German artillery pieces they had been pulling, as if this were a nineteenth-century war; an entire factory full of workers with shaved heads, laboring even as the war raged around them, wearing some kind of drab uniform, bent over machinery, not looking up or making eye contact with the passing Nisei; newly manufactured warplanes abandoned in the woods, some of them with no propellers but instead something the men had never seen and could not understand, jet engines; in a farmhouse, two dozen German troops caught unawares with two nude young women; in the basement of another house, another pair of young women, these ones wearing yellow cloth stars pinned to their clothing.

.   .   .

BACK IN ITALY, Rudy Tokiwa was taken to the army's Eighth Replacement Depot at Empoli, west of Florence, to convalesce. There he found himself living alone in a large pyramidal tent meant for a dozen men. As the days passed and his wounds began to heal, he became increasingly lonely, bored, and frustrated. Finally, he did what he had done when he'd found the tedium at the Salinas Assembly Center to be too great. He hobbled over to the mess tent and started to help out with the cooking.

Meanwhile on the front line, the 442nd, still taking casualties, absorbed the news of Franklin Roosevelt's death as they kept slugging it out with the retreating Germans. Many of them mourned the president's passing, some very deeply. Others, remembering the executive order that had deprived them and their families of their homes, had a harder time feeling grief, but they all knew his passing was a blow to the country. As they moved up the coast, crossed the Frigido River above Massa, passed through the marble-quarrying town of Carrara, and then fought their way laboriously back into the mountains—fighting again from peak to peak—Fred Shiosaki mostly thought about how much his legs ached and how very tired he was of climbing up and down mountainsides like the mules carrying their supplies.

On April 20, the 442nd closed cautiously on Tendola, another long, narrow village—a thousand years old—clinging precariously to the side of a mountain above a deep, forested valley. Most of the village's cobbled streets were so narrow that one could touch the ancient buildings on both sides just by spreading out one's arms. The glory of the town was the yellow spire of its church steeple, soaring elegantly above the village's red-tile roofs. It was the first thing in town to catch the light of a Tuscan dawn, the last thing to surrender its golden glow in the evening. It was also the perfect place for German snipers to hide out.

The next day, a thin gray sea haze hung over the coastal mountains as Lieutenant Daniel Inouye led a platoon of E Company men along a ridge east of Tendola and south of San Terenzo Monti. When a squad of German riflemen began firing on them from off to one side of his column, Inouye realized he had been flanked. As his men hit the deck, he stood taller, trying to spot a route to a better position. No sooner had he risen to his feet than a runner crouched behind him called out, "Hey, you're bleeding." Inouye checked his belly and sure enough it was bleeding. Without his realizing it, a German round, apparently from a distant sniper, had hit him in the gut. Feeling no pain from the wound, though, he motioned to his men to keep going. He had to get them out of there.

Then all hell broke loose. Three MG-42 machine guns suddenly opened up on them. As the machine guns raked his men, they dove again for cover. Inouye also threw himself on the ground, but then he began to crawl uphill into the German fire, closing to within five yards of one of the guns. Unclipping two hand grenades from his belt, he threw both in rapid succession into the German position. Both exploded, killing the Germans manning the gun. Before the next nearest gun could be brought to bear on him, he leaped to his feet, threw another grenade, and destroyed it as well. While his men rose to their knees and opened fire to distract the third gun crew, Inouye again dropped to the ground and crawled to within ten yards of it. As he stood, pulled the pin, and prepared to throw his final grenade, one of the Germans spotted him and fired a rifle-launched grenade directly at him. The grenade hit his right elbow and nearly severed most of his arm. His men tried to rush to him to render aid, but Inouye screamed at them to keep back, fearing that the hand on his severed arm would relax and release the lever on the grenade that it still clutched. With his other arm, he reached across his body, carefully pulled the grenade free from the grip of the lifeless hand, threw it at the German who had shot him, and killed him. Inouye was, by now, as he later said, "insane." He rose to his feet and stumbled forward with the one arm dangling useless from some sinews and shreds of uniform and his blood pumping in red spurts from a severed artery. Standing bolt upright, cradling his Thompson submachine gun in his remaining arm, he moved forward again with the wounded arm flapping at his side, unleashing repeated bursts of automatic fire at the remaining Germans until one of them finally shot him in the leg and he tumbled down the hill. There, lying in some brush as a few of his men gathered around him, he began to apply a tourniquet to his own leg and ordered them to resume the attack, growling at them, "Nobody called off the war!" Then, finally, he passed out.

THE NISEI SOLDIERS fought ferociously through the remainder of that day and all that night, trying to wrest control of the rugged terrain around Tendola from the Germans but taking heavy casualties. It was a battle that would, in the end, cause Rudy Tokiwa more grief than any other, even though he was far from the front, recovering at Empoli.

The worst of it came when a German artillery shell plunged directly into a mine shaft where I Company had established its command post. Five men were killed instantly and seven grievously wounded.* Among the dead carried out of the mine on a litter was Rudy's big, seemingly indestructible friend Lloyd Onoye, the kid nobody could bring down on the playing fields at Poston.

At dawn, as the first light touched the spire of Tendola's church, the Germans still held the town as fighting raged in the mountains all around them. By 2:00 that afternoon, patrols from K Company had maneuvered into positions both north and south of the town. Now they launched an all-out assault. It quickly devolved into a particularly nasty battle. The core of the opposition the Nisei faced here were battle-hardened German troops from the Kesselring Machine Gun Battalion, and they seemed determined to die in the ancient stone buildings of Tendola rather than return to a defeated Germany as prisoners of war.

---

*Because of the orientation of the opening to the mine shaft, there is some reason to believe that it might have been an American shell that killed Onoye and the others, but that has not been established.

As Fred Shiosaki fired mortar shells into German positions in the town, American artillery on nearby hillsides pounded the larger, stronger buildings where the biggest concentrations of Germans were holed up. All of K Company was committed to the battle now, and they began to advance on the town in a pincer movement, from both the north and the south. At the same time, Joe Hayashi, who had been one of Rudy and Fred's drill sergeants at Camp Shelby, led a squad of men up a steep, terraced hillside on the eastern side of town. Scrambling from terrace to terrace as machine-gun fire shredded the olive trees above him, Hayashi and his men lobbed hand grenades into three successive machine-gun nests, killing perhaps half a dozen Germans and causing many more to flee. But as Hayashi pursued the last of those to run, a burst of fire from a handheld machine pistol cut him down, and he died, bleeding into the rocky soil among the olive trees.

Fred watched in horror as one of K Company's medics, Hiroshi Sugiyama, dashed out onto the hillside where Hayashi lay dead. Unarmed and in full view, Sugiyama hunched over Hayashi for a moment, then moved on to another man, counting on the red cross on his armband to protect him. It didn't. A sniper, hidden somewhere in the village, shot him in the back, killing him instantly.

As the assault reached its climax, the people of Tendola huddled in cellars, under shuddering buildings, occasionally opening heavy wooden doors a crack to peer out at the bloody conflagration unfolding in their streets. One seven-year-old boy could not resist a better view. Mario Pomini crept out of a cellar where not just his family but many of his neighbors were pressed together in the dark, on their knees, praying. At the intersection of two narrow streets, he peered around a corner just in time to see a Nisei soldier clamber over a low stone wall, emerging from the terraced olive groves below town. The soldier started up the street, hugging the rough stone wall along one side. Glancing up, Mario saw half a dozen Germans waiting behind the open green shutters of a second-story window directly above the soldier. Waving, Mario caught the soldier's eye. The two locked eyes on each other for a brief moment;

then Mario gestured, a single, brief movement of his hand, pointing up at the window above the soldier. The soldier pressed himself tighter against the wall, hesitating, trying to make sure he understood. Then he unclipped a hand grenade, pulled the pin, stepped out into the street, and lobbed the grenade neatly overhead and through the window. The room above him erupted in flames and smoke. Fragments of stone flew across the street, slamming into another building, punching out windows. Then all was quiet. The soldier waited a few moments more and then began advancing up the street again when a German soldier leaned out of the blown-out window, leveled a machine pistol at his back, and killed him with a burst of fire.*

The battle dragged on into the night, devolving into house-to-house and sometimes hand-to-hand combat. Fred Shiosaki and his mortar team spent the night knocking down doors, climbing dark stone stairways trying to find firing positions, not knowing what might lurk on the next floor above them. All through the fight, though, Fred was distracted and in a simmering rage. He kept seeing that medic—Sugiyama—shot in the back, collapsing over another wounded soldier.

By the morning of April 23, the town seemed finally to have fallen. The only Germans anyone could find in town were dead, slumped over machine guns or splayed out on bloody cobblestones in the streets. Just north of town, I Company's Tadao "Beanie" Hayashi set out with his lieutenant, Sadaichi Kubota, on one last patrol, just to make sure the area was clear of enemy troops. Beanie was yet another of Rudy's friends from Salinas, but even more from Poston, where he had lived in Block 213, the same block as the Tokiwa family. He had been one of the boys who sat among the mesquite trees in the spring of 1943, listening to Harry Madokoro and Lloyd Onoye talk about why they all had to volunteer.

---

*Mario Pomini, then eighty-one, told his story—complete with a dramatic reenactment on the street where it happened—to me and a group of 442nd family members when we visited Tendola in April 2019.

Kubota had told Beanie earlier that morning that he didn't need to go along on the patrol, but Beanie had insisted. As they climbed onto a rocky knoll north of town, Kubota turned around to look at something off in the distance. As he turned back around, Beanie was already falling to the ground. A split second later, Kubota heard the report of the sniper's rifle. Four hundred yards away, a puff of white smoke drifted from the golden steeple of the village church. Beanie was the sixteenth and last of the young men from Poston to die in battle.

LATE THAT AFTERNOON, as K Company finished mopping up at Tendola, Fred's captain came to him, escorting the brother of the medic who had been shot in the back the previous day. Pete Sugiyama had just been informed of his brother's death, and he was in a bad way. The captain wanted to get him off the battlefield for a few days, to give him a chance to absorb the shock and grieve.

"Fred, you take Pete back to regimental headquarters."

"Well, yeah, God, I'll be glad to do that."

The two of them set off down the road. Before they got far, they came across a noncommissioned officer. He was leading a captured German at gunpoint.

"Hey, Fred, we captured a German here. Why don't you take him back, too?"

Fred agreed, but as the three of them walked on, something occurred to Fred. He studied the back of the German. He was a slight man, much older than Fred. He seemed scared, meek, and more than willing to comply with whatever Fred ordered him to do.

The regimental headquarters was nearly two miles away, and as they walked down the winding road, Fred realized they were out of sight of anyone, nearly out of hearing range, too. And nobody would notice the sound of one more rifle shot at any rate. He had his rifle trained on the German's back, and he couldn't stop thinking about Pete's brother getting killed the way he had. He wrestled with himself, thinking, "Pete, if you ask me to shoot that son of a bitch I'll shoot him." Fred glanced over at Pete, but he didn't say aloud what he was thinking, and Pete didn't return the glance or say anything at all. He just trudged along with his head bowed. Fred hung back a few steps, hoping maybe the German would make a break for it. He, too, just kept trudging along, his head bowed like Pete's. Again, Fred thought, "God, Pete, are you sure you don't want me to?"

In the end, they arrived at headquarters with the German POW still alive. As he walked back to rejoin K Company, Fred thought about it. He was glad he hadn't shot the man, but he grappled with how keenly he had wanted to, and how close he had come to doing it. It was a moment of clarity for Fred. He was still Fred Shiosaki, but he sure as hell wasn't the same kid who had left Spokane on a train two years before.

Meanwhile, at the headquarters he was just leaving, reports began to come in from U.S. reconnaissance aircraft flying just to the north of them. Large numbers of German and Italian fascist forces were moving north, retreating in disorder, abandoning equipment as they fled.

TWENTY-THREE

Most of all, I felt guilt for the transgression of mankind to do evil in the sight of God.

GEORGE OIYE

On April 25, as all three battalions of the 442nd continued driving north in western Italy and the 522nd plunged deeper into Germany, Solly Ganor and his father, dressed in their thin, lice-infested uniforms, trudged out through the gate at the Lager Ten slave-labor camp in Bavaria and began to walk toward Dachau. Many of their fellow prisoners were little more than walking skeletons really, their bones threatening to poke through the thin veneer of flesh still enshrouding them. Most were missing teeth, some entirely toothless, the results of scurvy. Their eyes were sunken—deep, dark hollows. Many had no shoes. Some had wrapped their feet in strips of burlap, but before long the burlap was soaked in blood. Guard dogs snarled and snapped at any stragglers. SS guards beat or kicked anyone who fell down, but Solly could see that the guards, for the first time since he had been enslaved, looked anxious. As the ragged column hobbled along the road, Allied warplanes occasionally roared overhead. Off in the distance, planes began to strafe and bomb a train crawling across the landscape until the locomotive finally exploded in a cloud of steam and shattered black steel and the rest of the train careened off the tracks.

By the next morning, they were marching through a leafy suburb where they could see German civilians peeking furtively out at them from behind curtains. Occasionally, someone ventured out of a house with a loaf of bread or a wedge of cheese and tried to hand it to the prisoners, but they hastily retreated inside as swarms of starving men fought over the food and SS guards screamed at everyone to get back in line.

Late that afternoon, they filed along a redbrick road and through a gatehouse with the same cynical motto that Solly had seen at Stutthof wrought in iron, *ARBEIT MACHT FREI.* A wave of dread washed over him. Dachau was different from Lager Ten. It smelled of death and ashes, of sewage and urine. It felt as if Lucifer himself lurked here. Solly and his father were herded, along with the other newcomers, between long rows of barracks toward the back of the camp. There they were ordered to undress for the shower room. Terror ripped at Solly's guts, and he saw terror in his father's eyes as well. Some of their fellow prisoners at Lager Ten had come from Auschwitz. They knew what the showers meant.

AT ABOUT 9:30 A.M. that same day, Kats Miho crossed the Danube with the 522nd at the prim and pretty Bavarian town of Dillingen an der Donau, about fifty miles northwest of Munich. Attached now to the Fourth Infantry Division, the battalion was racing across the countryside, pausing only occasionally to set up their guns and fire at the last desperate remnants of a rapidly disintegrating German army. They were moving so fast that the forward observers were having a hard time knowing exactly where they were. Sometimes as much as twenty-five miles ahead of the rest of the battalion and spread out over an area with a radius of perhaps thirty miles, they found themselves stopping at almost every junction, poring over road maps, trying to decipher the meaning of road signs written in Gothic script. Over the next several days,

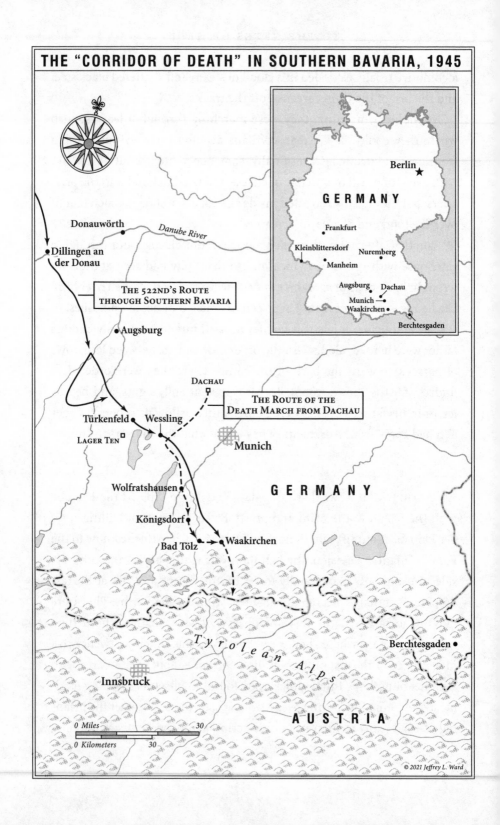

THE "CORRIDOR OF DEATH" IN SOUTHERN BAVARIA, 1945

GERMANY

Berlin ★

Frankfurt

Kleinblittersdorf · Nuremberg

Manheim

Augsburg · Dachau

Munich ·
Waakirchen ·

Berchtesgaden

Donauwörth · · · Danube River

· Dillingen an
der Donau

**THE 522ND'S ROUTE
THROUGH SOUTHERN BAVARIA**

· Augsburg

DACHAU ☐

**THE ROUTE OF THE
DEATH MARCH FROM DACHAU**

Türkenfeld · Wessling ·

LAGER TEN ☐

Munich

Wolfratshausen ·

GERMANY

Königsdorf ·

Bad Tölz · → · Waakirchen

$T_{y\ r\ o\ l\ e\ a\ n}$ Alps

Berchtesgaden ·

Innsbruck

AUSTRIA

0 Miles   30
0 Kilometers   30

© 2021 Jeffrey L. Ward

though, driving south, they advanced directly into what they would later call the Corridor of Death, a forty-mile stretch of lovely Bavarian countryside, lovely but for the sprawling network of slave-labor camps where more than sixty-seven thousand prisoners were now on the verge of death and many more than that were already dead.

IN NORTHERN ITALY, the 442nd was also moving fast, advancing up the Ligurian coast, sometimes marching on foot, other times riding in the backs of trucks or perched on top of tanks, facing only scattered pockets of resistance. Only mined roadways, blown-out bridges, and the necessity of bringing supplies forward kept them from advancing even more quickly. In every town and village now, crowds of civilians mobbed them, cheering them, showering them with flowers, embracing them, kissing them, thrusting bottles of wine into their hands. As they closed in on Genoa, the Nisei found that the city had already been liberated by Italian partisans, so they piled onto public streetcars, climbed into the backs of commandeered farm trucks, crowded into taxis, and rode into the city center, waving American and Italian flags to the cheers of thousands of civilians and hundreds of partisans lining the streets, wearing bright red scarves.

They did not linger in Genoa, though. To exploit the Germans' chaotic withdrawal, K Company was ordered to turn northeast and to advance through a range of low hills separating the coastal plain from the vast expanse of the Po valley. There, entire regiments of Germans were beginning to surrender en masse, and Benito Mussolini was about to die.

SOLLY GANOR AND HIS FATHER stood under a row of shower nozzles in a cold and barren room, waiting to die. Solly closed his eyes. His stomach had twisted itself into a hard knot. His father was clutching his hand so hard it hurt.

But then his father laughed. Solly opened his eyes, and his father gestured up toward the ceiling. A row of windows was open. A moment later, tepid water began to flow out of the nozzles over their heads. The Nazis were, in fact, giving them a shower, not gassing them. Standing under the flowing water as months of accumulated sweat and grime ran down into the drains, Solly rejoiced, marveling in the moment at the miracle of being alive, startled to realize how much he still craved life after all he had been through.

But even as the Nazis handed out new uniforms, doubt began to creep back in. What were they up to? Had animals become humans again? Solly fell asleep that night on the wooden slats of a bunk in one of Dachau's filthy barracks profoundly grateful for another night of life but wondering, was the nightmare really over?

In the morning, he found his answer. During the night, thousands of additional prisoners had arrived at Dachau from other sub-camps. These prisoners were given no showers. They were, as Solly had been hours before, dirty, lice-infested, and hollow-eyed. Many were profoundly emaciated, in some cases already half-dead. Judging by the languages they were speaking, they appeared to be a mixture of Lithuanian Jews like Solly, Ukrainians, Russians, and Poles. And with them, many more SS men had come into the camp during the night.

The new guards seemed extremely anxious, confused, and exceptionally ill tempered. They strode about the camp with snarling German shepherds and Doberman pinschers on leashes, issuing contradictory orders to the *Kapos*, beating prisoners randomly, looking up at the sky warily from time to time, talking to someone on radios in frenetic bursts of German laced with curses that Solly knew all too well from his time at Lager Ten.

By late afternoon, the guards seemed to have come up with some kind of plan. They lined roughly seven thousand of the stronger, healthier prisoners up in columns and began marching them back out through the main gates of Dachau, another long shuffling procession of ragged men in striped pajamas, some of them clutching thin, threadbare blankets, some of them wobbling on wooden clogs, some still limping along on feet wrapped in burlap, some barefoot. As Solly and his father passed through the gate, the sky ahead grew dark, and it began to rain, just showers at first, then a drenching downpour.

For the next five days, Solly and his father trudged south in a column of human misery that stretched out ahead of them for as far as they could see. Again, the SS walked alongside them with snarling dogs that lunged and snapped at anyone who stepped out of line. A few of the SS men carried bullwhips, but most carried submachine guns. Nobody knew where they were going or why. The obvious answer, that they were being led to some remote spot for a mass execution, seemed less likely the farther they went. If the guards had simply wanted to murder them all, they had already passed plenty of places that would suffice for that purpose. Some thought maybe they were going to Switzerland to be exchanged for German POWs. Others thought they would be put to work building some kind of defensive fortifications in the Tyrolean Alps, where the Nazis could make a last stand. None of it seemed to make much sense, and as Solly watched his SS guards become increasingly agitated and disorganized, it seemed most likely that they simply didn't know what they were doing.

By the end of the first day, their clothes and thin blankets were soaked through. When it became so waterlogged that he could no longer carry the weight of it, Solly's father had to abandon a precious coat he had somehow picked up at Dachau. That night, the SS forced them into a forest where they tried to sleep on the wet ground. In the morning, the SS shot those who could not or would not stand and resume walking. Occasionally, for variety's sake, instead of shooting them, the guards turned the snarling dogs loose and let them maul their victims to death. Trudging on, Solly and his father shivered continually, and their teeth chattered as temperatures dropped and the rain threatened to turn to snow. On the third day, a bitterly cold wind came up. By now, hundreds of them had begun to drop by the wayside, unable to go any farther as fatigue and starvation overcame them. As Solly and his father staggered on, they could hear almost continuous popping sounds from the rear of the column—the SS shooting those who couldn't keep up, leaving a trail of bodies lying by the roadsides of southern Bavaria. From time to time, American aircraft roared overhead, and the SS drove everyone into the woods. Off in the distance both the Germans and their captives could hear the rumble of artillery fire, and it seemed to be growing closer.

ON APRIL 29, U.S. troops—the Seventh Army's Forty-second and Forty-fifth Infantry Divisions and the Twentieth Armored Division—closed in on the main concentration camp at Dachau, where thirty thousand prisoners, many of them too weak to be marched out of the camp on April 26, still remained. The Americans could smell Dachau long before they could see it. As they approached the vast compound, they came across a railroad siding with thirty-nine boxcars filled with 2,310 corpses, all of them emaciated, some of them bloodied, as if they had been beaten. Men, women, children, and babies all lay heaped together in a macabre tangle of limbs. The train had arrived from Buchenwald the day before, but after more than three weeks crammed into the boxcars, most of those riding in them had already died of starvation, dehydration, and disease. As they peered into the boxcars, some of the GIs began to vomit. The stench—the sickly smell of death—was overwhelming.

The GIs, grimly silent but enraged, began to enter the Dachau camp itself. Some scaled its tall brick walls. Some entered by the railroad entrance at which the train had been pulled up. Others congregated in front of the main gate but hesitated to open it as thousands of prisoners in striped uniforms began to mass inside it, pushing at it, threatening to overwhelm and stampede their liberators. A tall, thin SS officer, Untersturmführer Heinrich Wicker—along with a Red Cross representative—came forward to negotiate the surrender of the camp. The Americans weren't disposed to negotiate anything. They marched Wicker to the trainful of corpses and demanded answers.

As they pushed deeper into the camp, the GIs' anger mounted as they came across things that until then they could not have imagined. Piles of naked white bodies, stacked up outside a building like firewood saved up for the winter. A mountain of shoes, many of them children's shoes. Some kind of interrogation room, its concrete walls splattered with blood and brain tissue. A crematorium, its brick ovens still full of bits of charred bones and ashes. And people, some of them rushing up to the GIs cheering, embracing them, dropping to their knees, and embracing their legs, others too weak to walk, crawling out of the barracks on hands and knees or remaining within, lying in their own filth in wooden bunks, more dead than alive, staring back at the GIs with eyes behind which no one now lived.

In Dachau's empty coal yard, a few GIs—in a cold and furious rage now—began to line SS men up against a wall and shoot them, killing several dozen, perhaps more, before a senior officer finally found them and put a stop to it. In other parts of the camp, prisoners took matters into their own hands, beating an unknown number of SS men and *Kapos* to death. Untersturmführer Heinrich Wicker was never again seen alive.

THAT SAME AFTERNOON, Kats Miho and other elements of the 522nd, riding in trucks, hauling their howitzers behind them, arrived at the village of Türkenfeld, fifteen miles southwest of Dachau and just two miles north of Lager Ten, where Solly Ganor had been imprisoned just days before. Since entering Germany, they had traveled almost five hundred miles and fired more than fifteen thousand rounds. Now, though, there didn't seem to be anything left to fire at. German resistance had all but evaporated.

U.S. troops were advancing so quickly, and in so many locations, that many of the 522nd's forward observers found themselves acting as scouts not only for the 522nd but for other infantry and armored units racing through Bavaria. They were now spread out across a swath of land perhaps thirty miles wide. And, gradually, they began to discover that

The 522nd hitching a ride near Dachau

more than a dozen Nazi slave-labor camps—sub-camps of the Dachau complex—were within a few miles of their command post in Türkenfeld, in all directions, north, east, south, and west.

There is no firm evidence that any of the 522nd participated in the initial breaching of Dachau's perimeter, but at least a few Nisei soldiers seem to have entered the camp by late that afternoon. Toshio Nishizawa recalled driving in through the open gates in a jeep and being shocked by what he saw—hundreds of living corpses lying on the ground or propped up against walls unable to rise, their eyes like those of furtive animals intently following the Nisei everywhere they went. Josef Erbs, an eighteen-year-old Romanian Jew, weighed only seventy-six pounds. As he lay sprawled on the ground, an American soldier with an Asian face bent over, picked him up, and carried him to an aid station. The face made an impression on Erbs. It was the first time he had seen an Asian of any sort. And he took note also of the shoulder patch on the man's uniform—blue, with a white hand holding a torch—the insignia of the 442nd RCT.

Not far from Dachau, Tadashi Tojo and Robert Sugai were scouting on behalf of a mechanized armor unit when they came across a compound surrounded by tall barbed-wire fencing. Inside there were barracks. An armored tank destroyer crashed through the gate, and dozens of gaunt prisoners in striped uniforms came stumbling out of the barracks, staring blankly at their liberators and wandering around aimlessly. There was no cheering here. The prisoners acted "like zombies," Tojo later reported. Someone threw a chocolate bar to one of them, who took a bite but then promptly threw up.

At another Dachau sub-camp, Ichiro Imamura watched as two of his fellow 522nd scouts shot the padlock off a locked gate on a compound surrounded by barbed wire. About fifty gaunt men in striped uniforms rose from the cold ground where they had been lying and wandered across a road to where two dead cows lay in a field. Within minutes they had cut strips of flesh from the carcasses and begun building a fire to roast the meat. Some of them, not waiting for the fire, began devouring the flesh raw.

The next day, April 30, as Adolf Hitler died a coward's death in a bunker in Berlin, the main column of the 522nd moved south again. Near the village of Wessling, they crossed the route along which Solly Ganor and the six thousand other Dachau prisoners had been marched just hours before. Here they began to come across bodies—scores of them, dressed in striped uniforms, splayed out in muddy fields, lying in ditches, scattered in pinewoods, many of them with gunshot wounds, a few with their throats torn out.

SOLLY DIDN'T NOTICE when his father stopped walking alongside him. He was in a stupor now, simply trudging blindly forward, trying to take the next step without falling down. He was aware of his hunger pangs, of the aching in his feet, of his own breathing, but little else. Perhaps an hour later, when he did finally realize that his father was no longer with him, he stopped and turned around, looking toward the rear of the column as the stream of walking dead parted around him. From the rear of the column, he could hear almost continuous rifle shots as the SS murdered more of those who couldn't keep up.

He stood still for a while. He wanted to lie down on the roadway and let the SS have their way. He understood now that he was ready to die. Death could not be worse than this life, and it would be so much easier than walking on. But he did walk on. Something in him demanded it.

At Wolfratshausen, on May 1, civilians peered out from behind blackout curtains at the long line of spectral figures that had suddenly appeared in their town. A few—risking the wrath of the SS—took hurried, candid snapshots of the passing spectacle. The column stumbled on through the town in a steady rain, passing neat, whitewashed homes with wide gabled roofs and beds of yellow daffodils and red tulips just now blooming. That evening, as they entered the ancient village of Königsdorf, with its tall white onion-domed church steeple, it began to snow.

There, for the first time in many days, Solly saw something that held his attention. Through the parted blackout curtains of a house, he caught a glimpse of an old man sitting in a rocking chair by a flickering

Clandestine photograph of the Dachau death march

fire, asleep with a large book open on his lap. The fire cast a warm golden glow on the man's face and seemed to fill the room. It was, Solly thought, so ordinary and yet so extraordinary. And perhaps the most beautiful thing he had ever seen. For a brief moment, it rallied his spirits. It reminded him that there was a better world, a world worth living in, somewhere beyond the ragged edges of the thin gray column in which he walked.

They passed through Bad Tölz, and darkness began to fall. Beyond the town, the Germans herded Solly and the others into a clearing in some woods for the night. Snow continued to fall, big wet flakes drifting silently down among the trees. Solly, surrounded only by strangers now, lay down and covered himself with his wet blanket. As he fell asleep, he heard the sound of rifle shots nearby. The Germans, apparently, had decided to kill the rest of them and be done with it. Solly, though, had given up on life again. He was just too exhausted to care.

ON THE MORNING of May 2, as Kats Miho, George Oiye, and Sus Ito approached the town of Waakirchen, nestled up against the foothills of the Tyrolean Alps, they began to see lumps in the snow alongside the road. Stopping to investigate, they brushed the snow from the lumps and found just what they had feared—more of the emaciated corpses dressed in striped pajamas that had littered the road the day before. In the woods just outside Waakirchen, they found even more. Some of the bodies beneath the snow had been shot; some had been badly beaten; some apparently had just died of exposure. As they continued brushing snow from the bodies, trying to find anyone who might be alive, more Nisei soldiers showed up, riding in jeeps and on top of tanks.

WHEN SOLLY GANOR awoke that morning, he thought for a moment he was in heaven. All he could see was a bright white light surrounding him on all sides. When he brushed the snow from his face, sat up, and

looked around, he realized he was alive and still in Germany. But there
was no sound. Nothing seemed to be moving anywhere in the woods
except for a bit of wind rustling the trees, bringing down little cascades
of snow. There were no snarling dogs, no Germans, no human voices,
just the absolute silence of the woods on a snowy day. He was surrounded by lumps in the snow, but he already knew what they were.
What interested him more was that on a rise in the distance he saw an
overturned cart with the carcass of a dead horse lying next to it. He got
up and staggered toward it. Next to the cart he found a German, a dead
civilian, and in the cart a pail with some potato peelings. Rummaging
through the dead man's clothes, he found a knife and a cigarette lighter.
He cut some strips of flesh from the dead horse and retreated to the
woods, hurrying now, certain the SS would find him before he could at
least enjoy one last meal. With shaking hands, he built a small, smoky
fire, put the horse flesh in the pail with the potato peelings and some
snow, and began to make soup.

The first sip of it tasted like a miracle. He became mesmerized by it,
staring at it bubbling in the pail, feeling it begin to warm his belly as he
drank it, seeing and hearing nothing else. The soup became his whole

Dachau survivors standing around a campfire,
with George Oiye on the left

world. When he finally heard voices and looked up and saw men in uniforms approaching him, riding on tanks, he resigned himself to the inevitable, resumed eating the soup, and waited for the bullet that would snuff it all out. Then he realized the voices were speaking English. He looked up again and saw an unshaven face, an Asian face, smiling down at him. Then several more. That did not make sense to him. He wondered again if he was dead, if these were some kind of Asian angels. One of the men hovering around him said, "You are free, boy." Solly grappled, trying to remember the English word.

"Who?" he finally croaked. Then again, "Who?"

Someone said, "Hey! He speaks English."

"Americans," another one of them said. "Japanese Americans."

One of the angels handed him a chocolate bar. Solly took it, but set it aside and resumed slowly drinking his soup. He would not eat the chocolate. That would be like eating a treasure. "You would not eat the *Mona Lisa*," he would later say.

PART SIX

HOME

Lieutenant Colonel Pursall and President
Truman reviewing the 442nd

TWENTY-FOUR

Do you mind awfully if I come over to your home to stay for the rest of my life—say about Thanksgiving Day?

CHAPLAIN HIGUCHI TO HIS WIFE, HISAKO

On the day that Solly Ganor crawled out of the snow, the German army in Italy surrendered unconditionally, taking a million German soldiers off the battlefield, and the Soviet army announced the fall of Berlin. The war in Europe was not quite over yet, though. Not until the German government formally surrendered.

As Kats and George Oiye moved with the rest of the 522nd into the town of Waakirchen that day, they found hundreds of survivors from the death march out of Dachau milling around aimlessly. A few, only recently imprisoned, were in better shape than most. The long march and the SS had killed the most emaciated and the sickest of them. But even here, some of the survivors were too far gone to be saved. The Nisei artillerymen were told not to give them their rations because their bodies could not process solid food. They needed to be fed only small amounts of soup at first, nothing more. It was hard for Kats to resist their imploring. Crowds of them gathered around the men at mess time, staring and begging with hand gestures and hollow, plaintive eyes. They snatched up food that fell to the ground and scavenged in the men's garbage sumps for potato peels, crusts of bread, anything remotely edible. Over the next few days—as the Nisei remained in the area and the U.S. Army scrambled to try to feed and shelter them—hundreds more of the Dachau inmates died of exposure or the effects of eating food their bodies could not handle.

Then the 522nd began to reconsolidate their forces, preparing to

Dachau survivors, with a 522nd jeep in the foreground

move southeast toward Berchtesgaden and Hitler's mountaintop retreat, the Kehlsteinhaus, where it was feared that SS fanatics might yet try to make a last stand.

AT 2:41 ON THE MORNING of May 7, Colonel General Alfred Jodl met Walter Bedell Smith at a small redbrick schoolhouse in Reims, France, and surrendered Germany's armed forces to the Allied Expeditionary Force. Though the final instrument of surrender would not be signed and ratified until just before 1:00 a.m. on May 9, the Third Reich was over. In Great Britain, where Germany had represented a threat to the nation's very existence since at least 1939, Winston Churchill learned of the surrender at about 7:00 a.m. but did not announce it publicly until

7:00 p.m. When he did, tens of thousands poured into Trafalgar Square and Piccadilly Circus, cheering and hugging each other. In Paris, enormous throngs of French civilians mingled with American and British soldiers, massing around the Arc de Triomphe, singing "La Marseillaise," and dancing down the Champs-Élysées.

News of the surrender arrived in the United States just in time to make it into the evening editions of many papers. Under banner headlines, millions read the Associated Press's lede, "The greatest war in history ended today with the unconditional surrender of Germany." That evening perhaps half a million jubilant people jammed into Times Square in New York, singing, dancing, holding copies of the evening papers high over their heads. Blizzards of torn paper and confetti drifted down from tall buildings at Rockefeller Center and on Wall Street, where more celebrants poured into the streets. Lacking paper, female workers in the garment district ripped open bales and threw thousands of yards of rayon, silk, and woolen fabric from windows, draping passing cars in strands of colorful cloth.

In most of the country, though, the response was more muted. Here and there church bells rang in small towns. People gathered in churches to offer up prayers of thanksgiving. As they had on December 7, 1941, Americans turned on their radios and then sat down to make phone calls to loved ones to discuss the news. They congregated in the evening air on front lawns and talked it over as moths drifted by in the dark. They gathered under humming electric streetlights on city corners. They sat in smoky taverns and bought each other congratulatory beers and exclaimed how glad they were that now at least some of the boys could come home. But all of them knew that this was not yet the moment they had been waiting for since Pearl Harbor.

THE 442ND WAS at Novi Ligure on the southern fringes of the Po valley when news reached them that the European war was over. Chaplain

Higuchi was in a communications tent late at night, and so he was the first man in the Second Battalion to hear the news. He asked his commanding officer for permission to address the men, once the announcement was official, and let them know.

The following morning, when the news was confirmed, Higuchi mounted a platform to address the battalion. The men were puzzled. It was odd for the chaplain to address them all together on anything other than a Sunday. Higuchi started by asking them to sing "America," leading them through the first few familiar lines:

> *My country, 'tis of thee,*
> *Sweet land of liberty,*
> *Of thee I sing.*

Then he told them, "Fellas, the war in which all our friends who slept with us and ate and died and wanted to see this day . . . the war is over." No one cheered. A soft sigh—a long, murmured, collective exhalation of breath—rippled through the ranks. But nothing more. Higuchi looked out at the upturned faces looking back at him and saw tears dribbling down cheeks. He knew what he was looking at. He felt it himself. He asked them to take a minute for silent prayer, to thank God for their deliverance but more than that to allow themselves to think of the men who were not there, who had died to make this day possible, and to think also of the folks at home who would never see their sons' return. When he dismissed them, a few of the men shouted and threw their hats in the air, but it was only a handful of the replacement troops, the ones who had not seen any fighting, who had not lost any friends, who had not seen young bodies torn open. The rest went back to their assigned tasks, happy it was over, but grim-faced. Nobody got out ukuleles; nobody danced hula.

Fred Shiosaki was in the Third Battalion's bivouac area when he got the news. Like the men in the Second Battalion, he couldn't manage to get too worked up about it. Too much had happened. Too many friends were gone. Too many bloody dreams haunted him at night. He thought, "Jeez. Well, I made it. I think I made it." Then he returned to the old schoolhouse where he was billeted and took a nap.

For Fred, and most of the Nisei soldiers in Europe, news of the end of the war in Europe was clouded not only by their grief and sheer exhaustion but also by the realization that—just as for the folks back home—the moment they were waiting for was still off in the future. Nobody could say how long the waiting would go on. That was a matter that would be decided in the Pacific. The same Associated Press story that announced the German surrender had stated it starkly with a single line printed in boldface, WAR ON JAPS CONTINUES.

Kats and the 522nd artillerymen in Germany reacted to the German surrender in the same way the infantry in Italy did. Not with indifference, but with a weary sigh and a sense of gratitude that they, at least, had somehow survived the whole ugly thing. Kats did notice one sudden change in the behavior of his buddies, though, when they climbed into a truck together for the first time following the news. Until then, the 522nd's drivers had typically driven their lumbering vehicles with a kind of wild exuberance, racing down the autobahns at breakneck speeds, careening around corners on narrow village streets, swerving around obstacles on winding mountain roads. Now, Kats noticed, the men in the backs of the trucks took to pounding on the roofs of the cabs, yelling, "Eh! Take it easy! We want to go home!" Many of the Nisei—especially the Buddhaheads—had gone to war carrying with them attitudes and beliefs they had picked up from talking with their Japanese fathers and watching samurai movies as boys. For the most part, they, in the tradition of those warriors, had not really expected to return alive. But now they did. They wanted to see their homes again, to taste their mothers' cooking, to kiss their girlfriends, to walk again on the beaches they had played on as children. And they didn't want some careless kid to swerve off a road and take all that away now.

. . .

AT POSTON, too, as at all the WRA concentration camps, the news of Germany's surrender was noted with relief but restraint, particularly by the Issei parents of young men serving in the 442nd. For weeks following the surrender, the *Poston Chronicle* and other camp papers continued to be filled with news of still more men who had died or been injured in Europe in the previous few months. As happy as everyone was to know that many of the rest of them might soon be coming home, there was an ever-increasing dread that there might not be any homes to return to.

In 1942, the chamber of commerce in Rudy Tokiwa's Salinas had conducted a survey and reported that only 1 of "approximately 10,000" Salinas residents supported the return of Japanese Americans to the Monterey-Salinas area. One respondent wrote, "There never was and never will be a Jap that was or ever will be loyal to the United States." In February 1945, an organization that called itself the Monterey Bay Council on Japanese Relations was incorporated specifically "to discourage the return to the Pacific Coast of any person of Japanese ancestry." And as the first few families started to return to the area in April 1945, threatening notices began to appear in the *Monterey Peninsula Herald*. The notices were anonymous, but they solicited funds and invited others to join the "Organization to Discourage Return of Japanese to the Pacific Coast," promising not only to lobby against allowing their return but to investigate the backgrounds of returning Japanese families, to work toward the deportation of any Japanese whose loyalties they might suspect, to insist on law enforcement's supervision of Japanese-language schools and societies, and to work to eliminate dual citizenship.

In response, a number of appalled community leaders launched a petition drive. On May 11, the *Herald*, under the headline THE DEMO-CRATIC WAY OF LIFE FOR ALL, printed a full-page open letter condemning the sentiments expressed in the ad and taking the *Herald* to task for

Graffiti on a garage in Seattle

printing it in the first place. Pointing specifically to the contributions of the 442nd, the letter said, "These families have made their homes here for many years and have been part of the life of the community. Their sons are making the same sacrifices as our own boys." Among the 440 signatories were John Steinbeck; Steinbeck's close friend from their time together on Cannery Row, the marine biologist Ed Ricketts; the photographer Edward Weston; and the poet Robinson Jeffers.

But by then copies of the *Herald* with the original notice had made their way to Poston, where families like the Tokiwas read them and shuddered, now terrified by the prospect that they would never be able to safely return to reclaim their remaining possessions and their way of life.

THE END OF THE WAR in Europe did not mean a quick trip home for the Nisei soldiers. A point system—based on length of service, number of dependents, and honors received in battle—determined the order in which men would be sent home and discharged. For some, the boat ride back to the States was still a year and a half away.

In winning the war, the Allies had inherited the consequences of what the Nazis had wrought—a massive humanitarian crisis. Much of Europe was in ruins. Hundreds of thousands of civilians were left destitute and homeless, wandering more or less aimlessly across the countryside, trying to figure out how to get back to their native countries and, more urgently, how to feed themselves. German POWs, again hundreds of thousands of them, were now incarcerated in camps and had to be fed, guarded, and interrogated as the Allies tried to figure out who among them had been most culpable in the atrocities the Nazis had inflicted on millions.

The 442nd traveled by truck convoy from Novi Ligure to the sprawling, dusty Ghedi Airfield east of Milan, where they were put to work processing more than eighty-five thousand German POWs as they were brought in from all over Italy. Many of the Germans were in bad shape— dirty, malnourished, suffering from various medical ailments. Fred Shiosaki spent long, hot days searching the POWs and confiscating any loot they had stolen from Italians, delousing them by dusting them from head to foot with DDT, and releasing them into a large stockade from which they would later be sent to smaller POW camps for additional interrogation and eventual repatriation.

In Germany, the 522nd artillerymen moved to the town of Donauwörth, northwest of Munich, and were put to work guarding a pontoon bridge over the Danube and searching for SS men hiding among the thousands of displaced people streaming over the Danube trying to find their way back to their home countries. It was tedious work, but there were compensations. Frequent three-day passes allowed them to visit an army rest and recreation camp at Königssee, an exquisitely beautiful lake surrounded by jagged granite peaks in the Tyrolean Alps, formerly a luxury retreat for Nazi officials. From there it was only a mile up a winding road to Berchtesgaden, where they could pose for photographs and poke through what was left of Hitler's private hideout, the Kehlsteinhaus. And closer to their base in Donauwörth was one of Germany's finest breweries, where they filled twenty-five-gallon rubberized canvas bags with beer before hanging them up in strategic locations throughout their quarters so that at any time of day or night they could fill their canteens or tin cups with some of the best, freshest beer in Germany.

As the summer dragged on, men finally began to disappear, rotating out and heading back to the States. Among the first to go were those who volunteered for immediate service in the Pacific. They headed Stateside for additional training before redeployment. At the same time, young men from the 100th, those who had fought all the way up the Italian peninsula beginning in the fall of 1943, began to head home.

Then, finally, the first 442nd men began to pack up. The goodbyes were hard. Harder than any of them had anticipated. As happy as they were to be going home, they all knew that whatever else life held in store for them, nothing would ever equal the intensity of what they had been through together, and that whomever else they might come to love, they would likely never love anyone in quite the same way that they loved one another.

ON THE OTHER SIDE of the war-torn world, on the morning of August 6, 1945, Fumiye Miho waited impatiently for the next train into Hiroshima. She was agitated. It was a warm humid morning, with only a thin sheen of scattered cloud cover graying the light of the rising sun. By noon, she knew, it would be stifling hot. She had already missed her usual 7:20 a.m. train so that she could watch Tsukie's children while Tsukie put in her mandatory early morning hours working in the woods collecting pine oil. Then she had just missed the 8:15 train. Now she was going to be seriously late for work.

In the last few months, life had only gotten harder for Fumiye, for everyone in Japan. Most recently, in March she and Tsukie's family had barely survived yet another devastating American firebombing of Tokyo, so her brother-in-law had packed up all his dental equipment and moved them to a village fifteen miles outside Hiroshima, the village from which Katsuichi and Ayano had immigrated to Hawai'i thirty-four years before.

But things had deteriorated further after they left Tokyo. They lived communally in a Buddhist temple now, along with four other refugee families from the city, their living spaces separated by curtains. The only water available had to be carried uphill in buckets from a dirty stream. Her brother-in-law had already fallen ill with typhoid fever from drinking the water. Tsukie's two infants were perpetually sick and hungry, and there was little food to be had except for potatoes and parsnips. The village authorities did not much care for having city people living among them, and local officials conscripted all the adults in the family into arising at 5:00 every morning to collect pine oil in the woods, for the manufacture of fuel for the kamikazes. The only saving grace was that Fumiye had secured a job in the city center of Hiroshima, translating English news broadcasts for the Japanese government. And that August morning she was late for it.

As she approached the ticket booth to inquire about the next train into Hiroshima, a flash of light unlike any light she had ever seen nearly blinded her. Everything turned white, almost translucent, just for a moment, before the normal yellow light of a summer morning flickered back on. The world went silent. She turned instinctively in the direction from which the white light had come. An old lady scrambled madly across the railway platform, as if crazed by something. A long, low rumbling sound arose in the distance, growing louder and louder until it became a sustained roar and the ground beneath the railroad platform seemed to quiver. Then the gray morning sky over Hiroshima resolved itself into what Fumiye thought in the moment was the most exquisitely beautiful thing she had ever seen, a towering tulip-shaped cloud, vaguely violet in color but at the same time somehow reflecting all the hues of the rainbow as it continued to rise higher and higher in the sky before finally darkening and flattening out into something vaguely like a mushroom. Confused, Fumiye ran back to the Buddhist temple, where she found Tsukie trembling, terrified, and, like Fumiye, utterly confounded as to what had happened.

By that afternoon, word reached the village that all of central Hiroshima had somehow been destroyed after an American warplane appeared over the city. Village authorities commanded everyone to return to the rail station at 5:00 p.m. to help with the wounded being evacuated from the city center. Many of the area's schoolchildren were on vacation and had gone into the city to do community service work that day, so the platform was packed with anxious parents when Fumiye arrived. When the first train pulled in, a long wailing arose from the crowd. Almost none of the parents could recognize the blackened, disfigured children who stumbled off the train or were carried off on litters.

The next day, Fumiye, in search of friends from work, took a train to within two miles of Hiroshima and then walked the rest of the way. Even before she got into the flat, empty wasteland where the city center had been, she could smell the overwhelming stench of burned flesh and see black columns of smoke rising from the ashes. Because it was August and they were afraid decomposing bodies would cause an outbreak of disease, men were already stacking bodies up, intermingling them with timbers pulled from collapsed buildings, and making enormous bonfires of them. On the Motoyasu River, men in motorboats were making their way through rafts of bloated bodies and pulling them out of the water so others could carry them to the pyres.

For the next week, Fumiye walked through the ruins of Hiroshima, wandering among other wanderers almost too disfigured to be recognized as human beings, sleeping at night on the charred lawns of what had been city parks, trying to find something, anything, she could do to help. She used funnels to pour water and orange juice into the mouths of people with no faces. She helped children search through heaps of bodies, looking for their mothers. She tried to ease the dying of an old woman who had turned purple and blue from what she would only later learn was radiation poisoning.

. . .

THREE DAYS LATER, on the morning of August 9, the United States dropped a second atomic bomb on Nagasaki. That same morning, in the predawn darkness, the SS *Waterbury Victory*—with the words "Go for Broke" painted on its starboard side—pulled up to Pier 40 in Honolulu Harbor, carrying the first 241 men and officers of the 442nd RCT to return to Hawai'i. As the sun rose over O'ahu, Hawaiian music began to play over the ship's PA system. Young women from the USO came aboard and handed out doughnuts and pineapple juice. But it was the women who followed them up the gangplank that caused the men to cheer—a bevy of young women in grass skirts and bathing suit tops, with plumeria and hibiscus flowers in their hair, carrying leis draped over their arms. They hung the leis around the necks of grinning young men wearing crisp khaki uniforms with arrays of medals and decorations on their chests. Then they danced hula, swaying on the foredeck as the men pulled out guitars and ukuleles and climbed up onto hatches, dancing along with them, singing the familiar songs of home.

After some speechifying by local officials, Alfred Pursall led them down the gangway to a motorcade that whisked them away to the

A hula dancer welcomes a veteran home aboard the SS *Waterbury Victory*

stately grounds of ʻIolani Palace, where thousands waited—parents, siblings, buddies, girlfriends, who showered them with more leis, and kisses, and embraces. There, finally, they sat under the banyan trees on the green grass and ate *kālua* pork and *laulau* as the *manu-o-Kū* birds again circled above them in graceful white loops against a blue Hawaiian sky.

ON AUGUST 14—THE fifteenth in Asia—news swept around the world that Japan had surrendered. Now, finally, Americans were able to celebrate as they had never celebrated in the history of the nation. In New York, the largest crowd the city had ever seen poured into Times Square. Men climbed lampposts waving American flags. Young women kissed marines and soldiers and sailors whom they did not even know. In San Francisco, a pair of young women tore off their clothes and leaped into a fountain utterly nude, to the enormous delight of sailors standing nearby. In Seattle, it was a bright blue day. Sirens wailed and car horns honked as people streamed out of offices and storefronts into the streets. A parade of civilians and young men in uniforms wended their way through the crowds on Third Avenue singing "Hail, Hail, the Gang's All Here." A B-29 Superfortress roared overhead. In New Orleans and Boston and Chicago and Los Angeles, in every city, midsized town, and tiny hamlet in America, it was the same—a massive, unstoppable outpouring of unrestrained relief and joy.

In Hawaiʻi that evening, Hisako Higuchi ran to the window of her apartment in Pearl City. Looking out over Pearl Harbor, she watched in astonished delight as the battleships in the harbor began to rake the sky with enormous searchlights. Sirens shrilled, and deep, sonorous boat horns sounded. The sky blossomed with fireworks and flares. Sailors poured out into the streets below her window yelling, cheering, shouting, "We're going home! California, here I come! Set the table, Mom!" Church bells rang. Neighbors pounded on her door to share their joy— the Satos, the Tatekawas, the Yoshidas. The Higuchis' son, Peter, peered up at his mother and burbled joyfully, "Now, Mama, we can have metal and rubber toys again!"

As things calmed down, late that night, she sat down to write to Hiro: "All I could think of when the news came was of you, wondering where you were and hoping that you felt the same thankfulness that was in my heart and to hold you again and have you close." But as she wrote, she noticed that Hiro's mother was sitting silently in a corner with tears in her eyes, thinking perhaps of her friends and family in Hiroshima and Nagasaki.

FRED SHIOSAKI GOT THE NOD to head for home in late October. In Livorno that fall so many GIs were trying to get across the Atlantic that the army put them on pretty much anything that would float. After waiting for weeks, Fred wound up on a particularly small, old, and slow Liberty ship. Quarters were so tight that he bunked with the ship's crew and ate their grub, which consisted largely of rancid meat and stale biscuits infested with black weevils. By now it was December and the ship crawled through monstrous North Atlantic seas for more than twenty days. And yet Fred had finally found his sea legs and never felt a twinge of seasickness. He arrived back in Newport News on Christmas Eve. From there he traveled by train to Washington, D.C. In Union Station, a soldier wearing the patch of the Texas Division approached him, pointed to Fred's 442nd patch, and said, "Hey, you're with the 442nd."

"Yeah."

"Were you at the Lost Battalion?"

"Yeah, I was there. I was in there."

The soldier offered his hand and said he had been one of the Texans on the mountain. Fred stared at the hand. He stammered, "Do you know how many men we lost getting you guys out of there? Do you know how many of my friends died in there?"

"Well, anyway, I want to thank you."

Fred turned away and looked out a window. He wasn't about to shake the man's hand. Later he would say he was not proud of the moment and regret how he had behaved, but standing there in Union Station at the time, he just wasn't ready.

On January 4, he boarded a military transport bound for Fort Lewis, south of Seattle. En route, the plane landed in Spokane, about four miles from the laundry in Hillyard. Fred sprinted off the plane and made a quick phone call home. On the other end of the line, he could hear his mother and his sister, Blanche, screaming in delight. "I'll get in the car and come right down!" Blanche yelled. But Fred had to climb back on the plane and continue over the Cascades to Fort Lewis to be discharged.

Two days later, though, he was back in Spokane. When he opened the door and walked into the warm, familiar, steamy smells of the laundry, his whole family was there. His older brother, Roy, had just returned from serving in Europe himself. His mother and sister, gleeful and laughing, embraced him. His father shook his hand, looked him in the eye, and said simply, "You did well." Then he went to the front of the laundry and took down the two blue stars hanging in the window.

WHEN RUDY LEFT ITALY for home, he was still hobbling from his injuries. And like so many returning soldiers, he soon found that not all his wounds were physical. As he passed through Chicago on his way west, a car backfired, and he and another GI nearby hit the ground at the same moment. He got up and dusted himself off, but he realized then, for the first time, that it might take him a while to get over the war, both physically and mentally.

When he arrived at Fort Douglas in Utah, he learned that the Poston camp had been closed up. Everyone had left, and no one could tell him anything about the people who had been incarcerated there. It was as if they had all just disappeared. He began making phone calls to friends in Salinas, but nobody knew where his parents had gone. Alarmed, concerned, and frustrated, Rudy decided to head for the place his father had always talked about eventually settling, San Jose.

At the bus station in San Jose, he spotted a young woman at a Red Cross stand set up to aid returning GIs. As he approached the booth, her back was to him, but he started up a conversation.

"Ma'am, I'd like some help."

"What can I do for you?"

"Well, I've just come back from overseas and my parents were in one of those concentration camps. And the camps are closed. So I'm trying to find them. I'm just wondering if there's any way, a place or a way . . . I can ask questions about it?"

The woman finally turned around and looked at him for the first time. She studied him for a moment.

"There's a place on Fifth Street. A bunch of Japs are livin' there."

A sailor, standing behind Rudy, waiting in line, pushed his way forward.

"Are you calling this man a 'Jap'? Do you see his ribbons and stuff? He fought overseas! Who do you think you are?"

And with that the sailor leaned over the counter and slapped the woman across the face. Rudy grabbed his arm and said, "Oh no! We don't want to cause trouble. All I'm doing is, I want to find where my parents are."

The sailor put Rudy in a cab that took him to the Buddhist church on Fifth Street. And there, sure enough, when he limped into a small bedroom upstairs, Rudy found his parents. His father remained seated, looking him over, and then said simply, "I'm very glad to see you home. Are any of your wounds bad?" Rudy assured him he would be okay. But his mother leaped up and draped her arms around him, not crying as Rudy had expected, but instead murmuring, "*Kamisama* has awarded this to me, for what I have done."*

Rudy had no idea what she meant, but she explained her painful early morning cold-water rituals in Poston: "If you are the mother of a

---

Kamisama refers to a deity or multiple deities in Japanese.

soldier, you do everything you can. Whether it looks foolish or looks like a *bakatare* doing it, you do it to try to bring him home."*

Rudy made no mention of it that day, but as he sat down and chatted with his family, pinned to his chest, along with a Purple Heart and a Combat Infantry Badge, there was a Bronze Star. Before he left Italy, the army had awarded him the medal in a large ceremony at Empoli, with fifteen thousand GIs and a number of colonels and generals on hand to watch. It embarrassed Rudy a bit to stand on a platform as soldiers marched past, saluting him. But as he stood there, watching them, something surged in him that had not been there when he'd left Poston three years before. He had been angry then—angry at the country that had incarcerated his family, that had humiliated his parents, that had cost them their farm and their livelihoods, that had treated him as a second-class citizen. In many ways, he was still angry and would remain so for a long time. But standing there with the medal on his chest and a brass band playing behind him, with the 442nd colors and American flags fluttering in the breeze, he had a moment of peace and pride that surprised him and that he would long remember. "You know," he thought, "it's coming out to be, it doesn't make no difference what you look like, it's what you're doing and what you've done for the country that counts."

IT WAS DECEMBER 1945 before Kats and most of B Battery's artillerymen were able to start for home. They sailed from Marseille aboard a Swedish liner, the MS *John Ericsson,* with six thousand other homeward-bound troops, then flew from the East Coast to California on a DC-3. In Southern California, they were marched one evening into a darkened auditorium. When the lights came up, they were astonished to find themselves on a CBS soundstage with Frank Sinatra introducing them to his radio audience, along with a singer whose career had taken a meteoric rise while they were overseas, Peggy Lee. By the time they left the

---

*Bakatare means "idiot" or "moron" in Japanese.

auditorium, Kats had both Sinatra's and Lee's autographs scrawled on the back of a ration ticket.

Then, finally—two years and nine months since they'd left Honolulu— they sailed for Hawai'i. As the boat approached O'ahu and rounded Diamond Head at 3:00 a.m. on January 15, 1946, Kats and nearly all of the 232 servicemen aboard crowded the rails. None of them could sleep. A nearly full moon hung low over the sea to the west, and all of them wanted to catch that first glimpse of the Aloha Tower and the city skyline and the white sands of Waikīkī in the moonlight. At 8:00 a.m., Kats walked down a gangway toting his duffel bag on his shoulder. There were no hula dancers to greet the men this time. Sailors and soldiers had been returning to Hawai'i for so many months now that only a few newspaper photographers bothered to show up to cover the arrival of yet another boatload. Roy Fujii, Kats's cannoneer, took the Honolulu bus token off the chain on which he had worn it around his neck throughout the war, gave Kats a wave, climbed on a bus, and headed for his parents' home up in the hills.

Kats looked around for his own parents. And there they were, waiting and waving. Both of them. Kats knew that the war years had been hard on his family. His father had just been released from the camp in Santa Fe. His mother had had no choice but to sell the Miho Hotel. Now the two of them were scraping out a living picking macadamia nuts for a commercial farm on O'ahu, just as Katsuichi had done decades before when they first arrived in Hawaii. Katsuaki was dead, and nobody knew how Kats's sisters in Hiroshima were faring. It was going to take a lot to put their lives back together. But for now, Kats savored the moment. Just being there in his parents' presence, luxuriating in the warm tropical breeze, smelling the sea, seeing the morning mist clinging to the green-humped mountains above the city, was enough. It was a moment of pure, overwhelming joy.

Three days later, Kats walked onto the campus of the University of Hawai'i, across University Avenue from Atherton House, entered a classroom, and tried to pick up where he had left off on that morning in December 1941 when the whole world had suddenly fallen away beneath his feet.

EPILOGUE

Naturally gratitude and thanksgiving filled our hearts. But we also felt reverence and a special aloha for the buddies we would be leaving behind, their resting place on foreign soil marked with white crosses.

CONRAD TSUKAYAMA

Whenever I write a book, I try to visit as many as possible of the locations where the story I am telling unfolded. That's how it was that on a warm, translucent spring morning in 2019 my wife and I climbed into the back of a vintage 1942 U.S. Army jeep and joined a convoy of similar jeeps starting up a rutted dirt road in northern Italy. Driving the jeep was a young Italian man wearing an enthusiastic smile, an olive-green helmet, and a World War II U.S. Army uniform bearing the red-white-and-blue shoulder patch of the 442nd Regimental Combat Team. He, along with a dozen of his fellow Italian World War II reenactors, specializes in re-creating the exploits of the 442nd. Their mission that day was to escort a group of the sons, daughters, and grandchildren of Nisei veterans to the top of Monte Folgorito, where the 442nd broke the fearsome Gothic Line and began to drive the Germans toward the Po valley and the inevitable end of the war in Italy. My wife and I were privileged to join them.

As we made our way up the mountain, the rutted road quickly became little more than a goat trail strewn with boulders. The jeep bounced from one precarious foothold to another. On her side of the jeep, my wife closed her eyes and clutched my hand each time the jeep went slightly airborne. On my side, I peered nervously at the edge of the trail where, inches from the tires, the mountainside fell away abruptly to a boulder field hundreds of feet below. Eventually, we arrived at a lovely little green meadow just a few hundred feet below the top of Folgorito. From there, we climbed up the last bit of the mountain on foot, hauling ourselves over rock ledges, clutching at shrubs and roots. On the way, we stopped to examine a small cave that the Germans had hacked in the stony side of the mountain seventy-five years before, a space just big enough for three or four men with machine guns to crouch and wait in ambush for anyone trying to cross the meadow below.

When we finally clambered onto the summit, I stood for a moment just catching my breath. Then I looked around, and I was stunned. Below me to the west, the mountain's green foothills tumbled down toward the brilliant turquoise expanse of the Ligurian Sea. To the southwest, I could see all the way to Livorno; to the north, all the way to the buff-colored cliffs of the Cinque Terre. To the northeast, the great spires of Monte Altissimo loomed above us like stony fangs, their edges seemingly razor sharp, as if they had just been freshly chiseled out of gray stone yesterday. What really arrested my attention, though, was what lay between me and those peaks—a deep chasm, its abrupt sides cloaked in dark vegetation, dropping thousands of feet from where I stood, at an angle of perhaps sixty degrees. At the bottom were the red-tile roofs of houses in what looked like a toy village.

The village was Azzano, and it was out of that abyss that the Nisei soldiers of the 442nd RCT had climbed in the middle of the night seventy-five years before, lugging their weapons, prepared to fight and if need be to die. Standing there, I struggled to comprehend the sheer audacity of it, pondering what exactly enabled those young men to do something like that. But in almost the same instant I knew the answer.

It was something simple and powerful and irreducible. It was who they were at their cores. Those young men were the living embodiments of the spirit that has always animated America, the spirit that has held us together for more than two centuries—the striving, the yearning, the courage, the relentless optimism, the willingness to chip in and lend a hand, the fair-mindedness, the inclusiveness. They knew that they had been called upon to defend a set of simple but profound ideals—the highest ideals of America and the Western democracies—and having heard the call, they answered it, as did millions of young men in the first half of the 1940s. Most of them fought for those ideals on the battlefield; some, like Gordon Hirabayashi, fought for them in courtrooms.

But do not forget this. As American as they were, in some ways and to varying degrees, they were also proudly Japanese. As they stood up and ran into the fire, many of them carried with them values that their immigrant parents had taught them—not just the samurai's code of Bushido, but a host of related beliefs and attitudes—*giri* and *ninjo* and *gaman* among them. Indeed, it was largely because they held those other, "foreign" values that many of them were able to do what had to be done. On Monte Folgorito, in the Vosges forest, among the hills of Tuscany, at Monte Cassino, time and again they selflessly offered up their best selves. And the selves they offered up—the lives they put on the line—grew from both American and Japanese roots. Whether they lived or died in the endeavor, they reminded us yet again that we Americans are all composed of varied stuff, a multitude of backgrounds and identities forged together in the furnace of our national tribulations and triumphs.

In the end, they helped win for us a far better world than the one in which they found themselves when Japanese bombers first appeared over Pearl Harbor on the morning of December 7, 1941. Now, more than a generation later, it is up to us to cherish and protect what they won, to devote ourselves yet again to the principles they defended, to surmount our own mountains of trouble, to keep moving upward together on the long slope of our shared destiny.

· · ·

By most reckonings, the 442nd RCT was the most decorated military unit of its size and length of service in American history. The true scope of their contribution to the war effort, though, remained hidden from the world for more than half a century. The only member of the regiment to be awarded the Medal of Honor in the immediate aftermath of the war was Sadao Munemori, who had thrown his body on a hand grenade near Pietrasanta in the assault on the Gothic Line. The medal was presented to his mother on March 13, 1946. It took more than half a century and a sustained lobbying campaign in Congress before President Clinton, on June 21, 2000, finally conferred Medals of Honor on another twenty members of the regiment—some of them posthumously—saying, "Rarely has a nation been so well served by a people it has so ill served." Among those receiving the Medal of Honor that day were Daniel Inouye; the medic James Okubo; two men from K Company—Ted Tanouye and Joe Hayashi—and William Nakamura, for whom, the following year, the federal courthouse in which Gordon Hirabayashi had been convicted would be renamed the William Kenzo Nakamura Courthouse.

When they did finally come, the medals dramatically underscored the Nisei soldiers' disproportionate valor during the war. Of the roughly 16 million Americans who served in World War II, only 473 have received Medals of Honor. But 21 of those medal recipients came from the ranks of the 18,000 men who ultimately served in the 442nd. So in the end, the 442nd, representing just over 0.11 percent of the U.S. military force, earned 4.4 percent of the Medals of Honor.

In addition, the regiment earned 29 Distinguished Service Crosses, 560 Silver Stars, 28 Silver Stars with oak leaf clusters (in place of a second Silver Star), 22 Legion of Merit Medals, 4,000 Bronze Stars, 1,200 Bronze Stars with oak leaf clusters, 36 Army Commendation Medals, 87 Division Commendations, and more than 4,000 Purple Hearts. On October 21, 1963, Governor John Connally made the entire 442nd RCT honorary Texans.

None of that, though, had much effect on the stark realities that most of the Nisei vets experienced when they got home, particularly those who returned to the U.S. mainland. There it would take decades to fully win their own and their families' rightful place in American life. Millions of employers still refused to hire them. What jobs were available to them were mostly low paying and menial. Slurs and slights still met them everywhere they went. At the end of the day they were still "Japs" to the vast majority of their countrymen.

And all the medals and honors earned by their sons and brothers did little to alleviate the trauma that thousands of families had experienced in the camps or ease the shock of what they found when they, too, tried to return home. Up and down the West Coast, thieves had looted possessions left in storage. Vandals had shattered the glass in nursery greenhouses, destroyed stocks of merchandise, and spray-painted threats on their property—"Japs Keep Out!" Squatters had occupied homes and refused to leave. Opportunists, paying only fire-sale prices, had taken over prosperous businesses and secured leases on thousands of acres of fertile farmland that had first been cleared and worked by Issei immigrants. Neighborhoods from which they had been excluded by covenants and ordinances before the war were still legally closed to them, and in their absence their old neighborhoods had been occupied by other ethnic minorities, leaving little housing available to them. With many landlords, even in these neighborhoods, now refusing to rent houses or apartments to them, families had to live in the attics of friends, or in Christian and Buddhist churches, or in schools. In Seattle, roughly thirty families with no other options crammed into a Japanese-language school in the International District, renaming the property the Hunt Hotel, sleeping on cots, and in many ways living no better than they had in the camps.* As months went by, a rash of suicides began to take a toll among the displaced, particularly among the Issei.

---

*Named thus because most of the residents there had come to it from the Minidoka concentration camp, which had a Hunt, Idaho, postal address.

It would take decades for the country's leadership to broadly recognize and formally address the wrong that had been done to them.
But there was at least the beginnings of a shift in attitude among some
at the highest levels of government, particularly among those aware of
what the Nisei soldiers had accomplished. The new administration of
President Harry Truman pushed for a restoration of property and civil
rights for Japanese Americans. Shocked by reports of vigilantes attacking returning families, Truman wrote to Eleanor Roosevelt, "These disgraceful actions almost make you believe that a lot of our Americans
have a streak of Nazi in them." In Congress, in 1948, Truman pushed
through the Japanese American Evacuation Claims Act, though cumbersome regulations and red tape would render the act largely ineffec-
tive in terms of compensating people for their losses. Truman also strove
to gain greater public recognition for what the 442nd had done. On a
gray blustery day on the Ellipse—the fifty-two-acre oval park south of
the White House—in July 1946, walking with Pursall in review of the
442nd, Truman told the Nisei soldiers, "You fought not only the enemy,
but you fought prejudice—and you've won. Keep up that fight, and we'll
win." They were noble words, doubtless well intended and sincere, but
on the city streets, in the small towns, and on the farmlands of America, many hearts were still hard, racism still flourished, and a tough
road still lay ahead for most Japanese Americans, civilians and veterans
alike.

At the same time that he strove to restore the civil rights of those who
had been incarcerated in the camps and to valorize the Nisei soldiers,
Truman also reassessed the government's stance toward those Nisei
who had been imprisoned for resisting the draft. Finally recognizing
the fundamental unfairness of the circumstances surrounding their
convictions and acting on the recommendation of an amnesty board,
Truman pardoned all of the Nisei draft resisters in December 1947. For-
giveness, respect, and understanding from within the larger Japanese
American community, however, came more slowly, as many families

whose sons had served in the 442nd as well as organizations like the JACL, which had loudly condemned the resisters during the war, only gradually began to recognize their role as defenders of the Nisei's civil rights. In May 2002, in a ceremony in San Francisco, the JACL formally apologized to those who had resisted conscription.

FRED SHIOSAKI MOVED BACK into the apartment over the Hillyard Laundry with his parents and resumed taking classes at Gonzaga University. Right from the start, he struggled to find his footing. Many nights he awoke to find his mother hovering over him, saying, "You were screaming again." Sitting in classrooms at Gonzaga, he could not focus. His mind kept drifting back to moments from the war, moments he could not quite move past. One of his professors, a Jesuit priest, made a comment one day about "a bunch of Japs," and Fred sank deep into his seat, trying again to be invisible, as he had when the campus was full of naval cadets before the war. A friend, Bill Nishimura, introduced him to a vivacious young woman named Lily Nakai who had just recently graduated at the top of her high school class. But when Fred took her on a date to a skating rink, someone made a comment about "dirty rotten Japs." Friends had to pull Fred off the kid hurling the epithet.

Within a year, though, the nightmares started to die away, and his grades at school started to improve. He and Lily began to date steadily. Fred graduated with a degree in chemistry in 1949, but when he struggled to find a job, he broke up with Lily, concerned that he wouldn't be able to support a family, and went back to work at the laundry. Finally, he landed a job with a pharmaceutical company in Spokane and got back together with Lily. The two of them were married, and Fred moved on to a position with Kaiser Aluminum and eventually became the city chemist for Spokane.

In 1952, when passage of the McCarran-Walter Act meant Japanese immigrants were finally allowed to apply for citizenship, Fred and his siblings coached their parents, quizzing Kisaburo and Tori on civics and American history for their exams. When they both became American citizens, it was a moment of profound pride for Fred. He knew well that what the 442nd had done had paved the way for the moment. Watching his parents raise their hands at their swearing-in ceremony in May 1953, he thought to himself, "By God, you had a piece of this."

Kisaburo died of cancer in 1958. Tori survived him by nearly twenty years, passing away in 1977. In the interval, Fred and Lily had two children—Nancy and Michael—and Fred's career as a public servant accelerated. In 1967, he became executive director of the Spokane County Air Pollution Control Authority, then chairman of the Washington State Ecological Commission. In 1999, Governor Gary Locke appointed him to the Washington Fish and Wildlife Commission, a role that Fred—who had loved fly-fishing and fly tying since the days when his father had taken the family on expeditions to the lakes outside Spokane—particularly relished. When his son, Michael, moved to Seattle, Fred took over Michael's large backyard garden and became an avid gardener, growing everything from dahlias to enormous pumpkins that he gave away to neighborhood kids for Halloween jack-o'-lanterns every October. In the 1980s, Fred and Lily began traveling every winter to Hawai'i, where he reconnected with many of his K Company buddies, and it was only then—after decades of forbidding the topic within his family—that he began to talk about what he had done and what he had seen during the war.

When their father died, Fred's brother, Roy, took over the running of the Hillyard Laundry. The family continued to operate it until finally selling it to another laundry company in the 1990s. In 2011, Fred and many of his surviving comrades traveled to Washington, D.C., where the Nisei soldiers of World War II were presented with Congressional Gold Medals. Lily passed away on the Fourth of July 2016. Fred now lives in a retirement home in Seattle, where he remains spirited, tenacious, warmhearted, and, as he once described himself, "a 6-foot, 8-inch lumberjack housed in a 5-foot, 6-inch body."

. . .

RUDY, LIKE NEARLY EVERYONE who fought in that war, came home changed. His sister Fumi was shocked, at first, by how coarse his language had become, especially when he got together with his fellow vets. His temper, always short, was now a tiny fuse on a large stick of dynamite. Like so many of the other vets, he had nightmares. In his case it was almost always the same one. Night after night, he found himself back on Hill 140, running from something unknown but indescribably horrific.

For the next several years, he tried his hand at various occupations. He worked for a time as a farmhand in Sunnyvale, California. Then he learned to be a diesel engineer and traveled to South America on a banana boat as the engineer. He tried to get a job with Caterpillar in San Jose but was told he had to join a union. The union, like many on the West Coast, had a long history of discrimination against Japanese Americans and wouldn't accept him. Eventually he began working for Mount Eden, a large commercial nursery owned and run by a Japanese American family that had been incarcerated at Tule Lake. He married, fathered four children—Roy, Robin, Russell, and Rochelle—eventually divorced, had a brief second marriage, and then in the 1980s settled in with his partner for the remainder of his life, Judy Niizawa, a speech pathologist and community activist who had been born at the Amache concentration camp in Colorado.

As he moved on in life, though, Rudy was hindered by one overwhelming fact. As the years passed, shrapnel lodged in his body periodically shifted position and caused him long sieges of excruciating, debilitating pain and sometimes even paralysis. It got so bad at one point that he wound up in an iron lung, then in a full body cast, and finally dependent on crutches. Nine pieces of the shrapnel were eventually surgically removed from his body, but the pain remained a constant for the rest of his life.

Rudy was nothing if not tough, though. He persisted. He became active in Little League, the PTA, and the Boy Scouts of America, eventually becoming western regional director of the Boy Scouts. He advocated for Japanese American causes, serving as the founding president of the National Japanese American Historical Society of San Francisco and fighting for a national monument in Washington, D.C., to commemorate the sacrifices of the Nisei. His greatest postwar legacy, though, was what he did for the national redress movement in the 1980s.

Since shortly after the end of the war, there had been multiple efforts to persuade the U.S. government to formally apologize for the incarcerations and pay direct compensation to the families who had been affected. By 1980 that effort had finally gained traction with the creation of the federal Commission on Wartime Relocation and Internment of Civilians. In 1983, the commission recommended that Congress and the president issue a formal apology, establish a foundation to educate the American people on this hidden part of their history, and pay each surviving detainee twenty thousand dollars in partial compensation. But it still had to be passed into law, and that would entail a titanic lobbying effort.

In 1987, 120 activists began visiting congressional offices to make the case. Among them were a large number of 442nd veterans. At the urging of his partner, Judy, Rudy joined the effort and soon found himself prowling the halls of Congress on his crutches, reunited with many of his old comrades. They decided to approach this mission, as they had approached so many missions during the war, with a "go for broke" spirit. "We're going to take the hill one way or another," Rudy told his hometown newspaper. They strategized with Japanese American members of Congress like Norman Mineta and Robert Matsui, solicited the help of Senators Spark Matsunaga and Daniel Inouye, and relentlessly tracked down wavering members, boldly pushing their way past heavy wooden doors into carpeted outer offices, politely but firmly demanding that they be heard.

As the critical vote approached in 1987, Rudy and a contingent of

Nisei vets entered the office of Congressman Charles Edward Bennett of Florida. Bennett had fought with distinction against the Japanese in the steaming and bloody jungles of New Guinea. While overseas he had also contracted polio, and he was now dependent on leg braces and crutches in order to get around. When he walked into his office that day, he glanced at Rudy and his buddies and growled, "What the hell are you sons of bitches doing in my office?"

The Nisei vets began to explain their mission, but Bennett cut them off: "My goddamned government doesn't have to apologize to any son of a bitch. You understand what I'm saying?"

The others began to leave, but Rudy lingered. Bennett gestured for him to go. Instead, Rudy approached him on his crutches. Rudy had done some research. He knew that under his slacks Bennett was wearing leg braces.

"Sir, I just want to thank you," Rudy said, sticking out his hand.

"Thank me for what? I'm not going to do a goddamned thing for you guys."

"No, sir. . . . I wanted to thank you because you became a congressman right after the war ended. . . . And I happen to know . . . when you wake up in the damn mornings, you hurt like a son of a bitch. Sir, even with that, you take all this pain and everything, to help run our government. I'd like to certainly thank you, you're a damn good man. . . . I'd like to say thank you and I'll shake your hand."

Rudy shook his hand and left.

When the measure came up for a vote, Rudy was in the House, standing with his crutches in a section reserved for handicapped spectators. As Bennett entered the chamber, Rudy caught his eye. Bennett was a southern Democrat, generally conservative, and now quite senior and influential in the House. Seeing Rudy, he hesitated for a moment. He was scheduled to give a three-minute speech opposing the redress bill. Instead, he walked to the well of the House, lingered there for a moment, then walked out a side door. But as the vote tally began to show up on a tally display, Rudy saw that Bennett had voted for the bill. Moments later, more yes votes began to show up on the display. The measure had passed.

Rudy sought Bennett out in his office after the vote and thanked him: "Sir, I just want to thank you personally from my heart. I don't know what changed your thoughts, but damn I'm sure glad that you did."

"Ha, you son of a bitch, what the hell was I gonna do? I looked up there and I saw you in those goddamned crutches."

On August 10, 1988, after initially opposing the legislation, President Reagan signed the Civil Liberties Act of 1988, the language of which declares that the incarcerations of Japanese Americans were "carried out without adequate security reasons and without any acts of espionage or sabotage, and were motivated largely by racial prejudice, wartime hysteria, and a failure of political leadership." It still took three to five years for most of the 82,219 people then eligible to receive redress checks of twenty thousand dollars each.

For the rest of his life, Rudy continued to speak about his experiences in the war and to advocate for wider appreciation of what the 442nd had done. Not long before he died, he was asked in an interview what legacy he felt that he and the 442nd had left for subsequent generations, and he answered simply, "I think my job has been done. I feel that, now, I don't have to do anything more. I think we—not I but we—have proven ourselves." Rudy passed away on December 4, 2004.

LIKE FRED, Kats Miho had a hard time readjusting to student life when he walked back into a university classroom. He just couldn't seem to focus on his work. He lived with his brother Katsuro but spent most of his free time hanging out with his fellow 522nd vets, talking story and playing billiards in the back of the Owl Café in downtown Honolulu or holding beer busts with them on Sandy Beach, out east of Koko Head. By the end of his first semester, he was failing four of his five classes. It just seemed more important to spend time with his boys than with books.

By his second semester, though, his old imperative to get involved, to organize people, to speak out on issues, to make things happen, gradually reemerged. He buckled down to his studies. He became involved in organizing a veterans' club for the 442nd. He moved into a veterans' dorm and became its manager. He helped organize a university-wide carnival. And by his senior year he was again class president.

By the time he graduated, he was also becoming part of something much larger, something that would in time help to shape the future of Hawai'i. Having grown up in the exploitative plantation system, and having fought and bled for their country, many of the best and brightest among the 442nd veterans returned to the islands determined to fundamentally change the power structure of the territory. They started by going to law school. Daniel Inouye, Spark Matsunaga, John Ushijima, and Kats were just a few of the Hawaiian Nisei vets who took advantage of the GI Bill and headed for law schools on the East Coast. Kats and Inouye wound up at George Washington University, where they shared dinner at least once a week. At the same time, as many as twenty-five other Hawaiian Nisei vets were studying law at either George Washington or nearby Georgetown. As they returned to Hawai'i, the newly minted Nisei lawyers began to occupy positions of power in business, government, and the legal profession, and in doing so they began to lay the groundwork for a very different Hawai'i from the one they grew up in.

After passing the bar exam, Kats went to work for his brother Katsuro's law firm—Fong, Miho, Choy, and Robinson. Kats soon earned a reputation as a tough but fair-minded litigator, and people throughout the islands began to take note. In 1956, he met Laura Iida, the daughter of a prominent O'ahu businessman and banker. Kats first laid eyes on her at the gala opening of the Central Pacific Bank, of which Laura's father was the chairman. For the occasion, Mr. Iida had placed all his daughters in a row by his side, dressed in exquisite kimonos for maximum visual effect. But it was when Laura worked in the VA office in Honolulu that Kats got to know her better and set out to marry her. Mr. Iida had been incarcerated with Kats's father on the mainland, so the two men knew and admired each other, and that helped pave the way for a marriage. The ceremony was lavish, with Maine lobster flown in from the East Coast and more than a thousand people in attendance. With the rising success of the Miho brothers, it was widely seen as the merger of two of Oʻahu's most prominent families.

By the mid-1950s, led largely by the contingent of Nisei vets who had ascended to political power in the territory, many in Hawaiʻi were pushing hard for statehood. As part of that effort, Katsuro, now a member of the Hawaiʻi Statehood Commission, traveled to Washington, D.C., where he gave forceful, eloquent testimony before Congress on April 7, 1957. In June, a territorial referendum on statehood passed, with 132,938 eligible voters in favor and 7,854 opposed. The margin in the balloting was overwhelming, though on the ground enthusiasm for statehood was far from universal. Many native Hawiians, in particular, harbored well-founded resentments over the loss of sovereignty that they had experienced when their kingdom was overthrown by a U.S.-backed coup in 1893 and subsequently annexed by the United States in 1898. By the time of the referendum in 1957, though, the islands' indigenous people had been largely marginalized. Their numbers had been swamped by North American and Asian, especially Japanese, immigrants, and they lived, for the most part, in small, isloated communities in far-flung parts of the territory, well removed from the seat of power in Honolulu. They held little electoral power in their own ancestral land.*

Hawaiʻi was admitted to the Union on August 21, 1959, and Kats was elected to the first of five eventual terms in the new Hawaiʻi State House of Representatives. On the morning of August 31, 1959, wearing

---

*The memory of and desire for a sovereign Hawaiian nation has never really died, though. Beginning with a cultural reawakenng in the 1970s, there have been, in recent years, renewed calls for a return of Hawaiian sovereignty.

an enormous red lei, he ascended a platform in front of 'Iolani Palace, where the House of Representatives was to hold its first session. On a lower platform in front of him, Hawaiian and Tahitian dancers swayed to the sound of drums. The Honolulu Police Choral Group sang traditional Hawaiian songs. On the lawns beyond the stages, families sat on blankets under the banyan trees as flower women wandered among them handing out leis and weaving ti leaves and hibiscus flowers onto a long pole to form a *kāhili*, an ancient Hawaiian ceremonial emblem. Kats, remembering the day he had stood on that lawn in a khaki uniform more than a decade before, waiting to be shipped overseas, took it all in. His fellow legislators surrounding him on the stage were nearly as diverse as the islands they had come from. Though Hawai'i was far from a sovereign nation, its government, finally, was starting to look more like its people.

Before he finished with his legislative career, Kats had risen to become the House minority leader. When he finally left office in 1970, Governor John Burns appointed him to a judgeship in Hawai'i's District Family Court, a position in which he served for a decade before stepping down. He later served on the Hawai'i Public Housing Authority. As Kats continued the life of public service that he had first set his sights on as a student at Maui High, he and Laura raised a large brood of their own Mihos—Carolyn Mariko, Arthur Kengo, Celia Yukiko, and Ann Takako. Meanwhile, Kats worked tirelessly to co-found and develop the 442nd Veterans Club in Honolulu and devoted much of his free time to promoting sumo wrestling in Hawai'i. Kats's father died in July 1968. Ayano took her husband's ashes home to Hiroshima to be interred in the family grave site, but while there she died of what the doctors termed congestive heart failure and her children termed a broken heart. Their ashes were interred together.

Shortly before Kats passed away, on September 11, 2011, his old friend Daniel Inouye paid him a final visit in the hospital. Kats was buried at the National Memorial Cemetery of the Pacific, the "Punchbowl," not far from where his brother Katsuaki, Hiro Higuchi, Masao Yamada, and so many of his friends and comrades from the 442nd RCT now lie. Among them also lie the remains of dozens of servicemen who died in the attack on Pearl Harbor. On September 29, 2011, Governor Neil Abercrombie ordered that American and Hawaiian state flags be flown at half-staff throughout the islands in memory of Kats. Laura Miho still lives in the family home in the Mānoa valley in the hills above Honolulu and regularly attends lunches and reunions with the few surviving members of B Battery and their families.

FUMIYE MIHO RETURNED to Hawaiʻi in 1947. Transformed by her experiences in Hiroshima, she abandoned her Buddhist faith and joined the Religious Society of Friends, becoming a Quaker. Following in the footsteps of her brother Katsuso (Paul), she enrolled in Yale Divinity School. With a divinity degree in hand, she lived the rest of her life crusading for peace and justice, working at various times in slums on the East Coast of the United States, in orphanages, as a pastor on Maui, and, back in Japan, as the director of a center for refugees in Tokyo. She again returned to Hawaiʻi in 1991 but continued to travel the world lecturing on pacifism and racial justice. In 1992, in Paul's memory, she established the Katsuso Miho Fund for Scholarship in Peace-Making at Yale Divinity School. She passed away on October 31, 2010.

After the war, shaken and disillusioned by the horrors he had witnessed during his time with the 442nd, Hiro Higuchi seriously considered abandoning the ministry. But by 1950 colleagues had persuaded him to reconsider, and he undertook further studies in theology at Oberlin before returning to Kauaʻi, where he presided joyfully and with a renewed sense of faith over a small congregation in Waimea. From there, he went on to spearhead the development of another five churches around the new state of Hawaiʻi as well as to serve as chaplain in the U.S. Army Reserve, devoted to the end to the young men he had ministered to during the war. He died on November 10, 1981.

When Masao Yamada returned to Hawai'i, he requested six months' leave from the ministry so that he could tend to the needs of the returning Nisei soldiers as they struggled to adjust to civilian life. He then moved to the Big Island, where he presided over a congregation at the Church of the Holy Cross in Hilo, later moving on to the Hawai'i State Hospital on O'ahu, where he served as chaplain to the hospital's mentally ill patients. He and his wife, Ai, became passionate orchid hobbyists, developing many new hybrids and teaching patients at the hospital how to raise and hybridize orchids as a form of therapy. He died on May 7, 1984.

George Oiye, like Fred, Kats, Rudy, and many of the 442nd vets, struggled to adjust to civilian life. When he got home to Montana, he found that his parents were barely eking out a living, selling vegetables from their garden. Jobs were still hard to find for anyone with a Japanese name. When he tried to deliver vegetables around the state, most buyers wouldn't even talk to him. So he enrolled again at Montana State University. That's when the nightmares and flashbacks began. Night after night he awoke screaming, trying to keep from being bayoneted, or listening to the screams of his buddies as shells burst in the nighttime darkness of his bedroom. He couldn't study, and to top things off, his ears rang constantly from tinnitus, the effects of working with the howitzers in the 522nd. Finally, partway through his second quarter in school, he suffered a nervous breakdown and had to withdraw from the university.

Over the next few years, he wandered about the American West, working for a time to develop some raw land in Tucson, then moving on to Southern California, where he revived his youthful interest in aeronautics. In time, he graduated from the California Aero Tech Institute in Glendale and began to find engineering jobs in the state's burgeoning aerospace industry. He became a born-again Christian. In 1951 he married Mary Toyoda, and the couple had two children, Tom and Nancy. Long after surviving stomach cancer in the 1970s, George passed away on February 28, 2006, but not before returning almost every year to the forests and streams of Montana to hunt and fish and visit with old friends.

When Sus Ito was married in 1952, George Oiye served as his best man. Sus worked as a mechanic in Cleveland for a time after the war, but he soon grew dissatisfied with that line of work and decided to take advantage of the GI Bill in order to enroll in college as a biology student. From there, his career skyrocketed. He earned a PhD in biology and embryology from what was then Western Reserve University, became a postdoctoral fellow at Cornell in 1955, and joined the faculty of Harvard Medical School in 1960. Thirty years later, he retired from Harvard as the James Stillman Professor of Comparative Anatomy, but even after retirement he continued to do pioneering research in Harvard's labs until 2014. He died on September 29, 2015, at the age of ninety-six. The *senninbari* that his mother made for him and that he carried into battle, with its thousand stitches in red silk, now resides at the Japanese American National Museum in Los Angeles.

SOLLY GANOR'S FATHER, like Solly, had in fact survived the death march from Dachau and was reunited with Solly in Waakirchen shortly after they were rescued by the 442nd. His mother, though, died of typhoid fever in the death camp at Stutthof on December 25, 1944, as her daughter hovered over her, applying a cold, wet rag to her feverish head, just as Solly's father had seen it unfold in his dream at Lager Ten that same day. After the war, Solly worked for the U.S. Army, helping them ferret out Nazis hiding among civilians in Germany.

When the state of Israel was formed, he moved to the new nation and joined the Israel Defense Forces. He later served in the Israeli merchant marines before moving to England to study English literature at the University of London. Returning to Israel, he married in 1963. For the next fourteen years he managed a textile factory in Israel while he and his wife, Pola, raised the couple's two children, Daniel and Leora. In

1977, the Ganors moved for a time to La Jolla, California, before finally returning to Israel in 1984. In the spring of 1992, a group of 442nd veterans—Rudy Tokiwa and George Oiye among them—journeyed with the historian Eric Saul to Israel to meet Solly. Seeing them, talking with them in the lobby of a hotel in Tel Aviv, Solly began to weep. So did the veterans. It was the first time since the war that Solly had been able to cry.

Since then Solly has lectured widely on his experiences during the Holocaust and written a book—*Light One Candle*—recounting his personal life story. On April 28, 1994, he returned to Waakirchen, where he was reunited with Clarence Matsumura and John Tsukano, two of the Nisei troops who had rescued him in 1945. Addressing the crowd assembled there, Solly said, "We together, the survivors from the camps and the Germans, who remember our bloody past and are not willing ever to forget it, to you we stretch out our hands in friendship for the coming generations. . . . Since Auschwitz we know what man is capable of. And since Hiroshima we know what is at stake."

Solly's wife, Pola, passed away in May 2019. Solly died in August 2020.

TODAY THE HUNDREDS OF rock climbers, campers, hikers, and birdwatchers who turn up Prison Camp Road outside Tucson each year no longer find the Catalina Federal Honor Camp, where Gordon Hirabayashi was incarcerated in 1943. Instead, among the stone foundations of the old camp, they find a U.S. Forest Service sign reading GORDON HIRABAYASHI RECREATION SITE, as well as an array of plaques and interpretive signs introducing them to the story of the Japanese Americans during World War II. One of those plaques quotes Gordon, summing up his life's endeavor: "I was always able to hold my head up high because I wasn't just objecting and saying 'no,' but was saying 'yes' to a prior principle, the highest of principles."

Gordon was released from federal prison shortly after the war ended. He returned to the University of Washington, where, in six years, he earned his BA, MA, and PhD degrees in sociology. His first teaching posts took him and Esther to Beirut and Cairo, where Gordon was surprised to find that for the first time his colleagues and students regarded him simply as an American rather than a Japanese American. In 1959, the Hirabayashis moved to Canada, where Gordon joined the faculty of the University of Alberta, eventually becoming the chair of the sociology department. He and Esther raised their twin daughters—Marion and Sharon—and a son, Jay, but eventually they parted ways, amicably separating and divorcing in the 1970s. In 1986, Gordon married Susan Carnahan, a freelance writer and photographer whom he met at a Quaker meeting in Edmonton. The following year, the Ninth Circuit Court of Appeals vacated his conviction when his defense attorneys proved that the government had suppressed, altered, and destroyed evidence in his original trial.

After retiring from teaching, Gordon continued to speak out in defense of civil rights for the rest of his life. He died in Edmonton, Alberta, on January 2, 2012. Ten hours later, in a hospital a block away, Esther Schmoe also passed away. On May 29, 2012, President Obama—standing in front of an embroidered gold curtain in the East Room of the White House, with Susan Carnahan and other members of Gordon's family looking on—posthumously conferred on Gordon the Presidential Medal of Freedom, the nation's highest civilian honor. As he presented the medal, Obama quoted from Gordon himself: "Unless citizens are willing to stand up for the Constitution it's not worth the paper it's written on."

ACKNOWLEDGMENTS

As many books are, this one was ushered into the world by a host of angels. How it is that I have been lucky enough to have had them at my side as I undertook to tell this story I do not know, but I owe them all an enormous debt of gratitude.

First and foremost, I want to thank Tom Ikeda of the Densho project in Seattle. It was largely through my early conversations with Tom that I came to fully understand how important it is for all of us—particularly in these times we are living through—to better understand the experience of the Japanese Americans before and during World War II. As I plunged headfirst into the astounding collection of oral histories, letters, newspapers, photographs, and other material that Tom has made available to the world on the Densho website, he provided invaluable guidance and advice. He also opened many doors and introduced me to a wide variety of people, many of them listed below, who have greatly facilitated my work. I also want to thank the staff at Densho— particularly Densho's outstanding historian, Brian Niiya, and operations director, Dana Hoshide—for all the help they have given me in making good use of the resources they tirelessly collect and curate.

I am particularly indebted also to Fred Shiosaki, one of the last 442nd men still standing and the very embodiment of their "Go for Broke" spirit, as well as the close friends and family members of some of the other young men whose lives I chronicle in the book—particularly Michael Shiosaki, Mariko Miho, Judy Niizawa, and Robin Tokiwa. Thank you all so much for spending so much time with me, for talking story, for sharing all those letters and yearbooks and photographs, for letting me into your homes and your lives, and most of all for entrusting me with your loved ones' amazing stories. I can only hope that I have done some small measure of justice to them.

Among the many people in Hawai'i who contributed in so many ways, my thanks go out to Leilani Dawson at the University of Hawai'i, Mānoa; Warren and Michiko Kodama-Nishimoto; Gwen Fujie; Shari Y. Tamashiro; and two remarkable gentlemen—Flint Yonashiro and Roy Fujii—both veterans of the 522nd's B Battery.

On the mainland, special thanks to Janet and Jim Ohta; David Takami; John C. Hughes; L. Stuart Hirai; Jamie Henricks; Kristen Hayashi; Anne Burroughs; Judy Rantz Willman; and Kiyomi Hayashi for all things Quaker and for keeping me ever in the light.

In the halls of academia, my sincere thanks to Erin Aoyama at Brown University; Tara Fickle at the University of Oregon; and Megan Asaka at UC Riverside for their careful readings of the manuscript and their many valuable observations, suggestions, and corrections. As always, any remaining omissions or errors are entirely mine.

In the world of book publishing, I can never think of words superlative enough to express again my deep, heartfelt gratitude to two tough, warm, ferociously brilliant women—my agent, Dorian Karchmar, and my editor, Wendy Wolf—so I'll just say again, thank you two so much for being who you are. I owe much also to Louise Braverman, Terezia Cicel, and the rest of the superb team at Viking. And in London, many thanks to Daniel Crewe for his rigorous and pleasantly British review of the text and the excellent insights that resulted from it.

And finally, at home, I have yet again been blessed by the love and encouragement of my family—my daughters, Emily and Robin, and my wife, Sharon. On this particular journey, Sharon has been with me every step of the way, not just offering her usual tolerance of the messes I create by scattering stacks of books and reams of paper around the house, but, more important, lending me her keen insights and her terrific instincts for good storytelling. She has traveled with me to remote battlefields in Italy, taken notes while I interviewed veterans, spent many hours sorting and scanning documents in dusty university archives, organized boxes full of photocopies, skillfully edited successive drafts of the manuscript, organized photographs, and annotated and curated troves of primary source materials, particularly the voluminous correspondence of Chaplains Yamada and Higuchi. More than ever, without her there would be no book.

RESOURCES

BEYOND THE BOOK

For a collection of resources pertaining to the people, places, and events in this book, including video interviews with Rudy Tokiwa, Fred Shiosaki, Gordon Hirabayashi, and Kats Miho, please see "Beyond the Book" at DanielJamesBrown.com.

ABOUT DENSHO

Densho is a nonprofit organization started in 1996, with the initial goal of documenting oral histories from Japanese Americans who were incarcerated during World War II solely on the basis of their ancestry. This evolved into a mission to educate, preserve, collaborate, and inspire action for equity. Densho uses digital technology to preserve and make accessible primary source materials on the World War II incarceration of Japanese Americans. Densho presents these materials and related resources online and free of charge for their historic value and as a means of exploring issues of democracy, intolerance, wartime hysteria, civil rights, and the responsibilities of citizenship in our increasingly global society. Densho is a Japanese term meaning "to pass on to the next generation," or to leave a legacy.

To explore Densho's extensive collections of photographs, documents, letters, newspapers, and video interviews, or to contribute to their efforts to preserve Japanese American history, please visit Densho.org. A portion of the author's proceeds from the sale of this book go to support Densho in its work.

NOTES

For the sake of brevity, I have used the following abbreviations to refer to some of the more frequently cited newspapers below: *NYT* (*New York Times*), *LAT* (*Los Angeles Times*), and *ST* (*Seattle Times*).

In regard to frequently cited interviews, I use the following abbreviations to indicate the organizations that conducted the interviews or now hold recordings of them: Densho (the Densho archives available at densho.org/archives/), GFB (Go for Broke National Education Center archives available at www.goforbroke.org), and Holocaust Museum (United States Holocaust Memorial Museum available at www .ushmm.org). The source or location of other interviews is cited individually.

FOREWORD, AUTHOR'S NOTE, AND PROLOGUE

The Rudy Tokiwa quotation is from his March 24, 2002, GFB interview. The Orwell quotation is from "Politics and the English Language," which was first published in *Horizon* in April 1946. The epigraph to the prologue is from Densho's interview with Fred Shiosaki, conducted on April 26 and 27, 2006.

CHAPTER ONE

The chapter epigraph comes from Ted Tsukiyama's Densho interview, Jan. 5, 2001. My characterizations of Kats's character here and throughout are drawn from many sources, including the several oral histories he left behind and noted below, but most particularly from my interview with Mariko Miho on Jan. 19, 2018. Details of what he was doing and thinking on Dec. 7, 1941, come largely from his GFB interview on Jan. 20, 2002, his interview with Michi Kodama-Nishimoto and Warren Nishimoto (hereafter cited as Nishimotos) on Nov. 16, 1989, and his compiled narrative on the Hawai'i Nisei Story website (hereafter cited as Hawai'i Nisei Story).

Details surrounding the Japanese attack on O'ahu are derived from a wide variety of sources. Among these are Gordon W. Prange, *December 7, 1941: The Day the Japanese Attacked Pearl Harbor*, with Donald M. Goldstein and Katherine V. Dillon (New York: Open Road Media, 2014), and Steven M. Gillon, *Pearl Harbor: FDR Leads the Nation into War* (New York: Basic Books, 2011). A chronology of events at the Opana mobile radar site can be found on the National Park Service's Pearl Harbor website. Lieutenant Kermit Tyler's remark "Don't worry about it" is recorded in John Martini's interview with Tyler, Dec. 8, 1991, on the same site. Michael Wegner's C-SPAN talk on Dec. 5, 2011, provides many more details about the attack on Kāne'ohe Bay Naval Air Station. The "This is no drill" quotation is from Gillon, *Pearl Harbor*, as is the "This is no shit!" quotation. "Praise the Lord and pass the ammunition!" is from Prange, *December 7, 1941*. The harrowing arrival of the B-17s is vividly documented in Fred Swegles's article "B-17 Pilot Flew Unexpectedly into the Middle of Japanese Attack on Pearl Harbor," *Orange County Register*, Dec. 6, 2017. The death toll figure is from "Civilian Casualties" on the National Park Service website. Wayne Yoshioka described the tragedy at the language school on Hawai'i Public Radio on Dec. 3, 2016, in an audio piece called "A Pearl Harbor 75th Anniversary Story." More details of the casualties aboard different naval vessels that day can be found in Prange, *December 7, 1941*, and Gillon, *Pearl Harbor*. Other details of the damage done and the response on different ships are drawn from "Proceedings of the Hewitt Inquiry—Congressional Investigation Pearl Harbor Attack: Hewitt Inquiry Exhibit No. 73." The Akiji Yoshimura quotation is from James M. McCaffrey, *Going for Broke: Japanese American Soldiers in the War Against Nazi Germany* (Norman: University of Oklahoma Press, 2013). "The nerve of these guys" is from Ronald Oba's narrative on the Hawai'i Nisei Story site. "This is no test" can be found in Lyn Crost, *Honor by Fire: Japanese Americans at War in Europe and the Pacific* (Novato, Calif.: Presidio Press, 1994), as well as in a Ted Tsukiyama talk broadcast on C-SPAN on Dec. 5, 2011. More on Daniel Inouye's thoughts and actions that day can be found in Crost, *Honor by Fire*, and in John Tsukano, *Bridge of Love* (Honolulu: Hawaii Hosts, 1985). Flint Yonashiro described his thoughts and actions during the attack when I interviewed him in Honolulu on Oct. 20, 2018. The "This is a Jap" quotation can be found in Hawaii Nikkei History Editorial Board, comp., *Japanese Eyes, American Heart: Personal Reflections of Hawaii's World War II Nisei Soldiers* (Honolulu: University of Hawai'i Press, 1998), 51. The "War, war, coffee, coffee" quotation is from Takejiro Higa's Hawai'i Nisei Story interview. Kats's remarks "Eh, what's going on down there?" are documented in his interview with the Nishimotos on Nov. 16, 1989, as well as in his narrative on the Hawai'i Nisei Story site. Ted Tsukiyama describes the scene at the University of Hawai'i that morning in his Holocaust Museum oral history, recorded on Dec. 21, 1987.

CHAPTER TWO

The epigraph is from Fumiye Miho's unpublished memoir. Kats Miho relates his experiences growing up on Maui in his interviews with the Nishimotos, his Holocaust Museum oral history, recorded on June 21, 1989, and his narrative on the Hawai'i Nisei Story site. Additional details are drawn from my interview with Mariko Miho on Jan. 19, 2018, and from Fumiye Miho's memoir. I derived a great deal of information about the layout of Kahului in the early twentieth century from a very detailed map produced by an unnamed student at the University of Hawai'i in fulfillment of a class assignment as well as from my own observations exploring the town as it is today. The map is now housed in the Hamilton Library's Special Collections at the University of Hawai'i, Mānoa. I also gathered information about the social structure of Maui from Katsuro Miho's interview with the Nishimotos on Nov. 16, 1989; from Fumiye's unpublished memoir; and from my interview with Mariko Miho, cited above. Additional information about the social stratification of Maui and the lifestyles of the island's white population came in part from Irma Gerner Burns, *Maui's Mittee and the General* (Honolulu: Ku Pa'a, 1991); from Tom Coffman, *The Island Edge of America: A Political History of Hawai'i* (Honolulu: University of Hawai'i Press, 2003); from an academic paper written by Katsuso "Paul" Miho while a student at the University of Hawai'i on June 2, 1937, titled "An Ecological Dissertation of My Little Community"; and from perusing many issues of *The Maui News*, circa 1929–1941.

Statistics about the ethnic composition of Hawai'i's population are from Coffman, *Island Edge of America*, 41. "When you are asked to go in the sun" is from Walter Dillingham's Senate testimony, Aug. 13, 1921, printed in "Hearings Before the Committee on Immigration," U.S. Senate, on S.J. 82 (Washington, D.C.: Government Printing Office, 1921). Additional details about childhood life on Maui and the Maui County Fair came from my interview with Janet and Jim Ohta on June 29, 2018, and from reading contemporaneous accounts in *The Maui News*. My understanding of student life at Maui High was enriched by perusing Kats Miho's yearbooks and by Jill Engledow, *The Spirit Lives On: A History of Old Maui High at Hamakaupoko* (2007).

CHAPTER THREE

The Laura Miho epigraph is from remarks she made in the film *Voices Behind Barbed Wire*, produced for the Japanese Cultural Center of Hawai'i, written, directed, and edited by Ryan Kawamoto, executive producer Carole Hayashino. The figure of forty-five million radios is from Gillon, *Pearl Harbor*, 66. My sketch of life in Hillyard was informed primarily by my interviews with Fred Shiosaki on April 10 and July 2, 2016; by his Densho interviews on April 26 and 27, 2006; by an excellent portrait of the man by John C. Hughes, "Fred Shiosaki: The Rescue of the Lost

Battalion," published by Legacy Washington, Office of Secretary of State, Olympia, Wash., 2015; and by Stefanie Pettit, "Hillyard Laundry Building Has Colorful Past," *Spokane Spokesman-Review,* Dec. 11, 2008. My account of Fred's personal experiences that day are drawn primarily from my 2016 interviews with him, as well as from his Densho interview referenced above and the Hughes portrait. For interesting background on John Charles Daly's famous radio call, "The Japanese have attacked Pearl Harbor," see the Dec. 7, 1999, recording of NPR's *All Things Considered,* in which the veteran newsman Robert Trout provides eyewitness testimony about how things went down at CBS News that morning.

My account of Fumiye Miho's experiences growing up on Maui, her life in Japan, and her experiences on Dec. 8, 1941, are drawn from her unpublished memoir, her interviews with Michi Kodama-Nishimoto in 2000, a recorded presentation she made at a Honolulu Friends Meeting in 1992, and my 2018 interview with Mariko Miho. Additional details are from Elaine Fogg, "Honolulu Is Home, Sweet Home, After Hiroshima," *Honolulu Advertiser,* April 13, 1947. The various man-in-the-street reactions to news of the Pearl Harbor attack all come from Time-Life Bureau, *War Comes to the U.S.—Dec. 7, 1941: The First 30 Hours as Reported from the U.S. and Abroad* (Norwalk, Conn.: Easton Press, 2014).

Details about the imposition of martial law in Honolulu are from Gillon, *Pearl Harbor,* and from Gail Honda, ed., *Family Torn Apart: The Internment Story of the Otokichi Muin Ozaki Family* (Honolulu: Japanese Cultural Center of Hawai'i, 2012). Other details about the atmosphere in Honolulu that night are from Tamotsu Shibutani, *The Derelicts of Company K: A Sociological Study of Demoralization* (Berkeley: University of California Press, 1978); from "Blacked Out Liner Wins Race with War," *Oakland Tribune,* Dec. 10, 1941; and from general reporting in the *Honolulu Star-Bulletin* on Dec. 8, 1941. Kats's personal experiences are drawn from his Hawai'i Nisei Story narrative, from his interview with the Nishimotos, and from his 2002 GFB interview. The Katsuichi Miho quotation—"Don't do anything that will bring shame"—is from Katsuro Miho's interview with the Nishimotos on Nov. 16, 1989.

The FDR quotation—"every Japanese citizen or non-citizen"—can be found in the article "Custodial Detention/A-B-C-List" in the Densho Encyclopedia, as can much of the historical information I present here. Additional historical context can be found in the entry "German and Italian Detainees," also in the Densho Encyclopedia. The incidents I recite of Issei men being taken away are from Time-Life Bureau, *War Comes to the U.S.;* Richard Reeves, *Infamy: The Shocking Story of the Japanese American Internment in World War II* (New York: Henry Holt, 2015), 12; Franklin Odo, *No Sword to Bury: Japanese Americans in Hawai'i During World War II* (Philadelphia: Temple University Press, 2004), 112; Sumi Okamoto's Densho interview on April 26, 2006; and Thelma Chang, *I Can Never Forget: Men of the 100th/442nd* (Honolulu: Sigi Productions, 1991), 84.

CHAPTER FOUR

The epigraph is from a radio script printed in Honda, *Family Torn Apart,* 45. The account of Fred Shiosaki's life in the days following Pearl Harbor is drawn from my 2016 interviews with him, the Hughes portrait, and his Densho interview. The WAR LIST BIG headline is from the Dec. 8, 1941, edition of the *Spokane Spokesman-Review.* "Kay, look at this!" is from Fred's Densho interview, as are the subsequent quotations attributed to Kisaburo Shiosaki that day.

My portrait of Japan in the late nineteenth century is drawn in large part from Yuji Ichioka, *The Issei: The World of the First Generation Japanese Immigrants, 1885–1924* (New York: Free Press, 1988), 42–45, and from Donald Y. Yamasaki, *Issei, Nisei, Sansei: Three Generations of Camp Life Pu'unene, Maui, Hawaii* (Kahului, Hawai'i: D&S, 2013), 42. Details of work conditions for railroad workers in Canada are from "The Chinese Experience in British Columbia: 1850–1950," a short article on the University of British Columbia's library website. My description of the interior of the Davenport Hotel is drawn from contemporaneous photographs published in a promotional brochure. I compiled the essential narrative of Kisaburo Shiosaki's early life in Washington from my interviews with Fred Shiosaki, the Hughes portrait, Fred's Densho interview, and Blanche Shiosaki Okamoto, "Promising New Future: Memories of Tori and Kisaburo Shiosaki," *Nostalgia,* Jan. 23, 2019.

For more on the capture of Ensign Sakamaki, see his account in *I Attacked Pearl Harbor,* Gary Coover, ed. (Honolulu: Rollston Press, 2019). Kats relates his experience of his first night on patrol for the Territorial Guard in his Hawai'i Nisei Story narrative. The story of Katsuichi and Ayano Miho's early years in Japan and Hawai'i is derived primarily from my interview with Mariko Miho but with significant additional detail from both Kats's and Katsuro Miho's interviews with the Nishimotos. Katsuichi's arrest and detention at Sand Island are chronicled in Kats's 2002 GFB interview with considerable additional information derived from my interview with Mariko Miho. Conditions at Sand Island Detention Center are described in Honda, *Family Torn Apart.*

For a detailed account of the sinking of the HMS *Repulse* and the HMS *Prince of Wales,* see Gabe Christy, "The WW2 Sinking of Two Mighty War Ships," on the War History Online website. The submarine attack on Maui is described in Coleen Uechi, "Remembering Pearl Harbor: We Were Scared," *Maui News,* Dec. 7, 2016. The racist signs, comments, and comics are from a variety of sources, including contemporaneous photographs and Reeves, *Infamy,* 19–21. The *LAT* editorial, including the quotation "A viper is nonetheless," appears in a National Park Service online article, "A Brief History of Japanese American Relocation During World War II." The "All Japanese nationals" quotation is from the Hughes portrait. The "This is a race war" quotation can be found in Reeves, *Infamy,* as can the Jed Johnson and Chase Clark quotations. The imposition of martial law in the islands is discussed at length in the article "Martial Law in Hawaii," in the Densho Encyclopedia. The "these people are our enemies" quotation is from Reeves, *Infamy,* 19. Much more about the effects of restrictions on the lives of Japanese Americans in the wake of Pearl Harbor can be found in Bill Hosokawa, *Nisei: The Quiet Americans* (Boulder: University Press of Colorado, 2002). Fred Shiosaki quotes his father saying, "Don't go where there are crowds," in his Densho interview.

Kats Miho talks about his pride in joining the Territorial Guard in his interviews with the Nishimotos and his narrative on the Hawai'i Nisei Story site. His daughter Mariko also spoke about it at length when I interviewed her. The Densho Encyclopedia article "Hawaii Territorial Guide" offers an extended explanation of the history of the unit. Kats talks at length about his experiences the night he was discharged from the Territorial Guard in his interview with the Nishimotos and also a Holocaust Museum interview on June 21, 1989. Ted Tsukiyama's comment, "If a bomb had exploded," is quoted in Odo, *No Sword to Bury,* 128.

CHAPTER FIVE

The epigraph is from Lily Yuriko Hatanaka's oral history interview conducted by the Nishimotos, Dec. 14, 2009. Rudy Tokiwa describes what he was doing and thinking on Dec. 7, 1941, in his 1998 Densho interview. Many other details come from my interview with Rudy's partner, Judy Niizawa, on March 17, 2017, as well as some from Judy's interview with Rudy's sister Fumi Tokiwa Futamase on Dec. 30, 1995. The account of Rudy's life in Japan derives from the same three sources. For details on life in prewar Japan, I consulted Eri Hotta, *Japan 1941: Countdown to Infamy* (New York: Vintage, 2013), and Winston Groom, *1942: The Year That Tried Men's Souls* (New York: Grove Press, 2018). Duke Tokiwa's status as a star quarterback is confirmed by the 1942 Salinas High yearbook. For more on the burning of dolls and other precious items, see Duncan Ryuken Williams's moving piece "Thus Have I Heard: An American Sutra," *Tricycle: The Buddhist Review* (Spring 2019). The "Them dirty Japs" quotation and subsequent exchange are in part from Rudy's Densho interview and in part from his June 3, 2001, GFB interview. My account of his encounter with the FBI in the Tokiwas' home is from the same two sources and from my interview with Judy Niizawa. The restrictions placed on Japanese Americans in the Salinas valley are documented in Sandy Lydon, *The Japanese in the Monterey Bay Region: A Brief History* (Capitola, Calif.: Capitola Book Company, 1997), 100–101, and from Fumi Tokiwa Futamase's interview with Judy Niizawa.

A detailed account of the various military installations on Maui during the war can be found in "The History of Maui During the War," on the National Marine Sanctuaries website. My telling of Kats's time working at Pu'unene is based on his interview with the Nishimotos and his narrative on the Hawai'i Nisei Story site as well as my interview with Mariko. I built my account of Fred Shiosaki's and his parents' experiences with the FBI based on his Densho interview, his interviews with me, and the Hughes portrait. The reference to the removal of the gong at the Buddhist temple in Salinas is in Lydon, *Japanese in the Monterey Bay Region*, 99.

Frank Knox's comment "I think the most effective fifth column" is documented, among other places, in "Remember Pearl Harbor and Learn," *LAT*, Sept. 30, 2001. John Rankin's quotation "I'm for catching every Japanese" is from the Congressional Record for Dec. 15, 1941. For more about the back-and-forth over the executive order, see "Executive Order 9066" and the "Franklin Roosevelt" entry in the Densho Encyclopedia. Walter Lippmann's extraordinary remarks "Since the outbreak of the Japanese war" were made in his nationally syndicated column, "Today and Tomorrow: The Fifth Column on the West Coast," Feb. 12, 1942. Pegler's remarks, "The Japanese in California," are from his column "Fair Enough," in the *LAT* and also syndicated on Feb. 16, 1942. The text of "Executive Order 9066 Authorizing the Secretary of War to Prescribe Military Areas" can be found at Marist College's online archives. The data from the National Opinion Research Center poll regarding removal of Issei and Nisei can be found in Shibutani, *Derelicts of Company K*, 50. Eleanor Roosevelt's feelings about the removal and the executive order are documented in the "Eleanor Roosevelt" entry in the Densho Encyclopedia. For more on the workings of the WRA, see David A. Takami, *Divided Destiny: A History of Japanese Americans in Seattle* (Seattle: University of Washington Press, 1998). The "Hey, you Japs!" comment is quoted by Reeves, *Infamy*, 70.

CHAPTER SIX

The epigraph appears in Louis Fiset, ed., *Imprisoned Apart: The World War II Correspondence of an Issei Couple* (Seattle: University of Washington Press, 1997). The details of Jisuke and Fusa Tokiwa's conditions and state of mind are drawn primarily from my interview with Judy Niizawa. Many details of the Rock Springs Riot are drawn from "To This We Dissented: The Rock Springs Riot" on the History Matters website and from "The Wyoming Massacre," *NYT*, Sept. 8, 1885. The *San Francisco Chronicle's* headlines are reprinted in Hosokawa, *Nisei*, 82–83. Phelan's perverse comment "They are tireless workers" and more like them can be found in the "Statement of Hon. James D. Phelan of California Before the Committee on Immigration and Naturalization, House of Representatives, Friday, June 20, 1919" (Washington, D.C.: Government Printing Office, 1920). Some of the information about the Pozzi brothers comes from the 1940 federal census. But their relationship with the Tokiwas and their conversations before the Tokiwas left their farm are detailed in Rudy's Densho interview, in Fumi Tokiwa Futamase's 1995 interview with Judy Niizawa, and my interview with Judy. The information about the Pozzi brothers' farm today

comes from a Dunn & Bradstreet business profile online. Rudy discusses the family's move to the Salinas Assembly Center in his 2001 GFB interview. Additional details concerning that day and initial conditions at Salinas come from my interview
with Judy Niizawa, Fumi Tokiwa Futamase's interview with Judy, Marion I. Masada's
Sept. 10, 2014, Densho interview, and Chiyoko Yagi's July 28, 2008, Densho interview.
Some of the physical details about the camp are from Jeffery F. Burton et al., *Confinement and Ethnicity: An Overview of World War II Japanese American Relocation Sites*
(Tucson, Ariz.: Western Archeological and Conservation Center, 1999), 368.

The "Jap Camps" reference here comes from *ST*, May 13, 1942, 1, but the term was
used by other papers throughout the war. See the "Santa Anita (Detention Facility)"
entry in the Densho Encyclopedia for much more about that particular camp. George
Oiye describes his sister's experience at Santa Anita in his March 24, 2002, GFB interview. My description of Camp Harmony derives, in part, from details provided in
Takami, *Divided Destiny*, 52, and from Louise Kashino's March 15, 1998, Densho interview. The voyages of the USS *Grant* and other ships transporting Issei detainees to
the mainland, as well as their experiences upon arriving at Fort Sill, are documented
in considerable detail in Honda, *Family Torn Apart*. Mr. Oshima's killing and the
subsequent events are related in Otokichi Ozaki's radio script from June 3, 1950.
This can be found in the Otokichi Ozaki Collection at the Japanese Cultural Center
of Hawai'i in Honolulu, box 4, folder 13, item A. The "we will become living corpses"
quotation is from Honda, *Family Torn Apart*, 66.

CHAPTER SEVEN

The epigraph is from Gordon Hirabayashi, *A Principled Stand: The Story of Hirabayashi v. United States* (Seattle: University of Washington Press, 2013), 127. My portrait of Gordon, as well as my account of the day he decided to violate the curfew, is
drawn from three principal sources: a series of interviews he conducted with Densho
between April 1999 and May 2000, his 1990 interview with Lois Horn, and his own
account in *A Principled Stand*. Fred Shiosaki discussed the postwar state of affairs at
the Hillyard Laundry and his father's interactions with Simpson in my interviews
with him and also in his Densho interview. Judy Niizawa related Rudy's early experiences at the Salinas Assembly Center to me. Other details and the "Ah, he's one of
the Japs" quotation are from Rudy's 2001 GFB interview, as is the "I will teach you"
quotation. Gordon related his early work helping people prepare for incarceration in
his Densho interviews and in *A Principled Stand*. The "Please put your principles" quotation and the subsequent discussion with his mother are from Hirabayashi, *A Principled Stand*, 61–62. Gordon's "Why I Refuse to Register for Evacuation" statement is
a stand-alone document dated May 13, 1942, and can be found in the University of
Washington's Special Collections. His interactions with the FBI, including the dia-

logue I relate here, are recounted variously in Hirabayashi, *A Principled Stand*, 67–68, in the Horn interview, in Gordon's Densho interviews, and in Dolores Goto's 1971 interview with Arthur Barnett, available online in the University of Washington's Digital Collections.

CHAPTER EIGHT

The epigraph is quoted in Reeves, *Infamy*, 107–8. A second soldier chewed out the first and helped Mrs. Tokushige off the bus with her baby, but the incident is indicative of how capriciously and vindictively authorities could and sometimes did treat the detainees.

The mountain of scrap metal in Seattle is described at some length in "Seattle's 'Scrap Mountains' Landmarks for Sightseers," *ST*, Oct. 20, 1942. Other scrap collection efforts are documented in the *LAT* on July 4, 1942, and in "Scrap Brigade Scrapped All but 35 Piles," *LAT*, Oct. 20, 1942. Some of the names of baseball players who served come from James C. Roberts, writing on the American Veterans Center website; others are from Groom, *1942*.

My account of Rudy's arrival at Poston is derived primarily from his 1998 Densho interview, his 2001 GFB interview, Fumi Tokiwa Futamase's 1995 interview with Judy Niizawa, and my interview with Judy, although I also consulted the oral histories of various others who arrived at Poston that summer for small details about conditions in the camp. For more about the Colorado Indian Reservation and those who call it home, see Jay Cravath, "History of the Colorado River Indian Tribes," on the Poston Preservation website. Additional details about the construction of Poston are from Burton et al., *Confinement and Ethnicity*, 215–16, and the "Poston" entry in the Densho Encyclopedia. The "Fill it up with hay" quotation is from Rudy's 1998 Densho interview, as is the "Rudy, how about cookin' here?" exchange and the following dialogue. Judy Niizawa related to me Rudy's determination to please his elders at Poston.

Gordon described his initial days in the King County Jail in Hirabayashi, *A Principled Stand*, 79–81. I also derived a great deal of information about this period of his confinement from his diary, written while in jail and dated June 22 to Oct. 12, 1942. The diary is housed in the University of Washington Special Collections. Gordon related his experiences as "mayor of the tank" both in his Dec. 1999 Densho interview and in Hirabayashi, *A Principled Stand*. The text of his Fourth of July 1942 statement is drawn directly from his diary. His parents' arrival at Tule Lake, the greeting Mrs. Hirabayashi received, and Mrs. Hirabayashi's prayers for Gordon are also documented in his diary, his Dec. 1999 Densho interview, and Hirabayashi, *A Principled Stand*, 114.

Kats's summer of discontent in 1942 is documented in his interviews with the Nishimotos, his narrative on the Hawai'i Nisei Story website, and my interview with

Mariko Miho. My account of Fred Shiosaki's life that summer and his failed attempt to enlist is drawn from the Hughes profile, my own interviews with Fred, and his Densho interview. The pay scale for people working within the camps comes from Greg Robinson's "War Relocation Center" entry in the Densho Encyclopedia. Rudy discusses his life as a cook at Poston in both his Densho and GFB interviews. Additional details come from my interview with Judy Niizawa. Some of the information about the improvised recreational facilities at Poston are from Tom Mine's Densho interview on July 29, 2008, and from Thomas Y. Fujita-Rony's "Poston" entry in the Densho Encyclopedia. The "If you want to live, Mac" quotation is from Rudy's Densho interview. Biographical information about Harry Madokoro and his mother is from the *San Bernardino County Sun*, March 2, 1945; Mas Hashimoto, "Onward," *Pacific Citizen*, July 12, 2019; and the *Poston Chronicle*, Sept. 7, 1944. Judy Niizawa also discussed Harry's influence on Rudy at great length in my interview with her.

Gordon describes the arrival of his parents at the King County Jail in Hirabayashi, *A Principled Stand*, 120–21, and in his 1990 interview with Lois Horn. The quotation "The case is clear" is from his prison journal, cited above. The opening of Gordon's trial is described in "Hirabayashi Trial Opens," *Seattle Star*, Oct. 20, 1942. Gordon also discussed it in his interview with Lois Horn, in his Dec. 1999 Densho interview, and in Hirabayashi, *A Principled Stand*, 124–25. The courtroom dialogue comes from the same three sources. Judge Black's finding can be found at "46 F. Supp. 657 (1942) United States v. Gordon Hirabayashi, No.45738 U.S. District Court W.D. Washington N.D. September 15, 1942" on the Justia website.

CHAPTER NINE

The epigraphs are from Fiset, *Imprisoned Apart*. Some of the details of Christmas 1942 are from Donnie Hudgens, "World War II Diary: Remembering Christmas, 1942 . . . 75 Years Later," *Calhoun Times*, Dec. 25, 2017. My description of that Christmas at Poston is based largely on "7,000 Children in Yuletide Remembrances," *Poston Chronicle*, Dec. 24, 1942, and "'Twas the Night Before Christmas," *Poston Chronicle*, Dec. 27, 1942. The atrocious spectacle of the SS Christmas at Auschwitz is based on "Christmas Eve in Auschwitz as Recalled by Polish Prisoners," Dec. 22, 2005, on the Auschwitz-Birkenau Memorial and Museum website. Many of the government memos related to the creation of an all-Japanese American fighting unit, now declassified and reprinted from the National Archives, can be found in the University of Hawai'i Special Collections housed at Hamilton Library, in the Ted Tsukiyama Papers, box 9, folder 9. The quotation "Americanism is not" is from Roosevelt's memo to Secretary of War Stimson, Feb. 1, 1943, a copy of which can also be found in the Tsukiyama Papers.

Katsuaki Miho's musings about his future—"Once in every man's life"—are from a journal he kept, a copy of which was provided to me by Mariko Miho. Kats describes the all-night argument and the dialogue with his brother in his Hawai'i Nisei Story narrative. Kats had also related it to Mariko, who in turn related additional details to me. The rush of Nisei men to enlist is described in Coffman, *Island Edge of America,* and in Crost, *Honor by Fire,* which is where the figure of ten thousand would-be enlistees is from. Not all ten thousand were ultimately accepted into the service.

My description of the old men at Poston derives in part from my conversations with Judy Niizawa and in part from Paul Okimoto, *Oh! Poston, Why Don't You Cry for Me?* (Xlibris, 2011). Rudy's experiences as a bootlegger are drawn primarily from his 1998 Densho interview. The account of Lieutenant Bolton's visit to Poston is drawn from the *Poston Chronicle,* Feb. 9, 1943. The meeting under the mesquite trees and the subsequent conversations within the Tokiwa family are described in Rudy's 2001 GFB interview and his 1998 Densho interview. Judy Niizawa also related additional information about the meeting to me when I interviewed her, particularly about the roles that Harry Madokoro and Lloyd Onoye played in Rudy's decision making.

Cherstin M. Lyon's article "Loyalty Questionnaire" in the Densho Encyclopedia has much more on the loyalty questionnaire and questions 27 and 28 in particular. The 93.7 percent figure is from the website of the Japanese American National Museum. For more about those who answered no or did not answer, see Brian Niiya's very informative entry "No-No Boys" in the Densho Encyclopedia.

Gordon Hirabayashi describes his jailhouse diet, his release on bond, and his trip to Spokane to meet up with Floyd Schmoe in his Feb. 10, 1981, interview with Roger Daniels, housed in the University of Washington's Special Collections. My portrait of Esther Schmoe is drawn from contemporaneous photographs, from "'I Love Him,' Says Bride of Japanese American," *New York Daily News,* Aug. 13, 1944, from "Hirabayashi 'Bowled Over' as Wife Has Twins," an undated newspaper clipping, and from Jay Hirabayashi's "Remembering Gordon and Esther Hirabayashi," published on the website of the National Association of Japanese Canadians. Gordon also elaborated on his relationship with Esther in his Feb. 17, 2000, Densho interview.

Fred Shiosaki discussed his time at Gonzaga and his decision to enlist in his 2016 interviews with me and in his 2006 Densho interview. I've drawn additional details from John Hughes's fine portrait of Fred.

Much of my description of the farewell ceremony at 'Iolani Palace is drawn from "2,600 New U.S. Soldiers Get Public Aloha," *Honolulu Star-Bulletin,* March 29, 1943, as well as from photographs taken that day. The "Be a good soldier" quotation is from Stan Akita's narrative on the Hawai'i Nisei Story site, but variations of what he heard from his father pop up over and over in the accounts other Nisei soldiers give of the last words they received from their fathers. Kats describes the march to the harbor and departure on the *Lurline* in his Hawai'i Nisei Story narrative. Other similar accounts are included in Chang, *I Can Never Forget.* The "We were not soldiers" quotation is from Daniel Inouye's June 30, 1998, Densho interview. Some details of the conditions on the *Lurline* are from Herbert Isonaga's narrative on the Hawai'i Nisei Story site. My brief overview of the general state of the war is based, in part, on Rick Atkinson, *The Day of Battle: The War in Sicily and Italy, 1943–1944* (New York: Henry Holt, 2007), 5–6. The grim statistics from Auschwitz-Birkenau are from "Timeline: The History of Auschwitz-Birkenau," posted Jan. 27, 2020, on the *Times of Israel* website.

Kats describes the voyage from Honolulu to San Francisco in his Hawai'i Nisei Story narrative. Additional details are from Daniel Inouye's 1998 Densho interview; Chang, *I Can Never Forget*, 53; and Thomas Tanaka's April 17, 2004, GFB interview. Several accounts of the train trip to Shelby also appear in Chang, *I Can Never Forget*, and Whitey Yamamoto recounts it in his interview with the Nishimotos and his narrative on the Hawai'i Nisei Story site. In his 1998 Densho interview, Daniel Inouye discusses the nervousness that some of the men felt about going to Mississippi.

The account of Fred's final days in Spokane and his departure is based on his 2017 interviews with me and his Densho interview. I also obtained information about his brother Roy's service from Roy's obituary in the *Spokane Spokesman-Review*, Jan. 2, 2016. Fred's sister, Blanche Shiosaki Okamoto, describes the laundry, including the two blue stars, in her article "Promising New Future."

CHAPTER TEN

The epigraph here, like a number that follow, is from one of the many letters Hiro Higuchi sent to his wife, Hisako, during the course of the war. The letters were donated to the University of Hawai'i by their daughter Jane and are archived in the Special Collections at the Hamilton Library.

The arrival of the Hawaiian Nisei soldiers in Hattiesburg created a strong impression on many of them. I have drawn here from Daniel Inouye's recollections in his Densho interview and a number of accounts given in Crost, *Honor by Fire*. The lynchings I describe are documented in "Shubota, Mississippi," *Pittsburgh Post Gazette*, Dec. 28, 2016, as well as in a number of contemporaneous newspaper accounts. See, for instance, United Press, "Two Boys, 14, Lynched by Mob in Mississippi," *Philadelphia Inquirer*, Oct. 13, 1942. DeWitt's "A Jap's a Jap" comment is quoted in many places, among them Bill Yenne's "Fear Itself: The General Who Panicked the Coast," on the HistoryNet website. The boys' initial impressions of Camp Shelby are drawn from accounts in Chang, *I Can Never Forget*, and from Whitey Yamamoto's interview with the Nishimotos. Rudy's comment about his mother buying his pants is from his GFB interview. His encounter with Sadao Munemori at MIS school and his subsequent journey to New Orleans and Camp Shelby are documented in his 1998 Densho interview and his 2001 GFB interview. Additional details are derived from my interview with Judy Niizawa. Rudy describes his first encounter with the boys from Hawai'i and his exchange with them—"Hey, do these boxes belong"—in his 1998 Densho interview. Yasuo Takata's experiences on Cat Island and his observation, "We didn't smell Japanese," are documented in Jason Morgan Ward, "'No Jap Crow': Japanese Americans Encounter the World War II South," *Journal of Southern History* 73, no. 1 (Feb. 2007). I have drawn many details of the Nisei soldiers' time at Shelby from a contemporaneous pamphlet, *With Hawaii's AJA Boys at Camp Shelby* (1943), written by the *Honolulu Star-Bulletin*'s reporter John Terry. Virtually all of the new Nisei soldiers at Camp Shelby talked later in life about the conflict between the Buddhaheads and the kotonks. Many of these accounts appear throughout Chang, *I Can Never Forget*. Additionally, Fred Shiosaki, in both his Densho interview and his interviews with me; Rudy Tokiwa in his Densho interview; the letters of Chaplain Higuchi and Chaplain Yamada; *The 442nd Combat Team Presents: The Album* (Atlanta: Albert Love Enterprises, 1945); and Daniel Inouye's account in his Densho interview are just a few of the many sources I drew on for telling that part of the story. Stan Akita talks in compelling detail about what it was like to grow up in a plantation town in his narrative on the Hawai'i Nisei Story site. Many details of life in the cane fields are drawn from Franklin Odo, *Voices from the Canefields: Folksongs from Japanese Immigrant Workers in Hawai'i* (New York: Oxford University Press, 2013), and Yamasaki, *Issei, Nisei, Sansei*. For more on picture brides, see the "Picture Brides" entry in the Densho Encyclopedia.

Fred Shiosaki described his first days at Shelby in my interview with him, which is the source of the "Eh, you man" comment. George Oiye's biographical information and my account of his early days at Shelby are drawn from his book *Footprints in My Rearview Mirror: An Autobiography and Christian Testimony of George Oiye* (Camarillo, Calif.: Xulon Press, 2003); his GFB interview on March 24, 2002; and an interview he gave for a student project on May 20, 2004, and published on the Telling Their Stories website. His role as quarterback on his high school's football team is documented in "Southern Six Man Grid," *Montana Standard*, Oct. 30, 1938. The quotation "Who are they?" is from his piece "Anecdotes for the 522nd," published in *High Angle*, a newsletter by and for veterans of the 522nd FAB, no date. The shootings in Arkansas are documented in Ward, "'No Jap Crow.'"

Gordon Hirabayashi relates Esther Schmoe's encounter with the laundry proprietor—"Hell no! We don't want"—in Hirabayashi, *A Principled Stand*, 139, and recounts his own encounter with the restaurant owner in Idaho in his May 4, 2000, Densho interview. He describes learning of the Supreme Court decision against him in his Feb. 10, 1981, interview with Roger Daniels. Justice Stone's words, "in time of war," are taken from his summation of *Hirabayashi v. United States* on the Oyez website. Gordon's disappointed reaction, "I thought that the *raison d'être*," is from Hirabayashi, *A Principled Stand*, 134.

My overview of the amenities and temptations available to soldiers in Hattiesburg is taken in large part from advertisements in various issues of the *Hattiesburg
American* published in the spring of 1943. Rudy's mother's injunction to Harry Madokoro, "Please take care of him," is from Rudy's 1998 Densho interview. In the same
interview, he also relates the incident with the Black American soldier, the commandeered bus ride, and the dialogue beginning with "Hey, Mac, how about." Judy Niizawa related the same anecdote to me when I interviewed her in 2017.

CHAPTER ELEVEN

The epigraph is from Hiro Higuchi's letter on the date indicated. The "Never let a
tick" anecdote is related in Dorothy Matsuo, *Boyhood to War: History and Anecdotes
of the 442nd Regimental Combat Team* (Honolulu: Mutual, 1992), 67. The nicknames
listed here came, variously, from Oiye, *Footprints in My Rearview Mirror,* 119; an
interview Harry Kanada gave on March 28, 2004, for the Japanese American Military History Collective, ndajams.omeka.net; Terry, *With Hawaii's AJA Boys at Camp
Shelby*; and my interview with Judy Niizawa. The names the 522nd FAB gave to some
of their guns are documented in *Fire for Effect: A Unit History of the 522 Field Artillery Battalion* (Honolulu: 522nd Field Artillery Battalion Historical Album Committee, 1998), 150. Both Chaplain Higuchi and Chaplain Yamada commented on the
downcast attitude of the kotonks during this period in a series of letters to their
wives. Flint Yonashiro related the "Why the hell don't youse guys" quotation and the
accompanying anecdote in my 2018 interview with him. Fred Shiosaki recounted to
me the anecdote about Captain Lesinski and the bayonet. It is also related in Matsuo,
Boyhood to War, 190. The "When this war's over" quotation is from Terry, *With Hawaii's AJA Boys at Camp Shelby.* The biographical information about Pence is from
the DePauw University Athletics Hall of Fame website and the Pence quotation
"We're going to get tough" is from a newspaper clipping with no date. See the Densho Encyclopedia entries for "Rohwer" and "Jerome" for more about the two Arkansas camps. Some of the details relating to the dance at Shelby are from "Hawaiians
Start Work After 1st Open House," *Hattiesburg American,* May 3, 1943. Others are
from Chaplain Yamada's letters to his wife, Sept. 19 and 20, 1943. The information
about training requirements is drawn from *The 442nd Combat Team Presents: The
Album.* Other details are from Terry, *With Hawaii's AJA Boys at Camp Shelby,* and
from Yamada's letter to his wife on Aug. 28, 1943. The statistics about the Nisei soldiers' performance and the Pence quotation "I'll take these men into battle" are from
Terry, *With Hawaii's AJA Boys at Camp Shelby.*

The "Japs purchased this place?" quotation is from Hirabayashi, *A Principled
Stand,* 141, and the "I'm going to make use" quotation is from *A Principled Stand,*
142. Gordon also briefly discussed the Suzuki incident in his May 4, 2002, Densho

interview. He outlined the discussions in Spokane about his traveling to Tucson in both the 1981 Daniels interview and the 1990 Horn interview. He tells of the trip south, his arrival in Tucson, and his reception at the Catalina Federal Honor Camp in Hirabayashi, *A Principled Stand*, 148–50, and in the Horn interview.

The local reaction to German POWs in Alabama and the quotation "They are fine-looking, clean-cut young fellows" are drawn in large part from "510 Prisoners of War Here to Help in Harvesting Peanuts," *Geneva County Reaper*, Sept. 9, 1943. More about the general reaction to the presence of German POWs can be found in Michael Farquhar's "Enemies Among Us: German POWs in America," *Washington Post*, Sept. 10, 1997. Details about guarding the POWs as they dug peanuts are from Whitey Yamamoto's interview with the Nishimotos and Stanley Akita's narrative on the Hawai'i Nisei Story site. Kats relates the story of Katsuaki's death in his narrative on the Hawai'i Nisei Story site and in his 2002 GFB interview. Weather and lunar information for Sept. 16, 1943, is from Dothan Regional Airport as recorded on the Weather Underground website. Some details of the accident are from "Two Nisei Killed as Truck Overturns," *Dothan Eagle*, Sept. 17, 1943. Chaplain Yamada describes the service for Katsuaki in a letter to his wife, Sept. 23, 1943. My interview with Mariko Miho gave me additional insight into her father's state of mind following his brother's death. Some of the information regarding Katsuichi Miho and the other incarcerated Hawaiian Issei is drawn from Tomi Kaizawa Knaefler, *Our House Divided: Seven Japanese American Families in World War II* (Honolulu: University of Hawai'i Press, 1995). Information about the Fort Missoula facility is from "Fort Missoula Alien Detention Center," on the Historical Museum at Fort Missoula website. Additional details are from Sigrid Arne's "Japs, Italians Don't Mix in Concentration Camp," *Sandusky Register Star News*, Aug. 3, 1942. Iwao Matsushita's role in the camp is discussed in Yasutaro Soga, *Life Behind Barbed Wire: The World War II Internment Memoirs of a Hawai'i Issei* (Honolulu: University of Hawai'i Press, 2008). My portrayal of Katsuichi's general state of mind while at Fort Missoula is based in large part on my interview with Mariko Miho. Kats describes the trip to Montana with his brother's ashes in his interview with the Nishimotos, on the Hawai'i Nisei Story site, and in his GFB interview.

CHAPTER TWELVE

The epigraph is from a letter Higuchi wrote to his wife on the date indicated and is also reprinted in Hawaii Nikkei History Editorial Board, *Japanese Eyes, American Heart*, 233. Much of the biographical information about Higuchi is from "Hiro Higuchi, How the 442nd Regimental Combat Team Brought Him Full Circle," on the 100th Infantry Battalion Veterans' Education Center website. Similarly, much of the biographical information about Masao Yamada is from "Masao Yamada, America's First

Japanese American Chaplain Served America's First All-Volunteer Japanese American Military Unit" on the same site. Additional information is from "Chaplains" on the Go for Broke National Education Center website and from the extensive correspondence of both men. Yamada's exchange with an unnamed commander—"I don't trust you"—is documented in John Tsukano, *Bridge of Love* (Honolulu: Hawaii Hosts, 1985), 65. It was Higuchi's daughter, Jane, who attested to the fact that taking the Buddhaheads to the camps was her father's idea. Kats talks about his visit to the Jerome camp in his narrative on the Hawai'i Nisei Story site. Additional details come from Daniel Inouye's account in Matsuo, *Boyhood to War*, 72–73, and Inouye's Densho interview. Yamada's comment to his wife—"They are lost"—is from an Oct. 4, 1943, letter. Inouye's comment—"You won't believe"—is reprinted in Matsuo, *Boyhood to War*, 73. Rudy's exchange with an unnamed Buddhahead—"Hey, Rudy"—is from his 1998 Densho interview.

My account of Gordon's time at the Catalina Federal Honor Camp is built from information in his interviews with Lois Horn and Roger Daniels. Additional information about the camp is from Burton et al., *Confinement and Ethnicity*. We know that the FBI was intercepting Gordon's correspondence from a partially redacted FBI report compiled by an unnamed agent dated March 31, 1944, a copy of which is in the Pacific Northwest Historical Documents collection at the University of Washington. The quotation—"Why was I put in the white barracks"—is from Hirabayashi, *A Principled Stand*, 153. The quotation from the exasperated warden—"I want this war to end"—is from the Daniels interview.

John Terry's "Moonlight flooded the meadows" passage is quoted in Matsuo, *Boyhood to War*, 128. Higuchi discusses the improving morale of the men in his letter to his wife on Nov. 26, 1943. Kats relates the pig hunt in his Hawai'i Nisei Story narrative, and it is also mentioned in Matsuo, *Boyhood to War*, 69. Mariko Miho also provided additional details. Yamada's "from the sublime to the ridiculous" comment is from his letter home on Nov. 6, 1943. The "If we should only become" remark is from Terry, *With Hawaii's AJA Boys at Camp Shelby*. Rudy's father's remark—"You chose your side"—is from "Go for Broke Memories of Real Heroes," *San Jose Mercury News*, July 29, 1983. A series of letters from both Higuchi and Yamada to their wives made frequent reference to the cold weather in Mississippi that fall and winter. Yamada related the "Before I was asleep" anecdote in a Dec. 16, 1943, letter. Higuchi quoted the unknown soldier—"Guess brother, it's just you and me now"—in a Jan. 7, 1944, letter. On Feb. 4, 1944, anticipating that he would soon be in Italy, Higuchi wrote, "Expect I had better start learning," and Yamada commented on George C. Marshall's visit to Shelby in a March 5, 1944, letter. Fred Shiosaki, in his interview with me, indicated that they all knew what Marshall's visit meant. Higuchi's injunction to his wife—"I would like to have him grow up"—is in a letter dated April 1944. His letter to his son is dated March 28, 1944. My account of the epic fight at the USO club in Virginia is based on Rudy's 1998 Densho interview, his 2001 GFB interview, and the accounts of several other Nisei soldiers who were there, the most important of which is Thomas Espineda's Jan. 30, 1999, GFB interview.

My account of the departure from Newport News and Hampton Roads is based in part on information in Reeves, *Infamy*, and McCaffrey, *Going for Broke*, 177–86; my 2016 interviews with Fred Shiosaki; Mark St. John Erickson, "Hampton Roads, Nonstop Pipeline to World War Two," *Newport News Daily Press*, June 17, 2017; and *Fire for Effect*, 31. The wording from FDR's letter—"the hope, the gratitude, the confidence"—is quoted in McCaffrey, *Going for Broke*, 177. Weather data is drawn from the Weather Underground's historical records. Yamada describes the orange peel leis and writes, "Now we knew," in a letter to his wife on May 1, 1944.

The 100th's role in the assault on Monte Cassino is described in Chester Tanaka, *Go for Broke: A Pictorial History of the Japanese American 100th Infantry Battalion and the 442d Regimental Combat Team* (Richmond, Calif.: Go for Broke, 1982), 34–36, and also "Rome-Arno (January 22–September 9, 1944)," on the Go for Broke National Education Center website. The casualty statistics are from Hawaii Nikkei History Editorial Board, *Japanese Eyes, American Heart*, 75. Tanaka notes the "little iron men" moniker in *Go for Broke*, 39. The 100th's chaplain Yost discusses the collecting of flowers in Israel A. S. Yost, *Combat Chaplain: The Personal Story of the World War II Chaplain of the Japanese American 100th Battalion* (Honolulu: University of Hawai'i Press, 2006), 144.

CHAPTER THIRTEEN

The epigraph is from Hisako Higuchi's letter to Hiro on the date indicated. We know about the note in Gordon's shoe from his own account in Hirabayashi, *A Principled Stand*, and also from the March 31, 1944, FBI report cited above. The "The cockroaches in whatever section" quotation is from Hirabayashi, *A Principled Stand*, 158. A photograph of the loyalty questionnaire can be found in the Densho Digital Repository. The "This questionnaire, which I am returning" quotation is from "Nisei Rejects Draft Board's Questionnaire," *ST*, Feb. 15, 1944. I also drew on "Failure to Return Form Charged," *Topaz Times*, July 5, 1944. Gordon discusses the concerns surrounding his marriage in his Feb. 17, 2000, Densho interview. The numbers of draft resisters in each camp are taken from the "Draft Resistance" entry in the Densho Encyclopedia.

Many of the details of the voyage to Europe are from my interviews with Fred Shiosaki. Other bits and pieces are from Minoru Masuda, *Letters from the 442nd: The World War II Correspondence of a Japanese American Medic* (Seattle: University of Washington Press, 2008), 24; from Oiye, *Footprints in My Rearview Mirror*, 127–31; and from the letters of Chaplains Yamada and Higuchi. Judy Niizawa related to me how Rudy picked up his "Punch Drunk" nickname. Rudy describes getting "gigged" in his 2001 GFB interview.

Some of the biographical information about Sus Ito is from his Dec. 11, 1991, Holocaust Museum interview; some from his July 3, 1998, Densho interview; some from the Japanese American National Museum's *Before They Were Heroes* video and profile on its website; and a great deal from his Jan. 3, 2015, interview on the Discover Nikkei website. Roy Fujii told me of the bus token in my interview with him. Sus Ito discusses the things he took with him—including the *senninbari*—in *Before They Were Heroes*. Rudy talks about the single grain of brown rice in his 1998 Densho interview. For more about the economy within the camps, see the "War Relocation Authority" entry in the Densho Encyclopedia. Rudy talks about his father's situation at Poston in his 2002 GFB interview. His position as janitor is documented in a roster titled "List of Evacuee Employees, October 1942–August 5, 1945." Information about Nisei women serving in the Women's Army Corps, the Army Nurse Corps, and the Cadet Nurse Corps is drawn from "Japanese American Women in the U.S. Military During WWII" on the GFB website; "Making a Difference: The U.S. Cadet Nurse Corps" on the National Women's History website; and "Japanese American Women in Military" on the Densho website.

Yamada discusses the incident with Chaplain West in a letter to his wife, May 21, 1944. The 522nd's arrival in Italy is described in Oiye, *Footprints in My Rearview Mirror*, 130–32, and Kats's narrative on the Hawai'i Nisei Story website. Higuchi—like nearly all the freshly arriving Nisei—commented on the plight of Italian civilians in a letter to his wife on June 4, 1944. Fred Shiosaki relates his first impression of Naples in his Densho interview. Additional colorful accounts are in Lawson Sakai's Aug. 30, 2002, GFB interview and Masuda, *Letters from the 442nd*, 26. Yamada mentions the "You are fat" remark in a June 1, 1944, letter to his wife and describes his trip into central Naples in a letter dated the day before. Kats also talks about their first days in the Naples area in his Hawai'i Nisei Story narrative. Fred Shiosaki described the trip from Naples to Anzio in his interviews with me and in his Densho interview. Some of the details of life in Anzio that spring are drawn from Ernie Pyle's magnificent *Brave Men* (New York: Henry Holt, 1944). Otherwise my account of the boys' arrival and first experiences in Anzio are based primarily on my interviews with Fred Shiosaki, Kats's interview with the Nishimotos, his narrative on the Hawai'i Nisei Story site, and Oiye, *Footprints in My Rearview Mirror*, 133. The "Hey! I dug so deep" quotation is from Yost, *Combat Chaplain*. Fred Shiosaki talks about feeling that the 100th Infantry Battalion soldiers were like big brothers in his Densho interview. This attitude is echoed in many similar interviews and accounts, prominently Rudy's 1998 Densho interview, but many other 442nd men expressed the same sentiment. Chang mentions Sus's happily inebriated state in *I Can Never Forget*, 142. Nearly all the men commented on their shock at their first sightings of dead Germans. Typical are Whitey Yamamoto's remarks in his interview with the Nishimotos.

CHAPTER FOURTEEN

The epigraph is from Harry Madokoro's letter to his mother on the date indicated. It has been published in several places, including the Discover Nikkei website. The first shot of the 522nd's engagement in the war is documented in *Fire for Effect*, 35. My account of the battle for Suvereto and the hills beyond is based, in part, on details provided by Captain Walter Lesinski in a letter written to Colonel Sherwood Dixon, the Third Battalion's commanding officer at Camp Shelby, on Aug. 20, 1944. In it, Lesinski, who was in command of K Company during the battle, complains bitterly about what he perceived as the incompetence displayed by some of his senior officers that day. My account of the 442nd's first few days of battle also draws on my 2016 interviews with Fred; his 2006 Densho interview; Rudy's 1998 Densho interview; Kats's 2002 GFB interview; *Fire for Effect*, 33–35; Masayo Umezawa Duus, *Unlikely Liberators: The Men of the 100th and 442nd* (Honolulu: University of Hawai'i Press, 1987); and Orville C. Shirey, *Americans: The Story of the 442nd Combat Team* (Washington, D.C.: Washington Infantry Journal Press, 1946). Some specifics of troop movements and casualties during these days are from monthly reports compiled by the 442nd's headquarters staff and made available online at the University of Hawai'i at Mānoa's Japanese American Veterans Collection. The events described in this chapter are recorded in the July 1944 monthly report. Additional information of a similar type is from "Battle Campaigns: Excerpts from the 442nd Journals," published on the www.ajawarvets.org website (hereafter cited as Battle excerpts). Rudy's killing of his first enemy soldier and his exchange with Major O'Connor are drawn from his Densho interview, with some added details from my interview with Judy Niizawa. He later described how sick he felt after his first battle in a letter to his high school adviser at Poston, Mrs. Mary Courage, printed in the school's newsletter, *El Bulador*, Feb. 21, 1945. Fred described the artillery barrage that left Lesinski in shell shock in his 2006 Densho interview. Higuchi's stunned summation of the day—"It's just hell"—is from a letter to his wife dated July 8, 1944. Mariko Miho informed me about Grover Nagaji's "Dear John" letter. Fred Shiosaki related Gordon Yamaura's death in our 2016 interviews.

Rudy Tokiwa talks about the survival tricks he and the other new soldiers learned from the 100th in his 2002 GFB interview. In the same interview, he discusses his foraging trips and his inability to kill a rabbit. Judy Niizawa also related other details about his fondness for foraging. Mariko Miho explained to me how important chicken *hekka*, in particular, was to the Nisei soldiers from Hawai'i. The dish is also described in Masuda, *Letters from the 442nd*, 45.

CHAPTER FIFTEEN

The raising of the American flag in Rome is described in "Flag of U.S. Capitol Flies in Rome Today," *NYT*, July 4, 1944. Some details about holiday celebrations and crowd sizes are from "Holiday Crowd on Homeward Trip Easily Handled," *NYT*, July 4, 1944. The fall of Garapan is detailed on the front page of the same issue. My description of the Fourth of July at Poston is drawn largely from the July 4, 1944, edition of the *Poston Chronicle*, which is also the source of the "They're coming home some day" and "The guys ought to get shot" quotations. For more on the general strike at Poston, see the "Poston (Colorado River)" entry in the Densho Encyclopedia. For more on the schisms within the camps, see Eric L. Muller, *Free to Die for Their Country: The Story of the Japanese American Draft Resisters in World War II* (Chicago: University of Chicago Press, 2001), 39–40. The government's concern over the situation at Poston is outlined in a pair of letters from Scott Rowley (project attorney) to Philip Glick (solicitor), War Relocation Authority, July 8, 1944, and Rowley to Ed Ferguson (acting solicitors), Nov. 6, 1944. An in-depth study of the resistance movement at Poston can be found in Eric Muller, "A Penny for Their Thoughts: Draft Resistance at the Poston Relocation Center," University of North Carolina School of Law Scholarship Repository, 2005.

For much more on conditions at Tule Lake, see the "Tule Lake" entry in the Densho Encyclopedia. The Okamoto shooting is outlined in Reeves, *Infamy*, 197–99, but my account draws many details from "Report of the Investigation Committee on the Shoichi Okamoto Incident" compiled for the Spanish embassy by a committee of incarcerated residents of the camp, with the approval of the WRA, July 3, 1944, and also from a transcript of the Modoc County Coroner's Inquest of May 25, 1944, which contains many eyewitness accounts. Some details of the subsequent court-martial proceedings are from "Sentry Found Innocent on Manslaughter Charges," *Tucson Daily Citizen*, July 7, 1944.

The battle for the approaches to Hill 140 and the assault on the hill itself left a big impression on all who survived them, and my account is based on a large number of sources, among them Kats's 2002 GFB interview; Fred's Densho interview; his interviews with me; Rudy's 2002 GFB interview; and detailed accounts in *Fire for Effect*, 35–36, Shirey, *Americans*, 36–38, and McCaffrey, *Going for Broke*, 201–5. Biographical information about Calvin and George Saito comes in part from Jay Mathews, "California Family Took Fear, Not Anger, to Camps," *Washington Post*, Dec. 6, 1991. George Saito briefly describes the circumstances of Calvin's death in a July 11, 1944, letter to his father. Kiyoji Morimoto discusses the German counterattack in a GFB interview on Feb. 29, 2002. Harry Madokoro's heroics that day are described in his Distinguished Service Cross citation and in the "Monthly Historical Report" issued by the 442nd's headquarters on Dec. 15, 1944. Ted Tanouye's similarly heroic actions are outlined in the "Ted T. Tanouye" entry on the Fallen Heroes website as well as in the documentary film *Citizen Tanouye*, Hashi Pictures, 2005.

The "time fire" barrage on Hill 140 is documented in detail in *Fire for Effect,* 117–18. The reference to Colonel Hanley jumping up and down in joy appears there and also in Matsuo, *Boyhood to War,* 102, and McCaffrey, *Going for Broke,* 203. The reference to soldiers discouraging others from viewing the gory scene at the top of the hill is from Matsuo, *Boyhood to War,* 103. Moonrise and moon phase data here and elsewhere are from the timeanddate.com site.

The letters between Calvin, George, and Kiichi Saito are gifts of Mary Saito Tominaga to the Japanese American National Museum in Los Angeles, and they are published here by permission of the museum. Rudy tells the story of first meeting Pursall and his impressions of the man in his 1998 Densho interview and his 2002 GFB interview. Judy Niizawa filled in additional details when I interviewed her, particularly in regard to the enormous influence Pursall had on how Rudy thought about problems. Rudy also relates his capture of the German officers in his 1998 Densho interview. Judy Niizawa was a participant in that interview, and she was able to provide me with additional details about that episode.

The 442nd's movements after Hill 140 are chronicled in Shirey, *Americans,* 38–42. For more on the critical role of the 442nd's engineers, see "232nd Engineer Combat Company" on the National Museum of the United States Army's website. Fred detailed his role in the attack on Luciana in his two interviews with me and also talks of it in his Densho interview. Harry Madokoro's actions at Luciana are mentioned in his Distinguished Service Cross citation and described in detail in Shirey, *Americans,* 41–42, and in the "Monthly Historical Report" issued by the 442nd's headquarters on Dec. 15, 1944. In describing the battle for Luciana, I also drew from Crost, *Honor by Fire,* 155, and Tanaka, *Go for Broke,* 54–55. Yamada describes the German POWs in a July 30, 1944, letter to his wife, including the quotation "We are of a master race!" Shirey, *Americans,* 41, mentions Lucy and includes a photograph of her. He also describes the fall of Livorno in the following several pages. Chaplain Higuchi sent his "Dear Mother of a German soldier" letter to his wife on July 25, 1944, but it is reflective of a growing awareness among American troops that the Germans were perpetrating atrocities in Italy. The figure of seventy-five hundred killed in Nazi massacres is from "SS Massacre: A Conspiracy of Silence Is Broken," *Independent,* July 2, 2004.

CHAPTER SIXTEEN

In regard to the epigraph, note that Jane Higuchi was born after Hiro left Hawai'i to serve, and so he did not meet her until his return to Hawai'i following the conclusion of the war. The heartrending letters of George, Calvin, and Kiichi Saito are housed at the Japanese American National Museum and are gifts to the museum from Mary Saito Tominaga. George's July 11, 1944, letter has been reprinted in a number of places, including in *Letters of a Nation: A Collection of Extraordinary American Letters*, Andrew Carroll, ed. (New York: Broadway Books, 1997).

Fumiye recollected her experiences in wartime Japan in her memoir and also in her interviews with the Nishimotos. Gordon discusses his wedding and his desire not to let it be well publicized in his Feb. 2000 Densho interview. Esther's "I love him" quotation is from "'I Love Him,' Says Bride of Japanese-American" in an undated newspaper clipping. The "The barriers of race" quotation is from the same article. The "attractive white girl" remark is from an Associated Press story, "White Girl Weds Japanese Youth," that appeared, among many other places, in the *Reno Gazette News,* Aug. 2, 1944. My brief portrait of Esther Schmoe is drawn in part from "'I Love Him,' Says Bride of Japanese-American," from "Hirabayashi 'Bowled Over' as Wife Has Twins," and from Jay Hirabayashi's "Remembering Gordon and Esther Hirabayashi," cited in the chapter 9 notes above. Gordon talks about the anonymous hate mail and the fifty-dollar gift in his 2000 Densho interview.

Shirey provides some details on the mission into Pisa in *Americans,* 42–43. Rudy relates his role in his March 2002 GFB interview. Judy Niizawa also provided me with additional details from notes she had taken during Rudy's retelling of it, including the "No, no, no, no, Hitler and Japan" quotation. Fred Shiosaki described the stay at Vada to me in our 2016 interviews. Additional details are from Kats's narrative on the Hawai'i Nisei Story site; from Bill Yenne, *Rising Sons: The Japanese American GIs Who Fought for the United States in World War II* (New York: Thomas Dunne Books, 2007), 119; and from assorted letters written by Chaplains Yamada and Higuchi during this time, most important, one from Higuchi to his wife on July 22, 1944, and one from Yamada to his wife on July 26, 1944. Chaplain Yost mentions listening to "Axis Sally," in *Combat Chaplain,* 139. Rudy also mentions listening to her at different times in his 1998 Densho interview, where he recalls her addressing the Nisei directly as "you little iron men." Higuchi tells the story of the soldier taking a flowering plant to the cemetery in an Aug. 14, 1944, letter to his wife.

My account of the patrol on which Harry Madokoro was killed was assembled from my interview with Judy Niizawa, from Shirey, *Americans,* 42, from the Aug. 25–26 entry in the Battle excerpts, and from an obituary/memorial posted on the Remembering Our Own: Santa Cruz Veterans Project website hosted by the Santa Cruz Public Libraries.

The 442nd's assault across the Arno, including the incident in which Chaplain Yamada was injured, is documented in the 442nd's official "Narrative of Events" for Aug. and Sept., 1944. Additional details of the assault come from Shirey, *Americans,* 49. Most of my account, though, is drawn from letters Yamada wrote to his wife about the incident on Sept. 1 and 3, 1944, and also in a letter to Colonel Dixon on Sept. 16, 1944. Rudy also discusses Yamada's brush with death in his 1998 Densho interview. Hiro Higuchi wrote to his wife on Sept. 27, 1944, talking about how solicitous of the chaplains' safety the men were.

The large-scale movement of the 442nd to southern France is documented in the regiment's official "Narrative of Events" for Sept. 1944; in Shirey, *Americans,* 51; and in Crost, *Honor by Fire.* See also McCaffrey, *Going for Broke,* 225–26. The "I can hardly wait to get back home" is from George Saito's letter to Miyoko Hayashi, Sept. 7, 1944.

CHAPTER SEVENTEEN

Oiye describes the jeep incident in *Footprints in My Rearview Mirror,* 139–40. Kats also talks about the arrival in southern France in his Hawai'i Nisei Story narrative. Yamada talks about being miserable in his pup tent and the boys offering him blankets in a Sept. 30, 1944, letter to his father. Similarly, George Saito also discusses the miserable weather in a letter to his father on Oct. 1, 1944. Esther Schmoe's payment of Gordon's bail is documented in "Bail Is Posted for Japanese," *Spokane Spokesman-Review,* Oct. 6, 1944. The memorial service for Harry Madokoro is described in the *Poston Chronicle,* Oct. 7, 1944.

The 442nd's movement north through France is detailed in the regiment's official "Narrative of Events" for Oct. 1944 and in Shirey, *Americans,* 51. The statistics here, including the two million troops and three thousand pillboxes, are from Rick Atkinson, *The Guns at Last Light: The War in Western Europe, 1944–1945* (New York: Henry Holt, 2013). Fred Shiosaki described the train trip north in the cattle cars in my interviews with him and also in his 2006 Densho interview. Kats related the 522nd's northward journey and his meeting with Inouye in his Hawai'i Nisei Story narrative. Mariko Miho shared with me more about the Miho-Inouye relationship and what it meant to Kats. More about the Thirty-sixth Infantry Division, including rosters of its men and officers, circa 1945, can be found on the Texas Military Forces Museum website. Inouye's first impression of the Vosges is documented in Hughes, "Fred Shiosaki." The letters between George and Kiichi Saito are both from Oct. 14, 1944. The 522nd's entry into the battle for the Vosges is detailed in a battalion newsletter article, "522d Fought Five Months in France," *High Angle,* July 14, 1945.

McCaffrey talks of Higuchi's prebattle service in *Going for Broke,* 241. The "You are already good Americans" quotation is from a biography of Higuchi on the Japanese American Veterans Association website. The battle for Bruyères is recounted in Shirey, *Americans,* 51–58; the regiment's official narrative for Oct. 1944; and in considerable detail in Pierre Moulin, *U.S. Samuraïs in Bruyères* (France: Peace & Freedom Trail, 1993), translated from the French edition, *U.S. samuraïs en Lorraine* (Vagney, France: Gérard Louis, 1988). Higuchi describes seeing George Saito's body—"A boy came in without"—in a letter to his wife on Oct. 18, 1944. Kiichi Saito's letter to George in which he says, "Three weeks passed since," was written on Nov. 4, 1944, a week after

George's death. The Third Battalion's direct assault on Bruyères is described in Mc-Caffrey, *Going for Broke*, 246–47, Shirey, *Americans*, 56, and Chang, *I Can Never Forget*, 30. Additional details are from Masi Okumura, "I Remember Company L 442nd RCT 1943–1945," an unpublished typescript, and from my interviews with Fred Shiosaki and his 2006 Densho interview. Rudy Tokiwa mentions the villagers thinking the Nisei must be Chinese in his 1998 Densho interview and talks about them greeting the Nisei soldiers with kisses in his 2001 GFB interview. Fred talks about the woman with soda pop in his Densho interview and in my interview with him. George Oiye talks about entering the town and mentions the woman with the broom in Oiye, *Footprints in My Rearview Mirror*, 140–42, and in his 2002 GFB interview. The 442nd's push beyond Bruyères is documented in the official narratives for Oct. 1944 and in Shirey, *Americans*, 58–62. The Ohama atrocity is described in Chang, *I Can Never Forget*, 34. The shooting of the high-ranking German officer is related in Chang, *I Can Never Forget*, 33, and in McCaffrey, *Going for Broke*, 251–52. The "I hope you don't get mad" quotation is from Rudy's 1998 Densho interview, as is the "I wonder" quotation. Judy Niizawa also spoke to me about Rudy's concern that the war might dehumanize him.

The incidents surrounding the awakening of first the Second Battalion and then the Third are related in Shirey, *Americans*, 58–63. In his June 3, 2001, GFB interview, Rudy also describes the situation and says it was he who was told to go wake up the K Company boys. Fred recounted the moment in both his 1998 Densho interview and his 2016 interviews with me.

CHAPTER EIGHTEEN

The epigraph is from Yamada writing to Colonel Sherwood Dixon, Oct. 30, 1944, quoted in C. Douglas Sterner, *Go for Broke: The Nisei Warriors of World War II Who Conquered Germany, Japan, and American Bigotry* (Clearfield, Utah: American Legacy Historical Press, 2015), 53. The biographical information about Dahlquist is drawn from "John Ernest Dahlquist," on the Arlington National Cemetery website, from the "John E. Dahlquist" entry in the Densho Encyclopedia, and from an article titled "100th Bn Losses Attributed to Poor Leadership," *Hawaii Herald*, July 16, 1982, posted on the Hawai'i Nisei Story website. The Young Oak Kim incident is drawn from Chang, *I Can Never Forget*, 30.

Several books focus to a large degree on the battle that is the subject of this chapter, and I have drawn on all of them, along with many firsthand accounts, for my telling of the rescue of the Lost Battalion. Among the most important of these are Major Nathan K. Watanabe, *The 110/442D Regimental Combat Team's Rescue of the Lost Battalion: A Study in the Employment of Battle Command* (BiblioScholar, 2012); Scott McGaugh, *Honor Before Glory: The Epic World War II Story of the Japanese American*

GIs Who Rescued the Lost Battalion (Boston: Da Capo Press, 2016); and Sterner, *Go for Broke*. For the initial attempts to reach the Texans, I have relied largely on Watanabe, *Lost Battalion;* Shirey, *Americans;* McCaffrey, *Going for Broke;* and Sterner, *Go for Broke;* as well as Crost, *Honor by Fire,* 191–93, the regiment's official narrative for Oct. 1944, and the firsthand recollections of Fred Shiosaki and Rudy Tokiwa in their respective Densho interviews.

Fred Shiosaki described the night climb into the mountains and the subsequent fighting both in my interviews with him and in his Densho interview. Sus Ito explains the difficulties the 522nd had in bringing effective fire to bear on the German positions in the Vosges in *Fire for Effect,* 86. McGaugh's *Honor Before Glory* focuses on the rescue of the Lost Battalion, and he gives excellent and detailed accounts of the Texans' plight, in particular from the point of view of Marty Higgins, throughout the siege. Matsuichi Yogi's heroics are outlined in his Distinguished Cross citation available online at the Hall of Valor Project website. George Oiye relates his almost accidental capture of a German soldier in *Footprints in My Rearview Mirror,* 114, and in his March 24, 2002, GFB interview. Rudy narrates his participation in the quest to rescue the Texans in his 2001 GFB interview, his 2002 GFB interview, and his 1998 Densho interview. For more on the conditions James Okubo and the other medics faced, see Masuda, *Letters from the 442nd,* 110. My account of the failed attempt to deliver supplies to the Texans with airdrops is drawn mostly from McGaugh, *Honor Before Glory;* McCaffrey, *Going for Broke;* and Watanabe, *Lost Battalion*. Kats discussed filling projectile points with supplies in his interview with the Nishimotos, and this is also documented in Shirey, *Americans;* McGaugh, *Honor Before Glory;* and a number of firsthand accounts. McGaugh mentions the mortally wounded soldier calling out, *"Okaasan, okaasan,"* on p. 140. Some of the men who were there that night also recalled hearing a German soldier calling out for help until he died toward morning. Higuchi's wavering faith was much on his mind that Oct. The "Going back to the pulpit" quotation is from a letter to his wife on Oct. 6, 1944. His "It's either you kill or get killed" quotation is from his biography on the Japanese American Veterans Association website, as is the "What is God to me?" quotation.

Dahlquist's "Let's keep them moving" quotation is from McGaugh, *Honor Before Glory,* 141. The oft-repeated "Come on, Punch Drunk, let's go" wording is from Rudy's 1998 Densho interview. My account of the subsequent confrontation between Pursall and Dahlquist is drawn from a variety of sources but predominantly Rudy's retelling in his Densho and GFB interviews. Wells Lewis's death is recounted in McCaffrey, *Going for Broke;* McGaugh, *Honor Before Glory;* Moulin, *U.S. Samuraïs in Bruyères;* and many firsthand accounts, with only minor variations. The "Lewis is dead" quotation attributed to Dahlquist is from McGaugh, *Honor Before Glory,* 149. The final exchange between Pursall and Dahlquist, ending with "Those are my boys you're trying to kill," is drawn from Rudy's Densho interview. The "I don't know. I'm not the boss" quotation is from Rudy's 2001 GFB interview. McCaffrey quotes Chester Tanaka—"My God! If that dumb"—in *Going for Broke*, 266, as does Crost in *Honor by Fire*, 193. Fred Shiosaki's next thoughts and actions are largely drawn from my interviews with him and his Densho interview. George Oiye's are drawn from his 2002 GFB interview. Pursall's exclamation—"There's the man!"—is from Yuki Minaga's narrative of events in *Fire for Effect*, 176. The *"Make! Make! Make!"* quotation is from McGaugh, *Honor Before Glory*, 158. Oiye talks about temporarily losing his hearing in *Footprints in My Rearview Mirror*, 146. Fred's state of mind during the charge and the "God, I'm hit" quotation are from his Densho interview and my interviews with him, as is his "Well, say goodbye to your mother" quotation. Orville Shirey describes the retreat of the Germans in a letter to Colonel Dixon, Nov. 30, 1944. Rudy relates his post-battle conversation with Pursall—"Hey, Colonel, you coulda got shot"—in his 1998 Densho interview. The losses in K Company are detailed in McGaugh, *Honor Before Glory*, 167. Rudy narrates the death of his replacement and the "Oh yeah. Look in the foxhole" quotation in his 1998 Densho interview. Kats talks about the consternation caused by Dahlquist calling in the wrong coordinates in his Jan. 20, 2002, GFB interview. Captain Billy Taylor also discusses the incident in considerable detail in a letter dated Aug. 5, 1987, in the Ted Tsukiyama Papers at the University of Hawai'i. McGaugh, *Honor Before Glory*, 172, describes the German smoke screen. My account of the breakthrough to the Lost Battalion is drawn from Chang, *I Can Never Forget*, 54–55, and from Edward Guy's Aug. 7, 2004, GFB interview, which is also the source of the "Do you need any cigarettes?" quotation; from contemporaneous newsreels; from a letter Yamada wrote to Colonel Dixon, Nov. 1, 1944; from McGaugh, *Honor Before Glory*; from McCaffrey, *Going for Broke*; and from Masuda, *Letters from the 442nd*, 111. The "Hey, the 442 guys are here!" quotation is from Moulin, *U.S. Samuraïs in Bruyères*, 108. The Higgins quotation, "Honestly, they looked like giants" can be found in Mc-Gaugh, *Honor Before Glory*, 180. The "Hey, kids. Some balls" quotation is from Moulin, *U.S. Samuraïs in Bruyères*, 109.

CHAPTER NINETEEN

The epigraph is from Higuchi's Christmas Eve letter to his wife in 1944. The eviction of Private Matsuda from the barbershop in Parker, Arizona, and Andy Hale's remarks beginning with "I don't want none of their business" are reported in "Wounded Nisei Reported Shoved out of Shop," *LAT*, Nov. 11, 1944, and "Wounded Nisei War Veteran Ejected from Barber Shop," *Pacific Citizen*, Nov. 18, 1944. Rudy's mother confessed her painful early morning shower ritual to Rudy after the war. The "It really was ironical" quotation is from "442nd Unit Saves 'Lost Battalion,'" *Poston Chronicle*, Nov. 11, 1944.

The 442nd's battle action immediately following the rescue of the Lost Battalion is detailed in the regiment's official narrative for Nov. 1944. The numbers of survivors from K Company and I Company are from Shirey, *Americans,* 71, and are also mentioned in the Hughes portrait of Fred Shiosaki. My brief sketch of Virgil Miller is drawn primarily from Joy Teraoka's "Memories of Col. Virgil Miller," on the 100th Infantry Battalion website. Rudy recounts Dahlquist's review of the survivors in his 1998 Densho interview. That is also where the "Colonel, I told you" quotation is drawn from. The "General, this *is* the regiment" quotation is from Daniel Inouye's Densho interview. Others who were there, including Chaplain Yamada, recalled seeing tears in the colonel's eyes, though some remember Pursall rather than Miller being the colonel in question. Some details of the scene are also drawn from the iconic photograph in this chapter, of the four Nisei soldiers presenting the colors that day.

The number of service men and women from Poston and information about casualties are drawn from a series of articles in the *Poston Chronicle,* Nov. 12–Dec. 12, 1944. Similar stories appeared in *The Pacific Citizen* and the other camp newspapers as well during this period of time. A wide variety of the extraordinary artworks and handicrafts people created while incarcerated at Poston and other camps can be seen in the Densho Digital Repository as well as at the Japanese American Museum in Los Angeles and in the collections of a number of other institutions. For an interesting article about just one particular craft, see "Gaman and the Story of the Bird Pins" on the Smithsonian American Art Museum website. My discussion of the Roosevelt administration's decision to close the camps is based primarily on the "Franklin D. Roosevelt" entry in the Densho Encyclopedia.

The Oct. 1944 casualty figures are taken from Watanabe, *Lost Battalion,* and McCaffrey, *Going for Broke,* 271. George Oiye describes the trip up into the mountains above the Riviera in *Footprints in My Rearview Mirror,* 141, and it is also described by a number of the 522nd men in *Fire for Effect,* most notably on p. 174, where they relate their trouble with the recalcitrant mules. Kats talks about his experiences on the Riviera at some length in his Nishimoto interviews and on the Hawai'i Nisei Story website, including his experience at Studio Erpé. The "Hey, Rosie, Captain wants" quotation and the subsequent dialogue are from Fred Shiosaki's Densho interview. A number of details concerning the "Champagne Campaign" are drawn from *Fire for Effect,* 191–94.

Higuchi wrote at length about the Dec. 18, 1944, Christmas party in a letter to his wife the following day. Yamada detailed the Dec. 23 festivities in a letter to his wife dated that same day, and Higuchi described the Dec. 24 candlelight service to his wife in a letter written later that night.

CHAPTER TWENTY

The epigraph is from a Feb. 14, 1945, letter to his wife in which Higuchi continued to wrestle with his faith.

Much of my account of Solly Ganor's life and experience is drawn from his very moving autobiography, *Light One Candle: A Survivor's Tale from Lithuania to Jerusalem* (New York: Kodansha International, 1995), but I gleaned additional details from Solly's April 27, 1993, interview with the Holocaust Museum and from the text of a speech he gave at the University of Hawai'i and at Temple Emanu-El in Honolulu on Nov. 21, 1995. The "No. They will stay in their underwear!" quotation and the following horrifying dialogue are drawn from Ganor, *Light One Candle,* 66–68. For more on the Kovno ghetto, see the "Kovno" entry in the Holocaust Encyclopedia on the Holocaust Museum's website. The "Your mother just died!" quotation is from Ganor, *Light One Candle,* 316.

My account of Gordon's arrival and stay at McNeil is based primarily on his Feb. 10, 1981, interview with Roger Daniels. Some details are from an AP story, "Hirabayashi Taken to McNeil Island," *Klamath Falls Herald and News,* Dec. 28, 1944. My discussion of the prosecution of the Nisei draft resisters is based on two principal sources: the "Draft Resistance" entry in the Densho Encyclopedia and Eric Muller's *Free to Die for Their Country,* 100–112 and 124–46. The "You Jap boys" quotation is taken from Muller, 104, and the "It is shocking" quotation is from Muller, *Free to Die for Their Country,* 143. Much of the background information about the MIS is drawn from the "Military Intelligence Service" entry in the Densho Encyclopedia. The "We simply want" quotation is from "Legion Erases Names of Nisei," *Spokane Spokesman-Review,* Dec. 2, 1944, as is the "Get your heart in America" quotation. The story of what happened in Hood River was published in papers large and small around the country that December. For more background about the incident, see the "Hood River Incident" entry in the Densho Encyclopedia.

Biographical information about Frank Hachiya is drawn from the "Frank Hachiya (1920–1945)" entry in the online Oregon Encyclopedia website. I should note that there is a different version of the Hachiya story. On May 21, 1963, Senator Hiram Fong read into the Congressional Record a version of events in which Hachiya had been dropped behind enemy lines on Leyte a month before the invasion and was making his way to meet the invading Americans with maps of the Japanese defenses when he was shot. It's possible this was the case and that his true role was classified and kept from the press at the time. However, the date of Hachiya's shooting was more than two months following the invasion, so I have not used that account, dramatic as it is. For much more on the Hood River incident, and the source of the headlines I quote here, see the corresponding entry in the Densho Encyclopedia. Some additional details are drawn from an analysis written by the War Relocation Authority, "Prejudice in the Hood River Valley, a Case Study in Race Relations," June 6, 1945, available in the archives of the State Library of Oregon. Figures related to the service of Nisei women are from "Japanese American Women in World War II" on the Japanese American Veterans Association website.

Some information about the Doi family is from the 1940 federal census. Additional information about the family's return to California, the assault on their property, and the subsequent trial is from "Sumio Doi, First to Arrive," *Auburn Journal*, Jan. 11, 1945; "Arrests Are Made in Japanese House Fire and Dynamiting," *Auburn Journal*, Feb. 1, 1945; "Jury Frees Terror Raiders," *Auburn Journal*, April 26, 1945; Gary Noy, *Red Dirt: A Journey of Discovery in the Landscape of Imagination* (San Jose, Calif.: Writers Club Press, 2002); and Shibutani, *Derelicts of Company K*, 67.

The skirmishes and sporadic battles the Nisei fought in the mountains above the Riviera that winter are detailed in an official "442nd Infantry Battle Casualty Report—January 1-31," a copy of which can be found on the 442nd Regimental Combat Team Legacy website. George Oiye discusses his delight in helping to take out the big German railroad gun in Oiye, *Footprints in My Rearview Mirror*, 149-50, as well as in his GFB interview.

I am indebted to Mariko Miho for sharing with me her father's state of mind here and throughout the war. George Oiye describes the 522nd's redeployment to northern France in Oiye, *Footprints in My Rearview Mirror*, 151, and both chaplains discussed it in their letters home that month. The mystery that surrounded the 442nd's next mission comes up in Masuda, *Letters from the 442nd*, 173, in Crost, *Honor by Fire*, 235, and in Shirey, *Americans*, 76.

CHAPTER TWENTY-ONE

The epigraph is from Yamada's letter on the date indicated, at which point he was reflecting on what had just transpired on the Gothic Line.

The statistics regarding the firebombing of Tokyo are drawn from Brad Lendon and Emiko Jozuka, "History's Deadliest Air Raid Happened in Tokyo During World War II and You've Probably Never Heard of It," CNN.com, March 8, 2020. My account of Gordon Hirabayashi's encounter with the prison authorities at McNeil is drawn primarily from his interview with Roger Daniels, as is the exchange beginning with "Get your stuff."

The 522nd's entry into Germany is documented in Crost, *Honor by Fire*, 239, as well as in a very detailed time line on p. 11 of *Fire for Effect*. Moonlight conditions for the night in question are again from timeanddate.com. George Oiye recounts his harrowing experience in the minefield that night in Oiye, *Footprints in My Rearview Mirror*, 151-52, and in a draft article he wrote for *High Angle*, attached to a letter from Oiye to Ted Tsukiyama on Feb. 5, 1998, and housed in the Ted Tsukiyama Papers at the University of Hawai'i, Mānoa. The incident with the soldier who stepped on a mine is also documented in *Fire for Effect*, 169.

Fred Shiosaki talked of his trouble with seasickness, in this instance and others, in my 2016 interviews with him. In his Densho interview, he discusses their arrival in Livorno, General Clark's eagerness to have them back in the Fifth Army, the issuance of equipment, and the secrecy surrounding their movements. The Mark Clark quotation, "The courage and determination," is drawn from a letter from Clark to Colonel Pence on Sept. 7, 1944. Michael E. Haskew explains the larger context of the 442nd's mission in "Breaching the Gothic Line," on the Warfare History Network website, as does Shirey, *Americans*, 78. Fred described the movement into Azzano in both his Densho interview and his interviews with me, though he did not recall the name of the village. The same movements are recounted in great detail in the Battle excerpts cited above for the relevant dates. Masaharu Okumura described the stay in Azzano, with particular reference to the pancakes, in "I Remember Co. L 442nd RCT 1943–1945," an unpublished typescript, 1995. Crost, *Honor by Fire*, 252–53, mentions the boys rubbing soot on their faces and other prebattle details.

The "If you fall" quotation can be found in McCaffrey, *Going for Broke*, 301. My account of the climb up the back side of Monte Folgorito is drawn principally from Shirey, *Americans*, 82–83; Chang, *I Can Never Forget*, 125; a letter from Yamada to his wife on April 19, 1945; and the Battle excerpts cited above. The "At ten to five" quotation is from a letter from Yamada to his wife on April 10, 1945. Fred detailed the inauspicious start of K Company's assault on the mountain in his Densho interview and his two interviews with me. Additional details are from the regiment's official narrative for April 1945; McCaffrey, *Going for Broke*, 302; and Shirey, *Americans*, 83.

Rudy talks about his relationship with Sadao Munemori in his 2001 GFB interview. See also Sterner, *Go for Broke*, 109–10. Details of Munemori's extraordinary actions that day can be found in many places, but I have relied primarily on Shirey, *Americans*, 83; Munemori's Medal of Honor citation; Chang, *I Can Never Forget*; Tanaka, *Go for Broke*, 123; the Battle excerpts; and Ben M. Tamashiro's "From Pearl Harbor to the Po, the Congressional Medal of Honor: Sadao Munemori," *Hawaii Herald*, March 15, 1985, republished on the Hawai'i Nisei Story site. Judy Niizawa explained to me the extent of Rudy's wounds and his uncertainty about exactly where he was when he suffered them.

CHAPTER TWENTY-TWO

The 522nd's drive into Germany is very well documented by a number of firsthand accounts in *Fire for Effect*, 51–65, and a very useful map on p. 76 indicating the battalion's headquarters' location on specific dates. For tracing the unit's large-scale movements, I have also drawn on Oiye's account in Oiye, *Footprints in My Rearview Mirror*, 151–56, and Kats's recollections in both his Hawai'i Nisei Story narrative and his 1989 Holocaust Museum interview. Flint Yonashiro, with much glee, told me of the chicken-rustling expeditions he and Kats made on multiple occasions. In his Hawai'i Nisei Story narrative, Kats talks at some length about the booty the boys found in the German warehouse. Oiye also talks about it, more briefly, in Oiye, *Foot-*

prints in My Rearview Mirror, 153. The reference to top hats and tails is in *Fire for Effect,* 175. Mention of the two nude young women is made in *Fire for Effect,* 177. Kats tells of finding young women with stars pinned to their clothing in his 2002 GFB interview. Additional details are from Wayne Muromoto, "The 522nd and Dachau: The Men of the 522nd Encounter the Holocaust," *Hawaii Herald,* March 19, 1993.

Rudy discusses his experiences at the replacement depot at length in his 2002 GFB interview. Judy Niizawa also provided me with additional details about this period of Rudy's life. My account of the action in which Daniel Inouye was wounded is based primarily on his 1998 Densho interview and his Medal of Honor citation. The "Nobody called off the war!" quotation is from "Daniel Inouye: A Japanese American Soldier's Valor in World War II" on the National Park Service website. The tragedy when a shell hit the mine shaft where Lloyd Onoye was sheltering is documented in the April 1945 Battle excerpts cited above. Judy Niizawa, in her interview with me, provided additional details about this incident. The battle for Tendola and the surrounding area is documented in the regiment's official "Narrative of Events" for April 1945. Some of the descriptions of the terrain and the town are drawn from my own observations during an April 2019 visit to the area. Mario Pomini's dramatic account of the death of a Nisei soldier who was shot in the back was told to me and others and translated on the fly by Mario Mariani. We do not know the name of the Nisei soldier whose death Mario Pomini witnessed, but based on casualty reports for that day, it might have been either Private First Class Takashi Ito or Private First Class James S. Okamoto. Tadao "Beanie" Hayashi's death is recounted in "WWII Vet Lived for Slain Comrade," *Honolulu Star-Bulletin,* Sept. 11, 2014, and his death is noted in the *Poston Chronicle,* May 12, 1945. In both his Densho interview and his two interviews with me, Fred talked about escorting the German POW and the temptation he felt to shoot him. The Densho interview is the source of the dialogue beginning with "Fred, you take Pete back."

CHAPTER TWENTY-THREE

The epigraph is from Oiye, *Footprints in My Rearview Mirror,* 155. My account of the forced march from Lager Ten and the arrival at Dachau is drawn primarily from Ganor, *Light One Candle,* 335–38, with some details from Solly's April 27, 1993, Holocaust Museum interview. The 522nd's movement toward Bavaria is chronicled on the time line in *Fire for Effect,* 11, along with firsthand accounts scattered throughout that book. Some of the details are from Kats's Hawaiʻi Nisei Story narrative. The relatively rapid advance of the 442nd toward and into Genoa is chronicled in great detail in Shirey, *Americans,* 86–91. Sus Ito, in his Dec. 11, 1991, Holocaust Museum interview also describes the movement and the collapse of the German army in front of them. Details of the scene in Genoa are from Masuda, *Letters from the 442nd,* 201.

My account of what came to be called "the death march" out of Dachau is drawn primarily from Ganor, *Light One Candle*, 339–43, with additional details drawn from Solly's 1993 Holocaust Museum interview and his 1995 speech in Hawai'i. My account of the liberation of Dachau is based on a number of sources, not all of which agree with one another in some particulars, but I have put the most weight on Felix Sparks's account in his monograph, "Dachau and Its Liberation," written on 157th Infantry Association letterhead, March 20, 1984, a copy of which is in the University of Hawai'i Special Collections. The movement of the 442nd's headquarters as outlined in *Fire for Effect*, 11, along with the map on p. 76, indicates that the Nisei artillerymen were in the vicinity of the main camp as early as the afternoon of April 29, but there is scant evidence that they were among those who first breached its perimeter. It appears to be the case, though, that at least a few Nisei soldiers did enter the camp at some point that day, as per the recollection of Josef Erbs as recounted in *Fire for Effect*, 63, and Chang, *I Can Never Forget*, 168, and the account of Toshio Nishizawa in "The Liberation of Dachau" on the 100th Infantry Battalion's website. I have also given a good deal of attention to an academic paper, Linda K. Menton's "Research Report: Nisei Soldiers at Dachau, Spring 1945," housed in the University of Hawai'i Special Collections. There is no question that before, while, and after the main Dachau camp was being liberated, the Nisei soldiers came across and, in some cases, entered or opened a number of sub-camps of the larger Dachau complex. For documentation of these incidents, see *Fire for Effect*, 61–70; Tadashi Tojo's account, "Dachau-1945," in the University of Hawai'i Special Collections; Wayne Muromoto's compilation of accounts in "The 522nd and Dachau," *Hawaii Herald*, March 19, 1993; Knaefler, *Our House Divided*, 40; "522 Liberates Dachau Prisoners," on the Hawaii Nisei Veterans' website; Kats Miho's narrative on the same site; Minoru "Min" Tsubota's Aug. 18, 2003, Densho interview; Melissa Tanji, "Nisei Veteran Recounts WWII Memories of Dachau," *Maui News*, Nov. 8, 2015; McCaffrey, *Going for Broke*, 317–18; and Joseph Ichijui's June 16, 1997, Holocaust Museum interview.

My account of the rescue of Solly Ganor and the death march survivors is again drawn principally from Ganor, *Light One Candle*, 344–49, with additional details from his April 27, 1993, Holocaust Museum interview, along with the personal accounts of Kats Miho in his 2002 Holocaust Museum interview; Sus Ito, in his 1991 Holocaust Museum interview; Oiye, *Footprints in My Rearview Mirror*, 155; and *Fire for Effect*, 68. It should also be noted that another survivor of the death march, Larry Lubetzky, gave an account very similar to Solly's and credited Sus Ito specifically with his salvation. His account can be found in *Fire for Effect*, 66–67, and in Ito's July 3, 1998, Densho interview. On June 27, 1945, Lubetzky sent a grateful telegram to Ito: "I hope you will even remember me being at your home back [*sic*]. You, as one of the U.S. Army have your part in delivering us from our suffering in the God damned Germany. Thank you!" His son, Daniel, published a photograph of the telegram and an accompanying story, "Kind Snacks Founder: The Japanese American Hero Who Saved My Family," CNN.com, April 29, 2020. Both Oiye and Ito subsequently took pictures of the liberated prisoners, and some of those can be viewed online in the Densho digital repository. The dialogue beginning with "You are free, boy" is from Ganor, *Light One Candle*, 346–47.

CHAPTER TWENTY-FOUR

Headlines like the *NYT*'s on May 2, 1945, BERLIN FALLS TO RUSSIANS, brought millions of Americans the most welcome news they had heard in more than four years. Five days later stories like that with the Associated Press's glorious lede "The greatest war in history ended today" on May 7 brought them even happier news. Many of the details I include in my account of the celebrations on those heady days are drawn from these two articles. Kats Miho, in his Hawai'i Nisei Story narrative, and Sus Ito, in his 1991 Holocaust Museum interview, talk about the desperate condition of the Dachau survivors and the traumatic effect that witnessing their suffering had on them. Hiro Higuchi's reaction to the end of the war, and that of the men he addressed, is documented in Loni Ding's film, *Nisei Soldier: Standard Bearer for an Exiled People*, produced by the Center for Asian American Media, 1984, and in considerable detail in a letter from Higuchi to his wife on May 8, 1945. Fred described his response "Jeez. Well, I made it" in both his interviews with me and his Densho interview. The WAR ON JAPS CONTINUES headline is from the same May 7 Associated Press story cited above. Kats's quotation, "Eh! Take it easy!" is from his narrative on the Hawai'i Nisei Story site.

For examples of the relentless stream of casualty reports reaching Poston (like other camps) in the days and weeks following the end of the war, see *Poston Chronicle*, May 5, 9, 12, and 16, 1945. The "There never was and never will be a Jap" quotation is from Geoffrey Dunn's "Forgotten Documents Reveal Views on Return of Japanese Internees to Monterey Peninsula," *Monterey Herald*, Nov. 9, 2013. The text of the threatening bulletin itself can be read in "Organization to Discourage Return of Japanese to the Pacific Coast," *Monterey Peninsula Herald*, April 23, 1945. The rejoinders, including the "These families have made their homes" quotation, with Steinbeck, Jeffers, and the others mentioned as signatories, appear in the *Monterey Peninsula Herald*, May 11, 1945.

Shirey traces the movements of the 442nd in Italy following the surrender in *Americans*, 93–98. Kats in his Hawai'i Nisei Story narrative, and George Oiye in Oiye, *Footprints in My Rearview Mirror*, 156–58, discuss the 522nd's activities in and around Donauwörth. Some of the details of Fumiye Miho's experiences leading up to and following the bombing of Hiroshima are documented in "Honolulu Is Home Sweet Home After Hiroshima," *Honolulu Advertiser*, April 13, 1947. But the bulk of my information here came from a series of interviews Fumiye did with Michi Kodama-Nishimoto in the summer of 2000, Fumiye's unpublished memoir, and her recorded talk delivered at the Friends Meeting House in Honolulu in 1992. Mariko Miho also filled in some crucial details in my interview with her. Some information about conditions surrounding the bombing, including the weather that day, is drawn from Pamela Rotner Sakamoto's *Midnight in Broad Daylight: A Japanese American Family Caught Between Two Worlds* (New York: HarperPerennial, 2016), 300–392.

The arrival of the first wave of 442nd soldiers returning to Hawai'i is covered in "Honolulu Acclaims 442nd," *Honolulu Star-Bulletin*, Aug. 9, 1945, and "Huge Crowd Greets 442nd at Ceremonies at Iolani Palace Grounds," *Honolulu Star-Bulletin*, Aug. 9, 1945. My account of V-J Day is drawn from Aug. 14 and 15, 1945, issues of newspapers around the country, including the *NYT*, the *ST*, and the *LAT*. A lengthy letter Hisako Higuchi wrote to Hiro on Aug. 16 is the source for my description of the reaction in her household and her neighborhood in Pearl City, including Peter Higuchi's quotation, "Now, Mama, we can have metal," and those that follow.

Fred recounted his journey home, including his encounter with one of the Texans and the exchange that followed, "Hey, you're with the 442nd," in his interviews with me and his Densho interview. He also describes his reception at home, and the dialogue quoted there, in his Densho interview. Rudy recounts his journey home, the incident with the Red Cross woman in San Jose, and his reunion with his family in his 1998 Densho interview. The ceremony in which Rudy received his Bronze Star is documented in "Utah Soldier Honored at Italy Ceremony," *Pacific Citizen*, June 9, 1945. Rudy discusses his feelings surrounding that event in his 2002 GFB interview, which is also the source of his "it's coming out to be" quotation.

Kats discusses his homeward journey and the Frank Sinatra incident in his Hawai'i Nisei Story narrative. Some details about the arrival in Honolulu are drawn also from "432 Soldiers and 46 Civilians Arrive Aboard Mexico," *Honolulu Star-Bulletin*, Jan. 15, 1946. Mariko Miho also provided me with additional information about her father's return, his emotions, the state of the family, and their reunion. Roy Fujii related the anecdote about the bus token to me when I interviewed him in Honolulu in 2019.

EPILOGUE

The Conrad Tsukayama epigraph is quoted from Hawaii Nikkei History Editorial Board, *Japanese Eyes, American Heart,* 28. The 442nd is often credited with having been awarded more decorations than any other units of its size and length of service. That very well may be true. I have qualified the statement just a bit here after conferring with Brian Niiya, the historian at Densho, only because it is a very difficult statement to prove empirically. As Brian points out, the statement began to be made in reference to the 100th Infantry Battalion in the fall of 1944 and then broadened out to include the entire 442nd RCT. Although it is beyond doubt that the entire regiment won a disproportionate number of honors during World War II, I have not seen a statistical, side-by-side analysis proving that no other unit ever received more. The awarding of Sadao Munemori's Medal of Honor was written up in "Nation's Highest Honor Given Japanese American Who Gave Life to Save Comrades in Italy," *Pacific Citizen*, March 16, 1946. The medal counts are from "Hall of Honor Statistics," on the Go for Broke National Education Center website. Some of my information about the Hunt Hotel is derived from Aubrey Cohen's "Japanese Center Holds Memories of Hunt Hotel," *Seattle Post-Intelligencer*, June 8, 2007. The Truman quotation—"These disgraceful actions"—appears in a number of sources, including the "Harry S. Truman" entry in the Densho Encyclopedia. That is also the source of the "You fought not only the enemy" quotation. My summary of the postwar treatment of the Nisei draft resisters is drawn primarily from the "Draft Resistance" and the "JACL Apology to Draft Resisters" entries in the Densho Encyclopedia.

Fred discussed his difficulties upon returning home in his 1998 Densho interview as well as in the interviews I conducted with him. The "You were screaming again" quotation is from the Densho interview, as is the "a bunch of Japs" quotation. I learned more about Lily Nakai from an obituary published by the Harvey Family Funeral Home in 2016. The "dirty rotten Japs" quotation is from the Hughes portrait, as is the "By God, you had a piece of this" quotation. Some of the detail regarding the Shiosakis' later lives is derived from email correspondence between me and Michael Shiosaki and from Patricia Bayonne-Johnson's online article "Northwest Railroad Pioneer Kisaburo Shiosaki" on the 4comculture.com website. Additional information about the laundry—and the "a 6-foot, 8-inch lumberjack" quotation— is from Stefanie Pettit's "Hillyard Laundry Building Has Colorful Past," *Spokane Spokesman-Review*, Dec. 11, 2008.

The characterizations of Rudy's state of mind when he returned home, including the nightmares, are drawn from my interview with Judy Niizawa and Judy's Dec. 30, 1995, interview with Rudy's sister Fumi Tokiwa Futamase. My recap of the rest of Rudy's life is also largely drawn from my interview with Judy along with Rudy's own account in his 1998 Densho interview and an earlier Densho interview on Sept. 13, 1997. Judy was an active partner with Rudy as they participated in the national redress movement, so she was able to provide me with a great deal of information about that as well as about Rudy's struggles with the aftereffects of his injuries. The "We're going to take the hill" quotation is from the *Salinas Californian*, July 27, 1987. The "What the hell are you sons of bitches" quotation and my account of the events surrounding it are from Rudy's 1997 Densho interview. The "carried out without adequate security reasons" language is quoted from the Civil Liberties Act of 1988 and can be found in a Densho Encyclopedia entry by the same name, authored by Sharon Yamoto. Rudy's "I think my job has been done" quotation is from his 2002 GFB interview.

Kats talks about his aimlessness when he returned to Hawai'i in his Hawai'i Nisei Story narrative. In my interview with her, Mariko Miho gave me much of the same information and also shared with me some of how her mother and father met, courted, and were married. She was also the source of much of my information about Kats's political career. The vote tally for the statehood referendum is from *The Island Edge of America*, 290. Some of my paraphrasing of Hawaiian political history is derived from the same source, 351–55. My account of the first meeting of the Hawai'i state legislature is drawn in large part from "State Legislators Well Aware They're Making Island History," *Honolulu Star-Bulletin*, Aug. 31, 1959, and in part from "First Hawaii State Legislature Convenes," *Honolulu Star-Bulletin*, Aug. 31, 1959. The information about Katsuichi's and Ayano's deaths, the last meeting with Senator Inouye, and Kats's death is all derived primarily from my interview with Mariko.

The details about Fumiye Miho's later life are drawn from a short, unpublished biography authored by her niece Mariko. The brief account of Hiro Higuchi's later life and that of Masao Yamada are drawn from biographies of each on the 100th Infantry Battalion Veterans' Education Center. My brief synopsis of the rest of George Oiye's life is drawn from snippets in Oiye, *Footprints in My Rearview Mirror,* 163–262, as well as from a Densho Encyclopedia entry under his name. The material on Sus Ito is drawn from John Fleischman's "Extraordinary Life of ASCB Founding Member Susumu Ito," on the American Society for Cell Biology website; from "Exhibit: Before They Were Heroes: Sus Ito's World," on the Japanese-American in Boston website; and from an obituary, "Susumu 'Sus' Ito 1919–2015," *Boston Globe*, Oct. 4, 2015. Solly Ganor talks about his mother's death in *Light One Candle*, 317. Additional facts about Solly's later life and the quotation—"We together, the survivors"—are drawn from Eric Saul's "Biography of Solly Ganor, the Author of 'Light One Candle'" on Mr. Saul's website at www.easaul.com. In my interview with Judy Niizawa, she also recounted details of the trip to Israel on which Rudy met Solly. I learned a number of facts about the Gordon Hirabayashi Recreational Site from Jim Erikson's story on the naming of the site in the *Arizona Daily Star*, Nov. 8, 1999, reprinted on Tuscon.com on Jan. 6, 2012. The "I was always able to hold my head up high" quotation appears on a photograph of one of the plaques included in Mark Duggan's article "The Kinds of Things He Believed, He Tried to Live," on the Open Range website. Additional biographical information about Gordon is drawn from Julie Garner, "Gordon Hirabayashi, 1918–2012," *University of Washington Magazine*, March 1, 2012. Still more biographical information can be found in the "Biographical Note" introducing the Gordon K. Hirabayashi Papers on the Archives West website. And finally, I am indebted to Jay Hirabayashi for his moving and informative tribute to his parents, "Remembering Gordon and Esther Hirabayashi," on the National Association of Japanese Canadians' website, for details about Gordon's last days. The final passage, "Unless citizens are willing to stand up for the Constitution it's not worth the paper it's written on," is President Obama quoting Gordon at the White House on May 29, 2012.

PHOTO CREDITS

INDEX